D0641593

INTERNATIONAL ENVIRONMENTAL LAW

IN A NUTSHELL

SECOND EDITION

By

LAKSHMAN D. GURUSWAMY

Professor of Law
University of Colorado at Boulder, School of Law

Mat #40105176

COPYRIGHT © 1997 WEST PUBLISHING CO.
COPYRIGHT © 2003 By West, a Thomson business
     610 Opperman Drive
     P.O. Box 64526
     St. Paul, MN 55164–0526
     1–800–328–9352
Printed in the United States of America

ISBN 0–314–14409–9

∞

PREFACE

While the corpus and the contours of International Environmental Law (IEL) have changed between the first and second editions of this book, the objectives of the Nutshell remain the same. The Second edition of this Nutshell remains a primer on International Environmental Law (IEL)[1] addressed to students, practitioners, teachers, law and policy-makers, and inquirers who wish to obtain a functional, as distinct from a theoretical, introduction to the subject. It is also intended to be used by students of IEL in conjunction with other treatises and course books on the subject.

The book commences with an introduction to the relevant concepts of international law. Our approach to international law has the modest objective of promoting a functional awareness and understanding of the more important and germane principles and rules. This functional approach is noticeable, for example, in the abridged attention we give to the theoretical and doctrinal, as distinct from practical concepts, of international law relating to treaties and customs.

1. The page constraints of this book, and the changing legal character of the European Union (EU) as it evolves from an international organization into a confederation, restraints us from exploring the substantive corpus of EU environmental laws.

The core of the Nutshell attempts to distill the socio-scientific evidence confronting law-makers, along with the resulting corpus of substantive IEL. The principles and rules of international law and the substantive law found in treaties and customary law have been amply addressed and covered by treatises. They have also been dealt with in the problem-orientated course book GURUSWAMY ET AL., INTERNATIONAL ENVIRONMENTAL LAW AND WORLD ORDER (2nd ed. 1999) in which we have been involved. Unfortunately, the need to recognize and grasp the socio-scientific context of environmental problems has not received the same attention. We have tried to remedy this shortcoming and have provided a more extensive review of relevant socio-scientific findings, and their causal importance to substantive law.

The *raison d'etre* for the development of IEL is the need for an identifiable corpus of law that addresses the phenomena of environmental degradation in a way that existing laws are unable to do. In responding to this challenge, negotiators and law-makers in all major treaties have adopted an integrated approach, which assimilates and incorporates the findings of physical, natural, social, and political scientists within an interdisciplinary framework. In contrast, a review of much of contemporary theoretical and academic writing addressing the global environment quickly reveals the extent to which different disciplines still remain fragmented in their outlook. Whether emanating from the physical, natural, social or political sciences, or law, the tendency is for writers to address those within their own disciplines. The result is a fractured outlook that contributes little toward the making or implementation of IEL.

In particular, students and practitioners in whose hands the future of IEL lies need to appreciate the interdisciplinary framework of IEL for two connected reasons. The first is pedagogic. An interdisciplinary perspective facilitates a richer appreciation of IEL because it reflects reality rather than an artificially separated legal segment. The second is professional. International environmental lawyers in their law-making or law-applying roles act as the gatekeepers of international society, who are constantly confronted with competing theories, ideas, and conclusions that clamor for admission into the law. Lawyers engaged in real life law making or interpretation do not have the luxury of ignoring the science or the politics surrounding them. They are compelled to make hard decisions about concepts and ideas, and an early introduction to the socio-scientific context equips them to better understand the tasks they will confront.

This Nutshell attempts to provide such an introduction. We hope it offers those venturing into IEL an enhanced comprehension of this new and diverse field. We also hope, as together we face these challenges, to motivate our readers into approaching the daunting problems of our global environment with vision and resolve.

ACKNOWLEDGMENTS

The Second edition of this work—written in the incomparable environs of Boulder, Colorado—could not have been completed without the help of a fine group of research assistants. I am especially indebted to the uniquely gifted Kevin Doran who discharged the difficult tasks thrown at him with characteristic skill, analytical prowess, enormous diligence and insatiable curiosity. I am also indebted to Sarah Hamilton, Trish Oeth, and Sam Sorkin for their insightful and able research assistance, and for the resourceful and skillful manner in which they dealt with a multitude of editorial and analytical tasks.

Most intellectual endeavors at the University of Colorado School of Law are hugely enriched by our Research Librarian, Jane Thompson. I am most grateful to her for the generous and abundant help she provided this project.

Finally, I am grateful for the 2003 summer research grant made possible by Dean Harold Bruff of the University of Colorado School of Law, as well as for the collegial support of my great colleagues.

LAKSHMAN GURUSWAMY

Boulder 2003

*

VII

OUTLINE

*

TABLE OF TREATIES

The following abbreviations are used throughout the table:

NYIF – Not Yet in Force
NLIF – No Longer in Force

Note: The ratifications category includes acceptances, accessions and agreements.

TITLE & CITATION OF TREATY / INSTRUMENT	NUTSHELL PAGE REFERENCES			
	Date Concluded	Signat-ories	Ratific-ations	Entry into Force
1 African, Caribbean and Pacific States-European Economic Community: Fourth Lome Convention, 29 I.L.M. 783	294, 319			
	12/15/89	86	77	9/1/91
2 African Convention for the Conservation of Nature and Natural Resources, 1001 U.N.T.S. 3	172			
	9/15/68	15		6/16/69
3 Agenda 21, U.N.Doc. A/CONF. 151/26 (1992)	39-44, 52, 58, 320, 471 476, 546, 560			
	6/14/92	182		
4 Agreement Between the U.S. and Canada on the Water Quality of the Great Lakes (1978 Great Lakes Water Quality Agreement), 30 U.S.T. 1383 (as amended in 1987)	464-66			
	11/22/78	2	2	11/22/78
5 Agreement Concerning the International Commission for the Protection of the Rhine Against Pollution (Berne Convention), 994 U.N.T.S. 3	460			
	4/29/63		6	5/1/65
6 Agreement for the Implementation of the Provisions of UNCLOS Relating to the Conservation and Management of Straddling Fish Stocks and Highly Migratory Fish Stocks (SFSA), 34 I.L.M. 1542	399, 400-02, 548			
	8/4/95	33	59	12/11/01
7	172			
Agreement on the Conservation of Nature and Natural Resources Adopted by the Association of South East Asian Nations (ASEAN Convention), E.P.L. 64	7/9/85	6	3	NYIF

check ←

49	ECE (United Nations Economic Commission for Europe)	456			
	Convention on the Protection and Use of Transboundary Watercourses and International Lakes (ECE Treaty), 31 I.L.M. 1312	3/17/92		20	10/6/96
50	General Agreement on Tariffs and Trade, 61 Stat. A–3, 55 U.N.T.S. 187	554			
		10/30/47		136	1/1/48 (prov.)
51	General Agreement on Tariffs and Trade, Final Act Embodying the Results of the Uruguay Round of Multinational Trade Negotiations, Legal Instruments-Results of the Uruguay Round vol. 1, 33 I.L.M. 1125	13, 49, 243, 295, 555			
		4/15/94			1/1/95
52	Interim Convention on Conservation of North Pacific Fur Seals, 314 U.N.T.S. 105	404			
		2/9/57		4	10/14/57
53	International Convention for the Prevention of Pollution from Ships (MARPOL Convention), 12 I.L.M. 1319 (amended)	64, 270-71, 346-48, 350-55, 373, 573			
		11/2/73			7/1/92
54		408-11			
55	International Convention for the Regulation of Whaling (ICRW), 161 U.N.T.S. 72	12/2/46		12	11/10/48
	International Convention on Civil Liability for Oil Pollution Damage (1969 CLC), 9 I.L.M. 45, 973 U.N.T.S. 3 (as amended by the 1992 Protocol)	66, 75, 88, 363-66			
		11/29/69		19	6/19/75
56	International Convention on Oil Pollution Preparedness, Response and Co-operation (OPRC), 30 I.L.M. 773	359-60, 362			
		11/30/90	15	22	5/13/96
57	International Convention on the Establishment of an International Fund for Compensation for Oil Pollution Damage (1971 Fund Convention), 1971 U.N. Jur. Y.B. 103	88, 366-67			
		12/18/71		15	10/16/78

58	International Convention Relating to the Intervention on the High Seas in Cases of Oil Pollution Casualties (Intervention Convention), 970 U.N.T.S. 211, 26 U.S.T. 765	360-62			
		11/29/69		19	5/6/75
59	Johannesburg Declaration o Sustainable Development, 41 I.L.M. 1480	540			
		9/4/02			
60	Joint Protocol Relating to the Application of the Vienna Convention on Civil Liability for Nuclear Damage and the Paris Convention on Third Party Liability in the Field of Nuclear Energy, 42 Nuclear Law Bulletin 66	533			
		9/21/88	13	10	4/27/92
61	Kyoto Protocol to the United Nations Framework Convention on Climate Change, 37 I.L.M. 32	28, 183, 186, 190, 191, 195, 197-202, 207, 209-25, 549-51			
		12/10/97			NYIF
62	Mexico-United States Agreement for Co-operation on Environmental Programmes and Transboundary Problems, 26 I.L.M. 25	318			
		11/12/86			1/29/87
63	Mexico-United States Agreement to Cooperate in the Solution of Environmental Problems in the Border Area (1983 La Paz Agreement), 22 I.L.M. 1025	431-32, 467-69			
		8/14/83			
64	Montreal Protocol on Substances that Deplete the Ozone Layer (Montreal Protocol), 26 I.L.M. 1550	6-7, 12, 13, 54, 60, 236-45			
		9/16/87	46	184	1/1/89
65	Montreal Protocol on Substances that Deplete the Ozone Layer-- Adjustments and Amendments (Copenhagen Amendments), 32 I.L.M. 874	28, 236, 239, 243			
		11/25/92			6/14/94
66	Montreal Protocol Parties: Adjustments and Amendments to the Montreal Protocol on Substances that Deplete the Ozone Layer (London Amendments), 30 I.L.M. 637	28, 236, 239, 243-44			
		6/29/90			8/10/92
67	North American Agreement on Environmental Cooperation Between the United States, Canada and Mexico, 32 I.L.M 1480	87, 89, 468			
		9/14/93			

68	North American Free Trade Agreement (NAFTA)	87, 89, 295, 468			
69	Organization of African Unity: African Nuclear-Weapon-Free Zone Treaty, 36 I.L.M. 698	498			
		6/23/95			
70	Protocol for the Prevention of Pollution of the South Pacific by Dumping, 26 I.L.M. 38	380			
		11/24/86		10	8/18/90
71	Protocol for the Protection of the Mediterranean Sea Against Pollution from Land-Based Sources (amended in 1996)	338			
		5/17/80			6/17/83
72	Protocol for the Protection of the South-East Pacific Against Pollution from Land-Based Sources	338			
		7/23/83			9/23/86
73	Protocol on Environmental Protection to the Antarctic Treaty (1991 Antarctic Environment Protocol), 30 I.L.M. 1461	172, 252, 253, 258, 260-61, 264, 265-73			
		10/3/91	10	29	1/14/98
74	Protocol on the Protection of the Black Sea Marine Environment Against Pollution by Dumping, 1992 WL 602572	338, 380			
		4/21/92		6	1/15/94
75	Protocol to Amend the Vienna Convention on Civil Liability for Nuclear Damage, 36 I.L.M. 1462	87-88, 537			
		9/12/96			
76	Protocol to the 1972 Convention on the Prevention of Marine Pollution by Dumping of Wastes and Other Matter 36 I.L.M. 1	376-79			
		11/7/96			
77	Protocol to the 1979 Convention on Long-Range Transboundary Air Pollution Concerning the Control of the Emissions of Nitrogen Oxides or their Transboundary Fluxes, (1988 Nitrogen Oxides Protocol), 28 I.L.M. 212	9, 422, 426			
		10/31/88	1	28	2/14/91

#	Treaty				
88	Treaty between the United States and Mexico Relative to the Utilization of Waters of Colorado and Tijuana Rivers and of the Rio Grande from Fort Quitman to the Gulf of Mexico, (1944 Colorado River Treaty), 3 U.N.T.S. 314	466-67			
		2/3/44		2	11/8/45
89	Treaty Between the United States and the Russian Federation on Strategic Offensive Reductions, 4 I.L.M. 799	504			
		5/24/02		2	
90	Treaty Between the United States and the U.S.S.R on the Elimination of Their Intermediate-Range and Shorter-Range Missiles, 27 I.L.M. 84	497			
		12/8/87		2	6/1/88
91	Treaty Between the United States on the U.S.S.R on the Limitation of Underground Nuclear Weapons Tests, 13 I.L.M. 906	500			
		7/3/74		2	12/11/80
92	Treaty Between the United States and the U.S.S.R. on the Reduction and Elimination of Strategic Offensive Arms (START I), 32 I.L.M. 246	497, 504			
				2	
93	Treaty Between the United States and the U.S.S.R on the Reduction and Limitation of Strategic Offensive Arms (START II)	504			
		5/23/92		2	4/14/00
94	Treaty Between the United States and the U.S.S.R. on Underground Nuclear Explosions for Peaceful Purposes, 15 I.L.M. 891	500			
		5/28/76		2	12/11/90
95	Treaty of Rarotonga on the South Pacific Nuclear Free Zone, 24 I.L.M. 1442	498			
		8/6/85	1	12	12/11/86
96	Treaty of Tlatelolco for the Prohibition of Nuclear Weapons in Latin America, 6 I.L.M 52	498			
		2/14/67			4/22/68
97	Treaty on the Final Settlement with Respect to Germany, 29 I.L.M. 1186	498			
		9/12/90	6	5	3/15/91

98	Treaty on the Non-proliferation of Nuclear Weapons (NPT), 7 I.L.M. 809	498-99, 521, 568			
		7/1/68		188	3/5/70
99	United States—Canada Air Quality Agreement, 30 I.L.M. 676	425, 428			
		3/13/91		2	3/13/91
100	United States-Mexico Agreement on Cooperation for Protection and Improvement of the Environment in the Border Area (Mexico-U.S. Hazardous Waste Agreement)	318			
		8/14/83		2	2/16/84
101	UNESCO Convention Concerning the Protection of The World Cultural and Natural Heritage (World Heritage Convention), 11 I.L.M. 1358	162-65			
		11/23/72	1	175	12/1/75
102	United Nations Convention on the Law of the Sea (UNCLOS), 21 I.L.M. 1261	10, 11, 13, 16, 19, 35-37, 86, 149, 328, 339, 350, 355-59, 363, 370, 372, 391, 392-406, 548			
		12/10/82	30	142	11/16/94
103	United Nations Convention to Combat Desertification in Those Countries Experiencing Serious Drought and/or Desertification, Particularly in Africa, 33 I.L.M. 1328	471, 476-83, 560			
		6/17/94	4	179	12/26/96
104	United Nations Framework Convention on Climate Change (UNFCCC), 31 I.L.M. 849	6, 7, 9, 11, 40, 52, 62, 65, 186, 188-214, 221, 377, 390, 552, 565			
		5/9/92		188	3/21/94
105	Vienna Convention for the Protection of the Ozone Layer (Vienna Convention on Ozone), 26 I.L.M. 1529	7, 35, 54, 61, 65, 234-36, 238			
		3/22/85		185	9/22/88
106	Vienna Convention on Civil Liability for Nuclear Damage, 7 I.L.M. 727, 1063 U.N.T.S. 265 (as amended by the 1997 Protocol)	66, 75, 87, 88, 93, 532-33, 537-38			
		5/21/63	6	33	11/12/77
107	Vienna Convention on the Law of Treaties , 1155 U.N.T.S. 331	6, 11, 19			
		5/23/69	19	94	1/27/80

check

*

INTERNATIONAL ENVIRONMENTAL LAW

IN A NUTSHELL

SECOND EDITION

*

CHAPTER ONE

SOURCES AND FORMS OF IN-TERNATIONAL ENVIRON-MENTAL LAW

International Environmental Law (IEL) bears a name that reflects its content. At its substantive core, IEL endeavors to control pollution and the depletion of natural resources within a framework of sustainable development. Although the presence of both the terms "international" and "environmental" in its name suggests parity between national and international laws, IEL is formally a branch of public international law—a body of law created by nation states for nation states, to govern problems that arise between nation states.

IEL possesses some features that distinguish it from traditional international law. First, its creation and vigorous, if uneven growth, owe much to national environmental laws and policies. Nation states frequently have entered into landmark international agreements and practices, driven largely by the momentum of law, regulation, and policies applicable to their own environmental problems, and not necessarily because of the gravity of international problems. Second, the law-making in IEL has been shaped primarily by bio-physical not geo-political forces, and this communal foundation has at times sheltered it from the disfiguring political dissension found in other areas of international law. These two factors have inevitably, albeit asymmetrically, infused the objectives of national environmental regulatory laws, and the conceptual frameworks of environmental sciences, into the corpus of IEL.

In the result, IEL, while remaining a division or tributary of international law, possesses its own characteristics and attributes arising as much from its relatively non-political subject matter—the environment—as from the greater influence of domestic law. It is a measure of IEL's stature and recognition that it sits shoulder to shoulder, if uncomfortably, with other principles of public international law developed over the last 50 years, including those controlling the use of force, self-determination, permanent sovereignty over natural resources, and human rights.

Whether casting a gentle glance or a hard look at IEL, it is difficult to avoid its substantive corpus and powerful presence, or the vigor and fast rate of its expansion. It already has spawned over 200 multilateral agreements and treaties, countless bilateral instruments, and a host of declarations and UN General Assembly resolutions, some of which express "soft" IEL, while others articulate and restate existing rules of customary law. Moreover, it boasts a small but growing body of judicial decisions (case law) and general principles of law. A look at the substantial documents supplements to course books and treatises, for example, offers ample evidence of this growing corpus of IEL. *See*, for example, Lakshman Guruswamy, Et Al., Supplement of Basic Documents to International Environmental Law and World Order: A Problem Oriented Coursebook (West 1999); Patricia Birnie & Alan Boyle, Basic Documents on International Law and The Environment (1997); Phillippe Sands, Principles of International Environmental Law, v IIA & IIB (2000)

Treaties, customary law, general principles of law and judicial decisions are usually referred to as sources of law. Article 38(1) of the Statute of the International Court of Justice (Statute of the ICJ), confirms that "The Court . . . shall apply:

a.   international conventions . . .;

b.   international custom, as evidence of a general practice accepted as law;

c.   the general principles of law recognized by civilized nations;

d.   . . . judicial decisions and the teachings of the most highly qualified publicists of the various nations, as subsidiary means for the determination of rules of law."

While these are sources of law in one sense, they are also differing forms in which IEL is expressed or cast. For example, the written form of a treaty, agreed to at a law-making conference, authoritatively reflects what was agreed upon by its parties. A treaty may therefore be considered a source of law because we go to it to find out what the law is. At the same time it is a particular kind of written form, among others, adopted by IEL. Customary law assumes a different, usually unwritten, form, though it also is a source of law. It consists of unwritten, uncodified, principles that are established by evidence of practice and *opinio juris*. Even where custom is codified or reduced to writing by a group of eminent jurists or publicists such as the International Law Commission (ILC) that was created to codify and develop international law (see Appendix), there may be doubts as to whether such a re-statement is an accurate reflection of customary law. Likewise, as we shall see, general principles of law and judicial decisions are both sources and forms of IEL.

A. TREATIES

While we have just referred to four major sources and forms of IEL, substantive IEL overwhelmingly consists of principles and rules creating preventive, precautionary, or remedial norms embodied in treaties. Treaties are written agreements governed by international law, entered into between two or more states, creating or restating legal rights and duties. Treaties are also described as conventions, protocols, covenants, pacts, etc. A question that needs to be answered before we commence our summary of the sources and forms of law is: Why are treaties the principle source of IEL?

The preeminence of treaties is largely attributable to the nature of environmental problems.

These problems range over a wide spectrum of future contingencies. Moreover, they demand continuous observation and monitoring, as well as quick legal action and implementation in response to ongoing and relatively rapid changes in scientific knowledge and conclusions. The socio-scientific context calls for substantive IEL that is able to deal with wide and varied kinds of investigations, scientific monitoring, assessments, and findings. The law should be capable of responding to complex international environmental problems with a mix of generality, specificity, and adaptability. None of the four sources of IEL can fulfill all of these requirements, although treaties are best able to satisfy at least some of them.

For example, customary law, as we shall see, is made up of state practice and *opinio juris* that usually takes time to crystallize, one issue at a time, and is carefully restricted to the specific facts. General principles of law take even longer to identify and ascertain. Even where customary rules or general principles are clear, these sources do not provide mechanisms for inducing compliance or considering infractions. Treaties, on the other hand, offer a superior framework for dealing with environmental issues by allowing for targeted laws, flexibility of law-making, machinery for inducing compliance, and non-compliance and dispute resolution mechanisms—all of which can be tailored to the problems at hand. Finally, the fact that treaties are reduced to writing, and are therefore more accessible and applicable, assumes great importance when approaching a subject that requires clarity and certainty of legal response.

The Vienna Convention on the Law of Treaties, May 23, 1969, 1155 U.N.T.S. 331 (1988) deals comprehensively with a number of complex questions about treaties. Of these, we refer only to those of particular importance to IEL. The first concerns the entry into force of a treaty, or the date on which it officially binds the parties. Even though signed, a multilateral treaty typically does not enter into force until a stipulated minimum number of states have deposited their ratifications. Ratification is the process by which the respective national governments give legal force to the signatures entered by their representatives. For example, a signature by a U.S. diplomat does not bind the U.S. to an agreement until it is ratified by the Senate. The Convention on Biological Diversity (Biodiversity Convention), June 5, 1992, 31 I.L.M. 818 (1993) (entered into force Dec. 29, 1993) (*see* Chapter Five) required 30 ratifications [art. 36], and the United Nations Framework Convention on Climate Change (Climate Change Convention), Dec. 31, 1992, 31 I.L.M. 849 (1994) (*see* Chapter Six) requires 50 ratifications [art. 23].

A party to a treaty may enter reservations to the extent that they are not prohibited. Reservations allow parties to agree to all of the provisions of a treaty except those specified in the reservation, provided the other parties agree to the reservation. Recent environmental treaties frown on reservations, and conventions such as the Montreal Protocol on Substances that Deplete the Ozone Layer (Montreal Protocol), Sept. 16, 1987, 26 I.L.M. 1541, (1987) (*see* Chapter Seven), the Biodiversity Convention (*see* Chapter Five), and the Climate Change Convention (*see* Chapter Six) disallow reservations altogether. Parties have attempted to get around this by making "interpretive declarations" such as those entered by Fiji, Kiribati, Nauru, and Tuvalu to the Climate Change Convention, and the United Kingdom to the Biodiversity Convention, but the legal effect of such declarations is undetermined.

Treaties may also be amended where allowed by their provisions, but amendments generally do not enter into force unless ratified or accepted by all the parties. The formal, very demanding treaty amendment procedure found in treaties has proved to be anachronistic, preventing existing treaty regimes from keeping abreast of new developments and technologies or incorporating new and essential scientific findings. In order to meet this deficiency, a number of environmental treaties are tiered into two or three parts consisting of: 1) a "framework treaty" which usually functions as a constituent instrument containing general principles; 2) "protocols" that supplement or implement the framework treaty; and 3) technical and scientific "annexes" containing details that may need quick amendment according to changing needs. The Vienna Convention for the Protection of the Ozone Layer (Vienna Ozone Convention), Mar. 22, 1985. 26 I.L.M. 1529 (entered into force Sept. 22, 1988), for example, has a number of innovative procedures relating to the amendments of its protocols [art. 9] and annexes [art. 10] that do not require unanimous approval.

1. INTERPRETATION OF TREATIES

Like other areas of international law, many principles of IEL embodied in treaties are vague and nebulous for a number of reasons. Among the more important of these reasons is that treaties are drafted not by gods, but by humans who are unable to anticipate and provide for every factual or legal contingency that might arise in the future. To meet unforeseen contingencies, resort is made to abstractions and concepts of wide scope which almost by definition lack specificity and exactitude, and require interpretation before they can be applied to the facts of a case. When a novel case arises, the extent to which it might be covered by existing provisions through interpretation may be contentious.

In addition, there is a tendency for drafting conferences to resort to aspirational and hortatory expression when they cannot agree upon specific obligations. Furthermore, and conversely, when parties to a treaty want to move beyond the aspirational to the obligatory, but are unable to agree on the formulation of such an obligation, they sometimes leave it to be resolved by interpretation on a later occasion.

Consequently, treaties are replete with a variety of verbal formulations that do not amount to obligations of effect. These include: aspirational norms;

general norms containing inchoate and open-textured obligations; and formulations of rules or principles that codify contentious or competing rules.
Illustrations of aspirational and inchoate obligations
abound in environmental treaties. For example, according to the Climate Change Convention (*see*
Chapter Six), parties, taking into account their undefined "common but differentiated responsibilities" shall include climate change considerations
"to the extent feasible" [art. 4(1)(f)]. The Biodiversity Convention (*see* Chapter Five) is choked by
obligations of aspiration, such as "as far as possible
and as appropriate," [arts. 5,6,7] and "in accordance with its particular conditions and capabilities" [art. 6]. The Basel Convention on the Control
of Transboundary Movements of Hazardous Wastes
and their Disposal (Basel Convention), March 22,
1989, 28 I.L.M. 657 (1992) (*see* Chapter Nine) requires each party to take "appropriate measures"
to minimize the generation of hazardous wastes
[art. 4(2)(a)] and also requires that parties manage
wastes in an "environmentally sound" manner [art.
4(2)(d)]. The Protocol to the 1979 Convention on
Long–Range Transboundary Air Pollution Concerning the Emissions of Nitrogen Oxides or their
Transboundary Fluxes, Oct. 31, 1988, 28 I.L.M. 212
(1991) (entered into force Mar. 16, 1983) (*see* Chapter Fourteen) requires parties to "act as soon as
possible" in article 2(1) and "without undue delay"
in article 7.

While the previous citations serve as examples of
aspirational norms and inchoate or open-textured

obligations, the difficulties of interpretation are compounded by other provisions embodying general duties and competing norms that remain undefined. A possible variation, perhaps even conflict, in the way a general duty is expressed may be found by comparing corresponding provisions of the Biodiversity Convention and the United Nations Convention on the Law of the Sea (UNCLOS), Dec. 20, 1982, 21 I.L.M. 1261 (entered into force Nov. 16, 1994). Art 3 of the Biodiversity Convention (*see* Chapter Five) strikes a balance between the sovereign rights of states over natural resources and their duty toward the international environment by requiring that states "not cause damage" to areas outside their jurisdiction. This duty is formulated somewhat differently by art. 193 of UNCLOS (*see* Chapter Thirteen). Art 193 requires states "to protect and preserve" the marine environment. Such a divergence between the more onerous duty of "protecting and preserving" in contrast to the less exacting duty "not to cause damage" can create an interpretive problem when trying to ascertain the meaning and import of the general obligation of preventing transnational damage. It also invokes the need to reconcile the conflicting norms found in cognate treaties.

Two interconnected questions concerning treaty interpretation require further attention: 1) Who is empowered to interpret a treaty and 2) How, or according to what rules, is the law interpreted? Interpretation in IEL operates in a manner similar to national legal systems in which the interpretive task is undertaken by courts and judicial tribunals, as well as administrative agencies charged with implementing the statute in question.

The International Court of Justice (ICJ) is perhaps the best known among international courts, but the ICJ depends on the acquiescence of the parties for its jurisdiction [Statute of the International Court of Justice, art. 36, June 29, 1945, 59 Stat. 1031 (entered into force Oct. 24, 1945)]. Judicial or arbitral tribunals created by treaties such as UNCLOS or the Climate Change Convention are also empowered to interpret the law. Interpretation may further be rendered by the declarations of diplomatic conferences such as the 1972 Stockholm Conference on the Human Environment, the 1992 United Nations Conference on Environment and Development (UNCED), and the General Assembly of the United Nations. Increasingly, interpretation is made by the institutions created by environmental treaties including the permanent annual conferences of international regimes, or even expert organizations such as those mentioned in the Appendix.

The Vienna Convention outlines basic rules of treaty interpretation. Article 31 stipulates that a treaty shall be interpreted in good faith in accordance with the ordinary meaning to be given to the terms of a treaty in their context and in the light of its object and purpose. Article 32 allows for supplementary means of interpretation where interpretation according to article 31 leaves the meaning ambiguous or obscure, or leads to a result that is manifestly absurd or unreasonable. While these appear to be reasonably objective rules, they are not self-executing and need to be applied by an interpreter. The process of applying the rules creates an unavoidably subjective human element and can result in demonstrable differences in opinion.

For example, the ICJ in a recent decision [Legality of the use by a State of Nuclear Weapons in Armed Conflict, 1996 I.C.J. 66 (July 8)] denied the World Health Organization (WHO) standing to request an Advisory Opinion on the legality of the threat or use of nuclear weapons. The majority decision of the Court was based on a very narrow and restricted interpretation of the mandate of the WHO, and is dealt with more fully in Chapter Seventeen. On the other hand, as we see below, the Meeting of the Parties under the Montreal Protocol interpreted some of its provisions in an expansive and even non-textual fashion.

2. CONFLICT WITH OTHER TREATIES

Like the body politic of civil society within nation states, the international community is also subject to interest group politics, and commits itself through treaties to a variety of competing objectives and goals which are not integrated or even harmonized, and do not operate in unison. The clash of goals and objectives is vividly illustrated by the conflict between environmental protection and free trade (*see* Chapter Eighteen). For instance, a number of environmental treaties such as the Montreal Protocol, the Basel Convention, and the Convention on International Trade in Endangered Species and

Wild Fauna and Flora (CITES), Mar. 3, 1973, 12 I.L.M. 1085 (1973) (*see* Chapter Five) mandate trade restrictions to achieve their environmental goals. It is arguable that many of these trade restrictions could be justified under UNCLOS. Such trade restrictions, however, conflict with the GATT/ WTO regime that was restructured in 1994.

The Vienna Convention [art. 30] provides some guidance on how to interpret conflicting treaties dealing with the same "subject-matter." It focuses first on treaties that deal with the same parties and second on treaties that do not deal with the same parties. Where the parties to both treaties are common there are two rules: 1) a treaty that is later in time prevails; however, 2) where a treaty either states that it is subject to, or not incompatible with another treaty, that other treaty prevails. Where there is a conflict between a treaty to which both states are parties and another to which only one state is a party, the treaty to which both are parties will prevail [art. 30(4)(b)].

With regard to the Montreal Protocol, CITES and the Basel Convention, the last in time rule appears to give precedence to GATT/WTO, which was adopted more recently, but in the event of a GATT/ WTO *vs.* UNCLOS clash, the advantage swings to UNCLOS, which came into force even later. Still, a number of unanswered questions remain. For example, does the Basel Convention deal with the same subject matter as the GATT/WTO? If not, will the rule in Vienna Convention article 30(4)(b) apply? Can it be argued that the Basel Convention deals with a specialized area and must obtain precedence over a more general treaty dealing with trade in the round? What if an environmental treaty was to say that its provisions will take priority over other treaties dealing with the same subject matter? Although one might be tempted to answer these questions in favor of the Basel Convention, there are as yet no conclusive answers to such problems.

B. CUSTOM

Customary law, or custom, refers largely to unwritten law inferred from the conduct of states (practice) undertaken in the belief that they were bound to do so by law (*opinio juris*). In the words of the Statute of the ICJ, custom is "evidence of a general practice accepted as law" [art. 38(1)(b)]. Customary international law, therefore, is created by the fusion of an objective element, practice, and a subjective element, *opinio juris*.

Practice in IEL takes a number of forms, and the evidence necessary to establish it may be gathered, *inter alia*, from the following materials drawn from the legislative, executive, judicial, and administrative branches of a government: 1) national legislation; 2) diplomatic notes and correspondence; 3) statements and votes by governments in international organizations and forums of varying kinds; 4) ratification of treaties containing the obligations in question; 5) opinions of legal advisers; and 6) restatements of the law by scholars and jurists like the ILC. Evidence gathered from these sources will testify to what states actually do, and how they react when faced with a particular problem. In modern times, the *opinio juris* of states has been gathered from their declarations or admissions in international forums like the ILC and the General Assembly of the UN, in addition to the other more traditional sources listed above.

Suppose country A asserts that customary law establishes the right to take countermeasures with respect to an environmentally wrongful act. In order to establish such a claim it must first be proved that nations previously have resorted to such countermeasures following a pattern of conduct that is consistent, extensive, uniform, and general.

The next question is whether such practice was undertaken by states in the belief that what they were doing was compelled or mandated by law. This subjective element is referred to as *opinio juris*. If a practice is regarded as discretionary, or simply convenient or self-serving rather than obligatory, it is an example of usage that does not possess the critical element of *opinio juris* and therefore is not considered customary law.

The unwritten, uncodified form of custom is one of its chief weaknesses, and one way to remedy this shortcoming is to codify or re-state customary law, thus making it known and accessible. Re-statements of customary law are undertaken by the ILC, other scholars and jurists, courts, legal tribunals, conference declarations, and by treaties. A re-statement or codification by scholars and jurists serves the important purpose of reducing the law's uncertainty, but leaves open the extent to which it is accepted as accurate. Questions may arise as to whether the codification of a particular rule is a faithful and true reflection of the customary law, and as to the degree of consensus surrounding its codification. Such doubts weaken the authority of any re-statement of customary law.

Customary law is sometimes codified during a law-making conference, where it may take the form of a draft treaty which, if accepted, becomes binding as a treaty. For example, as we will see in Chapter Two, it is possible to assert that the 15–year process of negotiating UNCLOS led to the crystallization of customary IEL, and that Part XII, relating to the protection of the marine environment, is a codification of existing customary rules of law [*see* Louis Sohn & Kristen Gustafson, The Law of the Sea in a Nutshell (1984); Jonathan I. Charney, *Entry Into Force of the 1982 Convention on the Law of the Sea,* 35 Va. J. Int'l. L. 381 (1995)]. In such a situation the text of the treaty expresses both conventional and customary law, giving it a dual jural status. It is activated as a treaty only when signed and ratified, but it possesses the authority of customary law so long as it is accepted as law by the community of nations.

Important duties under customary IEL have been codified or restated in treaties and conference declarations as "principles" rather than "rules." In ordinary legal analysis, rules typically embody standards that are definitively applied to a specifically described state of affairs, and the application of such a rule frequently determines a particular controversy. Principles on the on the other hand are more abstract general norms from which specific rules or standards are derived, and embody reasons that argue for moving in a particular direction, rather than arriving at a specified result. Consequently, principles—unlike rules—do not themselves postulate obligations of result. Instead, principles are the foundations upon which rules incorporating obligations of result are built. One principle may be offset by another, and a principle may therefore be seen as only one among a number of considerations to be taken into account in reaching a decision [RONALD DWORKIN, TAKING RIGHTS SERIOUSLY 24–26 (1978)].

While many principles and rules have been espoused, only a few have been accepted into the corpus of customary IEL. The biggest impediment to the formation of customary law lies in the element of generality, which requires that the practice be widespread among at least a majority of states. This is difficult to establish in a world divided along cultural, economic, social, and religious lines. There are a number of principles that aspire to the status of customary law, but have not as yet attained that designation. They include the principle of common but differentiated responsibility, the polluter pays principle, the preventive and precautionary principles, and various principles of good neighborliness and cooperation. They are found in treaties, conference declarations, General Assembly resolutions, and the documents of various other international organizations and fora. These instruments of "soft," embryonic customary law play an important part in the development of IEL. They may not amount to customary law *per se*, but they do constitute a presence and a backdrop that facilitates the creation and interpretation of IEL in general. The more important examples are referred to in Chapter Eighteen, The Future of IEL.

In addressing the limited corpus of "hard" customary IEL, we first turn to the prohibition against transboundary harm. The obligation prohibiting transboundary harm is perhaps the most established of customary IEL obligations, and creates an obligation of effect—or a rule—premised on the broader principle of *sic utere tuo ut alienum non laedus* (use your own property in such a manner as not to injure that of another). It has been supported by the practice and *opinio juris* of states.

Nonetheless, it has generally been described as a principle, not a rule. This obligation is codified in Principle 21 of Stockholm, and is now entrenched in numerous provisions of treaties and declarations. It has been included as a "principle" in the Biodiversity Convention according to which: "States have ... the sovereign right to exploit their own resources pursuant to their own environmental policies, and the responsibility to ensure that activities within their jurisdiction or control do not cause damage to the environment of other States or areas beyond the limits of national jurisdiction" [Biodiversity Convention, art. 3]. A variation of it is also articulated as a principle in the Rio Declaration [Principle 2].

UNCLOS expresses the general duty, under customary international law, to preserve and protect the marine environment and its natural resources—including the obligation to prevent, reduce, and control pollution of the marine environment [UNCLOS arts.192–196]. This set of obligations meshes with others dealing with state responsibility. In the result, "[s]tates are responsible for the fulfillment of their international obligations concerning the protection and preservation of the marine environment" [UNCLOS art. 235].

It could also be argued that there is a customary law principle of notification and consultation before embarking on potentially damaging environmental activities (*see* Chapter Fifteen). Finally, the principle of sustainable development (*see* Chapter Two) lies at the foundations of modern IEL. This principle is more fully dealt with in Chapter Eighteen, The Future of IEL.

C. GENERAL PRINCIPLES OF LAW

We might expect article 38(1)(c) of the Statute of the ICJ, dealing with sources of international law, to be interpreted in accordance with its ordinary or plain meaning, in context, and in light of its object and purpose [*see* Vienna Convention, art. 31]. When so interpreted, "the general principles of law recognized by civilized nations" enjoy a parity of status with treaties and custom. Such a view is reinforced by its context in which a contrasting source of law, "judicial decisions," is relegated to the status of a "subsidiary" source [Statute of the ICJ, art. 38(1)(d)]. A persuasive case can therefore be made out that the courts, not states, now possess the power and discretion to enunciate relevant general principles of law by induction. [ANTONIO CASSESE, INTERNATIONAL LAW IN A DIVIDED WORLD 170–172 (1986)].

The inductive task of ascertaining general principles from legal systems around the world falls to the comparative lawyer, and involves the gargantuan task of studying all major legal systems to discover and distill general principles of law (note that the search is all-inclusive and not limited to "civilized nations"—an embarrassingly anachronistic phrase of the 1940s). The systematic study of all legal systems has been fitfully attempted, and is by no means complete, though it is possible to garner general principles from some areas of national law such as contract, criminal, and environmental law. However, international courts have not yet acknowledged that general principles of national law constitute a significant source of law that should be incorporated into international law. On the contrary, general principles have never been considered a major source of law, and have only been used in an interstitial manner to fill in very small gaps in procedural—not substantive—law.

The ICJ and other judicial bodies appear to have reasoned that general principles of domestic or "municipal" jurisprudence should be followed only so far as they are specifically applicable to relations between states [IAN BROWNLIE, PRINCIPLES OF PUBLIC INTERNATIONAL LAW 16 (5th ed. 1998)]. National or domestic laws, which on the whole are applicable to jural parties within a state, as distinct from inter-state relations, have fallen short of this standard and have largely been ignored.

General principles have the potential for assuming a new role under IEL. In Chapter Eighteen, "The Future of IEL," we envision IEL's merger with national environmental laws to become part of the Common Law of Humankind (CLH). A successful merging of IEL and national environmental laws which creates a CLH demands that general principles of national environmental law be recognized as such and be woven into the fabric of international law.

D.   JUDICIAL DECISIONS

As we have noted, the Statute of the ICJ restricts the role of judicial decisions to that of a "[s]ubsidiary means for the determination of rules of law" [art. 38(1)(d)]. One reason is that judicial decisions, including those of the ICJ, have no binding force "[e]xcept between the parties and in respect of that particular case" [art. 59]. In national common law systems, the best known of which developed in England, the common law is the customary law that is developed, modified and sometimes fundamentally redirected by the judges, the legal profession, and the courts. The common law system grew through *common law*

judicial decisions recorded by lawyers. Judicial decisions form the foundations of law and theoretically constitute the background against which statutes are introduced. Even civil law systems that repudiate the common law method of judge-made law possess hierarchical legal systems in which judicial decisions play a part and possess value because they contain principles of law that may be binding on subsequent courts.

It is evident that the international legal process lacks a hierarchical system of courts or a machinery of justice and cannot, therefore, adopt a strict doctrine of binding precedent. International judicial decisions are binding only on the parties. But it is also clear that judicial decisions play an important role in any system of customary law by restating, codifying, and clarifying the often uncertain and usually unwritten customary law. In a judicial decision we find an analysis of the evidence supporting the law, an articulation or declaration of what the law is, and a demonstration of how law should be applied to the facts. As such, a court or tribunal performs the difficult and valuable duty of collecting, examining, and assessing the evidence and arguments, deducing rules from amorphous general concepts, reducing them into written form, and arriving at conclusions derived from the application of law to facts. The art of judging is a strenuous, costly, and time-consuming job, requiring training, discipline, diligence, and expertise.

Where a court exercises its responsibilities and decides a case, it is a perfectly natural tendency to

learn from what has been achieved and to avoid
duplication. Moreover, it is foolish, for example, to
embark upon repeated investigations to re-discover
the wheel whenever we need to use one. The judicial use of precedents by international tribunals,
therefore, reflects a practical habit of mind that
avoids duplication and looks to past history for
guidance. Not surprisingly, subsequent international courts and tribunals have given earlier decisions
a persuasive authority that shades into a form of
precedent, albeit not of the strictly binding kind.

Judicial decisions have become part of the sub-
stantive corpus of IEL. Influential cases include: the
Trail Smelter Arbitration, (U.S. v. Can.), 3 R.I.A.A.
1938 (1949) (*see* Chapter Fourteen); Corfu Channel
Case (U.K. v. Alb.), 1949 I.C.J. 4; Case Relating to
the Territorial Jurisdiction of the International
Commission of the River Oder (Czech., Den., Fr.,
Ger., Swed., U.K., Pol.), 1929 P.C.I.J. (ser. A) No.
23, at 5; Lake Lanoux Arbitration (Spain v. Fr), 12
R.I.A.A. 281 (1957) (*see* Chapter Fifteen); Nuclear
Test Cases (I) (N.Z. v. Fr.), 1974 I.C.J. 253 (*see*
Chapter Seventeen); and the Case Concerning the
Gabcikovo–Nagymaros project [Gabcikovo–Nagyma-
ros Project (Hungary/Slovakia), 1994 I.C.J. 151
(Dec. 20)] (*see* Chapter Three). In 1993, the ICJ
created a new chamber for environmental law, and
a cluster of new IEL cases began to reach the ICJ.

Four recent decisions of the court have thrust the
ICJ to take a more active role in IEL. Those deci-
sions are: 1) the Request for an Examination of
Situation in Accordance with Paragraph 63 of the

Court's Judgment of 20 December 1974 in Nuclear Tests (N.Z. v. Fra.), 1995 I.C.J. 288 (Sept. 22) (Nuclear Test Cases (II); 2) the Legality of the Use by a State of Nuclear Weapons in Armed Conflict, 1993 I.C.J. 467 (Request for an Advisory Opinion by the WHO of Sept. 13); 3) The Legality of the Threat or Use of Nuclear Weapons, 1995 I.C.J. 3 (Request for an Advisory Opinion by the UN General Assembly of Feb. 1); and 4) the Legality of the Use by a State of Nuclear Weapons in Armed Conflict, 1996 I.C.J. 66 (July 8). Ambiguities in the decisions in Nuclear Test Cases (II) and the WHO Advisory Opinion (*see* Chapter Seventeen) raise doubts as to whether this is a challenge the ICJ is willing to accept in the future.

E. OTHER SOURCES OF LAW

Other subsidiary sources of international law include the writings of "the most highly qualified publicists" or scholars, again "as subsidiary means for the determination of rules of law" [Statute of the ICJ, art. 38(1)(d)]. The most influential example of this source would be the work of the ILC, empowered by Article 13 of the UN Charter to "initiate studies and make recommendations for the purpose of encouraging the progressive development of international law and its codification."

Further sources include resolutions, declarations, action plans, and agendas of the United Nations and other inter-governmental organizations, such as the Stockholm Conference and UNCED. We have already adverted to the way in which international organizations can interpret the law. In addition, it is possible for governments to create customary law by how they vote within international organizations. Where, for example, a nation votes in favor of a resolution affirming that it is illegal to build a nuclear reactor without consulting those who might be affected by an accident, that nation's supporting vote may demonstrate both practice and *opinio juris*. It would show *opinio juris* if the vote for the resolution was premised upon the assumption that there was no option but to vote for it because it embodies established law, or because the state now accepts that it is the law.

The possibility exists for such resolutions to assume a quasi-legal or "soft law" character in which the evidence surrounding a resolution does not give birth to law as of its passing, but takes it into a gray zone between gestation and labor. Although the terms "hard law" and "soft law" do carry fairly specific meanings, the underlying realm of international agreements defies such a clear dichotomy, rendering the terms somewhat deceptive. To begin with, the terms themselves refer to the type of *instrument*. Hard law is explained as treaties and custom, whereas soft law instruments include declarations of principle, codes of practice, recommendations, guidelines, resolutions, and standards [PATRICIA W. BIRNIE & ALAN E. BOYLE, INTERNATIONAL LAW AND THE ENVIRONMENT (2002)].

The criterion that is most commonly used to distinguish hard and soft law is that only hard law instruments are legally binding. International law scholars, particularly in the area of customary international law, have long recognized the importance of states' *recognition* that a particular instrument or rule is legally binding (*opinio juris*) [*see* Lakshman Guruswamy, *International Environmental Law: Boundaries, Landmarks, and Realities*, 10 FALL NAT. RESOURCES & ENV'T. 43, 77 (1995)]. However, when comparing hard and soft law sources it is important to remember that *opinio juris* is only one factor out of many that compel states to meet the obligations each type of instrument creates. States may feel just as bound by provisions of soft law instruments for a variety of other reasons. First, soft law instruments are negotiated in a political climate, implicating an intrinsic pressure to live up to their terms [Geoffrey Palmer, *New Ways to Make International Environmental Law*, 86 A.J.I.L. 259, 270 (1992)]. For example, when New Zealand and other Pacific countries sought a United Nations resolution banning driftnet fishing in the South Pacific, the earlier Langkawi Declaration on the Environment of 1989, a soft law instrument, gave them leverage to align support from the parties to that agreement, even though they never meant to be legally bound [*id*]. Also, states might choose to adhere to soft law norms out of concern for reciprocity—to ensure that the other parties to the agreement do likewise [RICHARD B. BILDER, MANAGING THE RISK OF INTERNATIONAL AGREEMENT (1981)]. Nations also seek to maintain an image of trustworthiness amongst other nations, both generally and for the purpose of preserving other nations' willingness to enter into further agreements [*id*]. Additionally, there often exists the threat of retaliation and other sanctions from other states in the event of noncompliance [*id*]. These and other pressures also operate to motivate states' compliance with hard law obligations.

The distinction between hard and soft law instruments is further clouded by the nature of compliance mechanisms in international law. There is no means of enforcing international legal obligations, even legally binding treaties, suggesting not that compliance is voluntary, but that political pressure, reciprocity, and other influences weigh more heavily on states than a sense of legal obligation, even for hard law. Furthermore, within supposedly "hard" treaties, the language used to create some of the obligations reveals that they are purely aspirational, and not meant to be legally binding at all. So, while the terms "hard" and "soft" law are useful for distinguishing between two different sets of documents, this classification is not particularly instructive as to what extent a particular document affects the behavior of the party states. A treaty, even one whose provisions are worded in an effort to create binding obligations on the parties, may be largely ignored following its entry into force. Likewise, a soft law instrument intended largely to be a political instrument may receive vigorous adherence by its member parties.

A second, less commonly used criterion for distinguishing between hard and soft law instruments is the degree of specificity of their provisions. In general the norms embodied in soft law instruments lack the precision and specificity of those found in treaties. Because of their elasticity, soft law norms may succeed in securing at least a preliminary consensus amongst nations with competing interests and views. By contrast it is much more difficult to obtain consensus for legally binding treaty obligations in a politically, culturally, and economically diverse world of nation states. Any form of agreement is valuable in and of itself, and the flexibility of soft law instruments permits nations, often with contradictory interests, to reach agreements which they might have balked at in more formal and demanding treaty instruments [Palmer, *supra*, at 269].

The preliminary consensus reflected in soft law agreements can serve as a catalyst to producing more binding agreements. The Helsinki Declaration on the Protection of the Ozone Layer sought successfully to reach a consensus that would ensure that meetings in London the following year would yield hard amendments to the Montreal Protocol [*id* at 269–70]. The UNEP Cairo Guidelines and Principles for the Environmentally Sound Management of Hazardous Waste, both soft law instruments, saw many of their provisions incorporated into the Basel Convention, and the Berlin Mandate acted as a precursor to the Kyoto Protocol to the United Nations Framework Convention on Climate Change. Most recently, Agenda 21 principles increasingly appear in new international agreements and judicial decisions. Craig H. Allen, *Protecting the Oceanic Gardens of Eden: International Law Issues in Deep–Sea Vent Resource Conservation and Management*, 13 GEO. INT'L ENVT'L L REV 563, 600 (2001).

Consequently, it is no longer possible to confine the corpus of IEL to the formal and traditional sources of international law such as treaties, custom, general principles and judicial decisions. As we have seen from the forgoing discussion, IEL has witnessed the growth of a significant and increasing body of declarations and resolutions of international conferences that have shaped, and will continue to play an even more important role in influencing its new contours.

CHAPTER TWO

THE HISTORICAL CONTINUUM

The present is often illuminated by the past. Landmark developments of IEL from 1972 to the present form a historical continuum that helps us better understand the strengths and weaknesses of the subject. We examine these landmarks.

A. THE STOCKHOLM CONFERENCE ON THE HUMAN ENVIRONMENT 1972

The 1972 Stockholm Conference on the Human Environment, (Stockholm Conference), may well have been the chrysalis from which IEL emerged as a legal subject in its own right. Up to about the time of the Stockholm Conference, international environmental problems had been dealt with in a sporadic and ad hoc manner resulting in a few significant treaties. These treaties were isolated events that did not constitute a recognizable corpus of IEL. The development of IEL leading to the Stockholm Conference was influenced by the thinking, ideology, and culture of concern about the environment experienced the world over.

The themes articulated in Rachel Carson's book, SILENT SPRING (1962), Barry Commoner's, THE CLOS-

ING CIRCLE (1971), and Kenneth Boulding's *Spaceship Earth*, [*see generally, The Economics of the Coming Spaceship Earth, in* ENVIRONMENTAL QUALITY IN A GROWING ECONOMY 3 (1966)] resonated from the United States into the thinking of other industrial nations. Many of these and other themes were melded and expressed with crusading cogency within an international context in LIMITS TO GROWTH [MEADOWS, ET AL. (1972)], a computer modeled study sponsored by the Club of Rome, a private group of industrialists and world leaders. The Meadows project team painted an apocalyptic picture of the growth of population, pollution, and exhaustion of natural resources leading to a break down of the carrying capacity of the earth. Along with a growing awareness of environmental phenomena such as acid rain and the poisoning of Japanese fisherman in Minimata bay, these publications led to a realization of the frailty of the planet earth and fomented apprehension among a cross section of common people, influential elites and decision makers in the developed industrial world.

In the face of these concerns, the United Nations was moved to convene a special international environmental conference to discuss the human environment in 1972. Sweden, which had begun to experience transboundary acid rain, volunteered to host it in Stockholm. The overall sense of crisis crying out for global action was brilliantly captured in the book by Rene Dubos and Barbara Ward, specially commissioned for the Stockholm Conference. [*See generally* ONLY ONE EARTH: THE CARE AND MAINTENANCE OF A SMALL PLANET (1972)].

While concern about the environment motivated many rich, developed industrial countries (DCs), the poor, less developed countries (LDCs) did not share the view that environmental degradation was the biggest threat facing the planet. For the LDCs, poverty and the alleviation of misery remained a more poignant and real problem. In the preparatory meetings leading to Stockholm, the LDCs–which called themselves the Group of 77 (their original number)–sharply and forcefully articulated the view that the worst pollution was caused by poverty. LDCs believed that greater development leading to material prosperity far outweighed any damage that might be caused by resource use and pollution. They were particularly scornful of the claim that DCs were genuinely trying to steer them away from pitfalls into which the DCs had fallen. LDCs expressed resentment over the fact that the DCs— whose drive toward wealth had consumed a great part of the earth's resources and had led to devastating pollution—were now asking the LDCs to remain poor, and, more gallingly, to pay for the clean up, restoration, and conservation of the earth. Many LDCs feared, moreover, that new environmental standards adopted by DCs would effectively bar the entry of LDCs' goods into DC markets.

This ideological impasse presented a formidable challenge to international environmental diplomacy and the question was resolved, as best it might be, by way of a compromise worked out in a meeting at

Founex, near Geneva, Switzerland. The compromise held that economic development was not necessarily incompatible with environmental protection, and that development could proceed provided it avoided damaging the environment. The essence of that understanding was summed up in the Preamble to the Stockholm Declaration of the United Nations Conference on the Environment (Stockholm Declaration), June 16, 1972, 11 I.L.M. 1416. It stated that "[m]ost of the environmental problems of LDCs are caused by under-development" and that LDCs must direct their efforts to development with due regard to the priority of safeguarding and improving the environment [*id*. § I, ¶ 4]. Similarly, the industrialized countries were exhorted to make efforts to reduce the developmental gap between themselves and the developing countries. In sum, the LDCs successfully thwarted potential environmental laws and policies from damaging their efforts to develop and grow economically, whether by industrial progress or trade. They did not, however, obtain substantial bankrolling for environmentally conscious development or give pledges to protect the global environment. This early declaration also did not meaningfully advance the doctrine of "common but differentiated responsibility" [*see* Chapter Six] later accepted at the 1992 Earth Summit [United Nations Conference on Environment and Development (UNCED), Rio de Janeiro, Brazil] as a means of recognizing the different needs of LDCs and DCs.

The Stockholm Conference, under the direction of its dynamic Secretary–General, Maurice Strong, is

regarded as the best documented, best organized
UN conference of its time. For a number of reasons,
it may also be considered the cocoon of IEL. First,
the biosphere, or the planet, was identified as an
object and placed on the agenda of national and
international policy and law in a way that had
never been done before. Second, the conference was
widely attended with 114 of the then 131 UN members participating in it (the Soviet bloc abstained
from attending, not because it rejected the purpose
or mission of the conference, but because of the
status accorded to East Germany). Third, the Stockholm Conference resulted in the creation of the
United Nations Environment Program (UNEP)
(more fully described in Appendix A), the first international organization with an exclusively environmental mandate. The UNEP has been instrumental
in drafting, facilitating and negotiating a number of
environmental treaties. Fourth, it produced a conference declaration of twenty-six principles (Stockholm Declaration) that dealt with the rights and
obligations of citizens and governments with regard
to the preservation and improvement of the environment. Apart from the Stockholm Declaration,
which is generally considered an instrument of IEL
in that it either crystallized or generated customary
law, the Stockholm Conference also created an action plan containing recommendations for future
implementation.

A number of specific principles of the Stockholm
Declaration bear mention. Principles 1, 2, and 5,
dealing with responsibilities to future generations,

were undergirded by an obligation to conserve. Principle 1, albeit counterbalanced by Principle 11, recognized a nascent right to a quality environment. Principle 21 referred to the right of states to exploit its resources pursuant to their environmental (*not* developmental) policies, and affirmed their obligation not to cause transboundary injury. This was followed by Principle 22, positing that states shall cooperate to develop international law regarding liability and compensation for extra-territorial harm.

These Principles have been re-institutionalized in many post-Stockholm agreements. For example, Principle 21 has been incorporated in a wide range of treaties including the Biodiversity Convention, (see Chapter Five), Vienna Ozone Convention, (see Chapter Seven), the LRTAP (see Chapter Fourteen), and UNCLOS (see below). Furthermore, the post-Stockholm world has spawned a prolific number of environmental treaties. Over 100 post-Stockholm treaties mirror almost every concern that has been the subject of national laws or regulations including acid rain, hazardous waste, ozone depletion, sea pollution from land and vessels, toxics, resource conservation, and global warming.

B. UNITED NATIONS CONVENTION ON THE LAW OF THE SEA (UNCLOS) 1982

Even Before Stockholm, negotiations had commenced concerning the law of the sea. Those negotiations lasted until 1982, when UNCLOS was opened for signature. UNCLOS finally came into force on November 16, 1994. It is the strongest comprehensive environmental treaty now in existence or likely to emerge for quite some time [*Letter of Submittal of the Secretary of State to the President of the United States*, 7 GEO. INT'L ENVT'L L. REV. 77 (1994)]. Arguably, it possesses the fundamental and over-arching character of a constitution for the oceans because of the scope and reach of its 59 provisions obligating environmental protection and conservation, out of 320 provisions in all. It can be asserted that UNCLOS functions not only as a treaty, but as a codification and articulation of customary international rules applicable to the oceans, binding on both signatories and non-signatories [Jonathan I. Charney, *Entry Into Force of the 1982 Convention on the Law of the Sea,* 35 VA. J. INT'L. L. 381 (1995); LOUIS SOHN & KRISTEN GUSTAFSON, THE LAW OF THE SEA IN A NUTSHELL (1984)].

It is worth remembering in this context that the oceans occupy over seventy percent of the landmass of the earth, and are in many ways a proxy for the global environment. Most pollution released into the environment is eventually deposited into the oceans through direct and indirect pathways, although the control of land-based pollution is generally directed at environmental controls on land dealing with air, land, and water pollution. Notable areas of oceanic governance such as conservation of wetlands, coastal areas, and biodiversity are of critical significance to international environmental protection in general.

UNCLOS contains at least fifty-nine environmental provisions, ranging from the global to the specific, spread out over several parts of the text including the Territorial Sea and Contiguous Zone (Part II), Exclusive Economic Zone (Part V), High Seas (Part VII), Enclosed or Semi–Enclosed Areas (Part IX), The Area (Part XI), Protection and Preservation of the Marine Environment (Part XII), and Marine Scientific Research (Part XIII). They deal with the conservation and management of living resources, pollution prevention, reduction, and control, vessel pollution, and environmental management.

UNCLOS is an umbrella convention that brings other international rules, regulations, and implementing bodies within its canopy. At the substantive level of obligation and implementation, many of its provisions are of a constitutional or general character, and call to be augmented and supplemented by specific regulations, rules, and implementing procedures formulated by other international agreements and nation states.

C. WORLD COMMISSION ON ENVIRONMENT AND DEVELOPMENT

Despite the uneasy truce at Founex reflected in the Stockholm Declaration, the persistent clash of two cultures, environmental protection and. development, continued to obstruct the progress of IEL. In order to resolve this problem, the World Commission on Environment and Development (WCED or Brundtland Commission) was created by the General Assembly of the UN in 1983 and charged with proposing long-term environmental strategies for *sustainable development*. That elusive term was not defined by the UN, and, despite the efforts of the Brundtland Commission and the Earth Summit, still eludes satisfactory definition. After four years of deliberation and worldwide consultation, the Brundtland Report, *Our Common Future*, articulated the paradigm on which the Earth Summit, and indeed IEL, has since been based. In essence, it rejected the despairing thesis that environmental problems were past repair, spiraling out of control, and could only be averted by arresting development and economic growth: a policy of no growth. Instead, it argued that economic growth was both desirable and possible within a context of sustainable development. [WORLD COMMISSION ON ENVIRONMENTAL DEVELOPMENT, OUR COMMON FUTURE (1987)].

Although sustainable development was not clearly defined, some of its key attributes are identifiable. It calls for developmental policies and for economic growth that can relieve the great poverty of the LDCs while simultaneously protecting the environment from further damage. Such development and growth should be based on policies that sustain and expand the environmental resource base in a manner that meets the needs of the present generation

without compromising the ability of future generations to meet their own needs.

In order to draw up a global plan for sustainable
development, the Brundtland Commission called for
an international conference to act as the successor
to the Stockholm Conference and carry forward its
legacy. The UN General Assembly complied, directing the UNCED or Earth Summit to take account,
inter alia, of the Stockholm Declaration and further
develop IEL. An ambitious agenda was drawn up
for the Earth Summit that included the following
three endeavors: 1) an Earth Charter that would be
the successor to the Stockholm Declaration; 2) an
action plan for the planet called Agenda 21; and 3)
the ceremonial signing of two conventions on biodiversity, and climate change.

D.   UNITED NATIONS CONFERENCE
ON ENVIRONMENT AND
DEVELOPMENT 1992

The Earth Summit, by which name the UNCED
is popularly called, was held in Rio de Janeiro in
June, 1992, and attended by over 180 countries and
100 heads of state. It has since been heralded as the
greatest summit level conference in history. It lead
to these four institutional results: 1) the *Rio Declaration on Environment and Development* (Rio Declaration), June 13, 1992, 31 I.L.M. 874; 2) *Agenda 21*,
U.N. Doc. A/CONF. 151/26 (1992); 3) the *Non-
legally Binding Authoritative Statement of Principles for a Global Consensus on the Management,*

Conservation and Sustainable Development of All Types of Forests, U.N. Doc. A/CONF. 151/26, v.3 (1992); and 4) the ceremonial signing of the Climate Change and Biodiversity Conventions.

Initial Earth Summit assessments were for differing reasons generally favorable, while a few were almost unreservedly laudatory, even euphoric. Later, more considered evaluations are beginning to cast doubts on these reviews. We do not offer a studied and documented appraisal of that event. Instead, we very briefly advance some conclusions adverted to in the course of the book.

In our view, the legal results of the Earth Summit were, at best, mottled. Rio undoubtedly offered a great platform for environmental protection, but its contribution to IEL was more apparent than real. While it did draw universal attention to environmental protection and raised many issues onto the global agenda, the legacy of Rio—apart from the Climate Change Convention—remains unimpressive.

To begin, the "Rio Declaration on Environment and Development" (Rio Declaration) replaced the intended "Earth Charter," with the former diminishing the environmental resonance of the latter. Second, the tone of the Rio Declaration set a dubious foundation for IEL and effectively turned the clock back from the Stockholm Convention. For example, the nascent right to a wholesome environment embodied in the Stockholm Declaration was abandoned in favor of a right to development (Principle 2). Also, the obligation not to cause transfrontier damage contained in Principle 21 of the Stockholm Declaration was weakened in Principle 2 of the Rio Declaration by the addition of crucial language authorizing states "to exploit their own natural resources pursuant to their own environmental and *developmental* policies" (emphasis added). Following a similar theme, the obligation to *conserve* implied by the duty to protect the environment for the benefit of future generations found in the Stockholm Declaration is replaced in the Rio Declaration by a right to *consume* or develop. The Rio formulation refers to "developmental and environmental needs of present and future generations" (Principle 3). Disappointingly, this re-formulation impliedly negates or weakens the obligation to conserve expressed in the Stockholm Declaration. Finally, the Rio Declaration frowns upon action such as that taken by the United States under the Marine Mammal Protection Act of 1972, 16 U.S.C. §§ 1361–1421 (1994), to prevent the slaughter of dolphins by prohibiting imports of tuna caught in dolphin killing nets. Principle 12 of the Rio Declaration states that "unilateral actions to deal with environmental challenges outside the jurisdiction of the importing country should be avoided." While the substantive shortcomings of the Rio Declaration do not necessarily restrict the further development of IEL, the ramifications of the Rio Declaration need to be addressed and are referred to in Chapter 18.

Agenda 21, a non-binding agreement, typifies a noticeable trend in IEL toward "soft law" norms (as discussed in Chapter One, treaties and custom generally create binding obligations on nations, while soft law sources are largely aspirational). Just as the Rio Declaration incorporated several allowances for nations' developmental needs, perhaps at the expense of more environmentally protective provisions like those of the Stockholm Declaration, Agenda 21 has been shaped by the tension between development and environmental protection. Agenda 21 calls for the "integration of environment and development concerns and greater attention to them" [Chapter 1.1], but this monumental challenge has been aggravated by the differing interests of developed and less developed nations, and has witnessed only limited progress.

While Agenda 21 calls for the conservation and protection of resources, it also mirrors the Rio Declaration in acknowledging the unique position of economies in transition, affirming the priority of political and social challenges in developing nations [Chapter 1.5]. Specifically, Chapter 3.2 gives substantial deference to the use of natural resources to combat poverty. Chapter 39, which deals with the review and development of international environmental policy, stresses the importance of participation by developing countries in drafting new legal instruments, but reaffirms the need to weigh their developmental needs against the obligations that might be imposed by those instruments.

Agenda 21 is not, however, devoid of an environmental dimension. Chapters 9–22 are devoted to and deal *inter alia* with the protection of the atmosphere, combating of deforestation, and integrated approach to land management, managing fragile ecosystems, conserving biological diversity, managing toxic chemicals and the management of hazardous, solid and radioactive wastes.

E. WORLD SUMMIT ON SUSTAINABLE DEVELOPMENT 2002 (WSSD)

In August and September 2002, ten years after the Earth Summit in Rio, the nations once again gathered for a major international environmental conference. This summit, held in Johannesburg as a follow-up to Rio, discussed present progress and further implementation of Agenda 21.

The Johannesburg Summit as originally envisioned was intended primarily to stimulate implementation of Agenda 21. The focus of the WSSD, however, as reflected in the deliberations and the two documents produced by it, was more clearly riveted on the problems created by poverty as distinct from environmental degradation. The conference gave birth to just two documents: a political Declaration and an Implementation Plan. [*World Summit on Sustainable Development Plan of Implementation*, Sept. 5, 2002, available at http://www.johannesburgsummit.org/html/documents/summit_docs/2309_planfinal.doc].

The Implementation Plan incorporated several important new goals to be reached within the next twenty years, including meeting people's basic sanitation needs, production and use of non-harmful chemicals, restoration of the world's fish stocks, and reductions in the rate of loss of biological diversity. [*Id.*]. More importantly, the Declaration affirmed "a collective responsibility to advance and strengthen the interdependent and mutually reinforcing pillars of sustainable development—economic development, social development and environmental protection—at the local, national, regional and global levels" [art 5]. The same principles were endorsed in the Implementation Plan. [Ch. 1, Introduction, para 2].

What is most striking about this re-articulation of SD is that it introduces a third element into the definition of SD. Social development, which hitherto had been subsumed under the rubric of economic development, is now treated as a separate concept. This is a significant development to the extent that SD—which hitherto consisted of two legs (economic development and environmental protection)—has now been given a third (social development). Consequently, environmental protection, which had enjoyed rough parity with economic development, has now been reduced to a third part of a tripartite concept.

The WSSD also represented a step forward in implementation of Agenda 21's focus on non-state actors. Section III of Agenda 21 sets forth a novel, hands-on approach with an emphasis on the importance of major social groups in implementing new environmental policies. Unlike previous conferences on sustainable development, in which delegates were exclusively from nation-states, delegates to Johannesburg included not only 10,000 government delegates but also some 8,000 delegates from civil society, including representatives from NGOs, corporate interests, and other areas of civil society. In addition, parallel events incorporated conferences between interested parties representing NGOs, women, indigenous people, youth, farmers, trade unions, business leaders, the scientific and technological community and local authorities as well as Chief Justices from various countries. [UN/DESA, *Key Outcomes of the Summit*, Sept. 2002, available at http://www.johannesburgsummit.org/ html/documents/summit_docs/2009_keyoutcomes_ commitments.doc].

The Summit saw a new level of dialog between these factions that encouraged a deeper understanding of each sector's needs. NGO, IGO, and business delegates launched more than 300 voluntary partnerships in which they made firm commitments of resources and interest to the implementation of sustainable development measures. The Secretary–General of the Summit, Nitin Desai, hailed this development as a major step towards achieving tangible results in the field, noting that "the results of the Summit have been far more comprehensive than any previous outcome. We have put together not only a work plan, but we have identified the actors who are expected to achieve results" [*The*

Johanesburg Summit Test: What Will Change?,
at http://www.johannesburgsummit.org/html/whats_
new/feature_story41.html (accessed Mar. 4, 2003)].
NGO leaders were similarly optimistic about the
trend signaled by the Johannesburg Summit, and
hailed it as a harbinger of "a new way of governing
the global commons—the beginnings of a shift from
the stiff formal waltz of traditional diplomacy to the
jazzier dance of improvisational solution-oriented
partnerships that may include non-government organizations, willing governments and other stakeholders" [*Id.*, quoting Johnathan Lash, President of
World Resources Institute]. With time, the involvement of these sectors of society may enable greater
implementation and cooperation among factions
seeking to obtain the sometimes contradictory goals
of sustainable development.

Major international conferences are epochal
events that demonstrate the commitment, re-affir-
mation, and consensus of the international community for developing the living law of the environment. They offer an eagle's view of IEL, and
demonstrate the extent to which IEL is now a permanent feature of the geo-political landscape of the
international community of nations, and of international civil society. We have seen how some of
the ubiquitous themes of IEL have been developed
and re-shaped by these conferences. They include
evolving concepts such as sustainable development—embracing the tension between economic
and social development and environmental protection—along with obligations to prevent transboun-

dary damage, the concept of common but differentiated responsibility, the precautionary principle, the doctrine of State Responsibility, the growth of NGO's, and a host of other the themes that will continue to be developed and re-worked on the foundations established by these global conferences. It is to a closer examination of the constituent segments of IEL that we now turn.

CHAPTER THREE

IMPLEMENTATION

The various problems discussed in Part II of this Nutshell illustrate the extent to which national problems have become international ones and demonstrate why international answers cannot be separated from national responses. The international environmental problems that first arise within nation states often cause territorial harm to the peoples and civil societies within those states before creating extraterritorial damage. These environmental problems demand national legislative, administrative, and judicial measures. Any international action taken to abate extraterritorial harm must necessarily address the roots of the problem located within nation states.

Most international treaties require implementation within individual nation states. Implementation of treaty obligations, however, is hampered by the fact that the vertical command and control power structure governing domestic politics within nations is conspicuously absent within the international legal order. In international society, power or authority rests on a horizontal base made up of co-equal sovereign states, and can be built into a pyramidal structure only if these nations consent to and join in such an endeavor. While piecemeal building upon the base has resulted in the substantial corpus of IEL noted in Chapter One, there is no overarching pyramid of authority consisting of law-making, law-interpreting, law-implementing, or law-enforcing institutions.

The absence of institutions cloning those within nation states does not signify a complete void in international implementing institutions. On the contrary, what we have are international implementing agencies and mechanisms serving the international society in which we live. They merit examination, and we begin with the many international organizations that facilitate the implementation of IEL, and follow this by examining compliance mechanisms, diplomatic avenues and judicial remedies as methods of implementation.

A. INSTITUTIONS AND ORGANIZATIONS

Despite the impressive growth of IEL and its expanding domain, there is still no single institution or organization that serves environmental protection in the way that the World Trade Organization (WTO) advances, interprets, implements, and enforces the concept of free trade [General Agreement on Tariffs and Trade, Final Act Embodying the Results of the Uruguay Round of Multinational Trade Negotiations, Apr. 15, 1994, LEGAL INSTRU-MENTS—RESULTS OF THE URUGUAY ROUND vol. 1, 33 I.L.M. 1125 (Hereinafter GATT 1994)]. The institutions and organizations enlisted to advance IEL are fractured, fragmented, and divided along functional, regional, bureaucratic, and geo-political lines. It is useful to take note of the more important of these entities, and a fuller description of them is found in Appendix A, *infra*. They are classified as Global Organizations, Regional Organizations, Treaty Specific Organizations and Non–Governmental Organizations.

1. GLOBAL ORGANIZATIONS

The United Nations was founded in 1947 before the dawning of environmental awareness, and its Charter creates seven principal organs including the General Assembly, the Security Council, the Economic and Social Council (ECOSOC), and the International Court of Justice (ICJ) [Charter of the United Nations (UN Charter), art. 7, Oct. 24, 1945, 1 U.N.T.S. xvi]. The UN Charter neither creates an environmental organ nor specifically mandates the protection of the environment.

A number of international organizations created by treaty or agreement have been brought into a familial relationship with the UN pursuant to charter provisions, and are known as Specialized Agencies of the UN. They enjoy juridical personality and may exercise rights and duties as subjects of international law. A number of them have broadly interpreted their constituent treaties to adopt an environmental competence. Those presently assuming environmental responsibilities include the Food and Agricultural Organization (FAO), the International

Labor Organization (ILO), the World Health Organization (WHO), the World Meteorological Organization (WMO), the International Maritime Organization (IMO), the UN Educational, Scientific, and Cultural Organization (UNESCO), and the International Atomic Energy Agency (IAEA).

While the IAEA does not possess Specialized Agency status as such, it plays a role in advancing environmental protection along with other semi-autonomous UN bodies such as the UN Development Program (UNDP), the United Nations Institute for Training and Research (UNITAR), and the United Nations Conference on Trade and Development (UNCTAD). After UNCED, the General Assembly of the UN created the Commission on Sustainable Development (CSD) as a functional commission of ECOSOC. Perhaps the most important of the UN Organizations, the UN Environment Program (UNEP) was created by a General Assembly resolution, not by treaty or agreement.

UNEP was established to act as a focal point for environmental action and coordination, but possesses no executive power. All UNEP programs are financed directly by member states. Consequently, its mission is to persuade and convince states of the need for environmental action, provide information, expertise and advice, and sponsor treaties. It has carried out these limited objectives credibly.

Increasingly, incentives, financial mechanisms, and technology transfers have become part of the architecture of IEL, and it is necessary to take note of the more important of the institutions involved. The World Bank group consists of the International Bank for Reconstruction and Development (IBRD), the International Development Bank (IDA), and the International Finance Corporation (IFC). The World Bank has developed a bad record by encouraging environmentally damaging developments, but under growing pressure from activists and NGOs appears to be mending its ways. In 2001 it released its Environmental Strategy, entitled *Making Sustainable Commitments: An Environmental Strategy for the World Bank, 2001*, which was a comprehensive pledge to consider environmental factors while pursuing its overarching goals of poverty reduction and social growth. The Environmental Strategy of the World Bank also acknowledged the environmental shortcomings of its past decision making.

In addition, the Global Environment Facility (GEF) was established in 1990 on an experimental basis to provide financial and technical assistance to developing countries to promote environmental protection. It was restructured permanently in 1994 and is a potential source of green funds for *Agenda 21*, [U.N. Doc. A/CONF. 151/26 (1992)], the United Nations Framework Convention on Climate Change (Climate Change Convention), [May 22, 1992, 31 I.L.M. 849 (entered into force Mar. 21, 1994)], and the Convention on Biological Diversity (Biodiversity Convention), [June 5, 1992, 31 I.L.M. 818 (entered into force Dec. 29, 1993)].

A review of global environmental institutions would not be complete without a reference to two legal institutions: 1) the International Court of Justice (ICJ), and 2) the International Law Commission (ILC). The ICJ is the principal judicial organ of the UN system, and exercises jurisdiction by consent. It has now set up an environmental chamber and demonstrated in the Advisory Opinion on the Threat or Use of Nuclear Weapons that it possesses the authority to address vexing environmental issues and apply the law to changing situations [Legality of the use by a State of Nuclear Weapons in Armed Conflict, 1996 I.C.J. 66 (July 8)]. The ILC was created by the UN General Assembly to work toward the codification and development of international law, and it has reported on subjects of great importance to IEL such as state responsibility and international watercourses.

2. REGIONAL ORGANIZATIONS

A number of regional organizations are playing an important role in developing IEL. The most important of these is the European Union (EU), formerly known as the European Community (EC) and the European Economic Community (EEC). The EU is the most advanced form of international organization in the world and is evolving into a Continent-wide political confederation. It possesses three key attributes lacking in other international organizations: 1) law-making agencies; 2) law-interpreting and enforcing agencies; and 3) a court with compulsory jurisdiction. Clothed with explicit environmental jurisdiction, the EU has enacted a large number of environmental laws over a wide range of subject areas. The extent of its corpus of environmental law, and the changing jurisprudential character of the EU, deters us from dealing with EU law in this volume. Other regional bodies of note are the Council of Europe, the Organization for Economic Cooperation and Development (OECD), the Organization of American States (OAS), and the South Pacific Regional Organization. (SPREP)).

3. SPECIFIC TREATY ORGANIZATIONS

Many treaties set up institutional arrangements (or rudimentary international organizations) for their implementation. They range from *ad hoc* conferences to more permanent institutional structures. A number of them are called conferences of the parties, which include a permanent secretariat and a budget, and, in some cases, special science advisory bodies. Representative examples include the sporadic conference of the parties under the Vienna Convention for the Protection of the Ozone Layer (Vienna Convention on Ozone), [March 22, 1985, 26 I.L.M. 1529 (1988)] and regular meetings of the parties under the Montreal Protocol on Substances that Deplete the Ozone Layer (Montreal Protocol), [Sept. 16, 1987, 26 I.L.M. 1550 (1989)] (*see* Chapter Seven). Additionally, the Climate Change Convention (*see* Chapter Six) institutes an annual conference of the parties, and the Biodiversity Convention (*see* Chapter Five) provides for a conference of the parties on regular intervals. Finally, the Convention for the Protection of the Marine Environment of the North East Atlantic (OSPAR Convention), Sept. 22, 1992, 32 I.L.M. 1069 (*see* Chapter Ten) requires regular meetings of the Commission, while the Convention on International Trade in Endangered Species of Wild Fauna and Flora (CITES), [Mar. 3, 1973, 12 I.L.M. 1085 (1975)] (*see* Chapter Five) sets up a conference of the parties that meets at least every two years.

4. NON–GOVERNMENTAL ORGANIZATIONS (NGOS)

Global NGOs are playing an increasingly important role in IEL. We mention three out of hundreds to illustrate their diversity and spread. The World Conservation Union (IUCN) is a unique hybrid comprised of non-governmental conservation groups, states, and public law entities such as universities and research institutes. The World Wildlife Fund (WWF) is a non-governmental conservation group whose goals parallel those of IUCN. WWF finances conservation strategies throughout the world. A third is the Earth Council, endorsed by the UNCED in 1992, which assists grassroots organizations pressing for the implementation of sustainable development (*see* Appendix A). The changing role of NGOs in shaping IEL is reflected by the substantial extent to which NGOs participated in the recent World Summit on Sustainable Development 2002 WSSD (*see* Chapter 2). Although UN conferences have historically been attended exclusively by the representatives of nation-states, WSSD offered extensive opportunities for NGO involvement.

NGOs have become established actors in the implementation of environmental law for a number of reasons. To begin, they are closer to the people affected by environmental degradation, and have the ability to represent them more faithfully and diligently than their governments. Second, NGOs have played a major role in organizing the once invisible colleges of scientists for the purpose of studying the effects and impacts of various environmental problems, and have participated, unofficially but visibly, in the making of treaties. Not surprisingly, they profess a legitimate and well-founded interest in the implementation of IEL. Third, the international character of these organizations embraces the concept of a global civil society committed to environmental protection, and their large and vocal membership have given them an undeniable international political standing.

Although NGOs exert pressure on nations and international organizations to comply with IEL, they have not yet attained the status of states as subjects of international law. There are fundamental conceptual problems in their achieving theoretical parity with states within a legal system comprised of sovereign states alone. Furthermore, NGOs' claims to the moral high ground of politics have been criticized on the basis that they are not significantly different from other self seeking units of civil society like churches, civic groups, trade unions and corporations. These critics point out that churches, civic groups, trade unions and corporations seek to advance the interests of their members whether they be parishioners, union card holders, or stock holders in the same way that NGOs do. The critics further argue that the self interested propagation of false or inflated environmental claims and alarm-mongering resorted to by some NGOs to increase membership is morally opprobrious. At the very least, such tactics are a far cry from the unsullied virtue claimed by NGOs, and does not entitle them to any preferential standing than other civic groups.

Despite these critiques, on a functional level there ought not to be objections to states or international organizations allowing environmental NGOs, or other civic groups for that matter, from performing the role of private attorneys general empowered to protect the international environment. Some treaties point the way in this direction.

For example, the IAEA has granted consultative status to NGOs having special competence in the nuclear field [Rules on Consultative Status of NGOs with the Agency, IAEA Doc. INFCIRC/14, (1959)]. The Convention on the Protection of the Environment Between Denmark, Finland, Norway and Sweden (Nordic Treaty), [art. 2, Feb. 9, 1974, 1092 U.N.T.S. 279 (entered into force Oct. 5, 1976)] goes further and grants all legal persons, including individuals, and non-governmental organizations the right to protest and vindicate environmental rights and duties in the legal systems of the parties. So, too, does the European Union [*see* Treaty Establishing the European Community, Mar. 25, 1957, art 230 (as amended), *reprinted in* EUROPEAN UNION LAW SELECTED DOCUMENTS 95 (Bermann, Goebel, Davey, Fox eds., 2002); *see also* Case t–585/93, Stichting Greenpeace, et al. v. Commission, 695 B.O. 219 (Ct. First Instance 1995)]. The Convention for the Protection of the Marine Environment of the North–East Atlantic (OSPAR Convention) 41 I.L.M. 1519, goes even further by granting NGOs observer status—a role which entitles them to participate in the meetings of the parties, and to submit reports, but not to vote [arts. 11(1) & (2)].

Formal treaty provisions are not the only means of obtaining NGO input. For example, the CSD is required to accept input from NGOs relating to the implementation of Agenda 21 [UNGA Res. 47/91, ¶ 3 (h) (1992)]. The CSD has also invited extensive participation by NGOs in the recent WSSD, including opportunities for representative groups to address the plenary. NGOs are sometimes invited to attend and participate as non-voting observers at the negotiations for international agreements, such as the Stockholm Convention on Persistent Organic Pollutants [May 22, 2001, 40 I.L.M. 532]. Even more striking, the Inspection Panel of the World Bank was created to provide an independent forum for private citizens or organizations who believe that they or their interests have been or could be directly harmed by a project financed by the World Bank. In a number of cases the World Bank has taken action pursuant to the claims and reports of the Inspection Panel [Lori Udall, THE WORLD BANK INSPECTION PANEL: A Three Year Review (1997)].

B. COMPLIANCE MECHANISMS

The international organizations we have referred to do not enjoy or exercise the power and authority of national legislative, executive, and judicial bodies that supervise and enforce the implementation of laws within nation states. It is important, therefore, that the substantive rules of international law should first possess an internal force or dynamic that makes sense to the parties and invokes an attitude of compliance rather than non-compliance. We have discussed some of the factors inducing voluntary compliance with the obligations created by international instruments in Chapter One § E. Treaty negotiators try to formulate and endow substantive rules with some compliance-generating character based on an eclectic mix of self interest, inducements, promises, embarrassment, and threats that promote implementation without the need for external supervision. Second, conventions or treaties also create institutions and techniques that induce compliance, while conferring power on appropriate authorities to deal with non-compliance. Consequently, treaties display a variety of processes, procedures and techniques that encourage compliance. As we have seen, some set up their own institutions, while others delegate power to existing international organizations such as those mentioned above. Individual treaties contain varying baskets of measures addressing such tasks, and provide *inter alia* for the following: interpretation, research, information and data collection and/or dissemination, monitoring, reporting, reviews of performance, rule-making by experts subject to differing types of confirmation, and management by international organizations. These compliance mechanisms call for further description.

To begin, we have referred to the importance of interpretation as a method of implementing a treaty [*supra* in Chapter One § C]. The interpretation and implementation of the Montreal Protocol provides illustrations—more adventurous than others—of how interpretation and other processes can be used as compliance techniques [*see* T. Ghering, *International Environment Regimes: Dynamic Legal* Systems, 1 Y.B. INT'L ENVT'L L. 35, 47–54 (1990)]. The First Meeting of the Parties under the Montreal Protocol clarified and interpreted various treaty obligations, including those in Annex A, which expressly stated that the Ozone Depletion Potential (ODP) figure for one of the halons was "to be determined." Inserting an ODP figure technically required amending the Annex of the Protocol, and involved a circuitous procedure, plus ratification by two thirds of the parties. To circumvent these cumbersome amendment procedures, the parties inserted an ODP figure into the Annex of the Protocol by way of interpretation.

The Second Meeting continued further along these lines, as states adopted a comprehensive "Amendment" to the Montreal Protocol that came into force upon ratification by one third of the parties, even though the explicit language of the Protocol itself required amendments to be ratified by two thirds of the parties. They also established an Interim Multilateral Fund to support ozone-friendly technology in developing countries, even though there was no provision either in the framework convention or the Protocol that authorized such a step. The Second Meeting of the Parties also adopted a "non-compliance procedure" not provided for in the Protocol, that allowed for the amicable resolution of disputes to be finally determined not by a judicial body but by a decision of the Meeting of the Parties. Finally, the "noncompliance procedure" adopted by the Second Meeting of the Parties sets up an "Implementation Committee" which deals with non-compliance and reports to the Meeting of the Parties.

In addition to implementation, ongoing research to ascertain the true environmental impacts and effects of any activities identified in a treaty is crucially important to enable the parties to a treaty to comply with its provisions. This is particularly the case when dealing with a framework treaty that requires later protocols to deal with unfolding facts. Treaties are replete with references to research. For example, the parties to the Vienna Convention on Ozone (*see* Chapter Seven) undertake to carry out research and scientific assessments on a variety of activities that may affect the ozone layer. These assessments include research into the physics and chemistry of the atmosphere, health and biological effects, and effects on climate of a variety of chemicals that might have a potentially deleterious effect on the ozone layer [arts. 2 & 3 & annex 1]. The Climate Change Convention (*see* Chapter Six) calls for research on the causes, effects, magnitude, and timing of climate change, along with the economic and social consequences of various response strategies [arts. 4(g) & 5], and sets up a subsidiary body for scientific and technological advice [art. 9]. The Biodiversity Convention (*see* Chapter Five) seeks to promote research that, *inter alia*, contributes to the conservation and sustainable use of biological diversity [art. 12] and sets up a subsidiary body on Scientific, Technical, and Technological Advice [art. 25].

The three treaties mentioned above also call for data collection and the dissemination of research and data. The purpose of the dissemination of research and data is to facilitate compliance. Reporting requirements may include the information obtained from research and data collection, and can take the form of reports by a particular international treaty organization to the parties, or more often, reports by the parties to the international organization or the other parties. The objective of reporting is to bring compliance into the sunlight of scrutiny by other parties and the treaty machinery. The importance of reporting as a technique to secure compliance is illustrated in the Climate Change Convention. All parties are obliged to communicate to the Conference of the Parties a general description of steps taken to implement the Convention, including a detailed description of anthropogenic emissions by sources and removal by sinks [arts. 4(1)(a) & (j); 12(1)(a) & (b)]. The reporting responsibilities of developed countries are even more onerous [art. 12(2)].

Assessments and reviews of performance are tied to reporting. On the basis of the reports and research made available, the parties or a specific treaty organization may assess the extent of implementation, and the progress made towards objectives. The Climate Change Convention entrusts this responsibility to the Conference of the Parties [art. 7(e)], while the Montreal Protocol requires assessment and review of control measures based on the reports submitted by a panel of experts at least every four years [art. 6].

Where a framework treaty institutes an objective, or final goal, the task of approaching it is usually undertaken in steps and requires interim measures. The task of making these rules and drawing up other measures, or recommending what they should be, is sometimes delegated to a group of scientific experts. We have seen that panels of experts have been set up under the Montreal Protocol, while the Climate Change Convention and the Biodiversity Convention have each created special scientific bodies. In our discussion on the amendment of treaties (*see* Chapter One), we noticed how the use of protocols and scientific annexes is directed at avoiding the tortuous process of treaty amendment. We have also noted above how annexes under the Montreal Protocol are amended. In addition, Chapter Eight on Antarctica offers examples of how the Commission under the Convention on the Conservation of Antarctic Marine Living Resources (CCAMLR) is possessed of management powers that will help nations comply with that treaty regime.

International treaty rules inhabit a consensual legal order and the implications of non-compliance with such rules stand in sharp relief to the comparable non-implementation of statutory rules within national legal systems. In the absence of bodies empowered to enforce compliance, the pressing goal of the parties to a treaty is to persuade the defaulter to comply. A medley of diplomatic and administrative measures is employed to secure such compliance. Judicial supervision leading to court-type decisions are available but are resorted to only in rare instances, and many environmental treaties provide for negotiation, conciliation, and arbitration as alternatives or preconditions to court litigation.

C. DIPLOMATIC AVENUES

Many environmental treaties require that parties explore diplomatic and other means of settling their differences before resorting to judicial or quasi-judicial dispute settlement. Such treaties include: CITES [art. XVIII]; the International Convention for the Prevention of Pollution from Ships (MARPOL), [Nov. 2, 1973, art. 10, 12 I.L.M. 1319]; the Convention on International Liability for Damage Caused by Space Objects (Space Liability Convention), [Mar. 29, 1972, art. IX, 961 U.N.T.S. 187]; the

Vienna Convention on Ozone [art. 11(1)], the Climate Change Convention [art. 14]; and the Biodiversity Convention [art. 27(1)]. These provisions signal the importance of diplomatic means for securing treaty compliance, and a number of treaties in fact institutionalize consultation between parties: the 1974 Paris Convention [art. 9(1)]; the Nordic Convention [art. 11]; and the Convention on Long–Range Transboundary Air Pollution (LRTAP), [Nov. 13, 1979, (art. 5, 18 I.L.M. 1442 (1983))]. Thus, diplomatic pressures and consultations are part of the implementing architecture of IEL. So too is the preventive regime, discussed later in this chapter, being developed by the ILC.

D. JUDICIAL REMEDIES

Apart from regulatory regimes supervised by or through agencies established by treaty, judicial enforcement provides another avenue for securing compliance with the law. Judicial remedies may be used to obtain specific items of compliance and can act as deterrents by bringing embarrassment, perhaps ignominy, to bear on wrongdoing states. In a community of nations where good standing and reputation are important, judicial remedies may have some use even though they lack mechanisms for enforcement.

It is necessary, to note at the outset, that a few environmental treaties have instituted a system of civil liability that allows private individuals to prosecute claims for breaches of a treaty within national courts, [*see*, for example, the Nordic Convention, art. 3, the Convention on Third Party Liability in the Field of Nuclear Energy (Paris Nuclear Liability Convention), July 29, 1960, art. 3, 956 U.N.T.S. 251 (entered into force Apr. 1, 1968), the Vienna Convention on Civil Liability for Nuclear Damage (Vienna Nuclear Liability Convention), May 21, 1963, art. II, 2 I.L.M 727 (entered into force, Nov. 12, 1977), and the International Convention on Civil Liability for Oil Pollution Damage, art. III, Nov. 29, 1969, 9 I.L.M. 45 (entered into force June 19, 1975)]. This type of judicial remedy is more fully described under the rubric of "civil liability" in § D 2 (c) of this chapter. In Chapter Eighteen, The Future of IEL, we refer to the potential for developing national remedies for implementing international treaties.

More commonly, judicial or quasi-judicial remedies within IEL are invoked through inter-state litigation, and are based on the grievance remedial principles of "state responsibility" or international tort law that enables one state to demand *ex-post* compensation and other relief for harm caused to it by another state. We have dealt with this topic below under the rubric of "Accountability for Transboundary Environmental Harms". Typically, adjudication arising under international laws governing such questions is handled by international courts, tribunals, and arbiters, and not national courts or institutions. The ongoing efforts to enlarge the domain of public international law by giving standing to injured persons other than states, such as NGOs, corporations, and private citizens, received weak institutionalization in UNC-LOS where the Sea Bed Dispute Chamber may exercise limited jurisdiction over non-state parties [Art. 187]. However, apart from narrow exceptions, the actors in public IEL remain confined almost exclusively to state parties.

If a state decides to take the traditional grievance-remedial judicial route, it can demand reparations from the wrongdoing state, and ask for a termination of the specific harmful conduct. However, this kind of *ex post* judicial remedy is a flawed way of dealing with an endemic problem for a number of reasons. First, judicial remedies can only be granted by a judicial forum, and international judicial bodies suffer from an underlying constitutional infirmity: lack of compulsory jurisdiction. The lack of jurisdiction becomes evident when dealing with the more serious problems of the global commons like climate change, ozone depletion, or biological diversity. These problems require concerted and coordinated action by all relevant state actors, and judicial supervision must extend to all affected parties. Unfortunately, some states will not consent to being brought within the compulsory and binding jurisdiction of courts or tribunals established under the treaties addressing these problems.

1. JURISDICTION

The settlement of disputes by way of compulsory and binding judicial proceedings is optional under the Climate Change Convention [art. 14(2)], the Biodiversity Convention [art. 26(3)], and the Vienna Convention on Ozone [art. 11(3)]. UNCLOS, on the other hand, does establish a system of compulsory dispute settlement and it remains to be seen how vigorously it will be used. The ICJ also possesses some level of compulsory jurisdiction, but as of 1999 only 64 states had signed the so-called "optional clause" [art. 36(2)], giving the court general jurisdiction [ICJ website, *at* http://www.icjcij. org/icjwww/ibasicdocuments/ibasictext/ibasicdeclarations.htm]. Even where they have signed the optional clause, 75% of those doing so have entered reservations, some of the self-judging type, that allow a state to decline jurisdiction where it determines that a case involves questions of domestic jurisdiction or national defense.

Jurisdiction can prove to be a difficult obstacle. In the Legality of the Use by a State of Nuclear Weapons in Armed Conflict case, the ICJ defined the concept to include legal capacity or status, and held that it lacked jurisdiction because the World Health Organization (WHO) was unable to demonstrate legal capacity [1996 I.C.J. 66 (July 8)]. In that case, the WHO, a specialized agency of the UN, sought an Advisory Opinion from the ICJ. The Constitution of the WHO commits it to the attainment by all peoples of the highest possible level of health [art. 1], and it is required to take all necessary action to attain this objective [art. 2(v)]. The question posed to the Court was: "In view of the health and environmental effects, would the use of nuclear weapons by a State in war or other armed conflict be a breach of its obligations under international law including the WHO Constitution?''

In its majority opinion, the Court admitted that the WHO's Constitution authorized the WHO to deal with the effects of the use of nuclear weapons, or any other hazardous activity, and to take preventive measures aimed at protecting the health of populations in the event of such weapons being used [¶ 21]. Despite this, the ICJ determined that preventive action, including asking the Court for the present Advisory Opinion, was not of the kind that fell within the scope of the WHO's activity [¶ 22]. Furthermore, the authority to take preventive actions did not confer upon it ''[a] competence to address the legality of the use of nuclear weapons . . . or to ask the Court about them'' [¶ 21].

According to the Court, questions affecting the legality of nuclear weapons are matters of arms control and disarmament and they are not the concern of a ''specialized agency'' such as the WHO whose authority is restricted to the sphere of public health. Questions of arms control and disarmament are matters for the UN itself, not the specialized agencies [¶ 26]. Because the question posed to the Court was not one that fell within the scope of the WHO, the Court declared that it lacked jurisdiction to entertain the case [¶ 31].

This decision highlights a number of more general defects concerning the concept of jurisdiction, which enables judicial forums like the ICJ to widen or narrow access to justice. The granting of an Advisory Opinion is a discretionary remedy [art. 65], and the ICJ could have assumed jurisdiction and declined to grant an opinion because, for example, the petitioning party lacked standing, status, capacity, or authority. Instead, it broadened the concept of jurisdiction to include questions of standing, status, or authority of a party to bring an action, and thereby widened the opportunities for denying jurisdiction and restricting access to the Court.

Even if there is no jurisdictional challenge to a case judicial remedies addressing non-compliance suffer from other defects. Judicial remedies are confined to the facts of a specific dispute, and cannot deal with the whole or look at an individual case as part of a broader environmental problem. Furthermore, there is no mechanism for enforcing or systematically monitoring the implementation of the order of an international court. This is particularly unsatisfactory because most environmental problems occur on a continuous or recurrent basis. Finally, typical judicial decisions are restricted to containing damage after the fact rather than preventing it from happening in the first place.

Despite these defects, judicial remedies can prove to be an effective way of implementing the law if they are administered by a tribunal having compulsory and binding jurisdiction like the UNCLOS tribunals, and if the tribunals assume a more activist role in interpreting and applying the substantive law. Such tribunals ought not to model themselves on the ICJ. The WHO case gave the ICJ an admirable opportunity to demonstrate its willingness to grapple with difficult issues of IEL. Instead, as Judge Weeramantry pointed out in his powerful separate opinion, the Court took a peculiarly obtuse view of the scope of the WHO, and in so doing signaled its unwillingness to play a more vigilant role within IEL to those who might invoke its intervention.

2.　ACCOUNTABILITY FOR TRANSBOUNDARY ENVIRONMENTAL HARMS

The ILC shouldered the burden of codifying the law dealing with accountability for transboundary harms in 1955, and their work, though still unfinished, has laid the conceptual foundations of this notoriously thorny segment of international law. They began by dealing with this subject under the heading "State Responsibility," but have now divided the original subject into two segments (more fully discussed in § (b) below): one dealing with responsibility for harms resulting from violations of international law; and the other with the prevention of and international liability for harms not involving violations of international law. We shall refer to the first as SR and the second as IL. A third liability regime, known as civil liability (CL), not hitherto addressed by the ILC, places responsibility on the actual polluter. The rules and obligations governing CL, are discussed in § (c) below.

(a) Application of SR

When one nation brings another to court it relies on a form of international tort law called "state responsibility". Before examining the main features of SR, it is relevant to note that the considerable theoretical attention given to the concept stands in stark contrast to its conspicuous absence in environmental treaties. The stubborn fact is that questions of how to claim compensation for the breach of international environmental obligations, either in national or international forums, have been deliberately neglected or omitted. Cases where compensation is obtained are the exceptions, not the rule, and the absence of a willingness among states to develop principles of SR is yet another reason why judicial enforcement can prove elusive.

The foundational principle of SR, as of tort law, is the concept of an internationally "wrongful" act. A state commits an internationally wrongful act when it violates or acts in breach of an existing international obligation found in treaty or customary law. As such, an act's classification as "wrongful" depends not on its being morally unacceptable *per se*, but instead on the wrongfulness of breaching international law. In theory, all obligations, whether general or specific, contained in treaties as well as in customary law have the potential to give rise to SR. An obligation may be very general, and fail to specify exactly what a State should do. One such obligation is to supply security or to implement CL mechanisms as required by the nuclear treaties discussed below. On the other hand, some obligations are very specific, such as those relating to time tables for reduction of ozone-damaging chemicals, and monitoring or reporting of ozone levels which could also give rise to SR [*International Law Comm'n Draft Articles on State Responsibility*, Adopted by the International Law Comm'n at its 1642nd Meeting, arts. 20 & 21, U.N. Doc. A/35/10 (1981) (hereinafter draft articles on SR)].

According to the draft articles on SR completed in 2001, "Every internationally wrongful act of a State entails the international responsibility of that State" [Art 1], and "there is an internationally wrongful act of a State when [the] conduct ... [i]s attributable to the State under international law; and ... constitutes a breach of an international obligation of the State" [Art 2(a) & (b)]. Questions then arise about the nature of an international wrong, and particularly as to whether such wrongs should be based on fault as distinguished from objective wrongs that give rise to state responsibility despite the absence of any negligence or intent.

i.   Fault Liability

The ILC's commentary to these draft articles on SR raises the question whether fault constitutes a necessary element of the internationally wrongful act of a State. They answer that:

This is certainly not the case if by "fault" one understands the existence, for example, of an intention to harm. In the absence of any specific requirement of a mental element in terms of the primary obligation, it is only the act of a State that matters, independently of any intention [para 10].

The ILC, therefore, has divorced any fault component from its use of the term "wrongful." The approach of the ILC is consistent with general principles of interpretation. It makes eminent sense to examine the primary obligations created by treaties on a case by case basis to determine if fault is an ingredient or element of the breach giving rise to a wrong. If fault is an element or ingredient of a particular primary obligation, then it is a requirement of SR for the breach of that obligation. If not, we should imply fault only if there are other reasons for so doing. If, for example, the obligation we are examining is the one restated in article 21 of the Stockholm Declaration, [June 16, 1972, 11 I.L.M. 1416 (1972)], the fact that it does not require the transboundary harm to be caused intentionally or negligently suggests that fault is not a requirement.

ii. Strict and Absolute Liability

The concepts of strict and absolute liability have not been authoritatively defined, but standards of strict liability are less rigorous than absolute liability, and may constitute no more than a reversal of the burden of proof, allowing a defending State to establish circumstances precluding wrongfulness or liability. Absolute or objective liability on the other hand is more conclusive and prohibits, or very severely limits, evidence of circumstances precluding liability. For example, the Convention on International Liability for Damage Caused by Space Objects (Space Liability Convention) illustrates absolute liability under a SR regime [March 29, 1972, 961 U.N.T.S. 187]. Where damage is caused to the surface of the earth or to an aircraft in flight, it asserts that, "[a] launching State shall be absolutely liable to pay compensation for damage caused by its space object. . . . " [art. II]. The Space Liability Convention draws a distinction between absolute liability [art. II] and fault liability [art. III]. While absolute liability is imposed for damage to the surface of the earth [art. II], damage resulting elsewhere can result in liability only where fault is established [art. III].

Other examples are taken from regimes dealing with CL, discussed below, but are illustrative of the common distinction between absolute and strict liability. The 1969 International Convention on Civil Liability for Oil Pollution Damage (CLC) as amended by the Protocol of 1992, illustrates strict liability [May 30, 1996 *reprinted in* GURUSWAMY et al. 877]. It places liability for oil spills on the owner of the ship subject to exceptions in limited circumstances, such as war, hostilities, certain kinds of natural phenomena, and acts of a third party [art. III(2) of CLC]. Four conventions on nuclear liability: 1) the 1960 Paris Convention on Third Party Liability in the Field of Nuclear Energy [April 1, 1968, 956 U.N.T.S. 251]; 2) the 1963 Vienna Convention on Civil Liability for Nuclear Damage [Nov. 12, 1977, 1063 U.N.T.S. 265]; 3) The 1962 Convention on the Liability of Operators of Nuclear Ships, [not in force]; and 4) the Convention Relating to Civil Liability in the Field of Maritime Carriage of Nuclear Materials [July 15, 1975, 974 U.N.T.S. 255], each implement a system of absolute liability, even though that term is not expressly mentioned. Like the oil pollution agreement, they allow for certain very limited exceptions based on armed conflict and civil war.

iii. Attribution, Causation, Exhaustion of Local Remedies, and Reparation

Apart from proving the breach of an obligation, with or without fault, a wrongful act must be attributed to a state for SR to arise. In the case of environmental wrongs, the acts resulting in the wrong must be laid at the feet of the state or an agency of the state. The draft articles on SR stipulate that the legislative, executive, or judicial conduct of any state organ shall be considered an act of state [art. 6]. Because transboundary environmental wrongs are often committed by private parties, it is necessary to attribute the wrong to the agency or government department that authorized, mandated or failed to prevent the wrongful action. According to the draft articles on SR the actions of private parties shall be attributed to the state where they are acting under "the direction or control" of a state [art. 8]. Thus, for example, if an industrial plant owned by a private corporation subject to the regulatory direction or control of a State causes transboundary harm, such actions could be attributed to the State.

A state responsible for an internationally wrongful act is first obligated to cease a continuing wrong, and having done so to offer assurances and guarantees of non-repetition if the facts so warrant [Art. 30]. Second, it is required to make full reparation for the injury the wrongful act caused [art. 31]. Reparation takes the form, either singly or in different combinations, of three remedies: restitution, compensation and satisfaction [art. 34].

Restitution is the obligation to establish the situation that existed before the wrongful act was committed. Such a reinstatement of pre-existing conditions is subject to the proviso that it is not materially impossible, or "out of all proportion to the benefit deriving from restitution instead of compensation" [art. 35]. Where restitution is not feasible a state responsible for an international wrong is under an obligation to compensate. Compensation covers any financially assessable damage [art. 36]. Where an injury cannot be made good by restitution or compensation, an aggrieved state is under an obligation to give satisfaction that may take the form of "an acknowledgement of the breach, an expression of regret, a formal apology or another appropriate modality" [art. 37].

In addition, a claimant for judicial remedies, whether based on SR, IL, or CL must prove causation. This can prove difficult, particularly where there is more than one source of the impugned pollutant as illustrated by the case of acid rain. Sweden, for instance, had to resort to very elaborate monitoring and measuring devices to trace the source of acid rain to an implicated suspect country such as the United Kingdom or Germany, or both.

As to whether there is an additional requirement of damage, the ILC in its commentary states:

> It is sometimes said that international responsibility is not engaged by conduct of a State in disregard of its obligations unless some further element exists, in particular, "damage" to another State.

But whether such further event must occur depends on the content of the primary obligation, and there is no general rule in this respect. For example, the obligation under a treaty to enact a uniform law is breached by the failure to enact the law, and it is not necessary for another State party to point to any specific damage it has suffered by reason of that failure. Whether a particular obligation is breached forthwith upon a failure to act on the part of the responsible State, or whether some further event must occur, depends on the content and interpretation of the primary obligation and cannot be determined in the abstract.

Procedurally, there is also a rule, subject to exceptions, regarding the exhaustion of local (national) remedies before preferring an international action. According to the draft articles on SR, the responsibility of a state may not be invoked if "...the claim is one to which the rule of exhaustion of local remedies applies and any available and effective local remedy has not been exhausted" [Art 44(b)].

iv. Trail Smelter Arbitration

The Trail Smelter Arbitration, a well known public international law case dealing with transboundary pollution, is invariably cited in any discussion of state responsibility [(U.S. v. Can.), 3 R.I.A.A. 1938 (1949) (*see* Chapter Fourteen)]. The facts of that case also serve the double purpose of illustrating how a civil liability system under national law could have dealt with the transnational wrongs suffered in that case. In the Trail Smelter Arbitration sulphur dioxide fumes from a Canadian smelter were causing damage in the state of Washington in the U.S .. Farmers in the U.S. who suffered damage were prevented from bringing an action in U.S. courts because they would have encountered jurisdictional difficulties. The first of these jurisdictional problems arose from the fact that the company owning the smelters had its place of business and was a company registered in Canada. A second jurisdictional problem arose from the *locus delicti* or the fact that the act that initiated the damage, and therefore the tort, occurred in Canada.

Even if the plaintiffs had overcome this difficulty and persuaded a U.S. court to assume jurisdiction on the basis that the harm inflicted or damage suffered was in the U.S., they still faced other difficulties. One of these other problems is the "proper law" to be applied by the court. Should it be Canadian or U.S. law? If the applicable law was

Canadian, to what extent did Canadian law permit recovery of damages in cases where the harm suffered was in a jurisdiction different from that in which it originated? The doctrine of *forum non conveniens*, dealing with the appropriate forum for an action, raised another question. Were the U.S. courts an appropriate forum for deciding a case such as this? These were among the reasons why it was necessary for the U.S. to espouse and advocate the claims of the Washington farmers and negotiate a treaty in which Canada accepted responsibility for provable damage. An arbitral tribunal was created under that treaty to find a solution that was just to all parties. The principles articulated by that arbitral tribunal in deciding this case have become one of the pillars of state responsibility. The arbitrators determined that "under the principles of international law, ... no state has the right to use or permit the use of its territory in such a manner as to cause injury by fumes in or to the territory of another, or properties or persons therein when the case is of serious consequence and the injury is established by clear and convincing evidence." It went on to conclude that the "... Dominion of Canada is responsible in international law for the conduct of the Trail Smelter. Apart from the undertakings in the Convention, it is, therefore, the duty of the Government of the Dominion of Canada to see to it that this conduct should be in conformity with the obligation of the Dominion under international law as herein determined."

(b) International Liability for Injurious Consequences Arising Out Of Acts Not Prohibited By International Law

As we have noted, the ILC's SR regime limits the application of SR to wrongful acts (i.e. those cases where a state causes injury through an act prohibited by treaty or custom). In reality, however, the conduct of one state can give rise to injury within the territory of other states without violating any such rule of treaty or customary law. Responding to this challenge, the ILC is currently pursuing a set of draft articles aimed at defining a state's liability for damages caused by acts that are not violations of international law. We have called this the regime of international liability (IL). It should be noted from the outset that IL deals primarily with "non-wrongful" acts. The terms wrongful and non-wrongful can be deceptive because their usage typically invokes a moral component. But as we have noted, non-wrongful means only that the act in question does not happen to violate an existing rule of international law. The more difficult and largely unresolved task lies in defining the non-wrongful acts to which IL attaches.

The ILC's work on IL has been plagued by conceptual difficulties since its inception. Critics have argued that the division between SR and IL creates unnecessary complication, and rests on an infirm conceptual basis [*see, e.g.*, Alan E. Boyle, *State Responsibility and International Liability for Injurious Consequences Not Prohibited by International Law: A Necessary Distinction?* 39 INT'L & COMP. L.Q.

1, (1990)]. Such critics suggest that it would have been simpler to consider all injurious acts (whether wrongful or not) under the single rubric of SR. In their view, SR could form a continuum, giving rise to a spectrum of liability, depending on the gravity of the injury. An injured state would thereby be free to invoke a suite of remedies that included reparation as well as compensation.

In practical terms, the forging of a new rubric called international liability, as distinct from SR, may not have created significant new difficulties. This is because the real challenge is to define the non-wrongful acts (or one not prohibited by international law) to which international liability attaches. This is a ubiquitous difficulty that remains problematic whether encountered under the rubric of IL, as the ILC would have it, or under the heading of SR as the critics prefer. Moreover, the ILC's separate treatment of wrongful and non-wrongful acts affirms the "legal" character of international law by emphasizing the difference between acts that violate international law and those that do not.

The twin objectives of the ILC in undertaking the codification of international liability for non-wrongful acts was to provide compensation to injured states (liability) and, as well as to deter or prevent putatively liable states from undertaking the actions in question, or at least take adequate measures to minimize the risk of potential harms (prevention). The ILC focused primarily on the prevention objective, reasoning that "pride of place would be given to the duty to avoid or minimize injury, rather than to the substituted duty to provide reparation for the injury caused" [*Yearbook of the International Law Commission*, International Law Commission, 34th Sess., at 86, U.N. Doc. A/CN.4/SER.A/1982/Add.1 (Part 2) (1983)]. Impelled by the force of this logic, the ILC further divided IL into two topics: prevention and liability, and focused on the former rather than the latter. Pursuant to this decision, the ILC's work on prevention has led to a set of draft articles on the prevention of transboundary harm from hazardous activities, while progress on liability has not yet advanced as far.

Under the current draft articles on prevention, the ILC has come up with a procedure by which a state must notify, consult, arbitrate, and negotiate with potentially affected states before engaging in non-wrongful acts "which involve a risk of causing significant transboundary harm" [art. 1]. So far, the ILC has not compiled a more specific list of acts falling under the scope of their prevention articles.

The ILC submitted the current draft articles on the prevention of transboundary harm from hazardous activities to the General Assembly at the Assembly's fifty-sixth session in 2001, with the recommendation that a convention be held to produce a treaty on their basis. The General Assembly has not yet done so, and we are witnessing significant developments that await completion.

(c) Civil Liability

While states painfully and slowly struggle to set up rules of compensation under SR or prevention of transboundary harm under the rubric of IL, they have also set up a third set of rules and regimes based on CL that channel responsibility for an environmental wrong on the polluter rather than the state. CL regimes are usually established by treaty and place only residual duties (which could give rise to SR) upon states. These regimes of CL have the potential to be expanded into more effective vehicles of environmental protection than those based on SR or IL.

It is worth considering the extent and manner in which the injured farmers in the *Trail Smelter* case could have been compensated through other legal procedures. For example, the US and Canada could have entered into a treaty in which their respective courts were granted jurisdiction to hear cases where damage occurred outside their ordinary jurisdiction. This approach might follow the recommendations of the Organization for Economic Co-operation and Development (OECD), calling for access to domestic courts and remedies by national and foreign entities on a non-discriminatory basis [*Recommendation of the Council for the Implementation of a Regime of Equal Access and Non-discrimination in Relation to Transfrontier Pollution*, OECD, May 17, 1977, 16 I.L.M. 977 (1977)]. The parties could also have agreed that an order by a court vested with jurisdiction under the treaty could be enforced in either country.

This principle of non-discrimination has now been incorporated into the Convention on the Law of the Non–Navigational Uses of International Watercourses [not yet in force, reprinted in 36 I.L.M. 700]. Article 32 states that watercourse states shall not discriminate against injured parties on the basis of nationality or residence or place where the injury occurred in granting persons access to judicial or other areas of remedial justice.

Claims based on CL enjoy substantial advantages over those originating in SR or IL. To begin with, an individual victim of environmental damage has direct access to justice (whether courts or administrative agencies) and does not have to await espousal or adoption by his/her country. As we have seen, decisions to prosecute claims based on SR are taken only in rare circumstances and victims are often held hostage to the politics of their own country. Second, even where states premise their case on SR, the time taken in doing so often is inordinately long because the machinery of states is notoriously slow. Third, in SR, the victim is forced to rely upon the state and not an advocate or attorney of his/her choosing, to present and argue the case. Fourth, the absence of a liability regime in SR makes recovery of damages very difficult. Admittedly, a victim who files an action in a foreign state faces some obstacles arising from the differences of legal systems, language, procedure and execution. But the constitutive treaty establishing a CL regime can address these difficulties. The constitutive treaty could place duties on the contracting parties relating to non-discrimination, access to justice, security for payment of damages, and thereby remove or ameliorate these difficulties.

i. Treaty Overlay

Where CL regimes are created, the primary responsibility for environmental harm is usually placed on the polluter and not the state. It is important to note that modalities for doing justice to the aggrieved parties, by placing the burden of compensation on private corporations and individuals have in fact been created by a number of treaties. UNCLOS, which is emerging as a constitution for the oceans, requires states to "ensure that recourse is available in accordance with their legal systems for prompt and adequate compensation or other relief in respect of damage caused by pollution of the marine environment by natural or juridical persons under their jurisdiction" [Art 235(2)]. Civil liability remedies against private and corporate entities are also underscored by a number of other treaties.

The recent Convention on the Law of the Non–Navigational Uses of International Watercourses, following the OECD recommendation, expressed the "Non-discrimination" principle that domestic or national courts can and should grant environmental relief and compensation. According to Art 32 where a person suffers or is under a serious threat of suffering significant transboundary harm the state in which the harm originated should grant the injured person "in accordance with its legal system, access to judicial or other procedures, or a right to claim compensation or other relief. . . ."

The same principle is embodied in a cluster of other treaties dealing with a range of activities including the peaceful use of nuclear energy, the operation of nuclear ships, maritime carriage of nuclear materials, oil pollution; the carriage of dangerous goods by road, rail and inland navigation vessels [Bjorn Sandvik & Satu Suikkari, *Harm and Reparation in International Treaty Regimes: An Overview, in* HARM TO THE ENVIRONMENT: THE RIGHT TO COMPENSATION AND THE ASSESSMENT OF DAMAGES 57, 57–58 (Peter Wetterstein ed., 1997)]; North American free trade [*see*, North American Agreement on Environmental Cooperation (NAAEC), arts. 5–6, 32 I.L.M. 1480 (1993), a side-agreement to NAFTA]; and protection of the Antarctic [Convention on the Regulation of Antarctic Mineral Resource Activities, Art 8]. The legal regimes addressing the peaceful use of nuclear energy, and oil pollution also, are illustrative of this seam of law.

The treaties dealing with the peaceful use of nuclear energy include the Paris Nuclear Liability Convention, the Vienna Nuclear Liability Convention, the 1997 Protocol to Amend the Vienna Convention on Civil Liability for Nuclear Damage and the 1997 Convention on Supplementary Funding. (See Chapter Seventeen). What is important about these treaties is that they place primary liability not on the state, qua state, but on the operator of the nuclear installation. In the event of the state being the operator, CL will of course, attach to the state but not on the basis of SR. These treaties only place residual or ancillary duties on the state which could give rise to SR.

For example, the Vienna Nuclear Liability Convention places liability on the operator of the nuclear installation alone [Art. II (5)], and restricts jurisdiction solely to the courts of the state where the accident occurred [Art. 11]. Rather than being held responsible for the actions of the operator according to the principles of state responsibility, the state is under a more limited duty to ensure that any claims against the operator are satisfied through the availability of funds and the necessary security [*id.* art VIII; 1994 Protocol to the Vienna Convention on Civil Liability for Nuclear Damage, art. 9]. Failure to fulfill this limited duty, however, could give rise to SR.

The field of oil pollution is governed by a cluster of treaties, including the 1969 International Convention on Civil Liability for Oil Pollution Damage (1969 CLC), the 1992 Protocol to Amend the 1969 CLC, the 1971 International Convention on the Establishment of an International Fund for Compensation for Oil Pollution Damage (1971 Fund Convention), and the 1992 Protocol to the Fund Convention. Like the treaties dealing with civil nuclear power, these oil pollution treaties place liability for oil pollution damage on the owner of the oil or other individuals or corporations involved in the enterprise of the carriage of oil from one location to another [GOTTHARD GAUCI, OIL POLLUTION AT SEA: CIVIL LIABILITY AND COMPENSATION FOR DAMAGE 89–119

(1997)]. Again, these treaties do not establish a regime of SR under public international law.

The NAAEC also provides national remedies of a more limited nature. This environmental side agreement to NAFTA obligates each party to ensure that judicial, quasi-judicial and administrative proceedings are available under its laws to sanction or remedy violations of its environmental laws [NAAEC, Art 5(2)]. It grants access to and empowers interested private persons to seek relief by way of damages or injunctions in the courts of that state party, where the laws of that party have been broken [NAAEC, Art 6(2) & (3)]. While NAAEC opens the door to persons other than those within the jurisdiction of the state party concerned, the cause of action is limited to the breach of the laws of that party. Unlike the regimes dealing with civil nuclear power or oil pollution, the agreement does not create a new regime of environmental laws that can be vindicated in the national courts of any of the state parties.

ii. Civil Liability Litigation

A civil liability case from Europe, in which the plaintiffs claimed environmental damages based on tort, illuminates the extent to which national courts can deal with cases of transnational environmental injury provided they are vested with appropriate jurisdiction by international agreement. The international agreement that enabled this case to proceed was the Convention on the Jurisdiction and the Enforcement of Judgments in Civil and Commercial Matters (Enforcement of Judgments Convention) [Sept. 27, 1968, 29 I.L.M. 143]. This convention had established uniform jurisdictional rules for national courts in the Member States of the then European Economic Community (EEC), now the European Union (EU), regarding disputes between parties domiciled in different Member States.

In *Bier v. Mines de Potasse d'Alsace SA* [1976] ECR 1735, a French company in Alsace discharged massive amounts of chlorides into the Rhine. The chloride allegedly damaged nursery gardens in Holland, and the Dutch Supreme Court upheld the assertion of jurisdiction by a Dutch court despite the argument that releases of the chlorides into the Rhine were lawful at the points of discharge in Alsace, France. The European Court of Justice (ECJ) affirmed, basing itself on the Enforcement of Judgments Convention. Subsequently, a Dutch court applied Dutch law concerning environmental damage, and found for the complainants, rejecting the defense that the conduct was lawful [ANDREAS F. LOWENFELD, INTERNATIONAL LITIGATION AND THE QUEST FOR REASONABLENESS 30 (1996)].

In the case of the Sandoz fire, complainants also pursued CL claims instead of SR. [This section relies on Hans Ulrich Jessurun d'Oliveira, *The Sandoz Blaze: The Damage and the Public and Private Liabilities, in* INTERNATIONAL RESPONSIBILITY FOR ENVIRONMENTAL HARM 429, 434–43 (Francesco Francioni & Tullio Scovazzi eds., 1991)]. In October 1986, a fire broke out in a chemical warehouse belonging to Sandoz, a major chemical manufacturer in Switzerland. The warehouse, located on the banks of the river Rhine, contained large quantities of pesticides and other harmful chemicals, and the firefighters employed unsophisticated fire fighting methods, using huge quantities of water to extinguish the fire. Ten to fifteen thousand cubic meters of water, containing over 30 tons of toxic chemicals–including insecticides, herbicides, and fungicides, flowed directly into the Rhine due to the absence of a catchment area (customarily built as a precautionary measure to prevent this kind of direct discharge from chemical plants). The runoff resulted in serious damage to fisheries, killed off all eels, and severely damaged the fauna and flora of the Rhine. It also posed grave threats to human health in Holland (where the Rhine constituted the primary source of drinking water), France and Germany.

There are a number of treaties protecting the Rhine against pollution, to which Switzerland was a party. There is no doubt that numerous provisions of these treaties relating to the care, storage, auditing, and emergency measures pertaining to the chemicals in the warehouse had been violated. Despite this, there were no claims based on SR, and none of the injured states made any direct claims against the Swiss Confederation for damages suffered by them.

Professor Jessurun d'Oliviera has commented that the German, French and Dutch governments privatized their claims by seeking reparations against Sandoz rather than the Swiss government. His observations reinforce the political reality that states will not litigate issues based on SR for good reason. The majority of claims were settled out of court, with the help of the Swiss government, within three years. This contrasts to the 14 years taken over the *Mines de Potasse d'Alsace* case, and 10 years for the Amoco–Cadiz litigation [*id*. at 440–41.]. While the riparian states did not pursue actions based on SR, it is open to conjecture that the possibility of an action based on SR induced the Swiss government to exert pressure on Sandoz to settle the cases in order to avoid an action based on SR.

(d) Conclusion

The last few years have yielded remarkable developments in the regimes of SR and IL. The recently concluded "draft articles on Responsibility of States for internationally wrongful acts" have illuminated and clarified the complex and complicated laws dealing with SR, and have established the foundation on which the regime of SR can continue to be built. At the same time, the new directions in which IL has developed augur well for IEL. In re-stating the rules governing the prevention of transboundary harm from hazardous activities, the ILC has set the stage for the transformation of IEL from an *ex post* to an *ex ante law*.

These developments have been complemented by the emergence of new international laws based on CL that break away from the inherited system of state-controlled law that gave rise to SR and IL. We live in a world in which national and international laws and regulations governing corporations and individuals, in matters of trade, commerce, health, communications, and the environment have become more important than those controlling states. This must of necessity mean that SR and IL will lose their primacy as the principal legal instruments for governing environmental protection. CL opens the door to NGOs and other private parties to use the legal system to protect the environment in a way not permitted by SR or IL.

Such a development does not mean that remedies based on SR and IL completely lose their utility or their importance. Instead, SR and IL assume new significance and vitality when used as interlocking remedies in conjunction with civil liability (CL). Many CL regimes are established by treaties that place subsidiary (but nonetheless important) duties on states. For example, the 1963 Vienna Convention on Civil Liability, as amended, makes the operator and not the state liable for injuries and damage caused by any accident, but it also requires the state to provide adequate security to ensure that the operators will pay up. A state that does not provide such security will be violating an obligation that may be actionable under SR. Again, in the Sandoz blaze, the fact that SR could have given rise to actions against Switzerland may have prompted the Swiss government to pressure Sandoz into paying up. There can be little doubt that SR and IL will continue to play an important role in IEL.

E. THE EFFECTIVENESS OF INTERNATIONAL ENVIRONMENTAL LAW

1. INSTITUTIONAL CONCERNS

Hundreds of international treaties have established scores of rules, along with the institutional machinery for securing compliance and supervising non-compliance. Sometimes, as we have seen, the treaties also provide judicial remedies. Do all these legal measures make a difference to the way nations, corporations, and individuals behave? Much legal analysis centers on the jural nature of treaties, their interpretation and implementation, making the *a priori* assumption that treaties do shape and change the behavior of the relevant parties.

There is, however, a substantial body of *realist* thinking, subscribed to by some of the world's most eminent states-persons, that defines international behavior and practice in terms of geo-political power rather than law. According to the realists, nations agree to treaties and the rules therein embodied only because they codify the existing or intended behavior or practice of the parties [*see* POLITICS AMONG NATIONS: THE STRUGGLE FOR POWER AND PEACE (Kenneth Thompson ed., 1993)]. Parties conform their behavior to treaty provisions because it is in their self-interest to do so, and not because they are obliged to so by law. The realists argue that it would be a mistake to equate this spurious correlation with true causation, as international lawyers tend to do [*see* RONALD B. MITCHELL, INTENTIONAL OIL

POLLUTION AT SEA 28–29 (1994)]. Despite the strenuous exhortations and exertions of many international lawyers, the core of realist thinking, now backed by the critical legal studies (CLS) adherents popularly known as *crits,* is alive and well [Philip Trimble, *International Law, World Order, and Critical Legal Studies,* 42 STAN. L. REV. 811, 833–34 (1990)].

For the crits, or "new stream" of international scholars, the distinction between law and politics exists as an illusion [*see* David Kennedy, *A New Stream of International Law and Politics,* 7 WIS. INT'L. L. J. 1 (1988)]. Legal language—whether embodied in rules, treaties or aspirational principles—like all language, simply operates in the service of persuasion towards some practical end. As Martii Koskenniemi has suggested, international law is the "*practice* of attempting to reach the most acceptable solution in the particular circumstances of the case. It is not the application of ready-made, general rules or principles but a conversation about what to do, here and now" [MARTII KOSKENNIEMI, FROM APOLOGY TO UTOPIA 486 (1989)].

It may be reassuring for some students and practitioners to learn that empirical studies have attempted to repudiate the alleged cynicism of the realists and the crits. In one study, a political scientist evaluated the evidence drawn from the control of intentional oil pollution, and concluded that the empirical evidence "unequivocally demonstrates that governments and private corporations have undertaken a variety of actions involving compliance, monitoring, and enforcement that they would not have taken in the absence of relevant treaty provisions." [RONALD MITCHELL, INTENTIONAL OIL POLLUTION AT SEA, 299, 1994]. In response, a "new stream" proponent would argue that the "relevant treaty provisions" simply exist as a political arrangement—and that whatever "compliance, monitoring and enforcement" results from such an arrangement, does so out of further political expediency.

Finally, though debate continues as to causal impetus, it is worth reiterating that international law is a social force that commands respect in the form of compliance. Despite its renowned asymmetry with domestic law, and its publicized defects in lacking a law-making and law-enforcing sovereign, international law does invoke compliance because it governs a law-abiding community of very politically minded states—not a gang of bandits or bank robbers [*see* ROGER FISHER, IMPROVING COMPLIANCE WITH INTERNATIONAL LAW 16 (1981)].

F. THE RELATIONSHIP BETWEEN IEL AND DOMESTIC LAW

A proper grasp and clear understanding of the relationship of national law to international law is of crucial importance to the study of IEL. The subject is of the utmost practical importance in clarifying the law of treaties, which impinges so frequently on the domain of state law. The two principal theories dealing with the relationship of national law to international law are known as *monism* and *dualism*. According to monism, international law and the national law of states are concomitant aspects of one unified legal system. According to dualism, however, they represent two entirely distinct legal systems in which international law possesses a character intrinsically different to state law.

While it unnecessary to explore the theoretical complexities of this discussion, it is important to understand some of the difficulties in the implementation of international obligations arising from the absence of any vertical power structure in the international community. The U.S. adopts a mixed dualist-monist approach to the interrelation of national and international laws, and the mottled status of international law in the U.S. illustrates some of the difficulties surrounding these issues.

1. TREATIES AND DOMESTIC LAW

To begin, the U.S. Constitution effectively, but not explicitly, deals with the ratification of a treaty. The power to enter into treaties with other nations is governed by Article II, section 2 of the Constitution which provides that the President "shall have the Power, by and with the Advice and Consent of the Senate, to make Treaties, provided two-thirds of the Senators present concur." Although treaty negotiations between states may culminate in the actual signing of the treaty, most states require a domestic ratification procedure before the signature may be given any legal effect. Thus, in the U.S., ratification can only occur with a two-thirds vote of approval by the Senate. This separate ratification procedure offers some evidence of the dualist character of international law in the U.S.

Second, while treaties constitute law within the international legal system, their status within the realm of U.S. domestic law is more dubious. Article VI, section 2, provides that:

> This Constitution, and the Laws of the United States which shall be made in Pursuance thereof; and all Treaties made, or which shall be made, under the Authority of the United States, shall be the supreme Law of the Land; and the Judges in every State shall be bound thereby, any Thing in the Constitution or Laws of any State to the Contrary notwithstanding.

While the Constitution makes treaties automatically part of the "supreme Law of the Land" they are afforded parity of status, not supremacy, with the Constitution and acts of Congress. The Constitution does not limit the treaty power explicitly, and no treaty or treaty provision has ever been held unconstitutional. Nevertheless, it is generally agreed that such limitations exist. For example, the Supreme Court held in *Reid v. Covert* [354 U.S. 1 (1957)] that treaties may not contravene any constitutional prohibition, such as those of the Bill of Rights or in the Thirteenth, Fourteenth, and Fifteenth Amendments. The case of *Missouri v. Holland* [252 U.S. 416 (1920)] is especially worthy of note because it concerned the constitutionality of an *environmental* treaty, between the United States and Great Britain (for Canada) for the protection of migratory birds. The treaty provided that the United States and Canada would enact legislation prohibiting the "killing, capturing or selling" of birds except in accordance with regulations promulgated by the federal government. The State of Missouri brought suit to enjoin enforcement of a federal regulation enacted pursuant to the treaty on the grounds that the powers reserved to it under the Tenth Amendment had been invaded. Prior to this case, Congress had attempted to regulate the hunting of migratory birds through the interstate commerce clause, but the effort was voided on the ground that this was a subject matter left to the separate states under the Tenth Amendment. Thus, as the State of Missouri saw it, the treaty approach—giving to Congress what Congress did not have without a treaty— represented a usurpation of the power of the separate states and consequently a subversion of federal-state relations as envisioned by the Founding Fathers.

The Supreme Court largely disposed of the argument that the subject matter of treaties is limited by the Tenth Amendment. The court asserted that whilst the great body of private relations usually falls within the control of the State, a treaty may override state power where the national interest is at stake. The court held that where the national interest of very nearly the first magnitude is involved, it can be protected only by national action in concert with that of another power. However, it remains possible, as the Court hinted in *DeGeofroy v. Riggs* [133 U.S. 258 (1890)], that the treaty power may be limited by "restraints ... arising ... from the nature ... of the states."

In addition to granting the power to make and enter into treaties, the Framers of the Constitution provided that resulting treaties, together with the duly enacted laws of the United States, should constitute part of the "supreme law of the land." Thus, as well as giving rise to international legal obligations, treaties have force as domestic law, to be applied as federal statutes and consequently to prevail at all times over inconsistent state laws (assuming no conflict with the Constitution).

Still, not all treaties are automatically binding on American courts. Aside from the general constitutionality requirement, two additional conditions must obtain for treaties to have domestic effect. First, a treaty must not conflict with a subsequent act of Congress. This is in keeping with the judiciary's interpretation of the supremacy clause, ranking treaties and acts of Congress equally and therefore ruling that the law later in time prevails. With the sole exception of *Cook v. United States* [288 U.S. 102 (1933)], cases in this area have involved conflicts between an earlier treaty and a later statute, with the latter prevailing. The courts presume, however, that Congress does not intend to supersede treaties, and consequently the courts are disposed toward interpretations that will achieve compatibility between treaties and federal statutes on the same subject.

Second, for a treaty to bind courts it must be "self-executing" or, alternatively, "non-self-executing" but supported by enabling legislation. Such was the holding in *Foster v. Neilson,* U.S. 253 (1829). Judicial decisions vary widely in their application of this requirement, however. The distinction between "self-executing" and "non-self-executing" treaties is more easily stated than applied. A determination that a treaty fits one category or the other may be shown to depend on subjective, or even political, considerations.

Although the Constitution is silent on the question of who has the power to suspend or terminate treaties and under what circumstances, it is generally accepted that the President has such power, *without* the advice and consent of the Senate, based on the President's established constitutional authority to conduct the foreign affairs of the United States. A challenge to the President's authority in this connection has thus far arisen only in the one case of *Goldwater v. Carter* [481 F.Supp. 949 (D.D.C. 1979)], and that case was decided, on purely jurisdictional grounds, against the challenge.

2. CUSTOM AND DOMESTIC LAW

The status of customary international law within U.S. domestic law is even less certain than the position of treaties. One major reason for its dubious status arises from the omission of custom from such clauses of the constitution as the supremacy clause, quoted above. While the supremacy clause unequivocally includes treaty law within the realm of federal law, it does not overtly afford such parity of status to customary law.

The famous case of *The Paquete Habana, 175 U.S. 677 (1900)* offers a baseline from which to assess the place of international custom in U.S. law. In that case, the President of the United States ordered a naval blockade of the Cuban coast "in pursuance of the laws of the United States, and the law of nations applicable to such cases." *Id.* at 712. Two small Cuban fishing vessels were captured and sold in the U.S. as prize vessels. The original owners bought suit to recover those proceeds and the U.S. Supreme Court, sitting as a prize court wrote:

> International law is part of our law, and must be ascertained and administered by the courts of justice of appropriate jurisdiction, as often as questions of right depending upon it are duly presented for their determination. For this purpose, where there is no treaty, and no controlling executive or legislative act or judicial decision, resort must be had to the customs and usages of civilized nations. . . . [*Id.* at 700].

Relying upon the first sentence cited above, some commentators argue that this case gives custom an equal status with statutes and treaties [*see*, e.g., L Henkin, *International Law as Law in the United States*, 82 Mich. L.R. 1555, 1556 (1984)]. But such an argument faces a major analytical and legal difficulty. We noted in the first chapter that the establishment of customary international law is established by evidence of state practice and *opinio juris*. This means that proponents of an alleged rule of custom may need to rely upon the statements made by various heads of state, including the President of the U.S., as evidence of practice and opinion juris. The President's statements, therefore, can become powerful tools for creating binding international obligations in the form of custom. If that were the case, and custom enjoyed inter pares status with treaties, without even the safeguard of Senate approval required for treaties, the door may well be opened for the President unilaterally to create domestically binding law by executive action, and even overturn congressional legislation.

The more plausible possibility, that customary international law cannot supercede other sources of federal law, is supported by the second sentence form the *Paquete Habana* cited above. International rules of customary law became relevant in that case because the President had incorporated customary law into his order. The court, therefore, was relying on customary law to the extent that it had been adopted by the President.

In fact, U.S. courts will not give effect to customary norms whose existence is denied by the political branches. Moreover, U.S. courts will give special weight to the views of the executive branch in interpreting customary law. *See Restatement (Third) Section 112, cmt.c.*

We have tried to identify how the implementation of international environmental law, be it treaty or custom, can be influenced by the manner and form in which it is incorporated into the domestic laws of states. United States law illustrates some of the difficulties surrounding this issue, while accentuating the extent to which customary law may be treated differently from treaty law.

CHAPTER FOUR

POPULATION

A. NATURE OF POPULATION GROWTH

In the past 100 years, the global population has grown from 1.65 billion to over 6 billion people, with almost 80 percent of that increase occurring after 1950 [U.N. DEPARTMENT OF INTERNATIONAL ECONOMIC AND SOCIAL AFFAIRS, WORLD POPULATION MONITORING 2001: POPULATION ENVIRONMENT AND DEVELOPMENT at 9, U.N. Doc. ST/ESA/SER.A/203 (2001) (hereinafter WPM 2001)]. Today, approximately 6.2 billion people inhabit the world [U.N. POPULATION DIVISION, WORLD POPULATION PROSPECTS: THE 2000 REVISION, VOL. III: ANALYTICAL REPORT, at 5, ST/ESA/SER.A/200 (2002) (hereinafter WPP 2002)].

While it took until approximately 1804 for the global population to reach 1 billion, this figure doubled to 2 billion by 1927—a span of only 123 years. The global population reached 3 billion in 1960 (33 years); four billion in 1974 (14 years); and five billion in 1987 (13 years). It then took a mere twelve years for the global population to reach the current level of approximately 6 billion people in 1999 [WPP 2002, at 155]. As a result of this growth, the global population increased by nearly 2.5 times since 1950, with a peak growth rate of 2.04 percent during the late 1960's, and an annual increase of 86 million people during the late 1980's—the largest annual increase in recorded history [WPM 2001, at 10].

However, in the face of this historical trend the most recent estimates predict a significant decrease in the rate of population growth. According to projections based on the UN's medium variant, the global population will reach 7 billion by 2012—thirteen years after attaining 6 billion in 1999. The UN's medium projection variant estimates that global population will reach 8 billion in 2026 (13 years) and 9.3 billion in 2050 (24 years) [WPP 2002, at 155].

The populations of 39 countries are expected, by 2050, to fall below present levels. For example, the populations of Japan and Germany are expected to decrease by 14 percent, and Italy and Hungary by 25 percent [WPP 2002, at v]. Additionally, in all projection variants the global population growth rate is expected to experience a steady decline from 2000 onward [WPP 2002, at 157]. The implication of these projections is that population growth is declining to levels reminiscent of past centuries. If these projections hold true, the rapid growth of the second half of the twentieth century may prove a singular event in the history of humanity [WPP 2001, at 155–7].

In contrast to previous studies of global population trends, these figures bode well for the environment. However, population continues to grow despite a decline in its rate of growth. While the global population growth rate is expected to remain at 1.35 percent through 2005, as compared to a peak of 2.04 percent in the late 1960's, the world's population continues to increase by about 79 million people per year, with 97 percent of these individuals living in less developed regions [WPP 2002, at 158; WPM 2001, at 11]. In fact, only six countries account for half of this annual increase: India (21 percent), China (12 percent), Pakistan (5 percent), Nigeria (4 percent), Bangladesh (4 percent), and Indonesia (3 percent) [WPP 2002, at v].

Additionally, from 2000 to 2050 Western Asia is expected to increase by 236 million people, Northern Africa by 130 million people, and Central America by 85 million people. Northern America is expected to have a population of 438 million by 2050 [WPP 2002, 170–72]; and by 2025 China and India are expected to have aggregate population increases of 342.8 million and 196 million people, respectively [WPP 2002, Annex: Table 2, at 28–27]. In more general terms, the medium variant of the UN's projections predict the population of less developed regions will rise from 4.9 billion in 2000 to 8.2 billion in 2050. And while the total growth rate is expected to continue to decline to below 1 percent by the year 2025, the world's population could reach 8.4 billion by then, and possibly 10.9 billion by 2050 [WPP 2002, at 163–67]. Only in Europe do all projection variants anticipate a smaller population in 2050 than in 2000 [WPP 2002, at 167].

B. DECREASING RESOURCES

The rate of economic and industrial growth has generally kept pace with population increases, but as national populations and economies expand, basic resources are dwindling [WPM 2001, at 70]. Any environmental assessment of population growth must therefore evaluate the extent to which larger numbers of people consuming larger quantities of resources cause damaging environmental impacts, leading to the depletion, even exhaustion, of scarce natural resources. While resources can be grouped in different ways, the classification of resources as non-renewable versus renewable enables us to understand that resources are exhaustible, and that unlimited growth cannot be supported perpetually.

The impact of global population growth on a diminishing natural resource base may be analyzed from a neo-Malthusian perspective (as discussed below). For example, it is possible to assess the relationship between rates of population growth and resource depletion primarily in terms of the per capita consumption of these resources in select populations [WPM 2001, at 71]. While this analysis presents a gloomy prospect, there are other ways of analyzing the same phenomena. Some developmental experts see increased population as leading to greater economic development and more prosperity as a whole. The type of solutions offered to the problem of population growth and resource depletion will often depend on the rigidity with which an assessment—or a commentator—adheres to a particular focus. Thus, while the following offers a brief summation of assessments made using the perspectives more fully discussed below, it is important to keep in mind that no single perspective fully encapsulates the problems surrounding resource depletion and global population.

It is abundantly clear that richer people consume more natural resources than poorer people. In 1998 consumers in high-income countries spent $15.4 trillion of the total global private consumption amount of $19.3 trillion. Purchases by low-income countries represented less than 4 percent of all private consumption [WORLD DEVELOPMENT INDICATORS 2001, WORLD BANK (2001)]. India and the United States respectively account for approximately 17 percent and 5 percent of the world's total population [WPP 2002, at 178]. Yet in 1998 the per capita electricity consumption of the United States—one of the wealthiest per capita countries in the world—was 11,832 kWh, while the per capita electricity consumption of India during this same period was 384 kWh. Additionally, while the 1997 carbon dioxide emissions from the United States accounted for 22.6 percent of the world's total annual carbon dioxide emissions, the carbon dioxide emissions of India comprised only 1.1 percent of that global figure [UNITED NATIONS DEV. PROGRAMME (UNDP), HUMAN DEVELOPMENT REPORT 2001, 202 (2001)].

One study found that the environmental impact of an United States citizen was many times that of a citizen of India [WORLD RESOURCES INSTITUTE, WORLD RESOURCES: A GUIDE TO THE GLOBAL ENVIRON-

MENT 17 (1994) (hereinafter WRI 1994)]. For example, an average United States citizen consumes 43 times as much petroleum as an average citizen of India, 386 times as much pulpwood (used in paper production), and 11 times as much beef. As a nation, the United States consumes 25 percent of the world's energy but accounts for less than 5 percent of the world's population. The United States also is responsible for 25 percent of the world's greenhouse gases. The data clearly indicates that wealthy people, who comprise a small segment of the total global population, consume approximately two-thirds of global energy resources. From this perspective, overpopulation in the industrialized nations is the most important population problem.

At the same time, one cannot dismiss the actual impact of rapidly increasing numbers of human beings in developing countries. Larger numbers of people consuming larger quantities of resources leads to damaging environmental impacts and to the over-utilization of natural resources. From 2000 to 2035, the developing countries are expected to grow by 45 percent, as compared to the expected 2 percent growth of developed countries [WPM 2001, at 70]. The rapid increase of populations in developing countries has increased the usage of such environmentally damaging agricultural practices as deforestation and poor irrigation methods. Additionally, while the intent of these practices is often to meet the sustenance needs of a growing population, the end result is often a reduction in the agricultural yield the land is capable of producing. Biodiversity also suffers as a result of this cycle of diminishing returns. Regardless of how one measures the current and future rate of global population growth, it is apparent this growth will have adverse environmental consequences [WPM 2001, at 71].

In a seminal examination of natural resource policy [MEADOWS, ET AL., LIMITS TO GROWTH (1973)] researchers from Massachusetts Institute of Technology found that at least nineteen important natural resources were seriously depleted and would be exhausted in the foreseeable future. Though wrong about some conclusions, their original thesis about the finite nature of resources is buttressed by the fact that the physical environment is itself a resource. Global warming, loss of biodiversity, and depletion of the ozone layer are all related to consumption rates and growing populations whose demands for material needs are supplied by industry; industry in turn uses natural resources and causes pollution in a way that endangers the planet itself. Thus, an essential kernel of *Limits to Growth*, if not its entire thesis, remains true even today.

C. ENVIRONMENTAL THREATS

The environmental impacts of population growth are ubiquitous and universal. For instance, population growth has a direct impact on agricultural resources. The demand for food created from population growth has necessitated an increase in required cropland area at the expense of natural

ecosystems such as forests, grasslands, and wetlands. However, the food resources produces by
such increases are often incapable of keeping pace
with growing subsistence needs in developing
countries. While older FAO studies showed food
production lagging behind population growth, recent reports present a more optimistic face. A comprehensive study raised the question as to whether
enough food could be produced to meet demands of
a global population of 8 billion by the year 2030,
and answered affirmatively. According to the report, *"World Agriculture: Towards 2015/30,"* from
FAO's Global Perspective Studies Unit, remarkable
progress has been made over the last three decades towards feeding the world. While global population increased by over 70 percent, per capita food
consumption is almost 20 percent higher. In developing countries, despite a near doubling in population, the proportion of the population living in a
chronic state of undernourishment was cut in half,
falling to 18 percent in 1995/97. FAO anticipates
that this progress will continue. However, the absolute number of hungry will remain stubbornly
high. In 2015 there could still be about 610 million
people suffering from chronic undernourishment,
[Executive Summary www.stradanove.net/news/tes-
ti/biovisited April 21, 2003].

Another projection estimates that farmers, in order to meet the subsistence needs of the global
population in 2020, will need to produce 40 percent
more grain than in 1999 [P. PINSTRUP-ANDERSEN, ET
AL., WORLD FOOD PROSPECTS: CRITICAL ISSUES FOR THE

EARLY TWENTY-FIRST CENTURY (International Food Policy Research Institute 1999)]. As the average amount of grain land per person continues to fall, much of this will have to come from increased yield production on existing agricultural land [U.N. POPULATION FUND (UNFPA), POPULATION AND SUSTAINABLE DEVELOPMENT: FIVE YEARS AFTER RIO (1997)].

To increase agricultural productivity, scientists have developed "high-yield" varieties of crops and modified certain crops to be more resistant to adverse conditions, but have typically ignored genetic diversity. The use of irrigation and chemical pesticides and fertilizers has increased production, but has contributed to the depletion of arable land suitable for cultivation [*see* Laura Jackson, *Agricultural Industrialization and the Loss of Biodiversity*, *in* PROTECTION OF GLOBAL BIODIVERSITY: CONVERGING INTERDISCIPLINARY STRATEGIES (Lakshman Guruswamy & Jeffrey McNeely, eds. 1997); Robert Horsch & Robert Fraley, *Biotechnology Can Help Reduce the Loss of Biodiversity*, *in* PROTECTION OF GLOBAL BIODIVERSITY, *supra*; Lakshman D. Guruswamy, *Sustainable Agriculture: Do GMOs Imperil Biosafety?*, 9 IND. J. GLOBAL LEGAL STUD. 461 (2002)]. The use of harmful pesticides and fertilizers has also poisoned soil and water resources, while vermin have become resistant to chemical pesticides. Overuse of irrigation has resulted in salinization of the soil (buildup of salts and minerals) and waterlogging. The International Soil Reference and Information Center has determined that improper agricultural practices have moderately degraded 1.2 billion hectares of arable land world wide (10 percent of the earth's surface), while all higher life-forms have been eliminated on about 9 million hectares of once arable land (an area about the size of the states of Vermont and Connecticut combined) [WORLD RESOURCES INSTITUTE, WORLD RESOURCES: A GUIDE TO THE GLOBAL ENVIRONMENT 233 (1996)].

Many countries with a shortage of arable land also have a shortage of fresh water. Almost 75 percent of the world's fresh water now flows into irrigation, but diverting water for agricultural, domestic and industrial use usually means less water for aquatic environments like wetlands, lakes and rivers. While the oceans are vast and contain 97 percent of the earth's water, ocean water is not potable. Two of the remaining three percent of fresh water is trapped in the polar ice caps, leaving less than 0.008 percent of the remaining available for drinking. Compounding this problem, the use of fresh water has quadrupled between 1940 and 1990 [WRI 1994, at 181–82].

The largest direct user of water is agriculture, which accounts for approximately 70% of total global withdrawals and substantially more than this in many developing countries. To put this differently, while it takes 4–5,000 liters of water to produce the average daily diet of someone from a developed country, the global average water diet is 2,500 liters [WORLD WATER ASSESSMENT PROGRAMME, WATER SECURITY: A PRELIMINARY ASSESSMENT OF POLICY PROGRESS SINCE RIO, at 16 (2001) (hereinafter WWA 2001)]. Additionally, the latest estimates are that 1.2 billion people live on less than one U.S. dollar per day, and over 2.8 billion live on the equivalent of two U.S. dollars or less [WWA 2001, at 2]. Both directly and indirectly, these individuals use less water, but depend on its resources to secure their livelihoods far more than the rest of the global population. As of 2001, over a billion people still lack adequate water supplies, and more than twice this number lack adequate sanitation [WWA 2001, at 8].

While there have been significant areas of improvements in global environmental quality during the past 40 to 50 years, this progress has been countervailed by conspicuous deterioration in other areas. One group of experts believe that population growth is the major cause of such environmental deterioration [PAUL EHRLICH & ANNE EHRLICH, THE POPULATION EXPLOSION (1990); PAUL EHRLICH & ANNE EHRLICH, EXTINCTION: THE CAUSES AND CONSEQUENCES OF THE DISAPPEARANCE OF SPECIES 74 (1981)]. By contrast, others believe that the most powerful factor in determining the environmental quality is the technology used to produce goods and services, and that any chosen technology may cause either environmental degradation or improvement [Barry Commoner, *Rapid Population Growth and Environmental Stress*, 21 INT'L J. HEALTH SERVICES 199 (1991)]. It is difficult to deny, however, that population growth, even if not the single most important factor, does have a dramatic impact on the environment [PARTHA DASGUPTA, AN INQUIRY INTO WELL BEING AND DESTITUTION 269–96 (1995)].

D. REMEDIAL OBJECTIVES

1. THEORIES ON POPULATION GROWTH

Experts disagree on how to balance population growth and economic growth, but almost all agree that current usage rates of essential resources, and the attendant rates of environmental degradation caused by this usage, are not infinitely sustainable. As a corollary to this position, most experts also agree that without a substantial reduction in population growth or the development of resources capable of significantly attenuating its impact, this growth will eventually exceed the earth's carrying capacity—the maximum number of individuals that can be sustained by the earth's natural resources year after year without diminution in quality of life or resources. In general terms, contemporary theories of population growth can be grouped into three categories: (1) neo-Malthusian theories; (2) economic transition theories; and (3) redistributional theories. Prior to discussing these contemporary theories, however, it may be helpful to briefly canvass what is often considered the first modern theory of population growth—the theory expounded by Thomas Malthus.

(a) The Malthusian Apocalypse

Thomas Malthus' work entitled, "An Essay on the Principle of Population," published in 1798, expounds his theory on population growth. Malthus made two fundamental points: first, the rather obvious fact that food is necessary to human survival; and second, that human reproduction will persist at a consistent rate with only minor variations. Under the conditions assumed by these two postulates (and relying on census data obtained from the recently formed United States government) Malthus argued that while unchecked population growth increases geometrically, the food resources necessary to sustain that population increase only arithmetically.

In Malthusian terms, the inability of subsistence resources to match the rate of population growth ensured that a large portion of humanity would inevitably experience severe difficulties in meeting their basic needs. Thus, not only did the lack of resources operate as a consistent and powerful restraint on population growth, it rendered as impossible the Utopian ideal of a world free of hunger and poverty.

History has revealed the errors in the Malthusian view of population growth. Malthus, who wrote prior to the industrial revolution, did not foresee the dramatic impact technological advancements would have on food production. Increased crop yields, refrigeration, pesticides, mechanized farm equipment, and genetically modified organisms (GMO's) are just a few examples of the way in which the world has moved beyond the doom prophesied by Malthus. Nonetheless, starvation remains a significant problem in many portions of the world. And while technological advancements in agricultural products and practices have made possible

tremendous increases in food production, lack of
distribution has deprived much of the world of the
benefits made possible by these advances. Consequently, while population growth often exacerbates
the problems of grinding poverty and shortages in
food, clothing and shelter, in the world of today it is
often political factors, as much as population
growth, which ensures their continued existence.

(b) Neo–Malthusian, Economic Transition and Redistributional Theories of Population Growth

Neo–Malthusian theories predict disaster if population growth is not drastically reduced, but also
predict a technically and economically sustainable
society if the rate of population growth is significantly reduced [DAVID PEARCE & R. KERRY TURNER,
ECONOMICS OF NATURAL RESOURCES AND THE ENVIRON-
MENT 6 (1990)]. These predictions are premised upon
the neo-Malthusian theory that population growth
will exceed the food supply because the availability
of arable farmlands sets a limit to agricultural expansion. These experts believe that even technologies providing unlimited resources and reduced pollution would be insufficient to counteract the effects
of land overuse leading to decreased food production
and shortages [ROBERT CASSEN, ET AL., POPULATION AND
DEVELOPMENT: OLD DEBATES, NEW CONCLUSIONS (1994)].

Other theories are more optimistic and reject the
alleged alarmism and panic sown by the neo-Malthusians. The proponents of developmental theory
point to the continuing increases in food production

and output throughout the undeveloped world, and argue that these developments fly in the face of neo-Malthusian predictions of famine [Amartya Sen, *Fertility and Coercion*, 63 U. CHI. L. REV. 1035, 1050 (1996)]. One category of "developmentalists" believes that economic and social development, technical innovation, better management of resources, and market substitutes can overcome the limits of natural resources and accommodate continued population growth [PEARCE, *supra*, at 45–53]. They reject the position that economic development resulting in improved living standards causes rapid population growth *per se*.

Instead, these developmentalists subscribe to a theory of two-stage demographic transition. In stage one improved living standards reduce the death rate without creating sufficient economic security. A second stage follows in which the birth rate falls because of education, delayed marriage, and cultural changes. Some of these theorists point to prices of resources as indicators of scarcity, arguing that when prices become too high because of scarcity, a technology driven market substitutes an equivalent but cheaper resource. This theory, that prices will guide the market adjustment, depends on resources being owned, while the fact is that many resources such as water and the atmosphere are a "common pool" and are not owned. Consequently, others reject such price theories, and argue that there are often no incentives to conserve or protect such resources.

As distinct from the neo-Malthusians and developmentalists, "redistributionists" blame the problem associated with unsustainable growth and environmental depletion on inequities of consumption, and the unequal distribution of rights among the nations and peoples of the world [CASSEN, *supra*]. This group also believes in sustainable development, but maintains that the major cause of environmental depletion lies in a consumption explosion by the industrialized world rather than a population explosion in the Third World. This, they claim, is illustrated by the fact that 15 percent of the world's population enjoys 80 percent of the world's income. To them the problem is poverty rather than scarcity, and the solution is economic development that goes beyond providing technology. This third group claims that resources must be distributed more fairly between industrialized countries and developing countries. They emphasize that the population problem is not about an increase in the number of humans, but in a lack of human rights that include the right to a decent standard of living and the right of women to control their own reproduction.

2. THE WAY FORWARD

These theories and corresponding practical problems jostle for recognition within the new international framework of sustainable development. The approach fashioned and proclaimed at the "Earth Summit," the 1992 United Nations Conference on Environment and Development (UNCED), and the

World Summit on Sustainable Development (WSSD), hopes to integrate economic development, social development and environmental protection without compromising the needs of present and future generations (*see* Chapter Two). In a related approach, experts, governments, non-governmental organizations and international agencies worked for three years negotiating and revising a program to stabilize world population. Adopted, after some modification in Cairo, Egypt at the 1994 United Nations International Conference on Population and Development (1994 Population Conference), the result is a comprehensive plan that incorporates ideas from many theories [PROGRAMME OF ACTION OF THE INTERNATIONAL CONFERENCE ON POPULATION AND DEVELOPMENT, U.N. CONFERENCE ON POPULATION AND DEVELOPMENT, U.N. Doc. A/CONF. 171/13 Annex (1994) (hereinafter Program of Action); *Focus on Population and Development: Follow-up on Cairo Conference*, U.S. DEP'T ST. DISPATCH, Jan. 2, 1995, *available at* 1995 WL 8643457]. The Program of Action includes extending family planning facilities, improving women's education, health, and social status, encouraging sustainable economic development, and reducing the impact of population on the environment.

E. LEGAL RESPONSE

The above Program of Action was adopted at the 1994 Population Conference by consensus amidst controversy, and this dissension raises substantial doubts as to whether the Program of Action can become the *fons et origio* (source and origin) of a new international regime for population. Indeed, the legal response to population growth cannot be found in a discrete body of law dealing with population *per se*. Instead, it resides uneasily at the intersection of the laws dealing *inter alia* with sustainable development, social development, economic development, environmental protection, gender equity, health, education, and child welfare.

The 1994 Population Conference attempted to merge all of these strands of law into a comprehensive whole in its Program of Action. A handful of Islamic nations, however, were so opposed to it that they withdrew in protest, while parts of this document were strenuously opposed by a number of nations led by the Vatican [REPORT OF THE INTERNATIONAL CONFERENCE ON POPULATION AND DEVELOPMENT 146–149, U.N. Doc. A/CONF.171/13 (1994)]. The whole Program of Action, therefore, cannot be seen as a crystallization of customary international law, and may possess dubious value even as soft law.

The lack of agreement over population growth may seem surprising. All nations of the world, joined by the Catholic Church, recognize the environmental dangers of burgeoning populations—though the Catholic Church advocates population control through "natural family planning" [Gregory M. Saylin, *The United Nations International Conference on Population and Development: Religion, Tradition and Law in Latin America*, 28 VAND. J. TRANSNAT'L L. 1245, 1270 (1995)]. Moreover, there is international consensus, falling short of unanimity, that coercion be eschewed as a method of family planning [Program of Action, para. 7(3)]. Closer examination, however, reveals that a number of entrenched reasons block the creation of an international population regime.

The first of these arises from differing perceptions of the population question. As we have noted, neo-Malthusians fear that increasing populations will inexorably lead to shortages of food and natural resources and a failure of the carrying capacity of the planet. They demand immediate government intervention to defuse this time bomb in the form of family planning programs. This view is countered by "developmentalists" and "redistributionists" of varying stripes. In general, developmentalists see overpopulation as a symptom of underdevelopment, while the redistributionists argue that better distribution, more international equity, and less profligate consumption by the developed world would enable increasing populations to be sufficiently fed by an already adequate resource base.

Second, there are deep divisions separating the developmentalists and redistributionists. It is true they agree that the neo-Malthusians, ignoring strong evidence to the contrary, unwisely continue to sow panic. They also agree on the need for economic development and international equity. On social development, they agree on gender equity and the need for women to have improved health care. But the agreement stops there.

Developmentalists and redistributionists disagree fundamentally on well-established tenets of western feminism such as the empowerment of women through accessibility to abortion, contraception and education, and the assertion that "women are crippled by unbridled fertility" [DRAFT PROGRAMME OF ACTION OF THE INTERNATIONAL CONFERENCE ON POPULATION AND DEVELOPMENT, U.N. Doc. A/CONF. 171/L.1 (1994)]. The empowerment of women became a driving force at the 1994 Population Conference, and western feminists along with most developed countries saw this as a critical step in the move toward population control. For western feminists and developed countries, it is absolutely essential to give women reproductive freedom, emancipate them from anachronistic customs that bind women to the home, deny them an education, force unwanted children upon them, and then commit them to a lifetime of unrelenting labor of caring for those children.

For many religious traditionalists, whether Roman Catholic or Islamic, such a view insults the dignity of women. Religious traditionalists argue that western feminism seeks to limit a woman's freedom to bear children, denigrates motherhood, propagates immorality, promotes abortions, and assails the concept of a nurturing family: the very foundation of society.

While such doctrinal differences stand in the way of a legal regime controlling population growth, a third political reason militates against a legal regime instituting population control. In brief, such a regime may be seen as violating national sovereignty—encroaching on cherished notions of individual state control. And fourth, the Program of Action appears to have institutionalized, rather than resolved, deep controversies between feminist organizations, conservatives, environmentalists, religious traditionalists, and family planners.

Despite these problems, it is possible to point to some features of the sixteen-chapter Program of Action that may amount to a crystallization of customary law. For example, the sixth principle set out in chapter II of the Program of Action, which was accepted by the religious traditionalists, endorses the concept of sustainable development and requires that:

> [S]tates should reduce and eliminate unsustainable patterns of production and consumption and promote appropriate policies, including population-related policies, in order to meet the needs of current generations without compromising the ability of future generations to meet their own needs.

This may be viewed as a restriction on unfettered consumption by the developed countries, which according to some commentators significantly contributes to the population problem [Judith E. Jacobson, *Population, Consumption, and Environmental Degradation: Problems and Solutions*, 6 COLO. J. INT'L ENVT'L L. & POL'Y 255 (1995)]. Furthermore, even though the community of nations may disagree as to the means, a consensus exists that population growth should be controlled. Future population conferences may see greater agreement on the concrete steps necessary to achieve this objective. In the meantime, the implementation of policies aimed at sustainable development, gender equity, education, and health may all work in concert to reduce population growth.

CHAPTER FIVE

BIODIVERSITY

A. NATURE OF THE PROBLEM

Life on earth is supported by communities of plants, animals, and microorganisms interacting with each other within ecosystems, and with the physical environment [BIODIVERSITY 21 (E. O. Wilson ed., 1988)]. Biodiversity encompasses three concepts: the genetic diversity within each species, the diversity of species, and the diversity of ecosystems within a region. Biodiversity sustains life on earth by maintaining atmospheric quality, regulating local climates, absorbing pollutants, protecting watersheds, and generating and maintaining soils. The greater an ecosystem's diversity, the greater its capacity to support life and adapt to changing conditions.

Our anxiety over the loss of biodiversity may be based on the "use-value" of species and ecosystems, within economic, ecological, and aesthetic frameworks. Our concern may also be premised on ethical values, which are different than use-values and arise from a belief in the intrinsic worth of a species.

Within the use-value nexus, biological resources have economic value as food, medicines, chemicals, fibers, structural materials, fuel, and for other purposes. A benefit-cost figure can be calculated for preserving species with known economic values, and can even be estimated for those with unknown economic value; if a species is lost, the possibility of deriving use from it is also lost [BRYAN G. NORTON, WHY PRESERVE NATURAL VARIETY? 27 (1987)].

On the other hand, the ecological services provided by ecosystems are so diffuse and untraceable that actual economic value for those services cannot be estimated for individual species. Each species contributes to, and is interrelated and interdependent upon other species in the ecosystem. The ecological value of preserving biodiversity is based on the incalculable value of the essential services provided, for example by ecosystems, such as forests removing carbon dioxide from the atmosphere.

It should also be remembered that an ecosystem is vulnerable to the weaknesses of its species. For example, loss of genetic diversity within plant and animal species leads to uniformity that makes species more susceptible to diseases and pests. This weakness renders them less able to adapt to a changing physical environment, and in turn makes the ecosystem less stable [PAUL EHRLICH & ANNE EHRLICH, EXTINCTION, THE CAUSES AND CONSEQUENCES OF THE DISAPPEARANCE OF SPECIES 74 (1981)].

Biological resources also have aesthetic value as sources of recreation and beauty. Like economic and ecological values, aesthetic values are based on the uses provided by species and ecosystems. The value of nature is difficult to quantify, but can be assigned based on the value of a similar experience, such as the ability to visit a pristine North Slope in Alaska, or a preserved tropical rain forest, or what a person would be willing to pay for the experience, or be willing to accept for not having the opportunity. Even the aesthetic value of nature's spiritual effect on humans may depend on the "use-value" of nature.

In contrast, preserving nature for its own sake, as distinct from its use, depends on the intrinsic value of a species in its own right, independent of its value to any other. Ethical reasons for preserving biodiversity are based, quite simply, on the right of species and ecosystems to exist. Arguably, their enduring existence denotes the right to continued existence, which in turn carries responsibilities for humans. As the dominant species on earth, humans have a moral responsibility as caretakers or trustees to preserve other species.

B. ENVIRONMENTAL IMPACTS

The richest remaining areas of biodiversity are rain forests, coral reefs, and wetlands. Tropical forests contain 50 to 90 percent of the approximately 10 million species that live on earth. These ecosystems are threatened with rapid destruction as a result of pressure from growing local populations for agricultural land and fuel wood supplies, coupled with world markets for tropical hardwoods and animal products [NATIONAL ACADEMY OF SCIENCES, ONE

EARTH, ONE FUTURE (1990)]. The annual rate of tropical deforestation in the 1980s averaged 0.8 percent, with the greatest losses in Latin America, West Africa, and Southeast Asia. At this rate, scientists estimate that 5 to 10 percent of tropical forest species (hundreds of thousands) may face extinction by the year 2020.

Tropical deforestation to clear agricultural land is often accomplished by a *slash and burn* method which releases carbon dioxide and other gases that contribute to global warming and depletion of the ozone layer. Tropical deforestation may also lead to degradation of soil fertility and changes in regional hydrology, as watersheds are destroyed, and precipitation patterns change. However, the most serious long-term impact of tropical deforestation may be the loss of plant and animal species.

Coral reefs cover only 0.17 percent of the sea floor, yet they contain 25 percent of all known marine species. Coral reefs are created in tropical saltwater by animals called stony-coral polyps. With the aid of symbiotic algae living within the corals' tissues, the corals secrete the limestone reefs over thousands of years. The fragile coral reef ecosystems are vulnerable to both natural environmental threats such as disease and predation, and human activities that pollute or physically destroy the reefs.

Coastal wetlands which provide vital breeding, nursery, and feeding areas for marine species are threatened primarily by pollution, development pressures from expanding human populations (six out of ten people live within 40 miles of the coast), and rising sea levels predicted to result from climate changes and subsidence [WALTER V. REID & MARK C. TREXLER, DROWNING THE NATIONAL HERITAGE: CLIMATE CHANGE AND U.S. COASTAL BIODIVERSITY 8 (1991)]. For example, over half of the wetlands in the contiguous United States have been dredged or developed, destroying ecosystems valuable not only for fish, waterfowl, and endangered species habitat, but also for natural water purification and flood prevention systems.

C. CAUSES

The primary cause of the loss of biodiversity is habitat destruction resulting from the expansion of human populations and activities. Among terrestrial ecosystems, the expansion of agriculture and commercial harvesting has led to the destruction of forests, while overgrazing and conversion to agricultural crop land has significantly altered natural habitat. In aquatic ecosystems, dams have destroyed large sections of freshwater habitat, while coastal development is responsible for destroying reefs and near-shore marine habitat.

Other direct causes include invasion by introduced species, over-exploitation of biological resources, industrial agriculture and forestry, pollution, and potentially, global climate change. Clearly the introduction of predators, competitors, and pathogens into isolated ecosystems poses a serious threat to the survival of native species. Just as clearly, forest, marine, and wildlife resources have been over-exploited—sometimes to the point of extinction—not only for food but also for commodities such as elephant ivory and ceremonial objects such as tiger bones. In a related vein, industrial agriculture and forestry techniques use fewer varieties of plants to increase productivity; the result is a loss of biodiversity, and an increased susceptibility to pests. In addition, pollution of the air, soil, and water has led to the reduction, and even extinction, of some sensitive species which can, in turn, lead to the destruction of entire ecosystems. Finally, many species and ecosystems may not successfully adapt to predicted global climate changes brought on by air pollution.

D. REMEDIAL OBJECTIVES

The goal of species biodiversity conservation is to meet people's needs for biological resources while ensuring that those resources last indefinitely. As we shall see, remedial actions need to be based within global frameworks of equity and justice as well as sustainable development. Earlier treaty regimes attempted to deal with biodiversity as a self-contained problem, but subsequent geo-political developments demanded a different approach governed by two systemic principles that have become a foundational part of modern international environmental law. The two contrast starkly with environmental protection simpliciter.

The first principle is international equity or justice. It demands that the endemic problems of global poverty must constitute the bedrock of any discussion of other global predicaments such as environmental protection. The second principle is sustainable development. This is a new paradigm endorsed by the Earth Summit that generally allows for the use and exploitation of resources subject to environmental restraints (*See* Chapter Eighteen).

Consistent with a pattern established during the negotiations at the Stockholm Conference on the Human Environment (1972), the protection of biodiversity has become part of the North–South debate on equity and sustainable development, traversing the issues of development (economic growth) and global poverty. The experience of the Convention on Biological Diversity (CBD), June 5, 1992, 31 I.L.M. 818 (entered into force Dec. 29, 1993) signed at Rio in 1992, has demonstrated the near impossibility of segregating or surgically isolating the environmental or scientific problems of biodiversity from its socio-political milieu.

E. LEGAL RESPONSE

1. THE CONVENTION ON BIOLOGICAL DIVERSITY (CBD)

In 1987 the UNEP Governing Council asked an ad hoc working group to "explore the desirability and possible form of an umbrella convention to rationalize current activities" in this area. By umbrella convention, the Governing Council meant a treaty that would consolidate the existing treaties into a workable whole, eliminating jurisdictional overlap and filling perceived gaps. As this proved politically unattainable, the international community settled for the current CBD—a framework treaty which possesses only the power to seek "appropriate forms of cooperation" with the executive bodies of other biodiversity conventions [arts. 22(1), 23(4)(h)].

As a framework treaty, the CBD contains primarily aspirational provisions, with matters of substance left to future development by its own Conference of the Parties (COP). In fact, the CBD has received a great deal of criticism for its lack of substantive provisions, and because its most general obligations contain heavily qualified language. Others have defended the CBD by noting its resolution of long-standing problems such as access to biological resources—while reminding detractors of the forward-looking nature of the framework approach in setting the stage for future solutions among political difficulties.

In summarizing the provisions of this framework convention, for analytical purposes we have returned to the two overriding principles of (1) Equity and Resource Transfers, and (2) Sustainable Development (Conservation and Sustainable Use). Of course, the two principles are conceptually bound together, and one way that the CBD approaches that connection is by applying an underlying, if not expressly articulated, third principle known as Common But Differentiated Responsibility (CBDR).

CBDR links equity and sustainable development together by contemplating resource transfers such that "developed countries acknowledge the responsibility that they bear in the international pursuit of sustainable development in view of the pressures their societies place on the global environment and of the technologies and financial resources they command" [Principle 7, Rio Declaration]. In our analysis, we have located the specific commitments—including those based on CBDR—within a general discussion of the issues.

(a) Principles of Equity and Resource Transfers

In reviewing the outcome of equity issues in the CBD, we have noticed the differences in the background positions of the richer countries of the developed world, the North, and the poorer countries of the developing world, the South (*see* Chapter Two, Introduction). As most of the biological diversity in the world exists in the South, the South understandingly felt, and continues to feel, possessive of those resources. While accepting the importance of preserving biodiversity, they perceived outside attempts to curtail internal development as a threat to sovereignty; in addition, as these nations experience conditions of real poverty, the cordoning off of large tracts of land from development loomed as an impediment to alleviating deprivation through economic progress. Should the North—which has already consumed a substantial degree of its own biodiversity—now want the South to curtail its development in the name of biodiversity, the latter would exact a price. The South would embrace sustainable development only if the North would assume the costs, and only through projects that would not compromise a growing sense of sovereignty over natural resources.

On the other hand, the North viewed the protection of biological diversity less from the point of past sins, and more as a present global problem which entailed shared sacrifice. Thus, as the North had generally placed restrictions on development in its own countries—creating a series of protected areas such as parks, preserves and wilderness areas—it tended to believe that the South should do the same. Although the North recognized that the South should receive some financial help in its efforts to protect biological diversity, the North saw that protection as an outright obligation of each member of the global community, an obligation independent of financial transfer and ability to pay. Furthermore, in transferring financial resources to the developing countries, the developed countries wanted to retain control over exactly where that money would go; in other words, they wanted targeted and efficient use of their contributions.

i. Common Concern of Humankind

One outcome of the conflict between the developed and developing countries is expressed in the preamble of the CBD, which affirms that "the conservation of biological diversity is a common concern of humankind." Early in the negotiating process the parties dropped the phrase "common heritage" from consideration because of its connotation of community access to, and the sharing of proceeds from, the development of those resources. They rejected the formulation of the Food and Agricultural Organization of the United Nations (FAO), which had earlier confirmed that "plant genetic resources are a heritage of mankind ... [which] consequently should be available without restriction" [International Undertaking on Plant Genetic Resources, art. 1 (1983) (HEREINAFTER the Undertaking)]. Previously, both the Law of the Sea and the Outer Space Treaty employed the common heritage language calling for the sharing of proceeds from resources lying outside the area of national jurisdiction. These agreements were concluded, however, at a time when developing countries would benefit from such a concept. By contrast, in the case of biological diversity developing countries were dealing with resources within their own borders—resources to which they were reluctant to surrender sovereignty. Needless to say, due to its linguistic history the "common heritage" term did not gain favor. Even so, the "common concern" formulation—though less broad in scope—does recognize the loss of biodiversity as a major problem which the international community must attend to on a global basis.

ii. Access to Genetic Resources

The CBD therefore discards the principle of "free access" to genetic resources, a principle which maintained the right of a developed country to obtain and freely use the genetic material of a developing country. Though later annexes to the FAO Undertaking, referred to above, make clear that free access does not mean "free of charge," only with the CBD did the international community make a clean break from the original concept of free access. Under article 15(1) of the CBD, "the authority to determine access to genetic resources rests with the national governments and is subject to national legislation." The CBD adopts the principle of Prior Informed Consent, now a standard concept with regard to North–South environmental transactions [art. 15(5)], and developing country parties can negotiate with private companies or other parties on the "mutually agreed" price of access to genetic material [art. 15(4); *see* Chapter Nine, Toxic and Hazardous Substances for a discussion of Prior Informed Consent concerning hazardous waste transfers].

The provisions of the CBD dealing with access to genetic resources were firmly endorsed by two instruments. The first is the FAO's International Treaty on Plant Genetic Resources for Food and Agriculture, that was opened for signature in November 2001. This Treaty covers all plant genetic resources relevant for food and agriculture. Its objectives are the conservation and sustainable use of plant genetic resources for food and agriculture and the fair and equitable sharing of benefits derived from their use, in harmony with the Convention on Biological Diversity, for sustainable agriculture and food security. [http://www.fao.org/ag/cgrfa/itpgr. htm, visited April 14, 2003]. The second is the Bonn Guidelines on Access to Genetic Resources and Fair and Equitable Sharing of the Benefits Arising out of their Utilization, that was endorsed by the sixth Conference of the Parties in 2002. [http://www.biodiv.org/decisions/default, visited April 14, 2003]

On a related issue, genetic resources taken from the country of origin before the CBD's entry into force—such as those now held in gene banks throughout the world—are excluded from the present access provisions. The COP will soon take up the question of such resources, deciding what benefit, if any, developing countries will receive from genetic material previously removed from the country of origin.

iii. Biotechnology

Biotechnology, as considered in the CBD, "means any technological application that uses biological systems, living organisms, or derivatives thereof, to make or modify products or processes for specific use" [art. 2]. This ranges from the ancient practice of the selective breeding of animals and plants, to sophisticated DNA technology and genetic engineering. The CBD covers two important and controversial areas with regard to biotechnology.

Transfer of Technology

The CBD makes explicitly clear that "technology includes biotechnology" [art. 2], so that any reference to the transfer of technology also includes the transfer of biotechnology. The issue of access to and transfer of technology is dealt with in article 16—a convoluted article with a number of overlapping and cross-referenced provisions. As a first requirement, the article mandates that all parties, developed and developing countries, must "provide and/or facilitate" the access to and transfer of biotechnology [art. 16(1)]. The transfer of technology to developing countries must be made on "fair and favorable terms, including concessional and preferential terms where mutually agreed," and such transfer can occur by way of the financial mechanism [art. 16(2)]. Making the transfer available through the financial mechanism means that technology transfer qualifies as a fundable enterprise under the CBD. Finally, article 16(2) also provides that technology protected by an intellectual property right (IPR) in a developed country, if transferred, must receive "the adequate and effective protection" of that right in the developing country.

The controversy involving transfer of biotechnology again reflects fundamental differences of opinion between the North and the South. First, most biotechnology remains in the hands of private corporations in developed countries, and as market players within market economies, these corporations demand some remuneration for their investment. Second, biotechnology generally exists under IPR protection in developed countries, and corporations insist on similar protection in the developing countries. Without such protection, even payment for the technology will not suffice as the technology might be copied and pirated in the developing country.

In contrast, developing countries see the transfer of biotechnology as a main incentive for participation in the CBD. With transfer, over time they might develop their own biotechnology industries, developing the wealth of their own biodiversity. In addition, the South views IPRs as an impediment to technology transfer, as IPRs make the protected technology more expensive and thus more restrictive. They maintain that the level of IPR protection should be commensurate with an individual country's level of economic development, and thus a matter for national determination.

Resolution of the impasse concerning IPRs now rests with the new Trade–Related Aspects of Intellectual Property Rights (TRIPS) of the World Trade Organization. In effect, under this agreement developing countries must generally respect IPRs, but have a number of years in which to implement protective legislation. As for the channeling of resources to developing countries (who then might remunerate corporations involved in the transfer), article 16(2) makes clear that such projects are fundable by the financial mechanism—either for the cost itself and/or for the cost of the IPR protection foregone [*see* art.19]. In fact, the first COP listed the matter as a program priority for the financial mechanism to consider, giving emphasis "[i]n accordance with article 16 of the Convention ... [to] projects which promote access to, transfer of and cooperation in joint development of technology"

[*Decisions Adopted by the First meeting of the Conference of the Parties*, annex I(III)(4)(f), U.N. Doc. UNEP/CBD/1/17 (1994)].

Transfer of the Benefits of Biotechnology

As previously mentioned, the CBD provides for negotiations between developed country entities (usually corporations) and developing country parties concerning the price of access to genetic resources [art. 15(4) & 15(7)]. In this way, the CBD foresees a mechanism by which the developing countries might: (1) negotiate the acquisition of biotechnology developed from genetic resources [art. 16(3)]; (2) participate in research projects connected to genetic resources [art. 19(1)]; and (3) gain priority access to the results and benefits (such as royalties) arising from biotechnologies based upon genetic resources [art. 19(2)]. The governments of developed countries must facilitate the above outcomes, but on the whole negotiations will take place between private corporations and developing countries. Again, article 15(7) makes allowance for use of the financial mechanism to fund projects which share the research, development and benefits of genetic resources.

iv. Financial Transfers

Under the CBD, developed countries must pay "to enable developing country Parties to meet the agreed full incremental costs to them of implementing measures which fulfill the obligations of this Convention" [Art. 20(2)]. Again, as stated above, this provision enshrines the principle of Common

But Differentiated Responsibility (CBDR) as noted in Principle 7 of the 1992 Rio Declaration, in which developed countries acknowledge their greater financial responsibility in addressing global environmental degradation. Developed Countries, listed in an annex adopted at the first meeting of the COP, will channel their contributions through the newly restructured interim financial mechanism, the Global Environment Facility (GEF) [*see* Appendix A]. Following the Programme Priorities laid down by the COP, the GEF will then fund individual projects put forth by the developing countries—the "incremental cost" to be determined by individual negotiations between the GEF and the respective applicant. Also, developed countries may bypass the GEF through regional, bilateral and multilateral channels under article 20(3), but the extent to which such funding might meet a developing country's financial obligations under the CBD remains an open question for the COP.

(b) Principles of Sustainable Development (Conservation and Sustainable Use)

As our second operating principle, sustainable development functions as a prevailing force within, and ultimate objective of, the CBD. Reference to sustainable development is only made once in the treaty, but it is repeatedly inscribed within two common terms of the CBD: "conservation" and "sustainable use." These might be seen as the twin poles of sustainable development. On the one hand, sustainable use acknowledges the necessity of utilizing biological resources: "sustainable use" means the use of components of biological diversity in a way, and at a rate that does not lead to the long-term decline of biological diversity, thereby maintaining its potential to meet the needs and aspirations of present and future generations [art. 2]. On the other hand "conservation" is not defined in the treaty, but its usage clearly speaks to the preservation of biological diversity. For example, the treaty does define *in-situ* conservation as "the conservation of ecosystems and natural habitats and the maintenance and recovery of viable populations of species in their natural surroundings ..." [art. 2]. Thus, in combining the development connotation of "sustainable use" with the preservation connotation of "conservation," the CBD strikes the balance of sustainable development.

The treaty imposes various obligations with regard to sustainable development, weaving these through a myriad of overlapping provisions. In summarizing these commitments, however, one is immediately confronted with the qualifying language, "as far as possible" and "as appropriate," that accompanies nearly every obligation. These qualifications severely limit the strength of very important provisions, and create the perception of the CBD as an empty treaty. Particularly with regard to the obligations of developing countries, these qualifications greatly reduce their respective commitments—and, as most of the remaining biodiversity lies within their borders, significantly diminish the worldwide effort to save biodiversity. On the other hand, no treaty can go beyond the political realities of the time, and at least the framework approach to international law-making provides a flexible method to institute stronger measures.

i. All Parties (Including Developing Countries)

In implementing sustainable development under the CBD, the focus is on national action. In general, all parties must develop "national strategies, plans or programmes for the conservation and sustainable use of biodiversity" [art. 6(a)], and then must integrate these approaches into other relevant national programs such as forestry and agricultural planning [art. 6(b)]. As part of this process each country must also conduct studies to identify the components of biodiversity [art. 7(a)], and then must monitor those components most in need of conservation as well as those "which offer the greatest potential for sustainable use" [art. 7(b)].

More specifically, with respect to the conservation of *in situ* biodiversity—that is, biodiversity in its natural setting—the CBD in article 8 makes a number of important mandates, including the establishment of protected areas, the management of biological resources within and without such protected areas, the protection of ecosystems, and the maintenance of viable species populations. Responding to articles 19(3) and 8(g), the parties at COP II also committed themselves to the development of a Protocol on Bio-safety, recognizing that the advent of biotechnology may have adverse environmental impacts on the conservation and sustainable use of biodiversity [Report of the Open Ended Ad Hoc Group on Bio–Safety, UNEP/CBD/COP/2/7]. And, though the CBD stresses *in situ* conservation as the primary means of protecting biodiversity, a number of *ex situ* provisions also exist. *Ex situ* conservation includes gene banks, captive breeding programs and zoos. Under article 9, parties must adopt measures to promote *ex situ* conservation through the establishment of appropriate facilities and through the development of appropriate species rehabilitation programs.

Parties must also incorporate a consideration of sustainable development into their national decision-making, protect traditional cultural uses of biological resources, and encourage cooperation between the public and private sectors [*see* art. 10]. On a related issue, parties must also consider the implementation of environmental impact assessment (EIA) procedures for proposed projects that are likely to have significant adverse impacts on biological diversity—clearly a step forward in achieving the overall goal of sustainable development [art. 14].

Again, all of these critical provisions remain qualified with the phrase "as far as possible and as appropriate," except for the simple duty to create "national strategies, plans or programmes" which receives the arguably less evasive escape clause "in accordance with its [a specific nation's] particular conditions and capabilities." In overseeing the implementation of all these requirements, such as they are, the COP will receive reports from each party concerning its fulfillment of the provisions and objectives of the convention [art. 26]. The national reports—first, second and third—submitted by the Parties, have focused on the general measures for conservation and sustainable use under art. 6.

ii. Developed Countries

Following the concept of Common But Differentiated Responsibility (CBDR)—which as stated earlier links together the two principles of equity and sustainable development—the CBD creates additional commitments for developed countries. These primarily involve obligations of funding and technology transfer, outlined above, which developed country parties must discharge in furtherance of sustainable development. In fact, as stated clearly in article 20(4), the obligations of developing countries to fulfill their obligations depends on the "effective implementation of developed country Parties of their commitments under the Convention related to financial resources and transfer of technology." In other words, one might see the qualifying language of developing country commitments, such as "as far as possible and as appropriate," as contingent on the contributions of developed countries. In this way the North, in effect, controls just how "qualified" these "qualified" commitments are. If the North wants real action by the South on sustainable use and the conservation of biodiversity, it need only contribute a commensurate amount.

Of further note, the CBD also distinguishes between Organization for Economic Co-operation and Development (OECD) members and former Soviet bloc nations. The latter, those "countries undergoing the process of transition to a market economy," can voluntarily assume the obligations of developing countries over time [art. 20(2)].

(c) Institutions

The CBD offers the typical institutional arrangements of a framework treaty. The COP acts as the "all-powerful" legislative organ which makes decisions on a range of substantive, administrative and procedural matters. The COP, which meets annually, also votes on amendments, protocols and amendments to protocols. The method for adopting informal or "everyday" decisions—whether administrative or substantive—remains to be decided. Procedural questions are resolved by a simple majority vote. Amendments to the convention or to protocols are by at least a two-thirds majority of parties present and voting [art. 29].

The Secretariat functions as the administrative arm of the COP, working year round to coordinate action with other international bodies and preparing reports and material for the next meeting of the parties. The Subsidiary Body on Scientific, Technical and Technological Advice (SBSTTA) provides expertise to the COP, creating scientific and technical assessments of both the status of biodiversity and the effects of measures taken to implement the CBD [art. 25]. Significantly, the first meeting of the

COP also established a Clearing–House Mechanism for Technical and Scientific Cooperation, an institution that will act as a catalyst for collaborative research and joint projects under the CBD [art. 18(3)]. The pilot phase of the clearing-house mechanism was commenced for the years 1996–1997. Today the objectives of the Clearing House Mechanism are to promote and facilitate technical and scientific cooperation within and between countries, develop a global mechanism for exchanging and integrating information on biodiversity, and create necessary human and technological networks.

(d) Relationship to Other Conventions

As we shall see, the nations of the world have already created a number of international as well as regional treaties on specific subjects concerning biological diversity. Significantly however, the CBD would trump all other treaties, including the WTO (formerly GATT), where the exercise of rights and obligations under those treaties "would cause serious damage or a threat to biological diversity" [art. 22(1)]. The one exception to this is in regard to the marine environment, in which the rights and obligations of the CBD may not conflict with those created by the United Nations Convention on the Law of the Sea (UNCLOS), Dec. 10, 1982, art. 22(2), 21 I.L.M. 1261 [entered into force (Nov. 16, 1994)]. Thus, in effect we now have two dominant environmental treaties dealing with biological diversity: the CBD for terrestrial biodiversity and UNCLOS for marine biodiversity.

As the preeminent treaty with respect to terrestrial biodiversity, the CBD directs the Secretariat to seek "appropriate forms of cooperation" with the executive bodies of other biodiversity treaties. The goal is to (a) facilitate the exchange of information, (b) harmonize reporting procedures, (c) coordinate respective programs of work, and (d) consult on how such conventions can contribute to the implementation of the CBD (UNEP/CBD/COP/3/29). To this end, the CBD Secretariat has entered into Memoranda of Cooperation with a number of executive bodies of other treaties, including the Ramsar Convention, CITES, and the Bonn Convention (see below). The CBD presently has memoranda of cooperation with the following conventions and institutions: Convention on International Trade in Endangered Species of Wild Fauna and Flora; Convention on the Conservation of Migratory Species of Wild Animals; Convention on Wetlands of International Importance, especially as Waterfowl habitat and the World Heritage Convention. It also has similar memoranda with international organizations such as: Center for International Forestry Research For Scientific and Technical Co-operation; Intergovernmental Oceanographic Commission; Pan–European Biological and Landscape Diversity Strategy; UNCTAD—United Nations Conference on Trade and Development; UNESCO—United Nations Educational, Scientific and Cultural Organization; IUCN—World Conservation Union ; and FAO. Significantly, GATT/WTO is not among them.

[http://www.biodiv.org/convention/partners-back-ground.asp]

2.   CARTEGENA PROTOCOL ON BIOSAFETY

The objectives of the CBD as embodied in Art. 1 relate to "the conservation of biological diversity, the sustainable use of its components and the fair and equitable sharing of the benefits arising out of the utilization of genetic resources." The Conference of the Parties felt that biotechnology can make a contribution towards achieving the objectives of the Convention if developed and used with adequate safety measures for the environment and human health. In so doing, they paid special regard to Art 19(3) which stipulated that:

> The Parties shall consider the need for and modalities of a protocol setting out appropriate procedures, including, in particular, advance informed agreement, in the field of the safe transfer, handling and use of any living modified organism resulting from biotechnology that may have adverse effect on the conservation and sustainable use of biological diversity

Acting upon this mandate, the Conference of the Parties to the CBD negotiated and adopted a supplementary agreement to the CBD known as the Cartagena Protocol on Biosafety on 29 January 2000, 39 I.L.M. 1027. The Protocol seeks to protect biological diversity from the potential risks posed by living modified organisms (LMO's), also known as genetically modified organisms (GMO's), resulting from modern biotechnology. It establishes an advance informed agreement (AIA) procedure for ensuring that countries are provided with the information necessary to make informed decisions before agreeing to the import of such organisms into their territory. The Protocol contains reference to a precautionary approach and reaffirms the precaution language in Principle 15 of the Rio Declaration on Environment and Development. The Protocol also establishes a Biosafety Clearing–House to facilitate the exchange of information on living modified organisms and to assist countries in the implementation of the Protocol. The Protocol will come into force after 50 ratifications. As of December 13 2002, 44 countries had ratified it. [http://www.biodiv.org/biosafety/signinglist.asp?sts=rtf&ord=dt]

The Protocol creates a number of procedures and institutions. Among the more important of them is the advance informed agreement (AIA) procedure which places an obligation on the exporter of GMO's. This procedure must be followed (unless expressly waived by the party of import), prior to the first intentional transboundary movement of LMOs for intentional introduction into the environment of the Party of import [art. 7]. In these cases, the exporter must provide a detailed, written description of the LMO to the importing country in advance of the first shipment. The importer is to acknowledge receipt of this information within 90 days and then explicitly authorize the shipment within 270 days or state its reasons for rejecting it.

However, the absence of a response does not imply consent. The purpose of this procedure is to ensure that recipient countries have both the opportunity and the capacity to assess risks that may be associated with the LMO's before agreeing to its import.

However, a number of LMOs are excluded from the AIA procedure taking into account the specific activity or the intended use of the LMO involved. These are: LMOs in transit [art. 6]; LMOs destined for contained use [art. 6]; LMOs intended for direct use as food or feed or for processing [art. 7(2)]. The Meeting of the Parties to the Protocol may also decide in the future to exempt additional LMOs from the AIA procedure. However, the fact that these categories of LMOs are excluded from the Protocol's specific AIA procedure does not imply that countries may not regulate their import.

The Protocol established a Biosafety Clearing–House under the clearing-house mechanism of the Convention, in order to facilitate the exchange of scientific, technical, environmental and legal information on, and experience with, living modified organisms; and to assist Parties to implement the Protocol [art. 20(1)].

For LMOs intended for direct use as feed or food or for processing, the Protocol establishes a special procedure which requires countries to exchange information at an early stage, through the Biosafety Clearing–House, to give notice of domestic authorizations of LMOs and to make available copies of national laws and regulations concerning these LMOs [art. 11].

According to the Protocol, governments will decide whether or not to accept imports of LMOs on the basis of risk assessments. These assessments are to be undertaken in a scientific manner based on recognized risk assessment techniques [art. 15]. However, in case of insufficient relevant scientific information and knowledge, a country may decide to apply the precautionary approach and refuse the import of the LMO into its territory. The Protocol also recognizes the right of importing countries to take into account socio-economic considerations such as the value of biological diversity to its indigenous and local communities in reaching a decision on import of GMOs.

While the Protocol concentrates on international action, it recognizes that national measures are vital to making its procedures effective. Consistent with the emphasis on civil society, member governments commit themselves to promoting public awareness, ensuring public access to information, and consulting the public in decisions about biosafety. They must also take national measures to prevent illegal shipments and accidental releases of LMOs, and they must notify affected or potentially affected states in the event that an unintentional movement occurs.

The commercialization of biotechnology and the proliferation of genetically modified organisms (GMO's) has spawned multi-billion-dollar industries for foodstuffs and pharmaceuticals that continue to grow at a dramatic pace. Advocates of GMOs have argued that they offer one practical way of feeding the poor and advancing sustainable development. As we have noted the Cartagena Protocol permits restrictions and even the banning of the import of GMO or living modified organisms (LMO's).

On the other hand the Agreement on Sanitary and Phytosanitary Measures (SPS Agreement) of The World Trade Organization (WTO) also addresses trade in GMO's .These agreements form part of the GATT regime institutionalizing free trade. The proponents of GATT contend that free trade is the most important international machinery for advancing economic growth and sustainable development. To the extent that a decision to ban GMO**s** obstructs free trade, the SPS requires that such decisions be justified on principles of "sound scientific knowledge" based on scientific risk assessments. But, as we have seen, the Cartagena Protocol focuses on environmental protection not free trade. The Biosafety Protocol allows nations pursuing biosafety to ban GMOs by using the precautionary principle, even where strict scientific proof may be lacking.

Any judicial dispute over this issue will fall within the jurisdiction of the Dispute Settlement bodies of the WTO because neither the Convention on Biological Diversity nor the Cartagena Protocol create binding dispute settlement procedures. Environmentalists, including this author, have justifiably been suspicious about the judicial machinery of the WTO. To assuage such fears, it is necessary that any decisions taken by the judicial bodies of the WTO be based on the international customary law principles of fairness and reasonableness. (see Lakshman D. Guruswamy, Sustainable Agriculture: Do GMO's Imperil Biosafety *9 Ind. J. Global Legal Stud. 461 (2002).*)

3.   INTERNATIONAL TREATIES RELATED TO BIOLOGICAL DIVERSITY

(a) The 1973 Convention on International Trade in Endangered Species of Fauna and Flora (CITES)

The CITES convention, is one of the largest environmental treaties and boasts 161 parties [http://www.cites.org/eng/disc/what.shtml]. It is an early international treaty that attempts to protect endangered plant and animal species through restrictions on international trade [Mar. 3, 1973, 12 I.L.M. 1085 (entered into force July 1, 1975)]. Such trade has contributed greatly to the decline of those wild species that possess some commercial viability, including the high profile mammals of Africa. Ratified by most countries involved in this type of commerce, CITES creates a number of bureaucratic hurdles that prevent particularly harmful exchanges. In effect, CITES establishes a paper trail for all allowable trade in protected species, and any trade without proper documentation is considered illegal under the treaty.

To date, CITES protects literally thousands of species, with a large number coming from the developing countries of the South. To keep track of such a high volume of trade, the COP has established both a Plants Committee and an Animals Committee—recently reconfiguring the membership in these to allow for greater representation by developing or "producer" countries. In addition to protecting both plant and animal specimens, either alive or dead, the treaty also covers "any recognizable part or derivative thereof" [art. I(b)]. This latter provision restricts legal trade in coveted items such as rhino horns and elephant tusks, though a great deal of illegal traffic still occurs in by-products as well as in whole specimens.

i. *Commitments*

The treaty actually creates only a few substantive duties for the parties. To begin, each party must establish both a "Management Authority" and a "Scientific Authority"—whose collective job it is to administer the permit system as detailed below. Each party must also submit annual reports to the Secretariat of the convention documenting the number and types of permits granted, and biennial reports on the legislative, regulatory and administrative measures taken to enforce the convention [art. VIII]. Finally, each party must follow the procedures of documentation regarding the three appendices of protected species.

Appendix I "includes all species threatened with extinction which are or may be threatened by trade" [art. II(1)]. To engage in commerce involving an Appendix I species, a trader must obtain both an export and import permit. An importing state will grant an import permit only after its Scientific Authority advises that the import will not be "detrimental to the survival of the species involved" and that the recipient can suitably care for the specimen, if living [art. III(3)]. In addition, the importing nation's Management Authority must confirm that the proposed use of the specimen is not "for primarily commercial purposes" [art. III(3)].

Similarly, the exporting state may grant an export permit only after its Scientific Authority finds the exchange non-threatening to the survival of that species [art. III(2)]. Furthermore, its Management Authority must (1) discover no violation of its own species protection laws, (2) believe that the transfer will minimize the risk of injury, damage to health or cruel treatment, and (3) confirm the previous granting of an import permit [art. III(2)]. Thus, the CITES regime disallows most harmful trade in Appendix I species, and generates an intricate paper trail for permissible exchanges.

Appendix II of the convention includes species which may become threatened in the future without trade controls [art. II(2)]. For this category CITES requires only an export permit and not the additional burden of an import permit. Following the exact model for Appendix I, the exporting party may grant the permit only after its Scientific Authority deems the exchange non-threatening to the survival of the species, and after its Management Authority finds the specimen both legally obtained and safely transferable [art. IV(2)]. Therefore, though less involved for the parties than Appendix I exchanges, the treaty still generates a considerable paper trail for all legal trade in Appendix II species.

Appendix III includes those species "which any Party identifies as being subject to regulation within its jurisdiction for the purpose of preventing or restricting exportation" [art. II(3)]. To trade in a species on this list, one must obtain an export permit (if from a country listing such species in Appendix III) and a Certificate of Origin. The export permit in this case dispenses with the need for any determination by the exporting country's Scientific Authority, requiring only satisfaction by the Management Authority that no domestic laws were violated in the taking of the specimen and that the transfer would not involve undue harm [art. V(2)]. The convention, however, does require a Certificate of Origin for all trade in Appendix III species, even if the transaction does not involve a party having placed the species on the list [art. V(3)].

To amend either Appendix I or II requires a two-thirds majority of parties present and voting at a meeting of the COP [art. XV]. This includes transfers of a species from one appendix to another, as occurred with the "uplisting" of the African Elephant from Appendix II to Appendix I in 1989. In practice, this super-majority voting procedure provides the COP with a dynamic tool, allowing it to alter the protections of the regime as circumstances change. An amendment to Appendix III occurs simply by the communication of any party that it wishes to designate a species as such [art. XVI].

ii. Continued Trade in Listed Species

Despite the commitments cited above, legal trade under the treaty—not to mention illegal trade outside the treaty—still takes place in several different ways. A major loophole of the CITES regime lies in the ability of parties to file reservations against the listing of a species in Appendix I, II, or III—or in any parts and derivatives of Appendix III species [art. XXIII]. A reservation avoids the permit system with regard to that species, in effect placing the objecting party in the position of a non-party who can freely trade with other non-parties.

A second problem involves such non-parties (or an objecting party for a particular species), with whom parties may still engage in trade. Parties may do so, however, only when the non-party issues "comparable" documentation which "substantially conforms" to CITES permits and certificates—a practice which remains open to fraud by traders and non-parties [art. X].

The treaty also authorizes certain exemptions for listed species. Specimens, for example, acquired within an owner's usual state of residence and deemed "personal or household effects" generally are not covered by the treaty [art. VII(3)]. The convention also exempts specimens documented by an exporting state's Management Authority as acquired before that particular species became listed [art. VII(2)]. Of greatest significance, CITES also excuses from its restrictions species "bred in captivity" if the trader obtains a certificate of captive breeding from the state of export [art. VII(5)]. To prevent fraud in this exemption, the COP oversees a register of all operations that breed Appendix I species worldwide, and has successfully urged Parties not to receive certificates of captive breeding from unregistered facilities.

The COP also allocates quotas for range states for certain species—including Appendix I species such as the leopard, various crocodilians, and the cheetah—when it determines that trade within set limits will not be detrimental to the survival of that species [*see* Res. 9.21, Ninth Meeting (1994)]. The COP had recommended that range states with a population of African elephants establish quotas for the export of raw ivory [*id.,* Res. 9.16]. This reinstituted the quota system for raw ivory that was discontinued when the African elephant was "uplisted" to Appendix I in 1989. However, in 1997 the 10th Conference of the Parties allowed the down-listing of elephants from Appendix I to Appendix II, while instituting a monitoring system for African and Asian elephants that would provide information on the illegal killing of elephants. Again, the quotas should function so as to manage the resident population and not to the detriment of the species as a whole. In this way the CITES regime has acted to promote the principle of sustainable development—in effect rewarding those parties and local communities which have successfully protected their herds—by endorsing a managed and limited cull.

Overall, the CITES regime has performed well given its limited resources and broad scope. As the COP acknowledges, however, illegal trade in the most sought after species still continues at an alarming rate. Whether the treaty proves ultimately successful will depend on the North's greater financial commitment in promoting diligent enforcement in the South.

(b) The 1972 UNESCO Convention Concerning the Protection of The World Cultural and Natural Heritage (World Heritage Convention)

Another early environmental treaty, the World Heritage Convention [Nov. 16, 1972, 1037 U.N.T.S. 151] plays a small but important role in the conservation of biological diversity. The convention recognizes and protects examples of "cultural" and "natural" heritage, and as of January 2003 the parties have listed 144 "natural" and 23 "mixed" cultural/natural sites. For inclusion on the World Heritage List, a qualifying example of "natural heritage" must fit within one of the following categories specified in article 2:

> natural features consisting of physical and biological formations or groups of such formations, which are of outstanding universal value from the aesthetic or scientific point of view; geological or physiographical formations and precisely delineated areas which constitute the habitat of threatened species of animals and plants of outstanding universal value from the point of view of

science or conservation; natural sites or precisely delineated areas of outstanding universal value from the point of view of science, conservation or natural beauty.

As defined, "natural heritage" typically includes the habitat of endangered species, and most sites on the World Heritage List are national parks.

To obtain a listing, individual countries nominate a domestic site for the World Heritage List, and the World Heritage Committee (an elected group of 21 parties) then judges the request with the help and expertise of the World Conservation Union (IUCN). The Committee also administers a "List of World Heritage in Danger," which consists of sites "threatened by serious and specific dangers, such as the threat of disappearance caused by accelerated deterioration ..." [art. 11(4)]. Not only are developing country sites represented, but the Committee has included on this list both the Everglades and Yellowstone National Parks of the United States. The Convention additionally creates a World Heritage Fund which helps developing countries in the establishment and maintenance of sites on the two lists [arts. 15–26].

Commitments

As a matter of international law, the convention creates obligations both at the national and international levels. Domestically, the convention recognizes a duty for each party—"to the utmost of its own resources and where appropriate"—to identify, conserve, protect and transfer to future generations the natural heritage located within its jurisdiction [art. 4]. As this provision suggests, a party must fulfill this duty for every site it designates as natural heritage—regardless whether the site actually makes it onto the World Heritage List. Furthermore, each party must undertake specific actions to meet this obligation, such as legal and administrative reforms [art. 5]. The parties must also submit reports on the efforts that they have expended to comply with the convention [art. 29].

At the international level, while reaffirming territorial sovereignty the treaty recognizes that natural heritage "constitutes a world heritage for whose protection it is the duty of the international community as a whole to co-operate" [art. 6(1)]. This is an early example of the "common heritage" concept, which was downgraded in the CBD to "the common concern of humankind" [*see supra* E. 1. (a)]. In addition, the World Heritage Convention imposes a collective obligation on the parties to assist poorer countries, at the latter's request, in their efforts to fulfill the substantive obligations of the treaty [art. 6(2)].

Though the effectiveness of the World Heritage Convention remains limited by the narrow definition of "natural heritage"—in practice constraining its application to the establishment and protection of national parks—it has proven a helpful tool in the global effort to conserve biological diversity. To multiply its effect in the future, the treaty administration must closely coordinate its activities with the CBD. As we have noted the World Heritage

Convention enjoys a partnership arrangement with the CBD.

(c) The 1971 Convention on Wetlands of International Importance, Especially as Waterfowl Habitat (Ramsar Convention)

The Ramsar Convention, signed at Ramsar, Iran in 1971, is the oldest international treaty created solely for the protection of ecosystems [Feb. 2, 1971, 1976 U.N.T.S. 245]. The treaty specifically attempts to safeguard wetlands, with an emphasis in protecting those areas of "international importance to waterfowl" [art. 2(2)]. Like the World Heritage Convention, the Ramsar Convention establishes a list of protected sites called the List of Wetlands of International Importance (the List). Presently, the List contains 1268 wetland sites. The COP has also created a Record of Ramsar Sites (again, one can analogize to the List of World Heritage in Danger), which includes List sites most in need of conservation.

For inclusion on the List of Wetlands of International Importance parties designate sites, and the COP thereafter votes for approval (and removal) of such sites [art. 6(2)(b)]. To become a full party to the convention, each contracting party must designate at least one wetland for the List [art. 2(4)]. This latter requirement actually has proved an impediment to the accession of developing countries, which often cannot meet the expense of creating a reserve. To assist developing countries in the creation of reserves, the convention established the

Ramsar Wetland Conservation Fund in 1990. This move has attracted new parties from the developing world and total membership now exceeds eighty parties.

Conservation

In addition to designating at least one wetland for inclusion on the List [art. 2(4)], the Parties in general must promote the conservation of wetlands by establishing and maintaining nature reserves, whether included on the List or not [art. 4(1)]. The parties shall also "endeavor through management to increase waterfowl populations on appropriate wetlands" [art. 4(4)]. Concerning listed sites, the parties must inform the managing "Bureau" of any change in ecological character [art. 3(2)], and should a particular party delete or restrict the boundaries of a designated site, it should compensate for any net loss through the creation of additional reserves [art. 4(2)]. Finally, by recommendation of the COP each party must inventory and monitor its national wetlands.

Wise Use

In potential conflict with the obligation to conserve, the Ramsar Convention also mandates that parties "formulate and implement their planning so as to promote ... as far as possible the wise use of wetlands in their territories" [art. 3(1)]. In juxtaposing conservation and wise use, the treaty offers an early example of the protection/development schism found in the CBD. In 1987 the COP defined "wise use" in terms of "sustainable utilization,"

and since has promulgated a number of requirements toward this end. Most notably, parties should
adopt and apply the COP's Guidelines of 1990 and
1993 for Implementation of the Wise Use Concept,
including the establishment of National Wetlands
Policies. Additionally, each party must develop management plans for each Ramsar site, and recent
monitoring procedures require parties to file annual
reports concerning the health of threatened areas
on the Record of Ramsar Sites. The COP has also
instituted the rule of environmental impact assessment prior to any proposed development of national
wetlands.

Consultations

The convention further mandates that the parties
"consult with each other about implementing obligations arising from the Convention"—especially
emphasizing this requirement with regard to transboundary wetlands [art. 5]. The preamble also
makes the general point "that the conservation of
wetlands and their flora and fauna can be ensured
by combining far-sighted national policies with
coordinated international action."

Though wetlands continue to deteriorate worldwide due to development and population pressures,
the Ramsar Convention has achieved a significant
amount given its limited budget and its only recent
growth in developing country membership. With
greater resources channeled to developing country
parties—and with increased coordination of its efforts with other treaty regimes such as the CBD—

the convention can undoubtedly increase its contribution to the global effort of protecting wetland biodiversity.

(d) The 1979 Convention on the Conservation of Migratory Species of Wild Animals (Bonn Convention)

The Convention on the Conservation of Migratory Species of Wild Animals, known as the Bonn Convention after its signing at Bonn, Germany, covers the entire spectrum of animal species including birds, mammals, reptiles and fish [June 23, 1979, 19 I.L.M. 11]. After a slow start, the convention has recently made considerable strides in effecting range state cooperation to protect migratory species. As of March 1, 2003 it has 81 parties, though the bulk of its parties are still European. Many nations have not signed the treaty because they presumably consider migratory species sufficiently protected under other conventions, often bilateral in nature. Neither Canada nor the U.S. is a party, for example, because their own bilateral treaty (now including Mexico) arguably defends the flyways of most ducks and geese. Such a stance, however, does little to protect the numerous other species listed in the Bonn Convention's annexes and fails to recognize the continued threat to all migratory species. Despite this unequal participation, the treaty continues to gain adherents in the effort to protect migratory species.

Commitments

The Bonn Convention adopts an interesting wrinkle to the usual framework approach to international law-making. Rather than relying on the adoption of protocols, the treaty facilitates the creation of cooperative arrangements among range states. This strategy is employed for species listed in Annex II and is described more fully below. At a more general level, the convention contains perhaps the most evocative plea for inter-generational equity in international law, proclaiming "that each generation of man holds the resources of the earth for future generations and has an obligation to ensure that this legacy is conserved and, where utilized, is used wisely" [pmbl.]. The treaty then leaves its specific requirements for actions undertaken with regard to the two annexes.

Appendix I lists endangered species, creating broad duties for range states whose territory comprises any part of a listed species' range, or whose flag-ships hunt the species extra-territorially [art. I(1)(h)]. "Endangered" under the convention "means that the migratory species is in danger of extinction throughout all or a significant portion of its range" [art. I(1)(e)]. For Appendix I species, range states must endeavor to conserve and restore habitats; to minimize the adverse effects of activities or obstacles impeding migration; and to reduce or control further endangerment [art. III(4)]. Range states must also prohibit takings of Appendix I species except in exceptional circumstances [art. III(5)]. To monitor progress in protecting both Appendix I and Appendix II species, the treaty requires each party to submit reports on measures taken to implement the commitments [art. VI(3)].

Appendix II contains those species with an "unfavorable conservation status," a broad term which suggests all threatened migratory species (*see* arts. I(1)(c) & (d)). Rather than general protection duties, however, the convention requires that range states strive to enter into cooperative Agreements with other range states to promote conservation and restoration of selected species [*see* arts. IV & V]. Any Agreement should attempt to cover the entire migratory route of the species, and should remain open to accession by all range states, including those not party to the convention [art. V(2)]. To date, the parties have concluded six such Agreements, including three Agreements that entered into force in 1994: the Conservation of Bats in Europe, the Conservation of Small Cetaceans (whales and dolphins) of the Baltic and North Seas, and the Conservation of Seals in the Wadden Sea. These three Agreements have successfully attracted a significant number of range states as parties. One of the more ambitious of these Agreements deals with the Conservation of African–Eurasian Migratory Waterbirds which came into force in November 1999 has collected 117 range states—some nonparties to the Bonn Convention—as signatories to the final text in 1995.

One criticism of the Bonn Convention is that it has not fostered more of the Agreements required for Appendix II species. At least part of the problem rests with the formal quality of such arrangements.

As structured under the convention, Agreements for the protection of Appendix II species are themselves binding legal instruments, necessitating long, and often politically exhausting periods of negotiation and ratification. In lieu of such formal agreements, the COP has recommended that range states first develop informal Memoranda of Understanding (MOUs), a practice which might allow substantial cooperation until more formal arrangements come into being. To this end, the parties (and nonparties) have developed two recent Memoranda of Understanding: the MOU Concerning the Conservation of the Siberian Crane and the MOU Concerning the Slender-billed Curlew.

The Bonn Convention therefore has dramatically improved its record over the last five years, with a number of additional Agreements and MOUs in the development stage. The convention has also created a strong working relationship with the CBD, the Ramsar Convention and CITES. With increased party recruitment, especially in the Americas and Asia, it can continue to enhance its performance.

4. REGIONAL TREATIES AND AGREEMENTS RELATED TO BIODIVERSITY

In addition to the above international treaties, a number of regional agreements have emerged over the years. They include a cluster of treaties protecting the Antarctic such as the Antarctic Treaty, Dec. 1, 1959, 19 I.L.M. 860; Convention for the Conservation of Antarctic Seals, Feb. 11, 1972, 11 I.L.M. 251; Protocol on Environmental Protection to the Antarctic Treaty, Oct. 4, 1991, 30 I.L.M. 1461. Among the more important of the others are the Convention on Nature Protection and Wildlife Conservation in the Western Hemisphere, Oct. 12, 1940, 161 U.N.T.S. 193; the African Convention for the Conservation of Nature and Natural Resources, Sept. 15, 1968, 1001 U.N.T.S. 3; the Convention on Conservation of European Wildlife and Natural Habitats, Sept. 19, 1979, E.T.S. 104, *available in Westlaw* 1979 WL 42275 (the Berne Convention); and the 1985 Agreement on the Conservation of Nature and Natural Resources adopted by the Association of South East Asian Nations (the 1985 ASEAN Convention), July 9, 15 1985 E.P.L. 64.

Members of the European Union also remain bound by Council Directive 92/43 on the Conservation of Natural Habitats and of Wild Fauna and Flora [1992 O.J. (L 206/7 1)], as well as the more specific Council Directive 79/409 on the Conservation of Wild Birds [1979 O.J. (L 103) 1]. More recently, the European Community Biodiversity Strategy, adopted in 1998, attempts to define a framework for action. The Strategy focuses specifically on the integration of biodiversity concerns into relevant sectoral policies, in particular: conservation of natural resources, agriculture, fisheries, regional policies and spatial planning, forests, energy and transport, tourism, development and economic cooperation.

This proliferation of agreements, some effective and some not, has compounded the need for coordination and cooperation among these various entities. As stated above, the CBD was originally intended to be an umbrella treaty—one which would consolidate the present cacophony of treaties into a workable whole. Hopefully the existing CBD, though lacking any direct power over the other conventions, can still play a significant part in coordinating the diverse activities within the field.

CHAPTER SIX

GLOBAL CLIMATE CHANGE

A. CLIMATIC FACTS

Energy from the Sun drives the climate system of the earth within a complex inter-planetary heat exchange. About a third of the incoming solar radiation from the Sun is immediately reflected back by the clouds, the atmosphere and the earth's surface. Much of the remaining two thirds warms the earth's surface which returns part of this heat upwards into the atmosphere. A stable climate, of the kind we enjoy on earth, requires a balance between incoming and outgoing radiation or heat.

Greenhouse gases (GHG's), despite the fact that they comprise a very small part of the atmospheric mix, play a critical role in maintaining this balance. In the right quantities, GHGs help support life and ecosystems on earth by ensuring a relatively constant surface temperature that averages nearly 60°F. Where they are not present, as on Mars, the average surface temperature falls to a low 39°F; and where GHGs are present in excess, as on Venus, that average rises to a high 810°F.

The atmosphere above the earth contains a mixture of gases of which Nitrogen accounts for approximately 78% by volume, while Oxygen makes up

21%. The remaining 1% is made up of a variety of gases among which water vapor and carbon dioxide are the GHGs most relevant to our purposes. Water vapor accounts for approximately 60–65% of 1%, while carbon dioxide makes up the balance 35–40%. The importance of water vapor as a GHG, and its much larger volume in comparison to carbon dioxide may be overlooked if we remain fixated on carbon dioxide emissions alone.

GHGs in the atmosphere are largely transparent to incoming solar energy, but absorb most of the earth's emitted infrared energy. Unlike the surface of the earth which radiates energy only upwards, the atmospheric GHGs radiate both away from and toward the earth's surface. Thus some of the energy radiated by the surface into the atmosphere is trapped by GHGs which redirect the energy back toward the earth's surface. This process is known as the "greenhouse effect," as GHGs operate to increase the atmospheric temperature in much the same way that the glass in a greenhouse operates.

1. INCREASING GHG EMISSIONS

Each year human activities discharge six billion tons of carbon dioxide (CO_2) and significant quantities of other GHGs such as methane and nitrous oxides, altering the natural distribution of atmospheric gases that blanket the earth. By the year 2010 global CO_2 emissions are expected to rise to 7.9 billion tons per year, and are expected to reach levels of approximately 9.9 billion tons per year by

2020. Much of this increase is expected to come from developing countries where CO_2 emissions are projected to grow by an average of 3.6% per year between 1999 and 2020. A full 77% of the projected increase in global CO_2 emissions between 1990 and 2010 is expected to come from developing countries; and between 1990 and 2020 developing countries are expected to account for 72% of the projected increase in global CO_2 emissions [INTERNATIONAL ENERGY OUTLOOK 2002, ENERGY INFORMATION ADMINISTRATION, DOE/EIA–0484 at 13 (2002) (hereinafter IEO 2002)].

We know for sure that water vapor and carbon dioxide are the most abundant GHGs. Other GHGs include methane (CH_4), nitrous oxide (N_2O), ozone (O_3) and halocarbons (human-made compounds that contain chlorine or bromine and carbon atoms) [See INVENTORY OF U.S. GREENHOUSE GAS EMISSIONS AND SINKS, 1990–2000, USEPA 430–R–02–003 (2002)]. Since the beginning of the industrial revolution, or about 1750, the atmospheric concentration of CO_2 has increased by 31%—primarily as the result of fossil fuel combustion [INTERGOVERNMENTAL PANEL ON CLIMATE CHANGE, CLIMATE CHANGE 2001: SYNTHESIS REPORT 137 (2001) (hereinafter IPCC 2001 SYNTHESIS REPORT)]. We are also told that the present concentration of atmospheric CO_2 (measured at 370 ppm in 2001) has not been exceeded in the past 420,000 years—the span of time measurable in ice cores. And though we lack certainty of knowledge regarding CO_2 concentrations prior to this time span, it is likely that present concentrations of atmospheric CO_2 have not been exceeded in the past 20 million years. Concentrations of other GHGs have also rapidly increased. Since 1750 atmospheric CH_4 has increased by 151% and atmospheric N_2O by 17% [A REPORT OF WORKING GROUP I OF THE INTERGOVERNMENTAL PANEL ON CLIMATE CHANGE, SUMMARY FOR POLICYMAKERS 7 (2001) (hereinafter WGI SPM 2001)].

2. A WARMING TREND

A growing scientific consensus holds that atmospheric CO_2 levels will increase to between 540 ppm to 970 ppm by 2100, which is respectively 90% to 250% higher than the concentration in the late 1700s. Today's CO_2 concentration of approximately 370 ppm is about 95 ppm greater than the pre-industrial concentration [IPCC 2001 SYNTHESIS REPORT at 69]. This could correspond to a mean global temperature increase from 1.4°C to 5.8°C, an increase range that is two to ten times larger than the central value of observed warming over the 20th century [*Id.* at 61].

Climatic records have been kept for nearly 122– years, although systematic climatic instrumental recording only began in the 1950's. According to many scientists, eight of the 10 warmest years in the instrumental record have occurred since 1990 [AMERICAN METEOROLOGICAL SOCIETY, CLIMATE /ASSESSMENT FOR 2001 4–5 (2002)]. Over the past century, the data indicates the global mean surface air temperature increased 0.4°C to 0.8°C [NATIONAL ACADEMY

OF SCIENCE, CLIMATE CHANGE SCIENCE: AN ANALYSIS OF SOME KEY QUESTIONS 16 (2001) (hereinafter NAS CLIMATE 2001)]. While such temperature changes have yet to unambiguously impact the earth's environment, the global average surface temperature during the 21st century is rising at rates very likely without precedent in the last 10,000 year [IPCC 2001 SYNTHESIS REPORT at 138]. The larger temperature increases now predicted to occur over the next century may have far more discernable—and problematic—effects.

In 1988, the Intergovernmental Panel of Climate Change (IPCC) was formed jointly by the World Meteorological Organization (WMO) (*see* Appendix § X) and the United Nations Environment Programme (UNEP) (*see* Appendix § S) to assess the risk of human-induced climate change. The IPCC formally consists of three working groups and a task force on national GHG inventories. Since its inception, the IPCC has issued assessment reports on climate change in 1990, 1995 and 2001.

According to the IPCC evaluations, future climate change will have both beneficial and adverse impacts on human and natural systems. However, modeling scenarios indicate that with larger and more frequent climate changes comes an increased likelihood of adverse effects to all systems. In general, such adverse effects will likely impact developing countries the hardest. The IPCC notes that for many developing countries climate change is projected to have a negative impact on GDP, while developed countries may experience marginal gains in GDP as a result of climate change [IPCC SYNTHE-SIS REPORT 2001 at 74].

In all countries, however, the poor are most vulnerable to climate change. In many regions of the world, water is a scarce and precious commodity. For populations in such areas, climate change would likely exacerbate existing water shortage and quality problems—though it is possible the effect would be palliative in some areas. Those water systems most at risk to the adverse effects of climate change are predictably those with the least resources to prepare against those adverse effects. For tens of millions of people in low-lying coastal areas on small islands, climate change presents the risk of losing their homes and livelihood. With climate change comes the risk of increased sea levels, severe and chaotic weather events, flooding and erosion.

Many small islands face the risk of population displacement and infrastructure loss, and must bear the substantial cost of protecting their vulnerable coastal areas. Climate change is also expected to adversely impact the biodiversity of ecological systems by increasing the extinction rate of vulnerable species. Also, with increased temperatures comes the risk of expanded potential transmission areas for such diseases as malaria and dengue [*Id.* at 67–81].

B. HUMAN CULPABILITY

At their natural or historic levels, GHGs maintain the heat balance that is necessary to life on earth by trapping infrared radiation which warms the surface temperature while at the same time permitting excess heat to escape. A build-up of GHGs can upset this important equilibrium and cause a rise in surface temperature [*See e.g.*, F. Sherwood Rowland, *Atmospheric Changes Caused by Human Activities: From Science to Regulation*, 27 ECOLOGY L.Q. 1261, 1287 (2001)]. A large number of scientists using mathematical models forecast a high degree of climate change as a result of increased levels of CO_2 and other GHGs by humans.

Despite the fact that the awesome complexity of atmospheric mechanisms cannot be fully replicated by mathematical models, the overwhelming majority of the scientific community agrees that global climate change will negatively impact the earth's environment. Indeed, a strong general consensus exists among the international scientific community that some action should be taken now to limit or reduce atmospheric GHGs on a global basis, because to delay action may allow climate patterns to gain the inertial force sufficient to render ineffective any action taken to correct these trends [INTERGOVERNMENTAL PANEL ON CLIMATE CHANGE, CLIMATE CHANGE 2001: SYNTHESIS REPORT–SUMMARY FOR POLICY MAKERS 16–18 (2001) (hereinafter IPCC SPM 2001 SYNTHESIS)].

The Second Assessment Report of the IPCC concluded that on a balance of evidence there was a discernible human influence on global climate. They cautioned, however, that a number of uncertainties constrained them from coming to a more certain conclusion. The Third Assessment Report addressed these uncertainties, and even though some uncertainties continued to linger, the IPCC concluded that most of the observed warming over the last 50 years is likely to have been caused by the increase in GHG concentrations [IPCC, CLIMATE CHANGE 2001: THE SCIENTIFIC BASIS 61].

1. THE NAY SAYERS

The predictions of the IPCC have been challenged by a large group of scientists. Since the UNFCCC was signed in 1992, dissenting scientists have expressed themselves through four petitions culminating in the Oregon Petition signed by over 17,000 U.S. scientists. To begin, some scientists contend that despite the volume emitted by human activities, the accumulation of anthropogenic carbon dioxide is really a tiny constituent of our atmosphere, which as we have observed, amounts to no more than 4/100 of 1% of all gases present. [Andrew R. Solow, *Is There a Global Warming Problem?*, in GLOBAL WARMING: ECONOMIC POLICY RESPONSES 7, 8 (Rudiger Dornbusch & James M. Poterba eds., 1991)]. These doubters next claim that a number of factors related to climate change remain uncertain, including the effects of clouds formed by water vapor which is a more abundant GHG than carbon dioxide [Richard A. Kerr, *Greenhouse Forecasting Still Cloudy*, 276 SCIENCE 1040, 1040 (1997)].

Moreover, the skeptics argue, there are a number of non-greenhouse-related factors that may augment global temperature. For example, the IPCC has not paid sufficient attention to the astronomical causes of global warming caused by the earth's orbital eccentricities as well as variations in solar output. There are at least two competing orbital mechanism theories that explain the occurrence of Ice Ages in the earth's past. The first theory posits that cyclical changes in the earth's elliptical orbit shift the pattern of solar heating, affecting the buildup of ice sheets. This has been termed the Milankovitch mechanism [Richard A. Kerr, *Upstart Ice Age Theory Gets Attentive But Chilly Hearing*, 277 SCIENCE. 183, 183 (1997)].

The second theory posits that ice ages were stimulated by changes in the inclination of the earth's orbit relative to the plane of the solar system, causing the planet to be enveloped in clouds of cosmic dust [id]. Some scientists point to an apparent sun-climate connection resulting from the sun's eleven and twenty-two year sunspot cycles [Richard A. Kerr, *A New Dawn for Sun–Climate Links*, 271 SCIENCE. 1360, 1360 (1996)]. They further argue that carbon dioxide has been steadily increasing for the last 11,000 years, coinciding with an interruption in the ice age and the onset of global warming.

The nay-sayers also disagree with the IPCC about human culpability. It is admitted by the nay-sayers that a 0.45°C warming has taken place during this last century. What many of these scientists contend, however, is that the temperature rise took place before 1940, prior to the huge increase in carbon dioxide emissions, and that there has not been much change since 1940 [S. Fred Singer, *An Assessment of the Kyoto Protocol,* Transcript from Panel Discussion, April 15, 1999, 11 GEO. INT'L ENVTL. L. REV. 767, 771 (1999); Robert C. Balling, Jr., *The Global Temperature Data*, 9 RES. & EXPLORATION 201, 202 (1993)].

They point out that National Oceanic and Atmospheric Administration (NOAA) satellites have been measuring the temperature at a height of a few kilometers in the atmosphere essentially over the entire earth since 1979 [George C. Marshall Institute, *Uncertainties in Climate Modeling: Solar Variability and Other Factors* (testimony of Sallie Baliunas, Ph.D., Senior Scientist of the George C. Marshall Institute, before the Senate Committee on Energy and Natural Resources) (Sept. 17, 1996) *http://www.marshall.org/baliunastestimony.htm*]. These records, based on microwave sounding units (MSUs), have smaller systematic errors than the surface records, which, unlike the satellite records, come from a variety of instruments, techniques, and measurement histories, and whose coverage is sparse over large areas like the southern ocean [Roy W. Spencer & John R. Christy, *Precise Monitoring of Global Temperature Trends from Satel-*

lites, 247 SCIENCE. 1558, 1558 (1990)]. The very precise satellite record shows no net warming over the last seventeen years, contrary to the forecasts calculating the effect of the recent rapid increase in human-made GHGs. The results based on satellite data using MSUs are supported by researchers whose observations are based on radiosonde data (weather balloons) [Dian J. Gaffen et al., *Multidecadal Changes in the Vertical Temperature Structure of the Tropical Troposphere,* 287 SCIENCE 1242, 1242 (2000)].

An expert panel of the U.S. National Research Council (NRC) that attempted to reconcile the contradictory figures between surface and atmospheric measurements has offered only a partial explanation. In light of the panel's inability to explain the differentials, they recommended the implementation of a worldwide monitoring system. Until more light is shed on this issue, the discrepancies still remain largely unexplained [B.D. Santer et al., *Interpreting Differential Temperature Trends at the Surface and in the Lower Troposphere,* 287 SCIENCE. 1227, 1231 (2000)].

The nay-sayers further point out that temperatures have fluctuated over the centuries and while the last 600 years have been cold, it was warmer 1000 years ago, and even warmer 3000 years ago. According to them, it is untrue that the warming from rising GHGs is going to be unprecedented in both magnitude and rapidity [S. Fred Singer, HOT TALK, COLD SCIENCE: GLOBAL WARMING'S UNFINISHED BUSINESS 5–6 (1997)]. Ocean sediment data of the past 3000 years discloses temperature changes of 3°C (about 5°F) taking place in a matter of a decade or two. Such rapid temperature changes, they state, have happened throughout recorded human history.

Finally, the projections of the IPCC are based on scientific tools known as models. Climate models are used to simulate and quantify climate response to present and future natural and human activities [IPCC CLIMATE CHANGE 2001: THE SCIENTIFIC BASIS, 94–95 (2001)]. The IPCC admit that quantitative projections of future climate change can only be undertaken where models simulate all the important processes governing the future evolution of the climate. However, it is clear that the models employed by them do not do so. The IPCC's latest Scientific Basis report makes clear that two important climatic processes: dynamic vegetation and atmospheric chemistry have not yet been included in the climatic models on which their predictions are based [id. Box 3. 48–50]. Atmospheric chemistry is the science dealing with the formation and effects of clouds, and to base projections without taking a full and satisfactory account of water vapor and clouds, arguably, casts some doubt on the conclusions of the IPCC.

C. POSSIBLE IMPACTS

While the causal connection between anthropogenically forced climate change and the adverse effects on human and natural systems cannot unequivocally be ascertained, the IPCC is confident that we will face significant adverse impacts. These adverse environmental impacts include the rise of sea levels, threats to human health particularly to those in low income groups living in tropical climates, harm to ecosystems and the extinction of some vulnerable species, and a decrease of yields in tropical and sub-tropical regions. Global warming will create water shortages in some parts of the world, while those living in small islands and low lying areas are at particular risk from sea level rises and storm surges [IPCC, CLIMATE CHANGE 2001: SYNTHESIS REPORT, 67–74]. While the IPCC have modified the severity of some of these impacts, their critics question the seriousness of the impacts if the rise in temperatures are only modest. The impacts will depend on the extent of global warming and the IPCC scenarios shed considerable light on this issue.

The IPCC's actual future "scenarios"—in noticeable contrast to their rhetoric—do not show draconian increases either in GHG's or in temperature. The IPCC after a five year study presented a Special Report on Emission Scenarios (SRES) in March 2000 presenting a cluster of scenarios based on differing "story lines." These scenarios do not include any reductions of GHGs under either the UNFCCC or the Kyoto Protocol. In other words the scenarios assume that these legal treaties have led to no reductions of GHGs. Six possible emission scenarios, beginning in 2000 and ending in 2100 were included in the Third Assessment Report in 2001. Of the six, Scenarios B1 and A1B seem the most probable while a third: A1T, is not implausible.

Scenario B1 describes a world moving toward globalization in which population peaks mid century and declines thereafter. It is a world that favors a service and information economy with reductions in materials intensity and the introduction of clean and resource efficient technologies [SYNTHESIS REPORT, 202]. Under this scenario emissions of carbon dioxide (CO_2), nitrous oxide (N_2O), methane (CH_4), and sulfur dioxide (SO_2) will be lower in 2100 than they are today [id. 203]. Concentrations of carbon dioxide and nitrous oxide, however, will double, while methane will remain about the same. Temperatures will increase by about 1.5 degrees C, and sea levels rise by 0.3 m.

Scenario A1B envisions a world similar to B1, and strikes a balance between fossil and non-fossil sources of energy. Under this scenario emissions of carbon dioxide double, nitrous oxides and methane remain about the same, while sulfur dioxide is dramatically reduced. Concentrations of carbon dioxide double, while nitrous oxides and methane increase by about 75% [*Id.* 203, 204]. Temperatures increases of 2.5 degrees C are forecast [*Id.* 209]. Also, sea levels rise by nearly 0.4 m.

Scenario A1T is a world that has moved to non-fossil energy sources. While emissions of all GHGs come down by the year 2100 concentrations do not. Carbon dioxide nearly doubles, while methane and

nitrous oxides also show increases [*Id*. 203, 204].
Temperatures rise by nearly 2°C [*Id*. 212].

D. REMEDIAL OBJECTIVES

A cluster of remedial objectives have been set
forth in the United Nations Framework Conventions on Climate Changes (UNFCCC), [May 29,
1992, 31 I.L.M. 849 (entered into force Mar. 21,
1994]. First, Article 2 states that the ultimate objective is to achieve

"... stabilization of greenhouse gas concentrations in the atmosphere at a level that would
present dangerous anthropogenic interference
with the climate system. Such a level should be
achieved within a time frame sufficient to allow
ecosystems to adapt naturally to climate change,
to ensure that food production is not threatened
and to enable economic development to proceed in
a sustainable manner."

It is noteworthy that UNFCCC refers to "dangerous" and not simply to human interference that
might present a hazard, as distinct from a danger,
to climatic systems. This makes ample sense because any wastes that are not recycled or absorbed
by man made industrial and economic systems have
some kind of impact on the environment.

The first law of thermodynamics states that matter and energy are only transformed never destroyed. Since the burning of fossil fuels leads to the
discharge of waste carbon such wastes will have an
impact on the environment. The question then be-

comes: To what extent do these wastes constitute a dangerous interference with complex climatic systems? In finding an answer to this question the UNFCCC stipulates that "... where there are threats of serious or irreversible damage, lack of full scientific certainty should not be used as a reason for postponing such measures..." [Art. 3(2)] provided they are cost effective [*id.*].

Second, it is equally important that economic development should proceed in a sustainable manner. Art. 3(4) underlines the importance of economic development by asserting that "The Parties have a right to, and should promote sustainable development..." As we have seen in Chapter 2, SD has become the foundational norm of IEL and its contours have been re-defined by the WSSD. While SD began as a two sided concept based on environmental protection and economic development, it has now been enlarged to become a triangle based on economic, environmental and social development.

Third, climate change policies and laws should be based on equity and in accordance with the principle of "... common but differentiated responsibilities ..." [art. 3(1)]. This principle establishes the common responsibility of all nations for climate change, while the "... lead in combating climate change ..." meaning the financial and technological burden of doing so is placed on the developed countries [art. 3(2), 4(1), 4(2), & 4(4)]. It is deserving of emphasis, however, that in the UNFCCC developing countries accepted their "common" responsibility for climate change. UNFCCC refers to the "common but differentiated responsibilities" of all countries, and does not define such responsibility as the sole and exclusive obligation of developed countries.

Fourth, the measures taken to deal with climate change could range from actions taken to mitigate or arrest climate change [art. 3(3)] to others that seek to adapt to it [art. 3(4)]. Mitigation according to the UNFCCC should be directed to the sources and sinks of GHGs [art. 4(1)(b)], and is defined by the IPCC as "anthropogenic intervention to reduce the sources of greenhouse gases or enhance their sinks." [IPCC Synthesis Report, 294].

Accordingly, mitigation would be directed toward reductions in the emission and accumulation of carbon dioxide and other GHGs, either by cutting down on emissions, as the Kyoto protocol did, or by increasing the role of sinks such as forests or oceans that absorb GHGs. Adaptation on the other hand would seek to adjust natural and human systems to the consequence of climate change. Such adjustments could range over a spectrum of socio-economic policies including building of sea walls, moving cities, variations of crops, and changes in clothing, housing and infrastructure. UNFCCC states that adaptation requires integrated plans for coastal zone management, water resources, agriculture and rehabilitation [art. 4(1)(e)].

Finally, it is inescapable that the call for reductions of GHGs must be accompanied by monumental efforts to increase alternative fuels. It seems almost hopeless to demand fossil fuel cuts without creating new sources of fuel, dramatically increasing fuel efficiency, and improving conservation.

E. LEGAL RESPONSE

The international legal responses to the threat of climate change or global warming are found in the United Nations Framework Convention on Climate Change (UNFCCC), May 29, 1992, 31 I.L.M. 849, reproduced in GURUSWAMY ET AL, Basic Documents 506 (entered into force Mar. 21, 1994), and the Kyoto protocol to the UNFCCC, 10 December 1997, 37 I.L.M.32, reproduced in GURUSWAMY ET AL. Basic Documents 561 (not yet entered into force). To the extent that the UNFCCC is the parent or framework treaty which gave birth to the offspring protocol the UNFCCC will be treated as the foundation and Kyoto as the superstructure. We will first identify the key features of UNFCCC and Kyoto, and then address some outstanding issues of interpretation and implementation common to both treaties.

1. SUBSTANTIVE OBLIGATIONS

(a) UNFCCC

i. *History and Overview*

Completed at the earth Summit in 1992, the UNFCCC came into existence after an accelerated process of negotiation. As scientific concern increased over the prospects of global warming, international attention focused rapidly on the issue in the late 1980s. Then in 1990 the UN General Assembly created the Intergovernmental Negotiating Committee (INC), calling for the adoption of a global convention on climate change at UNCED in 1992. Though there was a substantial political base which desired long-term quantitative emission limits, eventually a "go-slow" approach prevailed. The short negotiating period, combined both with the enormous economic stakes and a substantial amount of scientific uncertainty, resulted in the adoption of only cautious controls in the final version of the treaty.

The UNFCCC, however, is not an empty framework treaty whose substantive details entirely await further elaboration. Instead, it is a framework convention with a number of built-in requirements. First, developed countries must strive to reduce their overall emissions of greenhouse gases to 1990 levels by the year 2000 [art. 4(2)(a) & 4(2)(b)]. Second, developed countries have a general commitment to make financial and technological transfers to developing countries [art. 3(2), 4(1)(c), 4(2), & 4(4)]. Third, all parties—both developed and developing countries—must create inventories of GHGs, as well as national mitigation and adaptation programs [art. 4]. The Climate Change Convention, however, provides different timetables and requirements for developed and developing countries with regard to inventories and other programs, and the COP has established different guidelines for the national reports communicating such programs to the COP.

In mandating different requirements for developed and developing countries, as well as making further delineations within those groups, the Climate Change Convention in contrast to the CBD, explicitly embraces the concept of "common but differentiated responsibility" (CBDR) [pmbl. para. 6, Art. 3(1)]. As we have seen, this principle recognizes that only international cooperation will help to resolve a problem of the magnitude of global warming, but that in responding to the problem different states have different social and economic conditions that affect their response capabilities. CBDR also incorporates the equitable notion that developed countries, which have the largest share of historical and current emissions of GHGs, should take the first painful actions to ameliorate the problem. As we shall see, however, the exact application of CBDR remains controversial.

In negotiating the appropriate response to be taken by developed countries, the parties struggled with a number of possible strategies. One such point of contention involved the Comprehensive Approach to GHG emissions, a discussion of which we have included here to show both the complexity of the problem and the difficulty of available solutions.

ii. *The Comprehensive Approach*

In the original push toward creation of the UNFCCC, the international community generally limited its focus to the reduction of carbon dioxide emissions. As we have seen, CO_2 is the primary GHG, and because its sources and sinks were better

understood than those of most other GHGs, controlling CO_2 seemed the prudent place to start. Late in
the negotiating game, however, the United States
presented a different approach: parties could choose
any mix of GHG reductions and removals by
sinks—not just CO_2 reductions—in meeting their
respective commitment to reduce their overall contribution to global warming. By this strategy, each
GHG receives a scientifically based value, known as
its global warming potential (GWP), which measures that GHG's contribution to global warming
relative to other GHGs. In order to calculate the
total emissions of any particular GHG, a party need
only multiply the GWP by the volume emitted for
each gas. In this way, a party can arrive at its total
emissions of all GHGs by adding up the respective
contributions of each individual GHG. Thus, to
reduce its net contribution to global warming under
the Comprehensive Approach, a party could then
choose any combination of GHG reductions and/or
removals by sinks.

In the end, on the emissions side of the equation,
the UNFCCC adopted language which ultimately
approves of the Comprehensive Approach. At two
junctures, articles 4(2)(a) & (b), the treaty refers to
the reduction of "anthropogenic emissions of carbon
dioxide and other greenhouse gases"—which,
though singling out carbon dioxide, also includes
the full panoply of GHGs. The ambiguity of this
language actually provided the COP under article
4(2)(d) with real latitude in attempting to develop

quantifiable emissions limits in the future, and this was accomplished by the Kyoto Protocol.

As to the inclusion of sinks in the equation, again the phrasing of the UNFCCC endorses the Comprehensive Approach in articles 4(2)(a), (b) & (c). Thus, a party is free to subtract appropriate sinks in its calculation of total emissions of GHGs, and the COP has developed methodologies that developed countries should follow in making this important calculation.

iii.   Commitments

In implementing the concept of CBDR, the UNFCCC creates several classes of parties through annexes. Annex I includes the wealthier Organization for Economic Cooperation and Development (OECD) countries, as well as the former Eastern Bloc countries "undergoing the process of transition to a market economy." Annex II includes only the OECD countries. By omission, therefore, all remaining parties not included in Annex I or II are developing countries. At several junctures, which will be noted below, the UNFCCC makes further special provision for "least developed countries" and "small island states."

A. All Parties (Developed and Developing Countries)

All countries, including developing countries, have a number of general commitments under the UNFCCC. These include a duty to "promote and cooperate in the conservation and enhancement, as appropriate, of sinks and reservoirs of all greenhouse gases" [art. 4(1)(d)]. Significantly, this commitment omits any special protection for forests—the most important GHG sink—due to the concern of developing countries that the treaty not impinge on their freedom to develop that resource. The parties must also cooperate in preparing for adaptation to the impacts of global warming [art. 4(1)(e)], and must promote and cooperate in research and development [art. 4(1)(g)], exchange of information [art. 4(1)(h)] and education, training and public awareness [art. 4(1)(i)]. To the extent feasible, each party must also take climate change considerations into account in domestic policies and actions, employing appropriate methods of environmental impact assessment [art. 4(1)(f)]. Furthermore, each party must create national programs to mitigate climate change by addressing GHG emissions, which would also contain measures to "facilitate adequate adaptation to climate change" [art. 4(1)(b)].

More specifically under the UNFCCC, all parties must undertake certain reporting requirements. To begin, all parties must "[d]evelop, periodically update, publish and make available ... national inventories of anthropogenic emissions by sources and removals by sinks of all greenhouses gases" [art. 4(1)(a)], and communicate these to the COP [art. 12(1)(a)]. In the creation of inventories, the treaty lightens the burden on developing countries, qualifying the requirement by the article 12(1)(a) phrase "to the extent [their] capacities permit." In these national communications, the parties must also include a general description of steps taken or envisioned so as to implement the convention, such as progress on the creation of national mitigation and adaptation programs [art. 12(1)(b)]. In addition, as stated above, the COP has established different guidelines for developed and developing countries in making the required national communications, and most developing countries are given until 1997 to meet this requirement (assuming that developed countries provide the necessary financial resources to create such reports), while "least developed countries" may submit their first reports "at their discretion" [art. 12(5)].

B. Annex I Parties (OECD and Former Eastern Bloc Parties)

For Annex I parties the UNFCCC stipulates limited targets and timetables, requiring that all such parties "aim" to return to 1990 emissions levels for all GHGs by the year 2000 [art. 4(2)(b), art. 4(2)(a)]. The obligation—qualified as it is by the word "aim" rather than "must"—had created some confusion as to its binding quality. The Kyoto Protocol cleared this confusion and all Annex 1 or developed countries must now reduce their emissions of Carbon dioxide to 5% below 1990 levels.

(b) THE KYOTO PROTOCOL

The Kyoto Protocol to the United Nations Framework Convention on Climate Change (Kyoto Protocol), signed in 1997, though not yet in force, constitutes the most important attempt of the international community to give concrete expression to the umbrella undertakings embodied in the (UNFCCC).

i. History

The First COP (COP–1) assembled on March 28, 1995, in Berlin to address additional commitments, financial mechanisms, technical support to developing countries, and administrative and procedural issues involving climate change. A pressing issue was whether Annex I Parties would be able to achieve the general emissions reduction goal heralded by the UNFCCC. As a result, the Berlin Mandate was passed, under which developed countries agreed to future negotiation of a protocol containing express targets and timetables for emissions reductions. The Berlin Mandate created an Ad–Hoc Group on the Berlin Mandate (AGBM) to meet periodically with the function of determining how to strengthen the commitments of Annex I Parties past the year 2000. This was to be concluded ultimately in the form of a protocol, to be adopted at COP–3. The AGBM met eight times between COP–1 in 1995 and the Kyoto Protocol conference in December 1997.

Further stimulus for negotiation of a protocol at COP–3 occurred when, in April 1996, the IPCC published its 1995 second assessment report finding that "the balance of evidence suggests a discernible human influence on global climate" [CLIMATE CHANGE 1995: THE SCIENCE OF CLIMATE CHANGE 3 (J.T.

Houghton et al., eds., 1996)] [hereinafter IPCC Climate Change 1995].

Subsequently, COP–2 convened in July 1996, produced several important developments. First, the Parties published the Geneva Declaration, calling for "legally-binding targets and timetables to ensure significant reductions in GHG emissions," similar to the Berlin Mandate. second, the U.S. shifted its position toward a legally-binding agreement to accomplish the objectives of the Berlin Mandate and UNFCCC, a stance that the European Union had been advocating for years. The remaining issue left for the COP–3 negotiations in Kyoto was the establishment of legally-binding targets.

In direct response to these developments, a unanimous Senate Resolution in July 1997 [S. Res. 98, 105th Cong. (1997), 143 Cong. Rec. S8113–05 (daily ed. July 25, 1997)], passed during the run-up to Kyoto in 1997, clearly and unequivocally declared that the United States should not be a party to any mandatory reductions of greenhouse gases unless the developing countries were also parties to such an agreement. Despite their full knowledge that any agreement required by the Berlin mandate would not be approved by the Senate, the Clinton Administration felt obligated by the Berlin undertaking, and publicly committed itself to an emission reduction agreement restricted to developed countries alone, while taking its case to the public over the heads of the Senate.

ii. Overview & Assessment

Significant steps in the global response to climate change were then taken at COP–3 in Kyoto in 1997 and at COP–4 in Buenos Aires in 1998. After intense negotiation at Kyoto, the developed countries agreed to reduce GHG emissions to five percent below their 1990 levels between the years 2008 and 2112 [*Kyoto Protocol, art. 3(1)*]. The United States agreed to a reduction of emissions of 7%, the Europeans to a reduction of 8%, and the Japanese to a reduction of 6% [Id. *Annex B*].

The Kyoto Protocol, embodying this agreement, also provided a basis for emissions trading, primarily between developed countries. The Kyoto Protocol allowed for two types of implementation based upon: (1) joint implementation between Annex I (developed) countries, including the creation of mechanisms such as the "bubble" for the European Union, and the clean development mechanism (between developed and developing countries), and (2) emissions trading between industrialized countries.

The Kyoto Protocol, however, has not been ratified by United States. Additionally, a number of the industrialized (Annex I) countries have failed to carry out the emission reductions to which they had aspirationally agreed under the UNFCCC. The faltering attempts made at COP–4 in Buenos Aries in 1998 did little to remedy this problem.

Currently, OECD projections show that Annex 1 countries will exceed their Kyoto commitments by nearly 30%. The steep rise in projected emissions illustrates the challenge that most OECD countries face in meeting their commitments under the Kyoto Protocol. Emissions in those OECD countries that signed the Protocol will reach 12.5 billion tonnes in 2010, the middle of the Protocol's target period of 2008–2012. That is 2.8 billion tonnes, or 29%, above the target. [World Energy Outlook 2002]

Consequently, the Kyoto Protocol's objectives of reducing GHGs, primarily carbon dioxide, to a level that is five percent below 1990 discharges by 2112, are receding into the distance and appear effectively unattainable. But what is even more disturbing is that even if the Kyoto Protocol were fully and faithfully implemented, GHGs will double to their pre-industrial levels by the year 2100, and quadruple within another 50 years [IPCC CLIMATE CHANGE 1995, at 25].

2. INSTITUTIONS AND IMPLEMENTATION

(a) Conference of the Parties (COP)

As is the general case with framework conventions, the COP functions as "the supreme body" of the treaty. In effect, it possesses the legislative power to create additional protocols and amendments to the convention, as well as the authority to make any other "decisions necessary to promote the effective implementation of the Convention" [art. 7(2)]. This last mandate, though not rising to the formal character of amendments and protocols, allows the COP broad authority to interpret or clarify vague treaty provisions without embroiling itself in the complicated political process of formal law-making. It also provides the COP with implied power to make any other "necessary" decisions, even if such decisions are not specifically delegated to the COP by the convention. This ongoing process of informal law-making—when coupled with the majority voting procedures outlined below—exists as a dynamic tool of the framework convention. For a general discussion of the dynamic quality of the framework convention, see Brent Hendricks, *Postmodern Possibility and the Convention on Biological Diversity*, 5 N.Y.U. ENVT'L. L. J. 1 (1996).

Regarding protocols, the voting procedure for adoption remains unstated in the UNFCCC, but the practice is that they be adopted by consensus—though only parties who actually sign on to the instrument are bound by its provisions. As for amendments, the UNFCCC requires the agreement of a three-fourths (3/4) majority of parties "present and voting at the meeting" [art. 15(3)], and again only those parties who sign will be bound. Annexes, limited to "lists, forms and any other material of a descriptive nature that is of a scientific, technical, procedural or administrative character," require a similar three-fourths majority as amendments. In a burden-shifting move, however, even opposing parties are presumed bound by annexes unless they file a "notification of non-acceptance" [art. 16 (b)]. With respect to the informal decision-making process noted above, the UNFCCC states that the COP "shall, at its first session, adopt its own rules of procedure ... which ... may include specified majorities" [art. 7(3)]. Nonetheless, the COP failed to do so at both its first and second meetings, and the majority voting procedures concerning such matters remain unsettled. In general, parties who fear the tyranny of the majority—who perceive themselves as having the most to lose if the UNFCCC imposes strict emissions limits or substantial financial transfers—have attempted to block the implementation of majority voting. Until the COP reaches agreement on the subject, it will continue to employ the consensus approach regarding such informal decision-making.

The UNFCCC also provides several noteworthy and specific requirements for the COP. First, the COP must help "facilitate" the development of joint implementation projects between parties [art. 7(2)(c)]. Second, the COP must continue to monitor the individual obligations of the parties and to assess the cumulative effect of their implementation [*see generally* art. 7(2)(a) & (b), and art. 12]. Third, where appropriate the COP must seek the help of competent international organizations and non-governmental organizations (NGOs) [art. 7(2)(*l*)]. In fact, this last requirement finds more specific expression in article 7(6), which mandates that qualified NGOs have access to the meetings of the COP "unless at least one-third of the Parties present object." Such participation by NGOs is generally the rule for framework conventions, and although

NGOs have no voting rights, they typically do have the right to speak and to distribute literature.

(b) Secretariat

The Secretariat of the UNFCCC serves as the administrative arm of the COP [art. 8]. It works to organize new meetings of the COP, to compile and transmit reports submitted by the Parties and to help find assistance for developing countries in compiling their respective reports. In addition, the Secretariat undertakes any further tasks as designated by the COP in the future. The Secretariat is institutionally linked to the UN and is administered under its rules and regulations.

(c) Subsidiary Body for Scientific and Technological Advice

The UNFCCC creates a Subsidiary Body for Scientific and Technological Advice (SBSTA), whose primary function is to advise the COP on technical matters [art. 9]. Given the high degree of scientific complexity regarding climate change, the SBSTA plays an important informational role. It must continually assess the state of scientific knowledge concerning climate change, as well as assess the effects of measures taken to curb climate change under the convention. Its mandate is to draw "upon existing competent international bodies"—ranging from the IPCC to qualified NGOs such as IUCN—in summarizing, compiling and synthesizing information for the COP [art. 9(2)].

(d) Subsidiary Body for Implementation

An innovative body created by the UNFCCC, the Subsidiary Body for Implementation (SBI) assists the COP in evaluating the implementation of the convention [art. 10]. In particular, the SBI considers the in-depth review reports of the national communications submitted by the parties under article 12, and makes broad assessments and recommendations concerning the overall aggregated effects of the steps taken by the parties. In effect, the SBI does not evaluate the individual efforts of parties—instead, it looks at the total picture of compliance in making suggestions to the COP. In developing the in-depth review reports, however, the Secretariat and nominated experts may critically evaluate an individual country's performance.

(e) Financial Mechanism

The UNFCCC names the Global Environment Facility (GEF) as the "interim" financial mechanism [art. 21(3)]—a status extended by the first meeting of the COP and to be reevaluated in 1999 [See the general discussion of the GEF in Appendix A, § D]. The present "restructured" GEF meets the criteria of article 11(2) that the financial mechanism have an "equitable and balanced representation of all Parties within a transparent system of governance." To summarize, the restructured GEF, the entity now has both a Council and an independent Secretariat. The Council employs a voting method known as "the double-weighted majority," in which affirmative decisions require a 60 percent majority of the total number of participants as well as a 60 percent majority of the total contributions. The Secretariat (under the authority of the World Bank) approves individual projects, submits them to the Council, and the projects become final unless four Council members wish to put the project before a full vote of the Council. In effect, the Council only possesses a veto power over individual projects.

As for the relationship between the GEF and the UNFCCC, the GEF functions "under the guidance of and [is] accountable to the Conference of the Parties" [art. 11(1)]. Significantly however, the COP cannot recommend individual projects to the GEF, but only specifies "policies, programme priorities and eligibility criteria" [art. 11(1)]. Nevertheless, as the 1996 Memorandum of Understanding between the COP and GEF makes clear, the COP does retain the power to have a specific project reconsidered for funding under article 11(3)(b). At the first meeting of the COP, the parties adopted initial guidance procedures for the GEF—entrusting it with the task of meeting "the agreed full costs of relevant adaptation activities" undertaken in formulating national communications. These may include "studies of the possible impacts of climate change, identification of options for implementing the adaptation provisions . . . , and relevant capacity building." Thus the GEF continues to work closely with the COP in channeling necessary resources to developing countries.

3. OUTSTANDING ISSUES

(a) Joint Implementation

A controversial issue that remains unresolved in the UNFCCC and Kyoto is that of joint implementation. Joint implementation simply means that states can work together to fulfill their commitments under the treaty. A number of very difficult questions lurk within this apparently benign concept. To begin, can developed countries only work with other developed countries, or can they also work with developing nations? In either case, how should the UNFCCC award credits for such action?

Let us first imagine an actual joint implementation scenario between two developed countries. Suppose that developed country A (which is already very energy efficient) can only return to 1990 levels of GHGs at a steep price, and suppose that developed country B (an energy inefficient state just "undergoing the process of transition to a market economy") can do so much more cheaply. Proponents of joint implementation argue that for reasons of economic efficiency, country A should be able to help pay for country B's movement toward energy efficiency, and that the two parties should share a negotiated percentage of the reduced GHG emissions as a result of the project. In effect, both countries would benefit: country A could apply the credit to the GHG reductions of its target, and country B could do so also, and receive financial assistance it would not otherwise obtain. The most cogent argument against an arrangement such as this is that states should first make adjustments at home before attempting to "buy" their way out of their obligations under the UNFCCC. In reality, however, not a great deal of political resistance exists to joint implementation projects between developed countries, though the question of credits does remain problematic and unsettled.

On the other hand, dramatic controversy surrounds joint implementation projects between developed and developing countries—if the developed country seeks a credit for the project against its present commitments under the UNFCCC. Proponents foresee a global system of tradable emission rights, while opponents remain staunchly against such a proposal. Let us suppose for example that developed country A above enters into a project with country C, a developing country, in which country A offers to pay country C not to develop a tract of pristine rainforest. In this scenario, proponents of joint implementation again point to the economic benefit to both sides, reminding those opposed of the inherent economic efficiency of the arrangement. Country C can reduce global warming more cheaply than country A by preserving the rainforest as a "sink," country C is willing to negotiate as to the price of foregoing development, and country A remains willing to pay an appropriate price to offset its extremely expensive obligations under the UNFCCC. The percentage credit gained by country A would most likely be set by the appropriate authorities under the UNFCCC.

Rather than an efficient economic arrangement between equal bargainers, the developing countries see this second example in a much different light. First, the developed countries have created the problem of global warming and, developing countries contend, they should not try to escape from the moral commitment to curb their profligate GHG-generating lifestyles. Thus, developed countries must begin by attending to the source of the problem at home, and should not attempt to soften the economic blow to their own constituencies by creating obligations for developing countries. Second, developing countries fear that joint implementation of this kind will stifle their future economic progress. Projects which force maintenance of "sinks"—and thereby prevent development—especially are perceived as continuing the neo-colonial dynamic which prevents developing countries from catching up economically. Third, if developing countries eventually have future net emissions targets under the treaty, developing countries fear that the developed countries would have already appropriated the cheapest and most cost-effective projects for mitigation. Finally, and at the most general level, the poorer nations perceive joint implementation projects as a threat to sovereignty—simply another case of developed countries telling developing countries what to do on their own soil.

The Kyoto Protocol while not bringing closure to this potential dispute, did go some way toward the adoption of market mechanisms. The Protocol establishes a number of "cooperative mechanisms" that deal with joint implementation, the Clean Development Mechanism (CDM) and emissions trading, that allow an Annex I country to fulfill its commitment through joint efforts with other countries. Three of these mechanisms are established in articles 3, 6 and 12 of the Protocol.

While these three interrelated concepts are layered with complexity, in general, Annex I countries can receive credit for reducing greenhouse gas emissions for carrying out either joint implementation or CDM projects, and such credits can be used to meet the Annex I countries' commitments to reduce emissions under art. 3. Under art. 3 Annex 1 countries shall *individually or jointly*, ensure that their aggregate anthropogenic carbon dioxide equivalent emissions of the greenhouse gases listed in Annex A do not exceed their assigned amounts, calculated pursuant to their quantified emission limitation and reduction commitments inscribed in Annex B with a view to reducing their overall emissions of such gases by at least 5 per cent below 1990 levels in the commitment period 2008 to 2012.

Other provisions in art. 3, specifically Paragraphs 10 and 11, provide a mechanism for calculating the Parties emissions limitation and reduction obligations under a joint implementation scenario involving the transfer of "emission reduction units". Art. 6 authorizes an Annex I country, or a private entity from that country, to invest in a climate change mitigation project in another Annex I country. With approval by the host country, the investing country receives "emission reduction units," which it can add to its assigned amount. Art. 12 authorizes an Annex I country, or a private entity from that country, to invest in a climate change mitigation project in a non Annex I country through the Clean Development Mechanism. The project must contribute to sustainable development in the host country. If it is approved, the investing country can add the resulting "certified emission reductions" to its assigned amount.

The government delegations that drafted the Kyoto Protocol in 1997 could not agree on all the rules and institutional arrangements necessary for the operation of those cooperative mechanisms. As a result, many provisions are ambiguously worded, and many details were left to be supplied by future decisions. Since 1997, delegations have continued to resolve ambiguities and flesh out details so that governments may ratify the Protocol.

(b) Technology Transfers & Financing

According to article 4(3) of UNFCCC, Annex II parties (OECD members only) must pay for all the reporting requirements undertaken by developing countries. This includes the developing countries' obligation to create national inventories of GHGs under article 4(1) and to communicate such information to the COP under article 12. In addition to the full costs of reporting, the Annex II parties must pay for the full incremental costs of projects undertaken by developing countries to fulfill the latter's general commitments pursuant to article

4(1). However, these projects—such as designating and maintaining a sustainable rainforest preserve— must be approved by the financial mechanism as outlined above.

With regard to technology transfer, at the UNFCCC the developing countries settled for a rather weak commitment in article 4(5), which stipulates that developed countries "shall take all practicable steps to promote, facilitate and finance, as appropriate, the transfer of ... environmentally sound technologies." The UNFCCC, therefore, contains a greater emphasis on financial costs than on the transfer of technology. Some transfer of technology is expected though, and it will either take place through joint implementation projects or through the financial mechanism itself. All Annex II parties must include measures taken for the transfer of technology in their national communications to the COP.

By contrast, the wording on technology transfer in the Kyoto Protocol does lay greater emphasis on technology transfer. The opening sentence in article 10(c) & (d) of the Kyoto Protocol requires that Parties should "Cooperate in ..." in contrast to the UNFCCC's exhortation to developed country Parties only to "take all practicable steps". It also expands on similar language in the UNFCCC by adding the general catch-all on "practices and processes pertinent to climate change" [10(c)]. Perhaps most significantly, it formally recognizes the role of the private sector and the need for an "enabling environment" to promote technology transfers [10(c)].

COP4 may prove more significant than the Protocol itself in light of the more focused agreement that addressed the roles of all Parties. It called for Annex B Parties (largely OECD countries) to provide lists of environmentally sound technologies that were publicly owned, and for developing countries to submit prioritized technology needs, especially related to key technologies for addressing climate change. All Parties were urged to create an enabling environment to stimulate private sector investment, and to identify projects and programmes on cooperative approaches to technology transfer.

Most importantly, the agreement on technology reached at COP4 called for a consultative process to be established to consider a list of 19 specific issues and associated questions, set out in an Annex [http://cop4.unfccc.int/]. The technology impetus was carried forward in COP 8 and the Delhi Declaration placed heavy emphasis the importance of technology transfers including those relating to alternative sources of fuel and energy [Delhi Declaration: Paras (h), (i), (j), (k), (l), & (m), http://unfccc.int/cop8/].

(c) Adaptation

According to the UNFCCC, Annex II parties have a fairly vague financial responsibility to developing countries adaptation costs—the costs involved in dealing with the effects of higher seas and higher temperatures. Article 4(4) merely states that Annex

II parties "shall also assist the developing country Parties that are particularly vulnerable to the adverse effects of climate change in meeting costs of adaptation to those adverse effects." Coupled with article 4(8), this commitment could require Annex II countries to pay for a number of adaptation measures, such as the construction of sea walls for small island countries.

Art. 11 of the Kyoto Protocol make reference to Art. 4(4) of UNFCCC, and by inference calls for financial and technological help for the purposes of adaptation to climate change. This view was confirmed at COP6 which included adaptation in the activities eligible for funding under the Global Environmental Fund (GEF), and even established a special adaptation fund [http://unfccc.int/issues/].

At the COP8 in November 2002, the developing countries re-affirmed that the alleviation of poverty remained the primary objective of developing countries, and applied that principle to the politics of climate change. This principle, as we have seen in Chapter Two, had received unequivocal confirmation at the World Summit on Sustainable Development (WSSD) in September 2002. As might be expected, the Delhi Ministerial Declaration on Climate Change and Sustainable Development, issued at the conclusion of the COP8, confirmed the need for sustainable development. But to the surprise and consternation of emission reduction (mitigation) supporters, the New Delhi Declaration re-affirmed the importance of adaptation and effectively afforded adaptation parity of importance with mitigation [http://unfccc.int/ cop8/latest/].

The New Delhi Declaration emphasized in Para e that adaptation to the adverse effects of climate change is of high priority for all countries, and requires urgent attention and action on the part of all countries. By so deciding the New Delhi Declaration offers support to the position taken by countries like the United States who balk at paying the high costs of emission reductions, and have argued instead for adaptation. Accordingly, the Delhi Declaration has been warmly welcomed by the United States   [http://www.gcrio.org/OnLnDoc/pdf/us_delhi_declaration.pdf. Visited Feb 2, 2003].

(d) Costs & Benefits

We have noted that the Annex 1 (developed) countries will not reach the reductions mandated by the Kyoto Protocol. We have also noted that Kyoto requires a reduction of carbon dioxide to between 5% and 7% of 1990 levels for Annex 1 (developed) countries by the year 2112. We have further observed that the costs of implementing Kyoto is a major reason for its lack of implementation and its non-ratification by the United States. What then are the projected costs and benefits of the carbon dioxide reductions required by Kyoto?

We have noted the considerable uncertainty surrounding the extent and impact of global warming. Consequently any responses to the challenge of climate change, must be made in the context of such uncertainty. Decision-makers are sometimes placed on the horns of a dilemma, either: a) taking action now which turns out to be too costly as more knowledge is gained or b) deferring action now to learn later that negative effects are greater than originally thought. In these circumstances, weighing the positives (pros) against the negatives (cons) of a planned course of action makes good common sense.

Cost-benefit analysis offers a technique for comparatively assessing the monetized costs of global warming, as against the benefits of the reductions obligated by the Kyoto Protocol. To use cost-benefit analysis in evaluating the merits of the Kyoto reductions requires translation of positive and negative effects to a common measure: dollars. The methods and assumptions needed to measure positive and negative effects and to translate such effects to dollars can make cost-benefit analysis a complex and controversial undertaking.

Moreover, cost-benefit analysis can be expensive and difficult to explain because indirect methods are usually employed to approximate monetary values to the required environmental impacts of global warming. When calculating the benefits of the reductions, indirect estimating methods are necessary because many public services and benefits have no private sector equivalents; consequently, no market prices exist for directly estimating benefits. Analysts approximate monetized benefits using various estimating and survey techniques. Human health data, statistical and engineering models, and laboratory experiments play various roles. Resulting monetary estimates vary widely and are subject to professional disagreement on methods. Measurement problems can also lead to some important cost-benefit categories being ignored, and results can be subject to wide interpretation in partisan debates.

For all these reasons, it would be natural to expect the IPCC to undertake such an analysis with a view to clarifying and illuminating the issues. While their earlier reports did address this important assignment, the third and most recent reports of the IPCC, for reasons that are not entirely clear, have declined to do so.

We have seen in Section C above dealing with "Impacts" that the IPCC devoted considerable attention to the adverse effects of climate change on agriculture, forests, fisheries, energy, water supply, coastal loss of land, biodiversity, drought, and human health. With regard to the costs of such impacts the earlier reports of the IPCC did attempt to estimate adaptation costs incurred in building sea walls, adapting crops, changing technologies etc, as well as the costs of damage caused where adaptation is not possible. Their 1996 report estimates the costs to be around 1.5%–2% of current global GDP [CLIMATE CHANGE 1995–THE ECONOMIC AND SOCIAL DIMENSIONS OF CLIMATE CHANGE: *Report of IPCC Working Group III, (1996)].* According to one commentator this amounts to between \$480–640 billion based on figures for the year 2000 [Bjorn Lomborg, THE SKEPTICAL ENVIRONMENTALIST, 300 (2001)]. Looked at differently, if global warming could be arrested the world would not need to incur adaptation costs and would, therefore, benefit to the extent of $480–600 billion annually.

To what extent will the Kyoto Protocol mitigate climate change and obviate the need for adaptation costs? Unfortunately, even if it is fully implemented, what Kyoto can accomplish is marginal. According to Lomborg, when compared to a "business as usual" no carbon dioxide reduction scenario, Kyoto will reduce temperature by 0.15% C, or less than $1/6^{th}$ of one degree, while corresponding sea level rises will be reduced by 2.5 cm (1 inch) by 2100 [Lomborg, id., 302]. According to another commentator who bases his conclusions on the IPCC models, Kyoto will result only in the avoidance of one-fifth of one degree of the predicted warming [Russell Jones, *An Assessment of the Kyoto Protocol, Transcript from Panel Discussion, April 15, 1999, 11 GEO. INT'L ENVTL. L. REV. 767, 777 (1999)*].

Approaching the Kyoto reductions from a different standpoint the view of yet another commentator is that the Kyoto Protocol may result in a 16% reduction of global warming if that reduction is held stable for the whole of the century [Henry D. Jacoby et al., *Kyoto's Unfinished Business*, 77 FOREIGN AFF. July/Aug. 1998, at 54, 63–64]. However, reductions cannot be held stable because developing countries are not subject to any reductions, and as we have seen, emissions of carbon dioxide by developing countries will overtake those of developed countries by 2030 at the latest.

Having ascertained how little Kyoto will do to reduce global warming the next question pertains to the costs of the carbon dioxide reductions required by Kyoto. In the absence of IPCC estimates the breach has been filled by others. One of them is Lomborg who bases his projections on the Stanford Modeling Forum—the largest effort to examine the costs of Kyoto. He claims that the costs of implementing Kyoto in 2010 will be $346 billion annually but that this figure will drop to $161 billion if trading is allowed [Lomborg, id., 303]. According to OECD estimates it will cost around 2% of GDP. [*OECD Green Model: An Updated Overview* (1994)] *http://sedac.ciesin.org/mva/iamcc.tg/articles/ LOM/LOM1994.html* Adjusting these figures to to-day's GDP this should compute to about $900 billion annually in 2050.

4. IMPLICATIONS

(a) Research and Development in Alternative Energy

One of the primary reasons why even the modest cuts called for by Kyoto are so expensive to implement is that there is no viable alternative to coal or fossil based fuels. As pointed out above in Section D on "Impacts" any plan to cut down on fossil fuels must envision and integrate a comprehensive research and development (R & D) program on alternative energy. What is required is a substantial R & D program to produce new technologies that could bring about deep global emissions reductions and still allow robust economic growth.

Some of the technological options for GHG substitution include replacement technologies, involving a 100% reduction in carbon dioxide emissions, and reduction technologies, which involve a reduction in emissions of carbon dioxide [Edward B. Barbier et al., *Technological Substitution Options for Controlling Greenhouse Gas Emissions*, in GLOBAL WARMING: ECONOMIC POLICY RESPONSES 109 (Rudiger Dornbusch & James M. Poterba eds., 1991)].

Such an effort should involve several wealthy participating nations. Candidate energy technologies include nuclear, solar, hydroelectric, geothermal, and hydrogen from fossil fuel. Methods for safe and economical long-term storage of carbon in subterranean reservoirs, the deep ocean, and forests are also important research areas, as are technologies that enhance energy efficiency. Carbon storage through afforestation remains effective, however, only for as long as the forest is expanding, otherwise carbon released by dying trees offsets that stored by new trees. Few of the alternatives currently under discussion, however, can be widely used at reasonable costs without fundamental improvements.

These concrete steps could be treated as part of an overall planetary plan to deal with climate change. Far more attention must be paid to the development of new technologies for reducing GHG emissions. It will be nearly impossible to slow warming appreciably without condemning much of the world to poverty unless energy sources that emit little or no carbon dioxide become competitive with conventional fossil fuels. [See Jacoby at 66.] Current U.S. efforts, as reflected in the present administrations *Comprehensive National Energy Policy* do not face up to the challenge.

Investment in R & D on new long-term technical options was barely discussed at the Kyoto Protocol. One phrase advocating "cooperat[ion] in scientific and technical research" was tucked away in the text, [art. 10(d)] and that was all; no nation was obliged to devote any resources to R & D. There is little commitment to the long-term development of greenhouse-friendly technology by those countries most capable of producing it. However, we have noted that COP 8 agreed on the need for a far more robust technology initiative and how this will pattern out will significantly determine the success or failure of policies to address global warming.

(b) An Inclusive Convention

The next step in moving toward a long-term solution to climate change is to include both developing and developed nations in this earth saving enterprise. The inclusion of the developing countries must rest on the concept of "common but differentiated responsibility" (CBDR) articulated in the UNFCCC. Any obligations to protect the climate need not fall disproportionately on the poor and the deprived. Given the enormous disparities of wealth amongst nations, equity, fairness, and efficiency require that discharging the burden of protection should fall differentially and more heavily on the richer nations. Climatic stability is a public good that is of critical importance to all humanity, and ought to be protected by the entire international community. In the absence of a system of international government that can act to protect public goods for collective benefit, other mechanisms should be found.

It may be necessary to work out a scheme that pays at least the poorest of the poor countries to reduce their emissions. There is much to commend the suggestion of one commentator that in appropriate circumstances, global environmental governance and international environmental law should move from a "Polluter Pay Principle" to a "Beneficiaries Pay Principle." [Jonathan Baert Wiener, *Global Environmental Regulation: Instrument Choice in Legal Context,* 108 YALE L.J. 677, 751–752 *(1999)*]. But this should go hand in hand with other more flexible credits to developing countries for reducing GHGs. For example, commitments to increased amounts of reforestation, population control measures, energy efficiency, more technology transfers, and more investment in R & D should be brought into any carbon dioxide reduction calculus.

(c) Realistic   Long–Term   Implementation   Strategies

The Kyoto Protocol requires dramatic, unrealistic carbon dioxide emission cuts by 2010, without regard to investment and technology cycles. A fundamental question, then, is whether it is economically efficient and environmentally effective to demand that a manufacturer or utility incur significant costs in retrofitting to meet a short-term deadline, as opposed to phasing in more efficient equipment and technology as part of the industrial cycle, as old machinery and processes become obsolete? The clear answer emerging from an examination of a number of industries is that it is not.

Any U.S. commitment to reduce emissions more than 30% below what they otherwise would be in 2010 will therefore entail enormous changes in industry and consumer practices. Under the time scale of the Kyoto Protocol, the question is whether such huge efforts will be made? The answer given by the Clinton administration was that tax incentives, research subsidies, and trading will allow the United States to meet its goal with price hikes of only 4 to 6 cents per gallon of gasoline. But this can be accomplished only if abatement costs are cut in half through emissions trading with other industrial countries, as well as by another quarter from trading with developing countries. By contrast the Bush administration has concluded that implementing Kyoto will be too expensive.

A doubling of the pre-industrial concentration of carbon dioxide poses only modest environmental and economic problems and little, if any, economic problems if counteracted with good planning [Rob Coppock, *Implementing the Kyoto Protocol*, 14 Issues in Sci. & Tech. 66, 68 (1998)]. This is because the rate of change will be slow. The temperature trend this century has been about 0.05° to 0.1° per decade. Investment cycles for most industrial sectors are rapid enough that suitable adjustments can be made along the way. Even agriculture ought to be able to cope. It takes about eight years to bring a new cereal hybrid into production, which would be needed to adjust to differences in soil moisture, and recent experience breeding disease resistant rice suggests that genetic engineering can reduce this time. It also will not be long before agricultural implements are able to make on-the-fly soil-moisture measurement and precision delivery of fertilizer to offset changes.

Clearly, a permanent rise in temperature will give rise to a number of problems that will need adaptive strategies. [Climate Change 2001 Synthesis Report 278–282] Rising warmth and moisture would also broaden the breeding grounds for insects, most notably mosquitoes, increasing the spread of diseases like malaria, dengue, and yellow fever [*Id.* at 259–261]. However, lifestyle and public health measures such as mosquito control, eradication programs, and piped water systems, which have wiped out these epidemics in the United States, could offset the effects of future climate change.

Even the effort to counter a possible sea level rise of 6 to 37 inches by the end of the next century is not likely to be catastrophic. In urban and industrial locations, the cost of protective sea walls, such as those used in Holland, will be cost effective. See Kathryn S. Brown, *Taking Global Warming to the People*, 283 Sci. 1440 (1999). Elsewhere the coastline can be left to find its new level. The previously valuable property on the waters edge will be replaced by formerly inland property that becomes newly valuable because it is now next to water. Obviously there will be winners and losers, but then there always have been. Urban expansion has created more winners and losers than moderate climate change will do.

CHAPTER SEVEN

OZONE DEPLETION

About 90 percent of all ozone is found in a layer of the earth's atmosphere 6 to 30 miles above the earth's surface called the stratosphere. Ozone is also found in the layer of atmosphere closest to the earth's surface called the troposphere. This bad "tropospheric" ozone down here can damage human health, vegetation, exacerbate the "greenhouse effect" and is a key ingredient of urban smog. By contrast the "good" stratospheric ozone up there functions as a necessary and beneficial shield against biologically damaging solar ultraviolet radiation.

Without ozone's protective shield, living organisms and humans on earth would be exposed to a range of adverse consequences. In humans heightened exposure to solar ultraviolet radiation can lead to more cases of skin cancer, cataracts and impaired immune systems [UNITED NATIONS ENVIRONMENT PROGRAMME (UNEP), ENVIRONMENTAL EFFECTS OF OZONE DEPLETION: 1998 ASSESSMENT 28 (1998)]. A decrease in the ozone layer has also has been linked to crop damage, phytoplankton destruction with repercussions up the food chain, increased ground-level ozone pollution, and increased damage to photoreactive materials such as plastics, rubber, wood and cotton. The present chapter deals with the depletion of stratospheric ozone.

A. THE NATURE OF THE PROBLEM

When solar ultraviolet radiation interacts with oxygen molecules (O_2) in the stratosphere, these molecules fracture into single oxygen atoms (known as atomic oxygen) which then bond to nearby oxygen molecules to form ozone molecules (O_3). This process ensures that stratospheric ozone is continually being produced via the interaction of energy from the sun and oxygen molecules [F.S. Rowland, *Atmospheric Changes Caused by Human Activities: From Science to Regulation*, 27 ECOLOGY L.Q. 1261, 1267–68 (2001)]. A number of natural compounds containing elements such as nitrogen, hydrogen and chlorine work to destroy stratospheric ozone. This process of stratospheric ozone formation and destruction maintains the existence and efficacy of the ozone shield.

For nearly a billion years, stratospheric ozone has protected life on Earth from harmful solar radiation. In the past half century, however, human activity has worked to disrupt the natural equilibrium of ozone formation and destruction, thus weakening the ozone shield's ability to absorb this harmful radiation.

In relative terms, the amount of ozone in the atmosphere is exceedingly small. On average, in every million molecules of air less than five are ozone molecules [ACTION ON OZONE 1 (2002)] While the introduction of ozone depleting compounds into the stratosphere is caused by both natural and anthropogenic factors, the evidence clearly establishes anthropogenic emissions as the dominating cause of observed deviations from the "optimal equilibrium" of ozone formation and destruction. [*See* EXECUTIVE SUMMARY, 2002 SCIENTIFIC ASSESSMENT OF OZONE DEPLETION 13 (2002) (hereinafter 2002 SCIENTIFIC ASSESSMENT); EXECUTIVE SUMMARY, 1998 SCIENTIFIC ASSESSMENT OF OZONE DEPLETION 25–26 (1998) (hereinafter 1998 SCIENTIFIC ASSESSMENT)]. However, without the natural introduction of ozone-depleting compounds into the stratosphere, the equilibrium of ozone formation and destruction necessary to human and other life would cease to exist [ACTION ON OZONE 2002, at 1–3].

In 1985, British scientists published findings on what has since been called the "Antarctic ozone hole" [J.C. Farman et al., *Large Losses of Total Ozone in Antarctica Reveal Seasonal ClOx/NOx Interaction*, 315 NATURE 207 (1985)]. While ozone concentrations fluctuate naturally by season, latitude and altitude, the British data showed that ozone levels over the Antarctic between September and November (springtime in the Antarctic) had fallen 50 percent compared with 1960's levels, and that this "ozone hole" (actually a localized thinning of the ozone rather than an actual "hole") covered an area larger than the United States. In 1994 NASA researchers analyzed three years of data collected by the Upper Atmosphere Research Satellite

(UARS) [*NASA Reveals New Evidence for Chemical Cause of Ozone Depletion*, GLOBAL ENV'T CHANGE REPORT, Dec. 23, 1994, *available in* DIALOG, File No. 1994 WL 2513797]. The data confirmed the British team's finding of a localized diminishment in ozone levels above the Antarctic during the springtime. The data also provided "conclusive evidence" that human activities, rather than natural factors, were the cause of ozone depletion above the Antarctic and identified anthropogenic chlorine as the chemical culprit. Based on measurements taken by UARS of hydrogen fluoride, which is produced when CFCs breakdown, NASA researchers calculated that natural (non-anthropogenic) sources accounted for only 17 percent of the total amount of chlorine in the stratosphere.

B.　CAUSES OF THE PROBLEM

Emissions from volcanic eruptions, ocean spray, biomass burning, and other natural sources do introduce chlorine into the stratosphere and thus contribute to the destruction of stratospheric ozone. However, in contrast to the causal questions that exist more explicitly in the context of climate change [*see* Chapter 6], research data has largely settled the question of what role humans have in causing ozone depletion: human activities are the predominant cause of those problems.

While major volcanic eruptions can inject matter directly into the stratospheric ozone layer, the volcanic particles emitted cannot deplete ozone on

their own. It is only upon interaction with anthropogenic chlorine that the volcanic particles become
enhancers of ozone depletion [1998 SCIENTIFIC AS-
SESSMENT, at 26]. Researchers have measured the
stratospheric presence of nearly all known gases
containing chlorine. These measures indicate that
introduction of chlorine into the stratosphere by
natural sources, when added to the much larger
contribution of anthropogenic halocarbons, could
account for the entirety of stratospheric chlorine
[*Id.* at 25]. Also, by analyzing air trapped in the
snow since the late 1800's, researchers have confirmed that non-industrial sources of halons, CFCs
and major chlorofluorocarbons were insignificant in
terms of their depletive effect [2002 SCIENTIFIC AS-
SESSMENT, at 2].

CFCs were first produced the late 1928 as the
result of efforts to find a nontoxic substance capable
of serving as an effective and safe refrigerant.
Freon, the DuPont trademark name for one of these
substances, replaced ammonia as the standard cooling fluid in home refrigerators and soon became the
primary coolant in automobile air conditioners
[Rowland *supra*]. Since the invention of CFCs, millions of tons of anthropogenic chlorine have been
added to the natural levels of stratospheric chlorine.

Unlike chlorine from natural sources, such as
volcanoes and ocean spray, CFCs are not water-
soluble and do not "wash out" of the troposphere.
Because they are chemically stable, they do not
break down in the lower atmosphere and may have
a lifetime in the troposphere of over 100 years.

They inevitably reach the stratosphere through atmospheric circulation. The two most important
ozone depleting chlorinated substances are CFC–11
and CFC–12. More recently, scientists developed
HCFCs as a less destructive (though still problematic) substitute for CFCs. Halons, methyl bromide,
carbon tetrachloride, also are ozone-depleting chemicals.

Approximately 350,000 to 400,000 ozone-depleting metric tons of CFCs were contained in refrigeration equipment in 2002; 450,000 metric tons of
halon–1301, and of 330,000 metric tons of halon–
1211 were installed in fire fighting equipment in
2002. [UNEP, REPORT OF THE TECHNOLOGY AND ECO-
NOMIC ASSESSMENT PANEL (TEAP), VOL 1, PROGRESS
REPORT 13, 27 (2002)]. Estimates based on current
recovery capacity indicate that less than 2.4 percent
of the millions of tons of ozone-depleting refriger-
ants could be recovered annually [*Id.* at 27].

Halons, another type of ozone-depleting substance, contain bromine which attacks the ozone
molecules in a similar fashion to chlorine. Halons,
however, destroy four to sixteen times more ozone
than CFC–11 during their atmospheric life. Methyl
bromide, unlike other controlled ozone-depleting
chemicals, has both natural and human-made
sources—including emissions from biomass burning
and soil fumigation. A final culprit, carbon tetrachloride is a non-chlorinated ozone-destroying com-
pound whose ozone depleting potential is approximately equal to that of CFC–11. Once employed in
dry cleaning, its application in industrialized coun-

tries is now restricted because of its toxicity, but it still finds common use in other countries [*Ozone-friendly?*, DISCOVER, Feb. 1995, at 20].

C. ENVIRONMENTAL IMPACTS

By enabling more solar UV radiation to reach the earth, ozone depletion effectively increases both the probability that adverse consequences will result from UV radiation exposure and the degree of harm effected by those consequences. Among these consequences are immune system suppression in humans and animals, skin cancer and other forms of cancer, inhibition of photosynthesis resulting in diminished plant growth, and damage to the marine ecosystem. More specifically, while is well established that exposure to UV radiation can diminish the efficacy of subsequent immunizations, recent data now indicates that even when successful immunization has occurred prior to the increased exposure, UV radiation can work to suppress the immune response [UNEP, ENVIRONMENTAL EFFECTS OF OZONE DEPLETION: INTERIM SUMMARY (2000)]. Inhibited photosynthesis means reduced plant growth, which not only translates into diminished food production, but also presents consequences for global warming trends. And as regarding the marine ecosystem, one example of the potential impact of increased UV radiation can be seen in phytoplankton and zooplankton, which form the base of the marine food web. Phytoplankton and zooplankton are highly sensitive to UV radiation exposure, and as phytoplankton play a key role in the uptake of carbon dioxide, a decrease in their numbers could also work to enhance the global warming [*Id.*].

Researchers estimate that a 10 percent decrease in stratospheric ozone would result in an annual increase of 300,000 non-melanoma skin cancers and 4,500 melanoma cases worldwide [*Health and global changes: What will the future of our children look like?*, Working Paper, Sixth Meeting of the European Environment and Health Committee (EEHC), June 13–14, 2002, EEHC6/8 at 2 (2002)]. For every 1 percent decrease in stratospheric ozone, some researchers predict the average annual incidences of non-melanoma skin cancers will increase by a range of 1 to 6 percent; for squamous and basel cell carcinomas, the incidence rate is predicted to increase by approximately 2 percent ± 0.5 percent [*Id.* at 3]. Ozone depletion also relates to the incident rate of cataracts. Without mitigating behaviors to compensate for the effect of increased UV radiation exposure, researchers estimate that for every one 1 percent decease in stratospheric ozone, incidences of cataracts will increase by 0.5 percent [*CFCs and Asthma Inhaler Regulation: Hearings Before the Senate Labor and Human Resources Committee*, 105th Cong. (1998) (testimony of Thomas Downham), *available at* 1998 WL 177904 (F.D.C.H.)].

D. REMEDIAL OBJECTIVES

In order to restore the ozone shield and prevent the further enlarging of the ozone hole, it is necessary to prohibit the use of damaging chemicals [*supra* § B.]. Beginning with the Vienna Convention for the Protection of the Ozone Layer (Vienna Ozone Convention), Mar. 22, 1985, 26 I.L.M. 1529 (entered into force Sept. 12, 1988) the international community has instituted such controls, and we have seen the development of a comprehensive scheme for phasing out CFC's by the year 2010 and restoring the ozone-shield.

The legal response to the problem of ozone depletion remains one of the most striking achievements of international environmental law. A number of factors have contributed to this success: (1) A growing scientific consensus as to the threat posed to the ozone layer by the release of anthropogenic chemicals into the atmosphere; (2) The role played by bellwether states like the United States, which had begun controlling CFCs well prior to the start of negotiations for the Vienna Ozone Convention; (3) The existence of a relatively small number of producing nations whose industry, after limited objections, eventually backed international controls; (4) incentives for industry experts and other private parties to participate in technology assessments and policy recommendations, thus enabling greater effectiveness through increased compliance; and (5) the development of innovative institutional mechanisms that have attracted reluctant parties and have allowed for more flexible decision-making [*Cf.* Edward A. Parsons, *The Technology Assessment Approach to Climate Change*, ISSUES IN SCIENCE AND TECHNOLOGY 65 (2002)].

E. LEGAL RESPONSE

1. THE VIENNA OZONE CONVENTION

Under the Vienna Ozone Convention of 1985 nations agreed to take "appropriate measures ... to protect human health and the environment against adverse effects resulting or likely to result from human activities which modify or are likely to modify the Ozone Layer;" [art. 2(1)] but the measures are unspecified. There is no mention of any substances that might harm the ozone, and CFCs only appear towards the end of the annex to the treaty, where they are mentioned as chemicals that should be monitored. The main thrust of the convention was to encourage research, cooperation among countries and exchange of information. What is most significant about the 1985 convention is that for the first time nations agreed in principle to tackle a global environmental problem before its effects were felt, or even scientifically proven.

Following recent trends the ozone regime reflected the framework approach to international law-making (*see* Chapter 6, Climate Change). Also known as the convention-protocol approach, this method proceeds from a treaty of generalities, signed by a range of parties, who then create a protocol (or protocols) of more specific and stringent application. In this case, the Vienna Ozone Convention attracted over 25 signatories in the first two years, including all the major producers of ozone-depleting chemicals except Japan. With the science still uncertain in 1985, the parties negotiated a treaty without specific controls that instead stressed cooperation and research [*see* arts. 2–4]. Of greatest significance, the treaty empowered its Conference of the Parties (COP) to adopt future protocols dealing with such controls [art. 6(4)(h); art. 2(2)(c)]. This was achieved in 1987 with the Montreal Protocol.

2.   THE MONTREAL PROTOCOL

After a series of rigorous meetings and negotiations, the Montreal Protocol on Substances that Deplete the Ozone Layer Montreal Protocol was finally agreed upon on 16 September 1987 [26 I.L.M. 1550 (1987), and was amended and adjusted in 1997.

The final agreement addresses the special developmental needs of less developed countries who did not want the Protocol to hinder their development, and makes special provision for additional financial resources and access to relevant technologies. It sets the "elimination" of ozone-depleting substances as its "ultimate objective." [Preamble]. The Protocol came into force, on time, on January 1st, 1989, and it has been ratified by 184 countries. [http://www.unep.org/ozone/ratif.shtml, visited Feb. 24, 2003]. The Montreal Protocol has been modified five times so far. Its control provisions were strengthened through four adjustments to the Protocol adopted in London (1990), Copenhagen (1992), Vienna (1995), Montreal (1997) and Beijing (1999), and these developments are discussed more fully in section 3 below.

A milestone in the field of international law, the Montreal Protocol creates mechanisms and incentives for institutional participation which are now included in virtually every environmental convention. It should also be seen as an example of the precautionary approach. While scientists had linked CFCs and halons to potential global ozone depletion and had also identified the Antarctic ozone hole, the atmospheric models remained inconclusive with no direct evidence of physical harm to humans or the environment. Yet despite this uncertainty, in 1987 the parties adopted a protocol with firm national commitments regarding specific regulatory controls on CFCs and halons. The protocol entered into force on January 1, 1989, with its ratification by 29 countries and the EEC—which together accounted for 82 percent of global consumption of ozone depleting substances. Pursuant to its original terms, the Montreal Protocol required parties to ensure that by 1999 their production and consumption levels of the five main CFC were 50 percent of those same levels in 1986. The protocol provided for this goal to be achieved through the use of interim reductions.

3. ADJUSTMENTS AND AMENDMENTS

A look at the difference between Adjustments and Amendments provides a window into the dynamic institutional machinery of the regime. Under the

Vienna Ozone Convention, while the COP may pass amendments by a two-thirds majority, these may not bind a party against its will [art. 9(3)–(4)]. Instead, following the traditional rule of consent in international law, each party must sign on to and ratify each amendment before becoming obligated [art. 9(5)].

Once an amendment is adopted under the Montreal Protocol, however, each party relinquishes its ability to avoid "adjustments." Adjustments include changes in the reduction and/or phase-out schedules of all controlled chemicals described in articles 2A–2H and listed in Annexes A–E, as well as changes in the ozone depleting potentials of the chemicals listed in Annexes A–E [art. 2(9)(a)(i)–(ii)]. Significantly, if the COP passes adjustments by a two-thirds majority vote which represents separate majorities of both the developed and developing countries present, the adjustments become binding on all the parties [art. 2(9)(c)–(d)]. In this way, the Montreal Protocol commits parties to specific numerical controls, regardless of whether they have voted for or against a successful adjustment. Some scholars have perceived the effect of this decision-making system as being an end-run around the formal doctrine of consent in international law. Others have argued that the parties have simply consented in the protocol to be bound against their consent to adjustments. Regardless, the COP has made many such adjustments over the years; Table 1 below presents some of the current requirements for parties not operating under article 5 (which sets forth compliance terms for developing countries) of the Montreal Protocol.

The protocol has also been the subject of four amendments. In 1990 the London Amendment added methyl chloroform, carbon tetrachloride and an additional range of CFCs to the phase-out schedules and established the means for conveying financial and technical assistance to developing country parties. The 1992 Copenhagen Amendment added hydrochlorofluorocarbons (HCFCs), hydrobromofluorocarbons (HBFCs) and methyl bromide to the phaseout schedules and formally recognized the creation of the Multilateral Fund as the official means for conveying financial and technological assistance. The 1997 Montreal Amendment instituted a licensure system for exports and imports of ozone-depleting substances, with the primary motivation being to discourage the growing illegal trade in the substances. And in 1999, the Beijing Amendment extended the regulatory controls on HCFCs to production and added bromochloromethane to the phaseout schedules.

As of 2003, the Montreal Protocol has been subject to nine sets of adjustments to the control measures designed to accelerate the phaseout of ozone-depleting substances, and is set out in the table below.

OZONE AGREEMENTS AND THEIR EFFECTIVE DATES			
TREATY	**MEETING WHEN TREATY WAS AGREED**		**ENTRY INTO FORCE**
	TITLE	**VENUE, DATE**	
Vienna Convention	High-level Diplomatic meeting	Vienna 22 March 85	22 Sept 88
Montreal Protocol	High-level diplomatic meeting	Montreal, 14-16 Sept 87	1 Jan 89
London Adjustment	2nd Meeting of the Parties to the Montreal Protocol	London, 27-29 June 90	7 March 91
London Amendment			10 Aug 92
Copenhagen Adjustment	4th Meeting of the Parties to the Montreal Protocol	Copenhagen, 23-25 Nov 92	23 Sept 93
Copenhagen Amendment			14 June 94
Vienna Adjustment	7th Meeting of the Parties to the Montreal Protocol	Vienna, 5-7 Dec 95	5 Aug 96
Montreal Adjustment	9th Meeting of the Parties to the Montreal Protocol	Montreal, 15-17 Sept 97	4 June 98
Montreal Amendment			10 Nov 99
Beijing Adjustment	11th Meeting of the Parties to the Montreal Protocol	Beijing, 29 Nov - 3 Dec 99	28 July 00
Beijing Amendment			25 Feb 02

UNEP, THE MONTREAL PROTOCOL CONTROL SCHEDULE AND ITS EVOLUTION 5 (2002)

The Montreal Protocol, as updated through the Seventh Meeting Parties (Dec. 1995), sets specific consumption and production controls for seven types of chemicals: CFCs [Montreal Protocol, at arts. 2A & 2C], halons [art. 2B], carbon tetrachloride [art. 2D], methyl chloroform [art. 2E], hydrochlorofluorocarbons (HCFCs) [art. 2F], hydrobromofluorocarbons (HBFCs) [art. 2G], and methyl bromide [art. 2H; *see generally* Report of the 7th Meeting of the Parties to the Montreal Protocol, Vienna, Dec. 5–7, UNEP/OzL.Pro.7/12 Decision VII/1–3 (1995)]. Originally, the protocol dealt only with halons and certain CFCs, and added articles 2C–2E in 1990, and articles 2F–2H in 1992 by amendment. Other amendments have included the listing of new Annexes, and changes involving trade restrictions and transfer of production allowances.

The Montreal Protocol offers special arrangements for developing countries. These nations generally have less stringent requirements under the Protocol, including later base level dates and longer phase-out periods. The Montreal Protocol also provides developing country parties with security that phase-outs will not leave them lacking necessary chemicals, as both developed and developing countries in most cases may continue production beyond a chemical's reduction date so as to meet the "basic domestic needs" of developing countries [art. 5, 8bis(a)–(b)]. These "basic domestic needs" provisions have helped to allay third-world fears of being left without proper substitutes under the Montreal Protocol.

Additionally, all parties, not just developing nations, are allowed "essential use" exemptions after the 100 percent reduction phase-out date for most chemicals. These exemptions are granted by the parties under Annex VI and cannot be taken unilaterally. For the year 2001, for example, the Technology and Economic Assessment Panel authorized 141 tons of "essential use" exemptions to Poland for ozone-depleting chemicals, as well as 292 tons to the U.S. and 1065 tons to the EU, respectively [UNEP, Report of the Technology and Economic Assessment Panel (TEAP), Vol 1, Progress Report 47 (2002)].

4.   TRANSFERS

The Montreal Protocol originally allowed small-producing parties to transfer or receive production in excess of the prescribed limits, as long as the combined levels of the two parties engaged in the transfer did not exceed production standards. The London Amendments extend this right to all parties, not just small producers, and for all controlled substances except HBFCs [art. 2(5)]. Identified in the protocol as industrial rationalization, this mechanism attempts to enhance efficiency between producers, allowing a shift of reduction and phase-out burdens from those least capable to those in the best position to do so. For those controls already at 100 percent reduction, this has the practical effect of allowing a transfer from one producer to another of that excess deemed necessary for the basic domestic needs of developing countries. With regard to HCFCs, the Copenhagen Amendments permit developed country parties who are small consumers to transfer excess consumption to other developed country parties [art. 2(5)bis.]. Again, as with all the provisions for industrial rationalization, the nations involved must notify the Secretariat of the terms and period of the transfer.

In a further nod to economic efficiency, regional organizations such as the EU may also "jointly fulfill" their consumption obligations as long as the combined levels remain within the mandated limits [art. 2(8)]. This resembles the notion of "joint implementation" developed under the Climate Change Convention (Chapter 6) by which parties may more efficiently share the burden of compliance.

5.　TRADE RESTRICTIONS

Though in possible violation of the 1994 WTO Agreement (formerly the GATT), the Montreal Protocol as augmented by the London and Copenhagen Amendments (and through the adjustments at the Seventh Meeting of the COP) bans all import of controlled substances from non-parties, except HCFCs and methyl bromide [arts. 4(1), 4(1)bis., 4(1)ter.]. In addition, the protocol now bans all export of these substances to non-parties [arts. 4(2), 4(2)bis., 4(2)ter.], and discourages the export of technology for their production or utilization [art. 4(5)]. The protocol also bans the import from non-parties of products containing the above substances—though a party who makes a timely objection to the Annex listing such products will not be bound [arts. 4(3), 4(3)bis., 4(3)ter.]. Finally, the parties through the COP must in the future consider the feasibility of so-called "process" trade restrictions, which disallow the import of products produced with, but not containing, the above controlled substances [arts. 4(4), 4(4)bis., 4(4)ter.].

6.   TECHNOLOGICAL AND FINANCIAL ASSISTANCE

By way of the London Amendments, the Montreal Protocol became the first environmental treaty to link the compliance of developing countries to the provision of technological and financial assistance by developed countries. Accordingly, the protocol now operates a "financial mechanism," including a Multilateral Fund to meet all "agreed incremental costs" of compliance by developing country parties [art. 10]. Though what constitutes "incremental cost" within a particular situation remains highly debatable, the term refers to the cost of compliance which a party would not incur but for its adherence to the Montreal Protocol. In this way, developing nations need not simply rely on the protections offered by article 5, but have a new incentive both to sign on to the protocol and to meet the relevant control provisions. The Multilateral Fund remains under the ultimate control of the COP, but the World Bank, UNEP and UNDP share in its administration.

F.   THE IMPACT OF THE REGIME

According to UNEP, the Montreal Protocol prevented ozone depletion by at least 50 percent in the northern hemisphere's mid latitudes, and 70 percent in the southern mid latitudes by the year 2050. If not for the Montreal Protocol levels global consumption of CFCs would have reached 3 million metric tones in 2010 and 8 million metric tons in

2060. Ozone-depleting chemicals in the atmosphere would have been approximately five times greater. These increases, had they occurred, would have made ozone levels approximately 10 times worse than current levels. They would effectively have doubled the amount of harmful UV radiation in the northern mid latitudes and quadrupled the amount in the south. It is estimated that such increases would have resulted in approximately 19 million more cases of non-melanoma cancer; 1.5 million cases of melanoma cancer; and 130 million more cases of eye cataracts [UNEP, BACKGROUNDER: BASIC FACTS AND DATA ON THE SCIENCE AND POLITICS OF OZONE PROTECTION 4 (Oct. 5, 2001)].

As reported by UNEP in 2002, the total combined effective abundance of ozone-depleting compounds in the troposphere continued to decline from a peak which occurred from 1992 to 1994. Levels of the atmospheric halon, bromine, have continued to increase, though at a rate slower than in previous years, while atmospheric chlorine levels have progressively declined. And while in 1998 total chlorine introduction from the major CFCs was on the rise, subsequent measurements indicate this growth trend may have ceased [2002 UNEP SCIENTIFIC ASSESSMENT, at 1].

CHAPTER EIGHT

ANTARCTICA

Geographers had posited the existence of a large southern continent long before seafarers first spotted Antarctica in the early 19th century. The ancient Greeks reasoned that in order to balance the major landmasses of the northern hemisphere, a great continent to the South must exist. Later European explorers, believing this fabled continent would prove hospitable to human settlement, set out to find *Terra Australis Incognita*—the Unknown Southern Land. However, the Antarctic continent—first reached by explorers during the late 19th and early 20th centuries—proved to be anything but hospitable [*see* Maria Pia Casarini, *Activities in Antarctica Before the Conclusion of the Antarctic Treaty*, *in* International Law for Antarctica 627, 631–32 (F. Francioni & T. Scovazzi eds., 1996)].

A. GEOPHYSICAL SKETCH

Antarctica is the coldest, windiest, iciest, driest and highest major landmass on Earth. The fifth largest continent in the world, Antarctica comprises around 9% of the earth's continental (lithospheric) crust and is approximately twice the size of Australia. However, only a tiny fraction of the continent itself is visible, as 98% of its 5.4 million square miles is buried beneath an immense sheet of ice. Over three miles thick in certain areas, the continental ice sheet has an average thickness of over a mile and contains 90% of Earth's ice. Two-thirds of all the fresh water in the world is contained within the ice of Antarctica [U.S. EPA, FINAL ENVTL IMPACT STATEMENT—PROPOSED RULE ON ENVTL IMPACT ASSMNT OF NONGOVERNMENTAL ACTIVITIES IN ANTARCTICA 2–6 (2001) (hereinafter EPA 2001); NSF, THE U.S. IN ANTARCTICA—REPORT OF THE U.S. ANTARCTIC PROGRAM EXTERNAL PANEL 9–25 (1997) (hereinafter NSF RE-PORT)].

Despite the abundance of fresh water in the form of ice, Antarctica is climatologically a desert. The interior of the continent averages less than two inches of precipitation per year—just slightly more than that of the Sahara Desert [EPA 2001, *supra,* at 2–3]. The continent is also regularly pummeled by strong winds. Antarctica also holds the record for the lowest recorded surface temperature in the world at–128.6°F (–89.2°C) [NAT'L CLIMATE DATA CEN-TER, NOAA, GLOBAL MEASURED EXTREMES OF TEMPERA-TURE AND PRECIPITATION (2000)]. While the average annual temperature of the continental interior is –70°F (–57°C), Antarctic temperature trends vary considerably according to region. For instance, in the northern regions of the Antarctic Peninsula average annual temperatures range from 50°F to 60°F (10°C to 15°C) during the austral summer, while temperatures in the interior high altitude regions range from –112°F to –130°F (–80°C to –90°C) during the austral winter [EPA 2001, *supra* at 2–3].

Unlike the Arctic polar region of the North, Antarctica has no indigenous human population; the continent is the largest single region historically uninhabited by humans. Itinerant researchers and a small but growing number of tourists constitute the visiting human population [GLOBAL ENV'T OUTLOOK PROJECT, UNEP, GLOBAL ENV'T OUTLOOK 2000 (1999)]. The terrestrial flora of Antarctica consists mostly of certain species of algae, mosses and lichens—though two species of angiosperms (flowering plants) grow in the relatively warmer region of the continent's northern-most extension called the Antarctic Peninsula [EPA 2001, *supra* at 2–14 to –15]. The Peninsula region supports the greatest diversity of flora and fauna on the continent—as well as the highest concentration of research stations [EPA 2001, *supra* at 15]. There are no exclusively terrestrial vertebrates capable of surviving an Antarctic winter. Tiny invertebrates such as mites, midges and springtails—as well as some 76 arthropod species (insects and the like), comprise the fauna that live exclusively on land. Scientists have also discovered a number of microbial species of bacteria and fungi native to Antarctica. Virtually all of these life forms—whether terrestrial flora, invertebrate arthropods or microbial bacteria—have habitats found only in Antarctica [NSF REPORT, *supra* at 11].

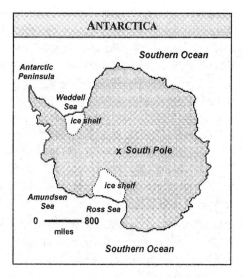

The continent of Antarctica is surrounded on all sides by the southern parts of the Pacific, Atlantic and Indian Oceans—a region commonly referred to as the Southern Ocean. The Southern Ocean encompasses an area of approximately 13.9 million square miles—or about 10% of the earth's total ocean waters [EPA 2001, *supra,* at 2–5]. In contrast to the biotic scarcity of the terrestrial environment, the waters of Antarctica have one of the highest concentrations of life in the world. The Southern Ocean is also home to numerous animal species whose survival depends upon their effective utilization of both the terrestrial and marine environments. In addition to an immense population of flying bird species, Antarctica is home to seven species of penguin—two of which breed exclusively in Antarctica—and six species of seal. The total bird population of Antarctica is estimated at 350 million, half of which are thought to be penguins. The aggregate weight of this prodigious bird population is estimated to be greater than 400,000 tons—more than the weight of all the seals and whales of Antarctica combined. Researchers have documented eight species of large cetaceans (whales) and nine species of small cetaceans (dolphins and porpoises) within the Southern Ocean—none of which are found exclusively within the region [*Id*. at 2–20 to –25].

Phytoplankton and zooplankton constitute the flora and fauna base of the Antarctic food chain—thus enabling the remarkable abundance of life within the Southern Ocean to exist. Within the dynamic of this food chain, zooplankton is an essential link between the region's primary producers (phytoplankton) and its major predators. Most prominent among the Antarctic zooplankton is the shrimp-like crustacean called the Antarctic Krill (*Euphasia Superba*). According to one study, krill comprise 75 to 90 percent of the marine invertebrate biomass within the Antarctic Peninsula region [*Id*. at 2–17].

B. SCIENTIFIC AND ARCHEOLOGICAL IMPORTANCE

Antarctica is an important location for conducting scientific research of global significance that benefits virtually all scientific disciplines. Because it has been less affected by human activity than any other continent, its near-pristine environment provides baseline for measuring pollution in populated areas of the world [NSF REPORT, *supra* at 1; *see also* SCI. COMM. ON ANTARCTIC RES. (SCAR), INFO. PAPER—SCIENTIFIC RESEARCH IN THE ANTARCTIC, *Agenda Item* 12, XXI ATCM]. Antarctic ice sheets hold valuable records of past global climates and help us to understand the effects of human activities on the global environment. Core samples in which a thin layer of ice, that once was snow during each calendar year, show evidence of industrial pollution and radioactive fallout, as well as volcanic eruptions from around the world. Meteorites, valuable for their planetary information, are easier to find in Antarctica because they accumulate and are more noticeable on the ice sheets. Nearly half of the 16,000 meteorites found on Earth were retrieved in Antarctica [COMM. FOR ENVTL PROTECTION (CEP), ANTARCTIC METEORITES, SCAR WORKING PAPER, XXV/ATCM/IP (Sept. 2000)].

The continent has terrestrial and freshwater ecosystems, unique in their simplicity, which provide valuable models for studying biological processes. Many important global environmental problems, such as stratospheric ozone and global warming, can be better studied in polar regions.

C. ECONOMIC CONCERNS

Based on their understanding of Antarctica's geological position, some scientists theorize that Antarctica may contain rich oil and mineral resources similar to those found in Australia and South Africa. A number of different minerals have been found within Antarctica by general geological surveys. Of the minerals Antarctica is known to possess, iron oxides and coal arguably comprise those that could be extracted, processed and distributed economically. Actual scientific data also suggests the presence of oil and gas beneath Antarctica's continental shelf.

The current international legal effort to prohibit oil and mineral exploration commenced some 50 years ago. It arose from the recognition that most drilling would occur on the continental shelf, in the very heart of Antarctica's biological productivity and that an accident—made more likely by Antarctica's harsh climate—would have a disastrous effect on most Antarctic ecosystems [Frank G. Klotz, *America on the Ice*, ANTARCTIC POLICY ISSUES 87 (1990)]. The principle of non-degradation of the Antarctic environment was implied in the Antarctic Treaty in 1959 [Dec. 1, 1959, 19 I.L.M. 860], which dedicated Antarctica to scientific research and peaceful purposes; the principle has been re-expressed in subsequent agreements. The Antarctic Environmental Protocol and various earlier conventions have committed the parties to a more comprehensive protection of the entire Antarctic environment [Protocol to the Antarctic Treaty on Environmental Protection, Oct. 3, 1991, arts. 2–3, 30 I.L.M. 1461].

Still, Antarctica remains economically attractive, but dangerous. Drilling rigs and well heads would have to withstand the most severe icebergs, high winds, and violent wave conditions in the world, making the prospect of oil or mineral development on Antarctica remote. Moreover, a lack of data, high financial costs and technical obstacles introduced by increased conservation efforts stymie mineral development. On the other hand, the ice sheet covering Antarctica contains 90% of the world's glacial ice, representing 70% of the world's fresh water, and may be a potential supply of fresh water if and when technology makes this economically feasible. Furthermore, Antarctica's growing tourist industry, which attracts thousands of tourists each year, could be economically significant, but poses its own environmental difficulties [*See also* INT'NL ASSOC. OF ANTARCTICA TOUR OPERATORS, OVERVIEW OF ANTARCTIC TOURISM, AGENDA ITEM 11, XXV ATCM/25IP073E (2002)].

D. ENVIRONMENTAL ISSUES

Antarctica is a microcosm of global environmental problems. For instance, Antarctica's coastal areas, where land is exposed, provide critical habitat and breeding grounds for seabirds and mammals. Human activities in the form of scientific bases and support facilities have contaminated the environment and disturbed seabirds and mammals, causing them to desert their nests or breeding grounds and alter breeding cycles for the year. Humans have also introduced foreign plant and animal species that disrupt Antarctica's ecological balance by competing with and sometimes destroying native species. Additionally, the Antarctic ecosystem remains especially fragile in that just one species, the Antarctic Krill, exists as the major food source of all higher species (whales, seals, fish, squid, penguins, birds) [Stephen Nicol, *Antarctic Krill–Changing Perceptions of Its Role in the Antarctic Ecosystem, in* ANTARCTIC SCIENCE: GLOBAL CONCERNS 144, 158 (G. Hempel ed., 1994)].

The Antarctic continent exerts a fundamental influence on the world's climate by regulating the average temperature of the earth. The immense Antarctic ice cap reflects up to 90% of the sun's energy, a primary reason Antarctica is so intensely cold. Oceanic and atmospheric currents work to carry this intense cold northward, thus cooling the waters of the Pacific, Atlantic and Indian Oceans, and significantly impacting the earth's weather conditions. Antarctica is also the principal "heat sink" of the global climate system, causing warmer air and ocean waters near the equator to move toward the colder air and waters at the pole, creating atmospheric and marine circulation patters in the Southern Hemisphere (in conjunction with the rotation of the earth). Any major change in the reflective properties of the continent (its "albedo") or the volume of the Antarctic ice sheet could have dramatic effects on the rest of the world, including climate change and a rise in sea level. [Henry Phillpot, *Physical Geography—Climate, in* KEY ENVI-

RONMENTS: ANTARCTICA 33, 36 (W. Bonner & D. Walton eds., 1985)].

Over the last half of the 20th Century, the Antarctic Peninsula region has grown warmer. Given that the 90% of the world's ice is located in Antarctica, were this ice to melt the sea level would rise some 200 feet—dramatically impacting human and other forms of life across the entire planet. [NSF REPORT, *supra,* at 14]. However, despite the observed warming trend within the Antarctic Peninsula region, data from a recent study—which contravenes earlier reports—indicates that between 1966 and 2000 a net cooling of the Antarctic continent took place [Peter Doran et al., *Antarctic Climate Cooling and Terrestrial Ecosystem Response,* 415 NATURE 517–20 (2002)].

E. GEO–POLITICAL SIGNIFICANCE

Protecting the Antarctic environment was made more difficult by the lack of recognized sovereignty over the entire continent. The primary international control strategies to protect Antarctica are collectively called the Antarctic Treaty System, initially developed by twelve countries that held conflicting views over the sovereignty of Antarctica. The Treaty System provides for cooperative international scientific projects, in which nations exchange information, facilities, and personnel. The Treaty System is a remarkable accomplishment in international cooperation. It suspends conflicting territorial claims, prohibits military use, and preserves the continent for scientific research [*see generally* U.S. DEP'T. OF STATE, HANDBOOK OF THE ANTARCTIC TREATY SYSTEM (H. Kohen ed., 9th ed. 2002)].

THE ANTARCTIC TREATY SYSTEM (ATS)

In addition to the 1959 Antarctic Treaty, the ATS consists of the following MEAs:

1972 CONVENTION FOR THE CONSERVATION OF SEALS

- Limits catches for three species and prohibits catching entirely for three species.
- Since 1964 no commercial sealing has taken place in Antarctica.

1980 CONVENTION ON THE CONSERVATION OF ANTARCTIC MARINE LIVING RESOURCES (CCAMLR)

- Identifies protected species and fishing regions, sets catch limits, fishing period and methods, establishes fisheries inspection procedures.
- Establishes Scientific Committee to provide technical advice on the setting of catch levels.

1991 MADRID PROTOCOL ON ENVIRONMENTAL PROTECTION

- Prohibits mineral resource activities, apart from scientific research, for a minimum of 50 years and requires Environmental Impact Assessments (EIAs) for all activities.
- Establishes Committee for Environmental Protection (CEP) to advise Parties on implementation. Technical annexes establish standards for, inter alia, EIAs, conservation of Antarctic fauna and flora, prevention of marine pollution.

F. LEGAL RESPONSE

1. OVERVIEW

As the forbidding continent of Antarctica gradually proved more accessible during the first half of this century, questions arose as to its legal status. Given the potentially vast rewards in the form of

mineral and living resources, seven countries made
various and conflicting claims of sovereignty. The
"claimant states," as these seven have become
known, were the United Kingdom (1908), New Zealand (1923), Australia (1933), France (1939), Norway (1939), Chile (1940) and Argentina (1942).
These countries based their claims on a diverse
assortment of theories, including the well-worn doctrine of "discovery" or "exploration," as well as
"contiguity" or proximity to the Antarctic land
mass. After World War II another group of five
countries—all with extensive contacts in the continent—asserted that they would neither maintain
nor acknowledge any territorial claims to Antarctica. Thus Belgium, Japan, South Africa, the
U.S.S.R. and the United States became known as
the "nonclaimant states."

Throughout the 1950's the dispute continued
over who would control Antarctica. Finally, in 1959
the twelve claimant and nonclaimant states met to
resolve their differences, eventually signing a compromise treaty. The result of these efforts, [the
Antarctic Treaty (1959 Antarctic Treaty), [Dec. 1,
1959, 19 I.L.M 860 (entered into force June 23,
1961)], has since given birth to a broader international regime for the continent, reflected in the
table above, which now includes the Convention for
the Conservation of Antarctic Seals (1972 Seals
Convention) [Feb. 11, 1972, 29 U.S.T. 441, 11
I.L.M. 251 (entered into force Mar. 11, 1978)]; the
Convention on the Conservation of Antarctic Ma-

rine Living Resources (CCAMLR), [May 20, 1980, 33 U.S.T. 3476, 19 I.L.M. 841 (entered into force Apr. 7, 1982)]; the Convention on the Regulation of Antarctic Mineral Resource Activities (CRAMRA), [June 2, 1988, 27 I.L.M. 859 (signed but unratified)]; and the 1991 Antarctic Environmental Protocol, Oct. 4, 1991, [30 I.L.M. 1461 (entered into force Jan. 14, 1998)].

It should be noted, however, that from the outset excluded nations have questioned the legal basis of the original parties to contract on behalf of the world community. To these nations, Antarctica exists as part of the "global commons," and though the treaty parties may bind themselves, they may not bind others who are not privy to their agreement. Though the number of parties to the 1959 Treaty has grown from the original 12 to 45 (as of Jan. 2003), it still remains unrepresentative of the entire international community as only nations who "conduct substantial scientific research" in the region achieve full voting status. Because of this exclusivity, some nations have suggested that the treaty system operates more as a "club" than an internationally sanctioned authority. Still, as the United Nations has not acted to co-opt or replace the present treaty system, it remains the sole governing regime for Antarctica [*see* Lee Kimball, *The Antarctic Treaty System*, *in* CONSERVATION AND MANAGEMENT OF MARINE MAMMALS 203 (J.R. Twiss & R. Reeves eds., 1999)].

2. THE 1959 ANTARCTIC TREATY

The 1959 convention only incidentally considers several environmental matters. More significantly, the treaty places in abeyance the territorial claims of all contracting parties—neither negating nor sustaining the former claims while at the same time providing that "[n]o new claim, or enlargement of any existing claim, ... be asserted while the present Treaty is in force" [art. IV]. In addition to the original "claimant" and "nonclaimant" states, the convention allows accession by any country, but again only those who conduct "substantial scientific research activity" in Antarctica may achieve full voting status [art. IX(2)]. In effect, this system has created two classes of participants to date: as of Jan. 2003, 27 Consultative Parties (voting) and 18 Non-consultative Parties (non-voting).

Concerning the environment, the treaty does prohibit nuclear explosions on the continent, as well as the disposal there of radioactive wastes [art. IV]. The treaty also names the "preservation and conservation of living resources" as a possible topic of further measures by the parties [art. IX(1)(f)]. The latter in fact led to the Certain Recommendations of Third Antarctic Treaty Consultative Meeting, Annex: Agreed Measures for the Conservation of Antarctic Fauna and Flora (1964 Agreed Measures), June 13, 1964, 17 U.S.T. 992. These measures designate the continent a "Special Conservation Area," and provide safeguards for both "specially protected species" and "specially protected areas" (these measures were later incorporated into the 1991 Antarctic Environmental Protocol). The 1964 Agreed Measures limit the taking of all animals, except with a permit, and disallow the issuing of a permit for "specially protected species" except for a "compelling scientific purpose" that neither threatens the ecosystem nor the survivability of that species [art. VI]. The 1964 Agreed Measures also severely limit the bringing into Antarctica of any non-indigenous plant or animal species [art. IX], and require that at all times parties take precautions not to disturb or disrupt the animals living there [art. VII].

Within "specially protected areas," parties have more stringent requirements. In these areas access is restricted, as parties must not allow their nationals to collect plants or drive vehicles except with a permit [art. VIII]. In 1989 the consultative parties added multiple-use planning areas (MPAs) to the protections offered under the 1959 Antarctic Treaty—establishing a larger zone for which parties must develop a management plan. In this way, and as altered and improved upon by the 1991 Antarctic Environmental Protocol, the treaty now requires the parties to work more closely together in the coordination of all activities within a given locale.

3. THE 1972 CONVENTION FOR THE CONSERVATION OF ANTARCTIC SEALS (1972 SEALS CONVENTION)

Within the 1959 Antarctic Treaty area, the 1972 Seals Convention limits harvesting of three species of seals (Crabeater, Leopard, Wedell), and prohibits harvesting of three others (Ross, Southern Elephant, Southern Fur seals). In point of fact, since the inception of the convention no commercial sealing has taken place—whether driven by the convention itself, politics or economics. As a result, the convention remains something of a "sleeping treaty"—but not one with the negative connotation that the term usually implies.

In addition to the harvesting measures, the convention creates a closed season and a sealing season, and stipulates sealing zones (which allow limited taking) and sealing reserves (which do not) for the harvestable species. A loophole, however, exists with regard to all seal species, for which a party may issue a special permit that allows taking for reasons of scientific research or to provide specimens for museums, educational or cultural institutions [art. 4(1)(b)–(c)]. If a party issues a permit under article 4, it must then report the number of seals killed or captured under these permits to the Scientific Committee on Antarctic Research (SCAR) [art. 4(2)]. SCAR also remains in charge of assessing the annual reports of the parties, as well as suggesting amendments to its technical provisions.

Should nations decide to resume commercial sealing in Antarctica, the parties would have to reconcile the provisions of the 1972 Seals Convention with those of the 1991 Antarctic Environmental Protocol (see below).

4. 1980 CONVENTION ON THE CONSER- VATION OF ANTARCTIC MARINE LIV- ING RESOURCES (1980 CCAMLR)

The objective of the 1980 CCAMLR is the con- servation of all living resources found south of the Antarctic Convergence, encompassing "fin fish, mollusks, crustaceans and all other species of liv- ing organisms, including birds" [art. I(2)]. In ef- fect, the CCAMLR provides an early, rather rudi- mentary example of the ecosystem approach to conservation—an approach that aspires to protect the ecosystems as a whole rather than focusing on individual species. The treaty, though not defining conservation, explains that the terms "includes ra- tional use" and lists "the following principles of conservation:

(a) prevention of decrease in the size of any harvested population to levels below those which ensure its stable recruitment. For this purpose its size should not be allowed to fall below a level close to that which ensures the greatest net annual increment;

(b) maintenance of the ecological relationships between the harvested, dependent and re- lated populations of Antarctic marine living resources and the restoration of depleted populations to the levels defined in subpar- agraph (a) above; and

(c) prevention of changes or minimization of the risk of changes in the maritime ecosys- tem which are not potentially reversible over two or three decades, taking into account the state of available knowledge of the direct and indirect impact of harvesting, the effect of the introduction of alien species, the effects of associated activities on the marine ecosystem and of the effects of environmental changes, with the aim of making possible the sustained conservation of Antarctic marine living resources."

[CCAMLR art. II(3)]. The treaty thus mandates a method of conservation that focuses on specific species, the interrelation between species, and the entire marine ecosystem. In addition, the mention of "sustained conservation" suggests an early move toward the concept of "sustainable development" in international law.

In order to implement these principles, the treaty creates two significant institutions—the Commission and the Scientific Committee. The Scientific Committee acts as the consultative body to the Commission, making recommendations concerning conservation matters [art. XV]. Here the CCAMLR makes an early gesture toward environmental impact assessment, requiring that among its duties the Scientific Committee gauge the "effects of proposed changes in the methods or levels of harvesting and proposed conservation measures" [art. XV(2)(d)]. The Commission then acts on the Scientific Committee's recommendations at its annual meeting, including the formulation of specific measures on the quantity of harvesting, method of harvesting, and the designation of protected species [art. IX].

Interestingly, the CCAMLR binds its contracting parties to the important provisions of the 1959 Antarctic Treaty—whether or not they are parties to that treaty [art. III, IV]. The CCAMLR also requires its parties to adhere, "when appropriate," to the 1964 Agreed Measures [art. V(2)]. The convention, however, makes clear that it does not derogate from the rights and obligations under either the International Convention for the Regulation of Whaling (ICRW) [Dec. 2, 1946, 161 U.N.T.S. 366 (entered into force Nov. 10, 1948)], or the 1972 Antarctic Seals Convention. The CCAMLR also remains intact after the 1991 Antarctic Environmental Protocol, though the parties to both must cooperatively reconcile the differences between the two instruments.

5.   1988 ANTARCTIC MINERAL RESOURCES CONVENTION (CRAMRA)

In contrast to the CCAMLR, CRAMRA never received the full support of its own signing parties, as both France and Australia refused to ratify the instrument because it appeared too weak in terms of its protection. Originally intended to establish a framework for ascertaining whether the wise utilization of Antarctic lands included the prospecting, exploration and development of minerals resources, CRAMRA in its final form set forth an extensive range of measures aimed at protecting the environment. In fact, the CRAMRA's provisions concerning liability for environmental damage, environmental impact assessment, and dispute resolution will continue to serve as models for future international environmental law treaties. In the end, however, the convention never came into force and so remains a dead letter, presumably supplanted forever by the 1991 Antarctic Environmental Protocol.

6. 1991 ANTARCTIC ENVIRONMENT PROTOCOL

As CRAMRA's prospects faded, and amid growing fears that the continent faced imminent environmental degradation, the Antarctic Treaty Consultative Parties chose to create an environmental protocol to the 1959 treaty. The 1991 Protocol, broad and ambitious in scope, incorporates a number of progressive environmental ideals and principles. Most significantly, the protocol establishes Antarctica as a "natural reserve, devoted to peace and science" and commits the parties "to the comprehensive protection of the Antarctic environment and dependent and associated ecosystems" [art. 2]. Though some nations lobbied for the designation of the continent as a "World Park"—a designation which presumably would offer greater protection—the classification of Antarctica as a natural reserve marks the first for any substantial area within the global commons. Among other principles the protocol places a premium on the planning and conducting of activities so as not to cause significant harm—an objective mandating prior assessment, effective monitoring and cooperation among the parties. Furthermore, the protocol acknowledges the intrinsic value of the continent, including its wilderness, aesthetic and scientific values [art. 3(1)]. In fact, some critics see an over-emphasis on scientific value, worrying that the "priority" given to scientific research in articles 3(1) & 3(3) could outweigh the prohibition against causing significant harm.

As for substantive requirements, the protocol adopts a 50 year moratorium on "any activity relating to mineral resources, other than scientific research" [art. 7]. Thus the protocol forbids all mineral exploration except that done for scientific purposes. While some parties sought a permanent ban on such activities, others, notably the United States, preferred some flexibility to pursue mineral resources in the future. As a result, after 50 years any Consultative Party may call a Review Conference to amend art. 7 (or any other provision), at which the parties may adopt any such amendment by a weighted majority [art. 25]. Otherwise, to change the moratorium before the expiration of the 50 year period, only the unanimous consent of the Consultative Parties will suffice [arts. 25(1); 12(1)(a) & (b)].

Other substantive provisions include the establishing of contingency plans in response to environmental emergencies [art. 15] and the filing of annual reports by each party outlining the measures it has taken to comply with the protocol's various requirements [art. 17]. In this regard, the protocol creates no international authority to verify and enforce compliance, instead relying on the adoption of national measures by the individual parties. The protocol does, however, create a Committee for Environmental Protection (CEP)—the primary function of which is "to provide advise and formulate recommendations" to the Antarctic Treaty Consultative Meetings on the specific operations of the protocol [arts. 11–12]. In general, CEP must oversee, though not verify or enforce, the more detailed substantive requirements found in the protocol's annexes. To date, annexes have been adopted on Environmental Impact Assessment [Annex I], Conservation of Antarctic Fauna and Flora [Annex II], Waste Disposal and Waste Management [Annex III], Prevention of Marine Pollution [Annex IV], and Area Protection and Management [Annex V].

(a) Environmental Impact Assessment (EIA)

The protocol makes EIA an integral part of each party's obligation to protect the ecosystem, subjecting all relevant activities to the assessment procedures set out in Annex I [art. 8]. Though the procedures themselves are fairly detailed, the parties conduct the evaluations without international oversight. First, if an activity is determined to have "less than a minor or transitory impact," then no further assessment need take place and the activity may proceed [Annex I, art. 1(2)]. If, however, the party cannot make such a determination, then it must prepare an Initial Environmental Evaluation

(IEE). Again, the purpose of the IEE—which in-cludes a consideration of alternatives and impacts—is to assess whether the activity will have "less than a minor or transitory impact" [Annex I, art. 2]. If the IEE suggests the activity may have more than minor repercussions, then the party must prepare a much more extensive draft Comprehensive Environ-mental Evaluation (CEE). The draft CEE must con-tain very thorough investigations and conclusions about the possible impacts through the entire dura-tion of the activity and beyond [Annex I, art. 3].

The party then must allow public comment for a period of 90 days while simultaneously forwarding the draft CEE to the CEP for consideration [Annex I, art. 3]. If the CEP chooses, it may then pass the document on to the Antarctic Treaty Consultative Meeting for further consideration [Annex I, art. 3]. In effect the party always retains the right to go forward with its proposed activity, but only after intense public scrutiny at various levels. Finally, if the party does go forward after preparation of a final CEE, it must continue to monitor the activity, assessing and verifying the project's consequences [Annex I, art. 5].

(b) Conservation of Antarctic Fauna and Flora

The protocol also includes an Annex on the con-servation of plants and animals, which revises the relevant provisions of the 1964 Agreed Measures. In keeping with the protocol's focus on national con-trol, each party oversees its own endeavors and issues its own permits through an appropriate authority. Annex II prohibits the taking of, or harmful interference with, both fauna and flora except with a permit (the 1964 Agreed Measures had concentrated on fauna) [Annex II, art. 3]. The Annex additionally contains an Appendix A which lists "Specially Protected Species" which cannot be taken without a permit, and then only for a "compelling scientific purpose" that neither jeopardizes the species nor uses lethal force [Annex II, art. 3(5)]. Further, the Annex precludes the introduction of exogenous plants and animals except with a permit and for all species but those listed in an Appendix B [Annex II, art. 4]. In actuality Appendix B names very broad categories—"domestic plants" and "laboratory animals and plants including viruses, bacteria, yeast and fungi"—thus the requirement remains primarily one of applying for a permit. And lastly, in a devastating blow to polar companionship, the Annex outlaws dogs from the continent, banning all canines from the Antarctic Treaty Area as of 1994 [Annex II, art. 4(2)].

(c) Waste Disposal and Management

In Annex III the parties have attempted to deal with the difficult problem of waste from human activities in Antarctica. As general obligations each party must strive to reduce the amount of wastes, to remove wastes, and to clean up past and present disposal and work sites [Annex III art. I]. More specifically, the annex creates three categories of wastes requiring different disposal methods. First, the most hazardous wastes—such as radioactive materials, fuel, and acutely toxic wastes—must be removed by the generating party [Annex III, art. 2(1)]. Second, for less hazardous liquid wastes and sewage and domestic liquid wastes, the generating party must work to remove these from the continent "to the maximum extent practicable" [Annex III, art. 2(2)]. Concerning other waste disposal on land the annex allows no disposal onto ice-free areas or into fresh water systems [Annex III, art. 4(1)], and "to the maximum extent practicable" no disposal of article 2(2) wastes onto ice-covered areas except by stations into deep-ice pits [Annex III, art. 4(2)]. On the other hand a party may still discharge sewage and domestic liquid wastes directly into the sea in most circumstances [Annex III, art. 5].

(d) Prevention of Marine Pollution

Annex IV of the protocol creates rules for the prevention of pollution from ships in the Antarctic Treaty Area. The annex applies to all ships flying a party's flag and to any other ship engaged in Antarctic operations [Annex IV, art. 2], but not to warships or other ships owned and operated by a state-party and used for government service [Annex IV, art. 11]. The annex envisions four specific types of discharges, that of oil, noxious liquid substances, garbage and sewage. For oil, the annex prohibits the release of oil or oily mixture from a ship, except in cases permitted under Annex I of MARPOL 73/78 [Annex IV, art. 3; *see* Chapter Eleven, Vessel–Based Pollution]. The prohibition does not apply to discharge due to damage to a ship or its equipment. For noxious substances—a category of more hazardous substances—the annex disallows discharge in any amount causing harm to the marine environment [Annex IV, art. 4]. Similarly all garbage release remains prohibited except for food wastes, which each ship must discharge at least 12 nautical miles from land or the nearest ice shelf [Annex IV, art. 5]. As for sewage, a ship may not dispose of any untreated wastes at sea within 12 nautical miles of land or ice-shelves, except where such a prohibition would "unduly impair" Antarctic operations [Annex IV, art. 6]. The qualifier, "unduly impair," obviously allows flexibility on the part of each party's implementation of article 6.

The annex further states that it does not derogate from any specific rights and obligations under MARPOL 73/78 [Annex IV, art. 14], and requires the parties to develop contingency plans for combating marine pollution, including oil spills from ships [Annex IV, art. 12].

(e) Area Protection and Management

In Annex V the protocol clarifies and updates the 1964 Agreed Measures, as well as later adoptions of the consultative parties, concerning area protection and management. The annex offers two types of designations—Antarctic Specially Protected Areas (ASPAs) and Antarctic Specially Managed Areas (ASMAs). An area may be approved as an ASPA so as "to protect outstanding environmental values, scientific, historic, aesthetic or wilderness values, any combination of those values, or ongoing or planned scientific research" [Annex V, art. 3]. The primary protection afforded by an ASPA designation, which includes areas formerly designated Specially Protected Areas and Sites of Special Scientific Interest, is to prohibit all access except by a permit [Annex V, art. 3]. On the other hand an ASMA, which may include one or more ASPAs, does not require a permit for entry but instead seeks to coordinate activities and improve cooperation among the parties [Annex V, art. 4]. A third designation, which is not an area designation as such, allows a party to propose a site or monument of recognized historic value as a Historic Site or Monument [Annex V, art. 8]. The value of such a listing protects these locations from damage, removal or destruction [Annex V, art. 8(4)].

To propose an area designation, any party (or certain institutions within the treaty system) must submit a detailed Management Plan to the Antarctic Treaty Consultative Meeting [Annex V, art. 5]. The Management Plan should contain the necessary measures to protect each area as appropriate, and the annex provides extensive guidelines in this regard. Thus the annex contains considerable potential protections, but again potential pitfalls remain. Perhaps the most significant drawback—a further example of the emphasis on national enforcement throughout the protocol—exists in the reliance on each party's appointment of "an appropriate authority" to issue permits for access to the critical ASPAs [Annex V, art. 7]. This of course leaves a great deal of discretion to the individual interpreter concerning what activities do and do not take place within the most fragile areas of the continent. As of January 2003, 26 out of in total 27 consultative parties had accepted or approved Annex V. The acceptance or approval of one additional consultative party (India) must occur before Annex V can enter into force.

The United States has ratified the 1991 Antarctic Environment Protocol, passing implementing legislation in September 1996. The bill, The Antarctic Science, Tourism, and Conservation Act of 1996 [16 U.S.C.A. §§ 2403a, 2413] [H.R.3060], mandates the application of the National Environmental Policy Act (NEPA) [16 U.S.C.A. §§ 2401, et. seq.]. Procedures for all governmental and non-governmental activities on the continent.

CHAPTER NINE

TOXIC AND HAZARDOUS SUBSTANCES

A. NATURE OF THE PROBLEM

Large quantities of almost any chemical substance can harm humans, living organisms, and the environment. Toxic and hazardous substances, on the other hand, can cause significant damage in small, even minuscule, amounts. There is no universally adopted or accepted definition of a hazardous or toxic substance, despite the fact that they are among the pollutants responsible for transboundary air and water pollution, as well as land-based pollution and dumping. Overlapping definitions and meanings attached to them have resulted in the terms toxic and hazardous being used interchangeably, conjunctively, and even disjunctively.

In general, the toxicity of a substance is identified by a number of factors including the length of time it will persist in the environment, how it tends to bioaccumulate or build up in the tissues of lower species, the extent to which it reacts with other substances to form a more harmful contaminant, and whether it produces a carcinogenic (cancer-causing), mutagenic (gene-altering), or teratogenic (birth defect-causing) effect in humans [G. TYLER

MILLER, LIVING IN THE ENVIRONMENT 397–402 (12th ed. 2002)]. Similarly, a chemical substance is considered hazardous where it exhibits certain characteristics that can cause injury, disease, economic loss, or environmental damage [Id. 46–53].

The two terms have been variably defined even within national legal systems. For example, in the United States the term "hazardous" is defined differently for each class of pollutant and for differing regulatory schemes within a plethora of controlling statutes that include: the Occupational Safety and Health Act, 29 U.S.C.A. §§ 651–678 (West 2003); Clean Air Act, 42 U.S.C.A. §§ 7401–7671 (West 2003); Clean Water Act, 33 U.S.C.A. §§ 1251–1376 (West 2003); Federal Insecticide, Fungicide, and Rodenticide Act, 7 U.S.C.A. §§ 136–136y (West 2003); Toxic Substances Control Act, 15 U.S.C.A. §§ 2601–2629 (West 2003); Hazardous Materials Transportation Act, 49 U.S.C.A. §§ 5101–5127 (West 2003); Federal Hazardous Substance Act, 15 U.S.C.A. §§ 1261–1276 (West 2003); Resource Conservation and Recovery Act of 1976 (RCRA), 42 U.S.C.A. §§ 6901–6991k (West 2003); and the Comprehensive Environmental Response, Compensation and Liability Act (CERCLA or Superfund), 42 U.S.C.A. §§ 9601–9675 (West 2003).

Specifically, hazardous waste is defined by RCRA as any solid waste which because of its concentration, quantity, or physical, chemical, or infectious characteristics may cause or significantly contribute to an increase in mortality or contribute to irreversible or incapacitating illness [RCRA, 42 U.S.C.A.

§ 6903]. Hazardous air pollutants are defined by the Clean Air Act as air pollutants which may present a threat of adverse health effects, including those substances which may be carcinogenic, mutagenic, teratogenic, neurotoxic, or those that cause adverse environmental effects through bioaccumulation or deposition [42 U.S.C.A. § 4712 (b)(2)(B)].

A few salient developments surrounding hazardous and toxic substances shed light on the meaning of those terms. First, if a material is regulated domestically, it will also be treated as hazardous under the Basel Convention on the Control of Transboundary Movements of Hazardous Wastes and their Disposal (Basel Convention) [Mar. 22, 1989, 28 I.L.M. 657 (entered into force May 5, 1992)], and the Bamako Convention on the Ban of Import into Africa and the Control of Trans-boundary Movement and Management of Hazardous Wastes Within Africa (BamakoConvention) [Jan. 29, 1991, 30 I.L.M. 775]. Second, the Basel Convention defines hazardous waste to include substances which are explosive, flammable, oxidizing, poisonous, infectious, corrosive, toxic, ecotoxic, or any substance capable of forming another material which possesses any of the previous characteristics after disposal [Annex 3]. Third, in addition to contaminants that possess these characteristics, a number of treaties such as the Basel Convention, [art. 1 & Annex I] and the Bamako Convention [art. 2 & Annex I] contain a list of wastes that have previously been identified as hazardous, including medical waste, organic chemicals or hydrocarbons, radioactive wastes, and materials that contain traces of heavy metals.

B. SOURCES

About 95 percent of all hazardous pollutants are created by industries that generate four primary groups of toxic and hazardous chemicals. They are: toxic metals, petrochemicals, pesticides and radioactive materials (a discussion of radiation is excluded from this chapter because it is dealt with in Chapter Seventeen).

Toxic metals include heavy metals and trace metals. Heavy metals are those metals such as mercury, cadmium and lead which are at least five times as dense as water. Trace metals are those metals present in the environment or the human body in very low concentrations such as zinc, copper and iron [JOHN B SULLIVAN, JR. & GARY R. KRIEGER EDS., CLINICAL ENVIRONMENTAL HEALTH AND TOXIC EXPOSURE 13 (2nd ED. 2001)]. Metals are present in nearly all rock types, are concentrated in ores, and enter the environment naturally through erosion and volcanic activity. Human activities have altered the natural cycle of metals and in many instances contributions from humans surpass those from natural sources. Metals, for example, are natural contaminants of coal and oil and when burned these fuels release vast quantities of metals into the air. Ore refining, trash burning and cement production also result in airborne metals. Additionally, discarded materials in dumps can leak metals into underground aquifers and groundwater, while arsenic and cadmium, found in pesticides and fertilizers, can enter our waters through run-off.

Humans use petrochemicals in goods as varied as food, medicine, cosmetics, lumber, household appliances, fuels, plastics, papers and innumerable other manufactured products. Chemical compounds are divided into two groups: organic and inorganic. Organic compounds are based on carbon atoms usually in combination with hydrogen, and the better known include ethylene, methylene chloride, formaldehyde, benzene, DDT, and polychlorinated biphenyls (PCB's). Inorganic compounds are not based on carbon, and examples of such substances include sulfuric acid, aluminum, and chromium. Chemical products enter the environment in a number of ways. The principal among these are intentional use as in the case of pesticides, incidental and operational releases of liquid discharges and gaseous emissions during the manufacturing process, accidental spills, and waste disposal.

Most pesticides are produced by the petrochemical industry, but their importance as a source of pollution arising from individual and agricultural use calls for separate treatment. Approximately 2.3 million metric tons per year of these pesticides are used worldwide to kill, repel, or control undesirable living organisms including rodents, insects, weeds, molds, bacteria, worms and birds [G. TYLER MILLER, LIVING IN THE ENVIRONMENT 503 (12th ed. 2002)].

Humans use pesticides as pest killers, and to date over 50,000 pesticide products exist. They include: insecticides (insects), herbicides (plants), fungicides (molds and mildew), rodenticides (rats and mice), acaricides (mites and ticks), bactericides (bacteria), avicides (birds), and nematicides (roundworms).

The most widely used insecticides fall into one of four chemical groups: organochlorines, organosphosphates, carbamates and botanicals. The most dangerous of these are organochlorines (chlorinated hydrocarbons) which contain chlorine, carbon, and hydrogen. Examples of organochlorines include insecticides such as DDT, chlordane, lindane, aldrin/dieldrin, and heptachlor. These compounds are considered persistent because they do not readily break down in the environment. They also tend to bioaccumulate in plant and animal tissues [JOHN B SULLIVAN, JR. & GARY R. KRIEGER EDS., CLINICAL ENVIRONMENTAL HEALTH AND TOXIC EXPOSURE 1057–1081 (2nd ED. 2001)].

Pesticides contain both inert and active ingredients. The active ingredient is the portion of the chemical that actually kills or controls the target organism [TRAVIS WAGNER, IN OUR BACKYARD 239–49 (1994)]. Presently, 700 active ingredients function within the 50,000 different types of pesticides on the market. Because pesticides are designed to kill a broad spectrum of organisms, they present a threat not only to the target organism but also to other animals, including humans [WORLD RESOURCE INSTITUTE, WORLD RESOURCES 1994–95 113 (1994)]. Unfortunately, less than 0.1 percent of insecticides and 5 percent of herbicides applied to crops by spraying actually reach the target organism. The remaining chemicals become toxic contaminants as they vaporize into air, run off into water, or leach into soil and groundwater [G. TYLER MILLER, LIVING IN THE ENVIRONMENT 507 (12th ed. 2002)].

C. ENVIRONMENTAL IMPACTS & PATHWAYS

1. IMPACTS

Toxics often impact ecological food chains by bioaccumulating in the tissues of aquatic organisms. The process of bioaccumulation begins when a toxic contaminant present in the soil or water is absorbed by plants that are later ingested by a lower animal. If not readily excreted by it, the contaminant will gradually increase in that animal beyond the level of the surrounding environment. This process of growing accumulation continues up the food chain. Generally, the higher the concentration of a toxic substance in the environment, the more it will be taken up by plants and passed from plants to plant-eating animals, culminating in very high concentrations in predatory animals [JOHN B SULLIVAN, JR. & GARY R. KRIEGER EDS., CLINICAL ENVIRONMENTAL HEALTH AND TOXIC EXPOSURE 17 (2nd ED. 2001)].

In the 1960's, for example, in the United States bald eagles, peregrine falcons, and other predatory animals died as a result of reproductive failure caused by excess DDT in their tissues. These birds did not feed on the farmlands where farmers had originally used DDT, but on fish that were at the end of a long food chain in which DDT had bioaccumulated. Rain run-off had carried the DDT into lakes and ponds where the pesticide passed from algae to plankton, eventually aggregating in fish which retained rather than excreted the poison. Finally the birds that fed on these fish developed even higher concentrations of the deadly chemical.

High concentrations of toxic metals in the environment also present a danger to human health. Metals are a unique contaminant because they are elemental compounds that never decompose. Therefore, they remain a threat that can resurface at any time. Human activities that move these elements into the air, water, and soil may create concentrations toxic to humans. The tragedy that took place in Minamata, Japan, in the 1950's offers a painful example. Japanese villagers in the fishing village of Minamata were poisoned by mercury (a heavy metal) that had been discharged into the water by a nearby chemical company, and had bioaccumulated in fish eaten by the villagers. This resulted in approximately fifty deaths and several thousand cases of permanent nervous disorders.

Toxic metals like mercury, cadmium, lead, and arsenic find their way into the air through the burning of coal and oil for energy, ore refining, trash burning, cement production, and the use of automobiles [JOHN HARTE, ET AL., TOXICS A TO Z 116–118 (1991)]. These elements can also leach into the soil and water when metal-containing products are buried in landfills. Fertilizers and pesticides often contain arsenic and cadmium which can run off into surface waters and may eventually end up in groundwater. The specific health effects of high metal levels in humans depend on both the type of metal and the organ involved. Lead poisoning can cause convulsions, brain damage or degeneration, and death. Arsenic, beryllium, cadmium, and chromium cause lung cancer. Long term exposure to metal dust may result in the formation of scar tissue in the lungs or cystic fibrosis [G. TYLER MILLER supra at 472; HARTE supra at 104.

Toxic chemicals are believed to cause long term health effects in humans, like cancer and cirrhosis of the liver, at low dosages over a long period of time. DDT and other organochlorine insecticides pose the greatest threat to human health because they persist in the environment from 2–15 years and tend to bioaccumulate in food chains [WORLD RESOURCE INSTITUTE, WORLD RESOURCES 1998–99 114 (1999)]. Rarely used in the United States now, these chemicals still remain in extensive use in lesser developed countries that export a large amount of agricultural products. One notorious type of organochlorine herbicide, 2,4,5–T or Agent Orange, contains dioxin, one of the most toxic chemicals ever made by humans. Studies indicate that dioxin can cause soft-tissue sarcoma, Hodgkin's disease, fetal death, and birth defects [HARTE supra at 116–18 (1991); MILLER supra at 554–55. Organophosphate and carbamate insecticides find more frequent use in the United States. These types do not bioaccumulate and tend to break down more quickly, though often they remain more acutely toxic to vertebrate animals.

Toxic and hazardous wastes take many forms: liquid, solid, semi-solid (sludge), and containerized gas. They are neutralized or sequestered through various physical, chemical, and biological processes of treatment and disposal. Some physical waste treatment or remediation technologies change the form of the waste and reduce its volume and weight. Biological and chemical facilities use living organisms (microorganisms) to stabilize waste materials employing aerobic (oxygen-using) and anaerobic (non-oxygen-using) methods [ENCYCLOPEDIA OF THE ENVIRONMENT: ACID RAIN-ZONING 314–315, 795–803 (Ruth Eblan & William Eblan eds., 2000)]. During remediation, the treatment process itself can constitute a source of pollution by creating gaseous and solid residues that need to be discharged into landfills, underground injection wells, or the oceans.

A typical example of treatment is to place the waste in large surface impoundments such as pits, ponds, or lagoons where it is filtered, solidified, degraded, or neutralized. If not properly lined, however, the surface impoundment or landfill may leach or migrate into the groundwater. Also, the waste may simply run off into surface waters if the cap on the structure breaks down. With regard to household waste and small scale industrial waste, because the generator's quantities remain small these wastes are not typically treated as hazardous waste, and therefore these often end up in landfills not designed to prevent migration into surface or groundwaters [TRAVIS WAGNER, IN OUR BACKYARD 135–36 (1994)].

Incineration is a more expensive method of treatment and disposal, in which wastes are burned at high temperatures. Depending upon the waste involved, incineration may offer a relatively safe disposal method, though the ash generated can contain toxic materials that require disposal. Furthermore, in some circumstances toxic gaseous and particulate materials may escape at harmful levels. [SULLIVAN and KRIEGER supra at 628.

Wastes are also discharged into water bodies, such as rivers, lakes and estuaries. Where hazardous and toxic chemicals are so disposed we have seen how they can bioaccumulate in the tissues of aquatic organisms. When humans consume animals with elevated concentrations of contaminants in their tissues the result may be serious health effects or even death [MILLER supra at 325].

Wastes not successfully dealt with by any other means may be stored in waste piles or tanks and then disposed of in landfills, in surface impoundments, or in deep wells. Deep-well injection involves the pumping of liquid waste into a well or a geologic formation located below underground sources of drinking water. Unfortunately, injected hazardous wastes may eventually migrate into the groundwater through cracks or fissures [HARTE supra at 161.

2. PATHWAYS

We have dealt with the environmental movements, or the routes or journeys traveled by chemicals through air, water or land, and their advance through food chains. By pathways we now refer to their points of entry into, and passage through human bodies toward target organs, giving rise to disease and illness. Human intake of pollutants discharged into the environment may occur through three routes. A person may inhale a substance, ingest it through water or food, or absorb it through the skin.

Once it enters the bloodstream, the contaminant circulates to all of the organs in the body. However, the extent of harm depends on the concentration and type of contaminant present. Some contaminants are easily metabolized by the body and become detoxified. Other contaminants, typically cancer-causing substances, become more toxic after metabolization. This is called bio-activation. The body may also reduce the toxic effect of a substance by storing it in fat tissue, but adverse effects may still occur if the body utilizes a large amount of fat for energy at one time. The acute effects of a contaminant may disappear because a number of chemicals will naturally bind with proteins in the bloodstream, thereby reducing the amount free to attack a certain organ. Nonetheless, this process may result in a chronic effect because the chemical may stay in the body longer, becoming unbound and harmful at a later date.

All substances can become toxic if they impact humans in sufficient concentrations, and scientists engaged in ascertaining the risk posed by a chemical try to measure the linkage between exposure to a chemical and disease by employing both epidemiological and toxicological data. Epidemiology involves the study of human populations to discover the relationship between various risk factors and the occurrence of disease in that population. Toxicology uses data collected from laboratory experiments on animals, bacteria, and cell or tissue cultures to identify the mechanism of disease and the way that the contaminant causes harm.

Establishing linkages is particularly difficult for a number of reasons. The potency of a substance, the degree of exposure, and the fact that certain groups of people are more sensitive to particular toxic substances complicates such assessments. A fourth difficulty exists for toxicological data derived from high dosages administered to test animals. A researcher must extrapolate such high dosages onto a fact situation involving humans, who possess different metabolisms than animals, and whose contact occurs at a lower level of the suspect substance [SULLIVAN, supra at 49–51].

Real-life exposure to toxic and hazardous contaminants can result in both chronic and acute health effects in humans. Acute effects, such as skin burns, rashes, and kidney damage, appear shortly after introduction to a large dose or concentration of a contaminant. Chronic effects are those which do not appear initially, but tend to last for many years after long-term exposure to low concentration levels or short-term exposure to extremely high concentrations [MILLER, supra at 450]. Contact with certain types of toxic or hazardous contaminants can result in chronic health effects such as cancer, inheritable diseases, birth defects, heart and lung disease, and nerve or behavioral disorders. Carcinogens remain extremely difficult to identify because of the complex nature of cancer as a disease and the broad range of chemicals and environmental factors encountered by humans. To date, common examples of these substances include asbestos, carbon tetrachloride, arsenic, and benzene. Mutagens, such as benzo-pyrene and ozone, can alter an organism's genetic code resulting in cancers or inheritable diseases like cystic fibrosis. Other chemicals and certain metals, including lead, cadmium, arsenic and mercury are classified as teratogens. [HARTE, supra at 30–33].

D.   REMEDIAL OBJECTIVES

Hazardous chemicals and wastes are the inevitable consequence of modern living. The life style enjoyed in developed countries depends to a significant degree on the use of chemicals for a variety of purposes. So many of the goods taken for granted— ranging from simple articles like knives, forks, and instant food, to more complex machines such as motor cars or computers—involve the use of chemicals. Chemicals are used in the extraction and refining of raw materials needed for these products as well as in the manufacturing and packaging process. They also find their way into the environment when these products are discarded or dumped.

The dangers associated with the use of hazardous or toxic chemicals and the waste they create can be controlled by a number of strategies. A primary goal should be to reduce demand for products that entail the use of such substances. Demand management exists as a painful but necessary step in any concerted attempt to find solutions. Second, it is necessary to adopt a comprehensive view of the problem by regulating and managing local, regional and global material and energy flows in products, processes and industrial sectors. Third, and this may be the more practicable of the objectives, integrated as distinct from fragmented pollution controls should be adopted.

Many international conventions have attempted to control pollution within the environmental media (air, land or water) in which it is found. Such a fragmented approach fails for a number of reasons. It concentrates on moving the pollution generated by polluting activities from one place to another. Unfortunately, such pollution transfers ignore the basic law of physics that matter is indestructible. The initial destination of pollutants may be altered, but ultimately they re-enter the flow of material within the environment.

Limitations on discharges in one medium, such as air, while correcting the immediate pollution problem within that medium, often do little more than shift the pollution from air to land without recognizing the adverse impact of transferred pollution. Such transfers can create even greater problems in the medium to which they are moved. Thus, control technologies aimed at achieving specific limits to pollution generate new streams of residuals which have adverse effects on other media. This is evidenced by the massive quantities of sludge created by existing pollution controls in the United States. For example, the provisions of the United States Clean Air Act directed at reducing sulphur dioxide had required the use of 'scrubbers' in smoke stacks. Huge quantities of lime, limestone solution, and water are sprayed on exhaust gases as they flow up power plant smokestacks. Sulphur dioxide in the gas then reacts with the spray and forms a solution from which the sulphur dioxide is later removed, strained, and disposed of in the form of sludge. The Environmental Protection Agency (EPA) has estimated that three to six tons of scrubber sludge may be produced for each ton of sulphur dioxide removed from the flue gas. Consequently, the problem of sulphur dioxide in the air has been replaced by the problem of sludge disposal. Municipal wastewater treatment and sewage treatment plants also produce large quantities of sludge. Some of this sludge contains toxic substances which are nondegradable and bioaccumulable.

Direct transfers are compounded by indirect transfers resulting from physical, chemical, and biological forces. Usually, fragmented controls assess the risk of a pollutant on the basis of a single chemical causing exposure in a single medium, but they do not consider the extent to which the risk to people is multiplied when subject to exposure in different mediums. Most international treaties ignore the multi-media risk posed by even a single substance. The bewildering and aggravated risk presented by the synergistic effects of thousands of substances circulating in the environment simply falls outside the pale of reckoning.

The present fragmented approach also lacks economic efficiency. Pollution controls already in place ensure that wastes cannot be discharged according to the best environmental option. This may led to inefficient use of the assimilative capacity of the environment. In the example previously considered we observed how the implementation of the Clean Air Act might lead to the creation of large quantities of sludge. Sludge can be disposed of in a number of ways. It can be discharged into a river or directly into the sea, or piped into a lagoon to settle and dry out as solid waste. What is germane is the possibility that current air pollution requirements might lead to water discharges, or solid waste disposal problems that cause greater overall damage to the environment than might be the case if the air pollution standards had been cognizant of cross-media impacts. In addition, water pollution and land waste disposal laws also could prevent the discharges into water or disposal as solid waste without further treatment. Setting independent standards for each medium that ignore the assimilative capacity of the environment imposes unnecessary and unjustified costs on the manufacturing process.

A more efficient and cost effective method of pollution control would be to distribute the wastes between the three media of water, air, and land in a manner that makes optimum use of the environment, and of any special or particular assimilative capacity it might possess. This policy would lead to a balanced approach to pollution control which would avoid the problems of standards that are overly stringent in some areas and unduly lax in others.

An increasingly urgent need for safe and cost efficient methods of disposal has arisen as industrialized countries continue to strengthen regulations on the disposal of hazardous waste. In the past, industrialized countries have either dumped this waste directly into the ocean or buried it on land, but increased awareness of the dangers associated with these methods led to strict regulation, forcing industries to look to lesser developed countries for a solution.

Industry has targeted countries located primarily in Africa, Latin America, and the Caribbean because these countries normally have less stringent pollution control regulations and are usually more willing to accept these wastes as a method to raise revenues. The cost of disposing of wastes in these countries is usually significantly lower than either instituting waste minimization techniques at the source or utilizing an approved disposal facility located in the generating country.

Obviously, however, this practice is not a solution to the waste problem because it merely transfers the environmental cost from industry to a group of people less qualified to bear it. Most countries that import hazardous wastes lack information as to the risks these wastes pose to human health and the environment, and also lack the knowledge or administrative capacity to manage them properly. In fact, in the past many countries have accepted hazardous chemicals for use and disposal without knowing that the chemicals have been banned in the generating country. Because of this overall lack of knowledge, developing countries may utilize disposal techniques that are not adequate to control the risks that these wastes present to their citizens and their environment. In addition to the dangers posed by improper disposal techniques, the long distance transportation of hazardous wastes across land and water presents an increased risk of harm to transit states and the marine environment from accidental spillage.

Waste trade with developing countries continues to decline as industrialized countries have developed and utilized waste minimization techniques. Further, nations have enacted a number of treaties and regional agreements in order to deal with the problems associated with the trade of hazardous waste. As we shall see, treaties such as the Basel Convention indicate that these countries increasingly agree to dispose of hazardous wastes at the source as long as the disposal can take place in an environmentally sound manner [arts. 4(2) (c), (d), (e), (g), 7, 8].

Therefore, both the Basel and Bamako Conventions allow for trade between similarly situated party states, but only if the exporting state lacks the capacity to dispose of the waste in an environmentally sound manner and the importing state gives its Prior Informed Consent (PIC) (see below). The importing state must also possess the ability to dispose of the waste in an environmentally sound manner and if an illegal trade occurs, the exporting state must accept the waste for re-import [Basel, arts. 6, 9; Bamako, arts. 4, 6, 7, 9]

These conventions correctly seized the basic concepts underlying an integrated approach when they called upon all parties to reduce the generation of hazardous and toxic wastes to a minimum. This can only be done by reducing the source of such wastes and "sources" embrace demand for a product. They also call for "environmentally sound management" which opens the door to integrated pollution control. Unfortunately, as detailed below, these requirements are left in the soft limbo of aspiration rather than of hard legal duty.

The Bamako Convention calls for a prohibition on the importation of hazardous waste into their regions from non-parties and attempts to regulate trade between parties to the convention. The right of states to ban imports is supported by other agreements such as the African, Caribbean and

Pacific States — European Economic Community: Fourth Lome Convention (Lome Convention) [Dec. 15, 1989, 29 I.L.M. 783 (entered into force Sept. 1, 1991)], which prohibits exports of hazardous waste to African, Caribbean, and Pacific state parties from the European Union. While the prohibitions on exports or imports of wastes express valuable if controversial aspects of IEL, it is well-settled that the requirement of Prior Informed Consent codifies existing customary law (see below).

A number of organizations—including the International Labour Organization (ILO), the Organization for Economic Cooperation and Development (OECD) and the European Union have participated in the international effort to control the harmful effects of pesticides and other toxic chemicals. In addition, the World Health Organization (WHO) has developed important guidelines for classification, and WHO works with both UNEP and the ILO in promoting the International Programme in Chemical Safety.

Another significant contribution is presently being made by the Codex Alimentarius Commission, which has developed regional and international standards regarding chemical residues in foods. The Codex Alimentarius standards, it should be noted, generally remain substantially less restrictive than those of developed states and are relied upon by developing countries when alleging the formers' protectionist restrictions of trade disguised as health and safety concerns. On the other hand, some domestic environmental organizations of developed countries have used the Codex standards as a rallying point against free trade agreements such as NAFTA and GATT/WTO. Despite these problems the Food and Agricultural Organization (FAO) and UNEP, have significantly impacted the behavior of nations.

E. LEGAL RESPONSE

1. TOXIC AND HAZARDOUS SUBSTANCES IN GENERAL

Before 1998, no international treaty existed regarding the distribution and use of hazardous substances across all media. In the absence of such a treaty, the FAO and UNEP filled this gap with two sets of voluntary guidelines. These influential regulations—prime examples of "soft law"—predominantly focused on the relative obligations of developed and developing nations regarding trade. Both sets of rules adopted a regulated trade approach to the interaction between exporter and importer, allowing transfers of substances banned in another country under the principle of Prior Informed Consent (PIC). In 1998, the Rotterdam Convention was adopted, making PIC legally binding. The Convention builds on the voluntary guidelines, and while countries may still import hazardous substances, they may do so only if they have been notified of the potential hazards and the reasons for its ban in the exporting country.

This approach contrasts with that taken by the 1991 Bamako Convention negotiated by the Organisation of African States. The Bamako Convention, discussed in detail in the section on hazardous wastes, prohibits African countries from importing *all* banned or restricted pesticides and chemicals from outside the continent.

2.   PRIOR INFORMED CONSENT

(a) 2002 FAO International Code of Conduct on the Distribution and Use of Pesticides

As pesticide exports continued to accelerate during the 1980s, the United Nations FAO sought to limit the harmful effects of improper use in developing countries. The 1985 FAO Code of Conduct, amended in 1989, forged a compromise between exporting and importing nations. As the Code identifies in article 1(1.1), it seeks to "set forth responsibilities and establish voluntary standards of conduct for all public and private entities ... particularly where there is no or an inadequate national law to regulate pesticides." The Code— which deals only with pesticides and not other hazardous substances—embraces the "necessary and acceptable use" of these chemicals, while striving to prevent "significant adverse effects on people or the environment" [art. 1(1.2)]. Non-binding in nature, the Code consequently employs hortatory and sometimes vague aspirational language and the threats posed by agro chemicals in developing countries continued. The revised code adopted by the FAO in November of 2002 [http://www.fao.org/WAICENT/FAOINFO/AGRI-CULT/AGP/AGPP/Pesticid/Code/PM_Code.htm] attempts to overcome some of these shortcomings.

Under the revised Code, governments retain ultimate responsibility for the distribution and use of pesticides in their countries, but also the pesticide industry—including manufacturers, marketers and traders—plays a significant role. Indeed, the New Code of Conduct reflects more strongly than ever the responsibility of governments, the chemical and food industry, traders, pesticide users, public interest groups and international organizations in reducing the health and environmental risks associated with pesticide. The Code addresses the need for a cooperative effort between governments of pesticide exporting and importing countries to promote good practices.

Art. 1 of the code aspires to a number of laudable objectives some of which are fleshed out in the body of the code while others are not. For example, it seeks to promote integrated pest management (IPM)[art. 1.7.6] but the exhortations in the body of the code [art. 3.7, 3.8 & 3.9] do not contain a strategy or operational modalities for doing so. Other objectives are in fact backed by norms. The code deals with the risk assessment and management of pesticides [art. 6.1.3] and requires the pesticide industry to carry out scientific testing [art. 4], and provide adequate data on the basis of which governments can conduct risk assessments and undertake risk management [art. 6.2].

In order to receive and evaluate these reports, governments of importing countries should possess or have access to effective analytical facilities [art. 4.2]. Governments of exporting nations, as well as international organizations, should strive to assist developing countries in establishing facilities capable of undertaking product and residue analysis [art. 4.3].

The Code also requires governments of importing countries to develop necessary regulatory legislation for the control of pesticides, including registration [art. 6.1.2] and rules on availability and safe use [art. 7]. The FAO Code of Conduct additionally requires that all pesticide containers be clearly labeled according to international guidelines (e.g. the FAO Guidelines on Good Labeling Practice, 1985) [art. 10.1]. In this regard industry should use labels that include appropriate symbols and pictograms whenever possible, in addition to written instructions, warnings and precautions [art. 10.2]. Likewise, the packaging, storage and disposal of pesticides should conform in principle to the applicable guidelines formulated by FAO and WHO, respectively [art. 10.3]. Industry is encouraged to dispose of toxic pesticide waste in an environmentally sound manner [art. 10.6].

Undergirding the provisions of the Code of Conduct is the principle of Prior Informed Consent (PIC). This principle requires that no pesticide banned or severely restricted by any government in order to protect human health or the environment be imported without the knowledgeable acquiescence of the importing country. The New Code of Conduct states that its standards include reference to participation in information exchange and international agreements, particularly the Rotterdam Convention (*See infra*) [art. 1.7.7]. The Code goes on to state that governments should facilitate the exchange of information regarding actions to ban or severely restrict a pesticide and the scientific and legal information concerning pesticides [art. 9]. Additionally, governments are encouraged to develop their own legislation and regulations that allow information about pesticide risks to be available to the public, and to encourage public participation in the regulatory process [art. 9]. Lastly, all parties are to "encourage collaboration between public sector groups, international organizations, governments and other interested stakeholders to ensure that countries are provided with the information they need" [art. 9.4.2].

As a soft law instrument that only provides voluntary standards of behavior, the FAO Code of Conduct must rely on persuasion rather than the threat of legal consequences. The FAO has steadily provided sound advice concerning the management of pesticides, and the institution has developed a considerable and well-respected expertise in the area. Though the Code, as such, has achieved broad political acceptance, NGOs have in fact documented routine violations of its provisions in developing countries.

(b) 1987 UNEP London Guidelines for the Exchange of Information on Chemicals in International Trade (1987 UNEP London Guidelines)

In substance the 1987 UNEP London Guidelines, UNEP/PIC/WG.2/2 at 9, UNEP ELPG No. 10, UNEP/GC/DEC/15/30 (1987) closely resemble the voluntary standards of the FAO Code of Conduct. Providing a broad definition of the term, the Guidelines state that " 'chemical' means a chemical substance whether by itself or in a mixture or preparation, whether manufactured or obtained from nature and includes such substances used as industrial chemicals and pesticides" [art. 1(a)]. Concerning pesticides, however, the Guidelines in fact defer to the FAO which is acknowledged as the primary source of guidance for the management of pesticides internationally [Intro. 7]. Thus the Guidelines seek in non-duplicative fashion to supplement and cooperate with the FAO regarding pesticides, while establishing the primary system of voluntary controls for other hazardous chemicals.

As an overriding principle, the London Guidelines state that both importing and exporting countries should protect human health and the environment against potential harm by exchanging information on chemicals [art. 2.(a)]. To this end the Guidelines also promote the principle of Prior Informed Consent (PIC) and establish formal PIC Procedures. On the other hand, the Guidelines make clear that nations may participate in the information exchange procedures without participating in the more formal PIC Procedures [art. 7.1(a)].

The Guidelines establish the International Register of Potentially Toxic Chemicals (IRPTC) as the general information clearinghouse and require all states, having taken action to ban or severely to restrict a chemical, to notify the IRPTC with information surrounding that action [art. 6]. Particularly an exporting state having taken any action should provide the Designated National Authority of the importing state with the relevant information through the IRPTC [art. 8]. Additionally an importing state participating in the PIC Procedures, when responding using the official PIC forms, "will have the opportunity to record their decisions regarding future imports of banned or severely restricted imports in a formal way" [art. 7.1]. For its part the IRPTC relays the decision to the exporting country, maintains a database of all important information, and provides such information for inclusion in the regular updates of the UN Consolidated List of Products whose Consumption and/or Sale have been Banned, Withdrawn or Severely Restricted by Governments [art. 7.4].

Beyond the use of the clearinghouse, states of export should directly provide information, advice and assistance to importing states regarding the sound management of hazardous chemicals [art. 13(b)]. States of export should, for example, as far as practicable supply precautionary information in the principle language(s) of the importing state, accompanied by suitable pictorial aids and labels [art. 13(d)]. The Guidelines recognize the desirability of exporting states using no less stringent requirements of classification, packaging and labeling than in their own countries—and in the absence of standards in the importing state, that the exporter employ classification, packaging and labeling standards in conformity with internationally harmonized procedures [art. 14]. Importing states, on the other hand, have responsibilities with regard to their own citizens, and should take measures to ensure that users at all levels are given the necessary information, advice and assistance to manage these chemicals safely [art. 13(c)].

The London Guidelines therefore closely follow the substantive standards offered by the FAO Code of Conduct, with FAO and UNEP working jointly to implement the PIC procedure. In fact, negotiations are presently underway to create a PIC Convention and in 1995 the Inter–Organization Programme for Sound Management of Chemicals (IOMC) was established to coordinate the efforts of all international and intergovernmental organizations involved in chemical safety. Even with such improvements, the distribution and use of hazardous substances remains one of the most under-regulated areas of international environmental law. As we shall see below, the world community has so far placed more energy and attention on the transboundary movement and trade in hazardous wastes.

In 1994, The Code of Ethics on the International Trade in Chemicals (Code of Ethics) was concluded. [1998 UNEP Report on the Status of the Application of the Code of Ethics on the International Trade in Chemicals (http://www.chem.unep.ch/ethics/english/rep-en1.htm)]. While the Code of Ethics is a complement to the amended London Guidelines, it is broader in scope. The Code of Ethics is a voluntary instrument aimed at private sector parties, who are expected to help achieve the goals of the London Guidelines. *Id.* Thus, these private sector parties seek to increase chemical safety through the exchange of information on chemicals in international trade. Specifically, these parties are to develop safer packaging and clear and concise labeling, end the production and trade in chemicals with unacceptable risks, reduce the use of hazardous chemicals, and take other steps to promote chemical safety through testing and assessment, quality assurance, providing safety information, and promoting education and training for safety purposes.

(c) Rotterdam Convention on the Prior Informed Consent Procedure for Certain Hazardous Chemicals and Pesticides in International Trade (Rotterdam Convention)

The Rotterdam Convention on the Prior Informed Consent Procedure for Certain Hazardous Chemicals and Pesticides in International Trade [38 I.L.M. 1734] was adopted on September 10, 1998 but has not got entered into force. It requires 50 instruments of ratification to come into force [art.

26(1)]; as of January, 2003, 38 parties had ratified the Convention. The Convention seeks to promote shared responsibility and cooperative efforts among the parties for the international trade of certain hazardous chemicals [art. 1]. The term 'chemical' is defined in accordance with the London Guidelines as "... a substance whether by itself or in a mixture or preparation and whether manufactured or obtained from nature," and includes pesticides and industrial substances [art. 2.(a)]. However, the Convention does not defer to the FAO to determine how pesticides should be managed internationally. Thus, while the Convention builds on the existing voluntary PIC procedure, its provisions are legally binding on the parties independent of other soft law instruments.

The primary principle established by the Convention is that a chemical covered by the Convention can only be exported with the prior informed consent (PIC) of the importing party. Additionally, the Convention provides for the exchange of information among parties about potentially hazardous chemicals that may be exported or imported. The principle of PIC applies to chemicals listed in Annex III of the Convention. The Conference of the Parties, which will meet within one year after the Convention comes into force [art. 18(2)], will decide which chemicals to list in Annex III [art. 7(2)]. Initially, twenty-two pesticides and five industrial chemicals are listed in Annex III, with the possibility that additional chemicals may be added with each meeting of the Conference of the Parties [art. 7(2)].

Once a chemical is listed in Annex III and is subject to the PIC procedure, importing countries receive a "decision guidance document" which contains information concerning the chemical and the regulatory decisions to ban or severely restrict the chemical for health or environmental reasons [art. 7(3)]. The importing countries must respond within nine months with either a final decision or an interim response [art. 10(4)]. The final decision must state the party's consent to import, not to consent to import, or to consent to import subject to specified conditions [art. 10(4)(a)]. The decisions of the importing countries are then circulated to exporting parties, who must then ensure that exporters within its jurisdiction comply with the decisions [art. 11(1)(b)].

As for exchange of information, the Convention requires parties whom have banned or severely restricted a chemical they wish to export to provide the importing party with information concerning said chemical [art. 12(1)]. The information the exporting party must provide includes the reasons for their regulatory action, a summary of the hazards and risks presented by the chemical to human health or the environment, and precautionary measures to reduce exposure to, and emission of, the chemical [Annex 5].

The Convention provides that, as soon as practicable, the Conference of the Parties shall develop procedures for determining non-compliance as well as treatment of parties found to be in non-compliance [art. 17].

3. HAZARDOUS WASTES

To date, international attention has focused primarily on the transboundary movement and trade in hazardous wastes The Stockholm Convention on Persistent Organic Pollutants is attempting to change this approach by requiring that certain hazardous pollutants be eliminated or reduced and is more fully discussed below.

(a) Transboundary Movement

In 1987 the Governing Council of UNEP adopted the Cairo Guidelines and Principles for the Environmentally Sound Management of Hazardous Wastes (Cairo Guidelines) [UNEP/GC/DEC/14/30, UNEP ELPG no. 8 (1987)], which function as "soft law" similar to the 1987 London Guidelines, discussed above. The same UNEP working group then developed the text of the 1989 Basel Convention on the Control of Transboundary Movements of Hazardous Wastes and Their Disposal (1989 Basel Convention), which came into force in 1992. Like the Cairo Guidelines, the Basel Convention originally adopted a broad managed-trade approach to hazardous wastes—allowing all transboundary transfers based on the principle of Prior Informed Consent. Opponents complained that the Basel Convention did little to restrict trade, and instead functioned more as a tracking system for continued transfers to developing countries, in effect licensing the dumping of hazardous wastes in the third world. The Basel Convention was amended in response to these criticisms in 1995 and Art. 4(a) now bans hazardous wastes exports for final disposal and recycling from what are known as Annex VII countries (Basel Convention Parties that are members of the EU, OECD, Liechtenstein) to non-Annex VII countries (all other Parties to the Convention). The Ban Amendment has to be ratified by three-fourths of the Parties present at the time of the adoption of the Amendment in order to enter into force (62 Parties) but has of date been ratified by only 36 countries and may not come into force in the foreseeable future.

African countries were most vocal against the managed-trade approach of the Basel Convention and collectively in 1991 adopted the Bamako Treaty—which strictly bans the import of hazardous wastes from outside the continent (see below).

(b) The Basel Convention on the Control of Transboundary Movements of Hazardous Wastes and Their Disposal (Basel Convention)

i. *Environmentally Sound Management*

The Basel Convention, though primarily dealing with the transboundary movement and trade in hazardous wastes, also contains general provisions regarding the environmentally sound management of such wastes. Under the convention "hazardous waste" means those substances or objects included in the categories set out by Annexes I and III, as well as those defined or considered as hazardous wastes by the domestic legislation of the party of export, import or transit [art. 1(1)]. Other substances or objects included in the categories of Annex II, such as those collected from households, are known as "other wastes" [art. 1(2)]. Under the treaty "environmentally sound management" is defined as "taking all practicable steps to ensure that hazardous wastes or other wastes are managed in a manner which will protect human health and the environment against the adverse effects which may result from such wastes" [art. 2(8)]. With environmentally sound management as the operative model, all parties must reduce the generation of hazardous and other wastes to a minimum—though the obligation remains qualified by the phrase "taking into account social, technological and economic aspects" [art. 4(2)(a)]. Each party also must strive to create adequate disposal facilities within its own boundary [art. 4(2)(b)] and must require its management personnel to take the necessary steps to prevent pollution and minimize its consequences [art. 4(2)(c)]. The convention further mandates that the parties cooperate: (1) in the exchange of information; (2) in the monitoring of effects; and (3) in the development of environmentally sound technology and its transfer [art. 10].

ii. Transboundary Movement

Concerning the transboundary movement of wastes, the convention creates a number of general obligations for parties. As a rule the Parties must reduce the transboundary movement of hazardous and other wastes to a minimum consistent with the environmentally sound and efficient management of such wastes [art. 4(2)(d)]. In this regard the amended preamble of the convention now states "that transboundary movements of hazardous wastes, especially to developing countries have a high risk of not constituting an environmentally sound management of hazardous wastes ..." [pmbl. 7 bis]. Parties additionally must not allow export to parties which have prohibited all imports, or which cannot manage the particular wastes in question in an environmentally sound manner [art. 4(2)(e)]. Likewise, importing parties must prevent import if the wastes cannot be managed in proper fashion [art. 4(2)(g)]. The convention also prohibits any transfers between parties and non-parties [art. 4(5)], except transfers that do not derogate from environmentally sound management as provided by the convention and are communicated to the Secretariat [art. 11].

This latter provision has enabled the United States, a signatory that has not ratified the convention because it has not passed appropriate implementing legislation, to continue exporting hazardous wastes to parties. In fact, the convention only allows transfers between parties in the following circumstances: (a) the state of export cannot dispose of the wastes adequately; (b) the wastes in question are required as raw material for recycling or recovery industries; or (c) the transfer is in accordance with other criteria to be decided by the Parties [art. 4(9)]. Finally, as remarked above the amended convention prohibits all transboundary movements of hazardous wastes not designated for recycling from all OECD and EU states to all non-OECD and non-EU states [art. 4A(1)]. Hazardous wastes designated for recycling must likewise be phased out between the same states by the end of 1997 [art. 4A(2)].

When transboundary movement does take place, the parties must conduct such transfers in a manner protecting human health and the environment [art. 4(2)(d)]. In this regard parties must ensure that packaging, labeling and transport conform with generally accepted international rules and standards [art. 4(7)(b)]. More broadly, in no way may generating states transfer the duty to manage wastes in an environmentally sound manner to states of import or transit [art. 4(10)].

In addition to these general obligations, the Basel Convention establishes a global paper trail for any transboundary movement of hazardous or other wastes. The state of export must notify (or require the generator or exporter to notify) any state of transit or import concerning the details of the transaction [art. 6(1)]. This is done by way of written instrument through each state's designated "competent authority" [art. 6(1)]. The written notification must contain all the declarations and information specified in Annex V A [art. 6(1)]. Upon receipt the state of import must respond to the notifier in writing—consenting to the movement with or without conditions, denying the movement, or requesting additional information [art. 6(2)]. Until the notifier has received written permission as well as confirmation of an environmentally sound contract from the importing state, the exporting state may not allow shipment [art. 6(3)]. The state of export must also receive written consent from the state of transit, though provisions are made for a state of transit which is also a party to opt out of this requirement [art. 6(4)]. With written consent of the states concerned, the state of export may use a less detailed general notification for regular shipments over a twelve month period [arts. 6(6)–6(8)]. Finally, if informed by the importing state that the contract cannot be completed as drawn, the state of export must receive the shipment back unless other arrangements can be made, and neither the state of export nor any party of transit may hinder that return [art. 8].

At their 1999 meeting, the Ministers set out guidelines for the 2000–2010 decade [Secretariat of the Basel Convention, *Basel Convention Basic Information, available at http://www.basel.int/pub/basics.html*]. They plan to place more emphasis on creating partnerships with industry and research institutions to create innovative approaches to environmentally sound management (ESM). *Id.* The main emphasis is on minimizing hazardous waste. Their goals include further reduction of the movement of hazardous and other wastes, the prevention and monitoring of illegal traffic, and active promotion and use of cleaner technologies and production methods. In another development the 1999 meeting adopted the Basel Protocol on Liability and Compensation for Damage resulting from Transboundary Movements of Hazardous Wastes and their Disposal (The Protocol). The objective is similar to the HNS Convention (*See infra*) in that it addresses those financially responsible for damage resulting from transboundary movement of hazardous wastes. The Protocol deals with financial responsibility in relation to each phase of a transboundary movement, from the point at which the wastes are loaded on the means of transport to their export, international transit, import, and final disposal. Currently, the Protocol has 13 signatures and will enter into force after twenty signatures.

As a framework treaty, the Basel Convention has benefitted from the cooperative impetus and flexible decision-making power built into the framework approach. Informal decisions of the Conference of the Parties, meaning those that do not call for ratification or other formal approval by each state, have led to a number of innovative mechanisms. Such innovations include "Model National Legislation" for the transboundary movement and management of hazardous wastes, a "Manual for the Implementation of the Basel Convention," and "Draft Forms" for the identification and tracking of illegal trade. In addition, the COP has swiftly moved to implement specific provisions of the convention, including the development of a Draft Protocol on Liability and Compensation, and the establishment of regional and sub-regional centers for training and technology transfer regarding both the management of wastes and the minimization of generation. In short, under UNEP guidance the Basel Convention has quickly evolved from a poorly ratified treaty into a relatively effective, if under-funded, hazardous waste regime.

(c) The Convention on the Ban of Imports Into Africa and the Control of Transboundary Movement and Management of Hazardous Wastes Within Africa (Bamako Convention)

Though born out of disapproval with the Basel Convention's managed-trade approach, the Bamako Treaty in fact closely follows its predecessor in most respects. It does however create more stringent rules for its African parties in several ways. The most significant difference from the original Basel Convention lies in the Bamako Convention's banning of all hazardous wastes into Africa from non-parties [art. 4(1)]. Of course this difference has narrowed considerably given the recent amendment to the Basel Convention involving OECD and EU nations. Additionally, "hazardous wastes" is defined more broadly and even includes banned or strictly regulated hazardous substances [art. 2(1)]. The convention also provides for unlimited liability as well as joint and several liability on hazardous waste generators [art. 4(3)(b)]. Other differences include a stronger commitment to the Precautionary Approach that emphasizes clean production methods rather than permissible emissions [art. 4(3)(f) & (g)], and the disallowal of general notification procedures for regular shipments of the same wastes [art. 6(6)]. Though the Bamako Convention creates more stringent conditions than the Basel Convention, an African nation may nonetheless become party to both. The Basel Convention clearly allows a party to impose "additional requirements ... in order to better protect human health and the environment" [art. 4(11)], and the Bamako Convention permits a party to enter into other agreements as long as these do not "derogate from the environmentally sound management of hazardous wastes" as required by the convention [art. 11(1)]. Therefore, as long as an African party follows the strict procedures of the Bamako Convention, it may also benefit from the transfer of resources through the Basel Convention. Indeed a handful of African nations have ratified both treaties as of this writing.

(d) The International Convention on Liability and Compensation for Damage in Connection with the Carriage of Hazardous and Noxious Substances by Sea (HNS Convention)

The International Convention on Liability and Compensation for Damage in Connection with the Carriage of Hazardous and Noxious Substances by Sea, May 3, 1996 [35 I.L.M. 1406], was designed to compensate for damage caused in connection with the carriage by sea of hazardous and noxious substances [prmbl]. The Convention provides for compensation on two fronts. First, the owner of the HNS is liable for any damage caused by the carrying of such substances by sea [art. 7(1)]. Second, if the owner is either not liable or cannot compensate the injured for the entire amount, the HNS Convention establishes an HNS Fund who will then provide compensation [art. 14(1)]. The Convention specifies the process by which the initial and annual contributions to the Fund will be determined [art. 16–20]. Owners and the HNS Fund must compensate for "damage," which includes death or personal injury, loss of or damage to property, loss or damage by contamination of the environment, and the costs of preventive measures [art. 1(6)]. Since liable owners are required to provide compensation, each owner must have insurance or other financial security, such as the guarantee of a bank to cover liability [art. 12(1)]. If two or more ships, each carrying HNS, are responsible for damage, then there is joint and several liability [art. 8(1)].

4. ELIMINATION AND REDUCTIONS AT SOURCE

The Stockholm Convention on Persistent Organic Pollutants, May 22, 2001, [40 I.L.M. 1531], which acknowledges the importance of precaution in its preamble, seeks to protect human health and the environment from persistent organic pollutants (POPs) [art. 1]. It was adopted on May 22, 2001, and requires fifty instruments of ratification to enter into force [art. 26(1)]. As of January, 2003, 26 parties had ratified the Convention.

The Convention endeavors to achieve its objective by eliminating existing POPs, avoiding further production and use of POPs, and minimizing emissions of POPs that cannot be eliminated. The Convention calls for the parties to eliminate chemicals listed in Annex A [art. 3(1)(a)], unless the party has obtained an exemption [art. 4(3)]. Even if there is an exemption, however, the party must prevent or minimize human exposure and release into the environment [art. 3(6)]. Additionally, parties may only import chemicals listed in Annex A and B if for the purpose of environmentally sound disposal or for a use permitted by Annex A or B [art. 3(2)(a)]. Such chemicals can only be exported to another party if for the purpose of environmentally sound disposal or the importing party is permitted to use the chemical under Annex A or B [art. 3(2)(b)]. If exporting to a state not party to the Convention, the exporting party must be sure that the importing country is committed to protecting human health and the environment and will comply with the measure to reduce or eliminate releases from stockpiles and wastes [art. 3(2)(b)(iii)].

An implementation plan must be submitted by each party within two years of the date on which the Convention enters into force [art. 7(1)]. Part of this implementation plan must include an action plan that pertains to the chemicals listed in Annex C [art. 5(a)]. The action plan must evaluate the current and projected releases of Annex C chemicals, evaluate the laws and policies of the party relating to the management of such releases, and contain strategies to minimize and ultimately eliminate releases derived from such chemicals [art. 5(a)]. Annex C designates certain chemicals which must have priority consideration in order to prevent formation and release of those chemicals, and also lists possible measures to achieve that goal [Annex C pt. V(A)]. The Convention also calls for "best available techniques" and "best environmental practices" for dealing with chemicals in Annex C [art. 5(d)]. "Best available techniques" is not meant to be any specific technique or technology, but rather is aimed at the consideration of the technical characteristics, its geographical location and the local environmental condition of the installation [Annex C pt. V(B)]. The consideration of best available technique must bear in mind the likely costs and benefits of a measure as well as consideration of precaution and prevention [Annex C pt. V(B)]. "Best environmental practices" is defined as "the application of the most appropriate combination of environmental control measures and strategies" [art. 5(f)(v)].

Finally, regarding chemicals listed in Annex A, B, or C, parties must develop strategies to identify and then reduce and ultimately eliminate releases of such chemicals from stockpiles and wastes [art. 6]. Such chemicals must be handled in an environmentally sound manner and disposed of in such a way that the POP content is destroyed or irreversibly transformed [art. 6(d)]. Additionally, parties must ensure that upon becoming wastes, the POPs are not recycled or reused or allowed to cross international boundaries without taking into account the relevant international rules, standards and guidelines [art. 6(d)].

5. OTHER REGIONAL AGREEMENTS

In North America, the United States has signed two pre-NAFTA agreements with its hemispheric trading partners. The Canada—United States Agreement Concerning the Trans-boundary Movement of Hazardous Waste, Oct. 28, 1986, 11099 T.I.A.S. 496 (amended in 1992) allows the "export, import, and transit of hazardous waste" across the border [art. 2], and requires notification of the importing country for any planned transfers [art. 3]. In a twist on the principle of Prior Informed Consent, however, silence is deemed consent and the exporter may proceed with the shipment if the importing country does not respond to the notification within thirty days [art. 3].

In a more traditional version of Prior Informed Consent, and one more in adherence with the relative positions of developed and developing countries, the Mexico—United States Agreement for Co-operation on Environmental Programmes and Trans–Boundary Problems, Nov. 12, 1986 (Mexico–U.S. Hazardous Waste Agreement) [26 I.L.M. 25] entered into force Jan. 29, 1987 as Annex III to the 1983 US–Mexico Agreement on Cooperation for the Protection and Improvement of the Environment in the Border Area) prohibits transfer of hazardous waste without approval by the importing country [art. III]. For its part, the importing party must respond within forty-five days and may choose to accept, accept with conditions, or reject the planned shipment [art. III].

Another significant regional instrument, the 1989 Lome IV Convention, prohibits all exports of hazardous wastes from EU states to African—Caribbean—Pacific (ACP) states [art. 39(1)]. In fact the treaty, which defines hazardous wastes according to Basel Convention standards [art. 39(3)], mandates that ACP states prohibit the import of hazardous wastes from all countries [art. 39(1)]. The obligations of art. 39(1), however, are without prejudice to other international obligations.

CHAPTER TEN

LAND–BASED POLLUTION

A. NATURE OF THE PROBLEM

At least 80 percent of all marine pollution comes from sources that are located on land [*Agenda 21*, June 13, 1992, U.N. Doc. A/CONF. 151/26, ch. 17]. Pollutants generated on land travel through numerous environmental pathways such as the atmosphere, rivers, canals, underground watercourses, and outfalls before eventually finding their way to the ocean. Urban expansion into coastal areas has exacerbated the problem of land-based marine pollution. Twenty two of the world's 35 largest cities are on the coast of an ocean or sea. Of these, seventeen are in developing countries. Sixty five percent of the cities with populations over two and one half million are situated on a coast. These urban centers and their supporting agriculture and development create various forms of pollutants that end up in the marine environment [IMO/FAO/UNESCO–IOC/WMO/WHO/IAEA/UN/UNEP: Joint Group of Experts on the Scientific Aspects of Marine Environmental Protection (GESAMP), PROTECTING THE OCEANS FROM LAND-BASED ACTIVITIES. 2.2.1 (Jan. 2001) (hereinafter GESAMP Report)]. Land-based pollution has loomed more problematic to the extent that urban growth has departed from principles of sustainable development, and environmental protection has been ignored or minimized by economic growth.

B. SOURCES AND ENVIRONMENTAL IMPACTS

In general, there are eight groups of pollutants that are deposited into the ocean from land-based sources: 1) chemical nutrients; 2) sewage and bacterial agents; 3) oil; 4) organic chemicals; 5) metals; 6) sediments and litter; 7) radioactive substances; and 8) heat. Nutrients, such as phosphorus and nitrogen compounds, are introduced into the marine environment by runoff from fertilized agricultural lands, discharges of domestic sewage, industrial effluents, and atmospheric emissions. Excessive nutrient concentrations can accelerate the naturally occurring process of eutrophication by which waters are enriched by nutrients. The introduction of excessive nutrients into the ocean, however, can unnaturally increase the productivity of the waters and lead to uncontrolled phytoplankton growth [GESAMP Report 2.2.3].

Uncontrolled growth of these species is popularly known as a red tide. This process will eventually cause the decomposition of organic materials which will in turn result in a serious depletion of the oxygen content of the waters and possibly the death of fish and many important species of marine life. Large fish kills create an even greater demand for oxygen as the fish decompose. Additionally, some species of phytoplankton emit toxins which, if present in high concentrations, will contaminate shellfish and damage certain types of fish. In the ocean, increased algal growth and a lack of dissolved oxygen may have a detrimental effect on coral reefs, which function as important repositories of biological diversity (See Chapter five).

Sewage and bacterial agents account for a significantly large portion of all marine pollution [GESAMP Report 2.4.1]. The principal pollutants contained in sewage include organic materials, nutrients, pathogens and trace metals. In developed countries, sewage is usually treated to remove solids and is sometimes chemically or biologically treated to produce a less harmful effluent. However, in lesser developed countries raw sewage is often discharged directly into watercourses. The pathogens present in sewage contaminate shellfish and may lead to serious gastrointestinal disorders. Recreational activities may also be affected in areas in which sewage discharge has led to high pathogen concentrations. Finally, the organic materials and nutrients in sewage lead to accelerated eutrophication.

Oil tanker spills are a highly publicized source of marine pollution, but the bulk of organic chemicals enter the marine environment from less publicized land-based sources such as industrial discharges, sewage disposal, river runoff, and atmospheric fallout from fossil fuel combustion. Natural seepages also have a significant impact [GESAMP REPORT

2.4]. For a more complete discussion of the aquatic effects of oil pollution, see Chapter Eleven, Vessel–Based Pollution.

Organic chemicals, such as DDT and PCBs, are introduced into the marine environment through rivers, pesticide runoff from agricultural land, atmospheric deposition, and municipal and industrial discharges. High concentrations of metals in the marine environment can be toxic to marine life and present dangers to human health. The principal sources of metals in the ocean are industrial and municipal discharges into rivers, coastal discharges, and atmospheric emissions. Concentration levels of these metals tend to be greatest in industrial areas and estuaries. The characteristics and impacts of these toxic metals, and how they advance up the food chain are also discussed in Chapter Nine, Toxic and Hazardous Substances.

Litter and debris from human activities enter the ocean through rivers, municipal drainage systems, and coastal recreational areas. Plastics are the major type of litter present in the marine environment. Marine fish and mammals are injured or killed by plastics when they ingest or become entangled in the debris. In addition, the debris often ends up on coastal areas where it mars the beauty of the natural environment [GESAMP Report 2.4.9]. Soil sediments from agriculture can cover and destroy the bottoms of rivers, estuaries, bays and even entire sections of ocean gulfs. An example of this phenomena is found in the Chesapeake Bay in the United States where agricultural sediments have damaged the marshes, fisheries and bottom ecologies [CHARLES GOLDMAN & ALEXANDER HORNE, LIMNOLOGY 327 (1983)].

Metals are a particularly vexing pollutant because they do not degrade even when they are diluted, and can bioaccumulate to form toxic concentrations. For a fuller discussion, see Chapter Nine, Toxic and Hazardous Substances.

Land-based radioactive waste is often dumped into the oceans from ships. Russian nuclear wastes have been dumped into the oceans, and this dumping blurs the distinction between land-based pollution and dumping [LAKSHMAN GURUSWAMY, ET AL. INTERNATIONAL ENVIRONMENTAL LAW AND WORLD ORDER (1999); *see also* Chapter Twelve, Dumping].

Some percentage of the radioactive material in each nuclear power plant escapes to the environment during normal operation, and finds its way into the oceans. The marine impact of radioactive wastes disposal is illustrated by the case of the Savannah River in the United States which divides South Carolina from Georgia. Radioactive waste dumps and military nuclear processing facilities along the Savannah River have introduced so much fissionable material to the river that it has been measured in the flesh of fish [William Booth, *Ecosystem Paradoxically Glows at Former Atomic Bomb Factory Site*, Washington Post, May 26, 1996, at A3]. These radioactive materials are carried in water, sediments and biota of the Savannah River into the Atlantic Ocean. Moreover, nuclear bomb testing—particularly atmospheric testing—has introduced significant quantities of radioactive material into the marine environment.

Electric power generation creates large quantities of excess heat. As a result, most power plants are located on or near large sources of water and the marine ecology surrounding the power plant is severely impacted. Still, the dangers of heat discharge remain relatively unexplored and undiscussed. The concept of heat pollution thus illustrates the need for a flexible, working definition of pollution [GESAMP Report 2.4].

With any polluting substance, the impact on the marine environment primarily depends on whether the pollutants are present on the open seas or in a semi-enclosed or coastal area. Pollutants in the open seas tend to have a less detrimental effect than pollutants in coastal areas because of the open sea's natural capacity to assimilate and dilute large amounts of pollution [GESAMP Report 2.4.1]. However, the ocean's assimilative capacity is not infinite because time must pass before the pollutant can be dispersed, diluted, or sedimented. In addition, some pollutants are impossible to transform into less harmful substances and others may tend to bioaccumulate in marine animals. Coastal areas are usually more sensitive to pollution because they receive higher levels of pollutants from more concentrated sources and tend to be more biologically productive [*id.*].

C. REMEDIAL OBJECTIVES

The control of land-based pollution is the most daunting task facing the international community for a number of reasons. First, it is the result of domestic pollution in all it aspects, embracing the three media of air, land, and water. Controlling land-based pollution thus exists as a proxy for controlling the sovereign rights of states to pollute their own territory—a restraint that states rarely accept. The problem stems from the extreme reluctance of states to surrender even a modicum of sovereignty with respect to actions within domestic boundaries, strongly preferring to retain control at the national level.

Second, the scientific difficulties of demonstrating pathways and sources are immense except in cases of single source direct outfalls and pathways. In situations with more than one set of contributors, apportioning responsibility to individual polluters is fraught with uncertainty. As an additional complication, chemicals released into air or water interact with each other and give rise to synergistic reactions and effects. The impact of such synergistic effects is greater than the sum of their individual effects, making it very difficult to establish cause and effect relationships. DDT, for example, is extremely soluble in oil but not in water, greatly multiplying the exposure for marine organisms in oil-polluted waters [THE ENCYCLOPEDIA OF THE ENVIRONMENT, 686 (RUTH A. EBLAN & WILLIAM R. EBLAN eds., 1994)]. Thus, where different nations are responsible for land-based discharges of DDT and oil, respectively, they often resist control measures by arguing that another state is the more culpable agent. Nations thus find it easier to resist controls arguing that the actions required to arrest land-based pollution often involve surmise and guesswork.

Third, environmental controls on the sources of land-based pollution—run-off from rivers, estuaries, and pipelines—generally require extremely expensive measures entailing significant economic sacrifice. Nations invariably balk at accepting such self-imposed controls. In light of these difficulties, states have focused less on the remedial objective of solving land-based pollution, and more on maintaining the widest possible flexibility to adopt measures as they see fit.

In sum, even where the political will to roll back or reduce land–based pollution is present, the implementation of such policies presents daunting scientific problems. The first relates to the identification of sources of pollutants, and their respective impacts. Second, the creation of mechanistic, statistical or stochastic models that are able to allocate pollutant reduction among sources. Third, a common understanding of such information that enables collective actions to be undertaken and monitored.

D. LEGAL RESPONSE

Though land-based sources contribute the highest percentage of marine pollution, the international commitment to controlling these wastes remains understandably low. As it stands at the international level, there exists little more than a framework for future regulation of land-based marine pollution, with occasional calls for a legally binding instrument on the subject. The most effective agreements remain regional ones, and these do not comply with the rigorous standards imposed both internationally and regionally with regard, for example, to dumping and vessel-based pollution.

1. THE UNITED NATIONS CONVENTION ON THE LAW OF THE SEA (UNCLOS)

UNCLOS [Dec. 10, 1982, 21 I.L.M. 1266 (entered into force Nov. 16, 1994)] defines pollution as:

the introduction by man, directly or indirectly, of substances or energy into the marine environment, including estuaries, which results or is likely to result in such deleterious effects as harm to living resources and marine life, hazards to human health, hindrance to marine activities, including fishing and other legitimate uses of the sea, impairment of quality for use of sea water and reduction of amenities.... [Art. 1(4)]

Despite this broad definition, UNCLOS provides only a general scheme for states to follow in attempting to reduce land-based marine pollution. The convention requires states to adopt measures "to prevent, reduce and control" such pollution, "taking into account internationally agreed rules, standards and recommended practices and procedures" [art. 207(1)]. The mandate that states "take into account" international constraints of course has little normative value, as states need only consider and not follow such rules. Regardless, no formal standards even exist at the global level for land-based pollution, and states which began by looking only at simple recommendations under the Montreal Guidelines for the Protection of the Marine Environment Against Pollution from Land–Based Sources (Montreal Guidelines) [UNEP/GC.13/9/Add.3, UNEP/GC/DEC/13/1811, UNEP ELPG No. 7 (1985)], have now strengthened their resolve by the Global Action program and Washington Declaration discussed below. UNCLOS also provides that states "[s]hall endeavor to harmonize their policies ... at the appropriate regional level" [art. 207(3)], and "shall endeavor to establish global and regional rules, standards and recommended standards and procedures" [art. 207(4)]. Again, however, that states "shall endeavor" does not mean that states "must" act to facilitate these ends. Moreover, the rules for enclosed or semi-enclosed seas [arts. 122–123]—areas which tend to be the most susceptible to Land–Based marine pollution—only offer the slightly more forceful requirement that states "should cooperate" in coordinating protective action.

2. MONTREAL GUIDELINES FOR THE PROTECTION OF THE MARINE ENVIRONMENT AGAINST POLLUTION FROM LAND–BASED SOURCES

The Montreal Guidelines are a set of recommendations compiled by a Working Group of Experts under UNEP auspices. Adopted as a UNEP Governing Council Decision in 1985, they present a broad range of specific suggestions which states may adapt to national legislation, regional agreements or any future global agreement on land-based pollution. As such, the Montreal Guidelines elaborate on the generalities of UNCLOS article 207—providing for the basic obligations to protect the marine environment, to adopt control measures, to cooperate with other states, and to not cause transboundary harm. The Montreal Guidelines also state the need to establish "specially protected areas" and to assist developing countries in their efforts to combat pollution. Interestingly, in an early recognition of integrated pollution control, the Montreal Guidelines warn against simply preventing one type of pollution (i.e. land-based marine pollution) by creating another (e.g. hazardous waste landfills). Additionally, the Montreal Guidelines echo UNCLOS' expansive definition of marine pollution referred to above [Montreal Guidelines § 1(a); *see also*, UNCLOS, art. 1(4)].

To give more specific advice to governments, the Montreal Guidelines provide fairly detailed information in the three Annexes attached to the document. Annex I, "Strategies for Protecting, Preserving and

Enhancing the Quality of the Marine Environment," gives a substantial account of the three control strategies of environmental quality standards, emission standards and environmental planning. In developing a program to combat marine pollution, the annex suggests that governments individually tailor an approach combining all three strategies. Annex II, "Classification of Substances," provides an overview of the typical method of rating harmful substances, advising the creation of a "black list" for dangerous substances, and a "grey list" for less dangerous substances. Annex III, "Monitoring and Data Management," presents valuable recommendations toward the creation of effective technical programs, gleaned from the experiences of the better regulated states.

3. THE GLOBAL PROGRAM OF ACTION FOR THE PROTECTION OF THE MARINE ENVIRONMENT FROM LAND–BASED ACTIVITIES AND THE WASHINGTON DECLARATION ON PROTECTION OF THE MARINE ENVIRONMENT FROM LAND–BASED ACTIVITIES.

As discussed above, UNCLOS requires states to address land-based sources of marine pollution. However, recognition among the international community of the problems posed by land-based pollution, and the need to implement the strategic framework of UNCLOS and the Montreal Guidelines resulted in a 1995 meeting in Washington.

This conference produced the Global Program of Action for the Protection of the Marine Environment from Land–Based Activities (the GPA), [UNEP (OCA)/LBA/IG.2/7], and the Washington Declaration on Protection of the Marine Environment from Land–Based Activities (Washington Declaration), [UNEP (OCA)/LBA/IG.2.6].

The GPA calls on all parties to take action on national, regional, and international levels. It is designed to serve as a source of conceptual and practical guidance for the parties in the development of these programs. It includes detailed recommendation for the regulation of sewage, persistent organic pollutants (POPs), radioactive substances, heavy metals, oils, nutrient, sediment mobilization, litter, and physical alternations and destruction of habitats. It also identifies steps for sharing knowledge and experience dealing with the combating land-based sources of marine pollution. Chapter II describes a methodology for problem identification and solution at the national level. Chapter III addresses regional considerations while Chapter IV contains approaches for dealing with numerous source categories of pollutants.

The other document resulting from the 1995 Washington Meeting is the Washington Declaration. The Declaration accords priority to the implementation of the GPA [art. 13]. Thus, its goals are similar to the Washington Declaration, in that the GPA, identifies the common goal of dealing with all land-based impacts upon the marine environment, specifically those resulting from sewage, POPs, radioactive substances, heavy metals, oils, nutrients, sediment mobilization, litter, and physical alteration and destruction of habitat [art. 1]. The Washington Declaration also focuses on the development and implementation of national action programs. Priority is given to the treatment and management of waste water through the installation of environmentally and economically appropriate sewage systems [art. 15]. Both the Washington Declaration and the GPA were endorsed by the General Assembly in December 1996 [U.N. GAOR 86th plenary mtg., U.N. Doc. A/RES/51/189 (1996)].

4.   REGIONAL TREATIES

A number of regional treaties have addressed the problem of land-based pollution, including those for the Baltic Sea, the North Sea, the Mediterranean Sea, the North–East Atlantic Ocean, and the South–East Pacific Ocean. As a general rule, states have had a difficult time in developing regional standards, and even when developed the standards do not bind objecting parties. Furthermore, even when parties agree to regional standards no higher authority exists to compel action, as all enforcement power remains in the hands of the national governments.

The Convention for the Prevention of Marine Pollution from Land–Based Sources (1974 Paris Convention), June 4, 1974, [13 I.L.M. 352 (entered into force May 6, 1978)] was perhaps the most developed and comprehensive example of regional cooperation on the subject.

Covering the area of the North–East Atlantic and the North Sea, the 1974 Paris Convention called for the elimination of pollution from a "black list" of dangerous substances, and the strict limitation of pollution from a "grey" list of less harmful substances [art. 4]. A supervisory body known as the Paris Commission (PARCOM) amends the contents of both lists binding parties who vote for its decisions, but not reluctant parties [art. 18]. Over the years PARCOM adopted a considerable number of broadly accepted measures, including a phased-out reduction of PCBs and a strong endorsement of the precautionary principle as applied to integrated ecosystem protection [PHILIPPE SANDS, PRINCIPLES OF INTERNATIONAL ENVIRONMENTAL LAW 21 (1995)].

The 1974 Paris Convention has been replaced, along with the Convention for the Prevention of Marine Pollution by Dumping from Ships and Aircraft (1972 Oslo Convention), Feb. 15, 1972 932 U.N.T.S. 3 (entered into force Apr. 7, 1974), by the Convention for the Protection of the Marine Environment of the North East Atlantic (OSPAR Convention), Sept. 22, 1992, [32 I.L.M. 1069] (*see* Chapter Twelve, Dumping). The OSPAR convention entered into force in 1998, and consolidates efforts to combat land-based pollution with those to control dumping—creating a single commission to oversee both activities.

Art. 2 of the Convention specifies the general obligations of the parties to comply with two principles: the precautionary principle and the polluter pays principle. The notoriously vague precautionary principle, (see Chapter 12), as defined in the OS-PAR Convention means that "preventive measures are to be taken when there are reasonable grounds for concern that substances or energy introduced, directly or indirectly, into the marine environment may bring about hazards to human health, harm living resources and marine ecosystems, damage amenities or interfere with other legitimate uses of the sea, even when there is no conclusive evidence of a causal relationship between the inputs and the effects". According to the Convention the polluter pays principle requires the "costs of pollution prevention, control and reduction measures are to be borne by the polluter".

Article 3 calls for the use of best available techniques (BAT) and best environmental practice (BET) and "clean" technology in the implementation of programmes and measures aimed at meeting the objectives of the Convention. In determining what constitutes BAT and BEP in a specific circumstance, the Commission first looks to the guidelines provided in Appendix I, with BAT as state of the art technology and BET as the most appropriate mix of measures and strategies taking environmental, social and economic factors into account. Next, in the setting of programs and time scales for the control of a specific substance, the Commission considers a series of criteria listed in Appendix 2, including persistency, toxicity and tendency to bioaccumulate. In this way, the Convention dispenses with the "black list—grey list" method, providing only a single, non-exhaustive list of substances to be regulated. This approach appears to offer more flexibility in controlling any particular substance and consequently may lead to greater acceptance of the Commission's arrived at standards. Even so, objecting parties still are not bound by the Commission's official decisions with regard to the annexes and appendices [art. 13], nor its amendments to the annexes [art. 17] or appendices [art. 19]. Without a doubt, however, the OSPAR convention does present a better chance for more effective control than the 1974 Paris Convention.

The OSPAR Commission works within the framework of the 1992 OSPAR Convention as well as five long-term strategies. In July 1998, the Commission committed itself to the elimination of inputs of hazardous substances and radioactive substances from humans into the sea by 2020. Additionally, the strategies include combating eutrophication, the protection of marine ecosystems, and managing mechanisms for offshore activities.

There has also been some movement towards protection of the aquatic environment from land based sources of pollution in the Arctic region. The governments of Canada, Denmark, Finland, Iceland, Norway, Sweden, the Russian Federation, and the United States of America all of which have territory north of the Arctic Circle, are working together to protect the "Arctic Region." The "Arctic Region" means the area north of 60 Latitude, including Labrador and the region in northern Quebec known as "Nunavik." In January 1990, the Arctic Council Panel was established in order to study the feasibility of an Arctic Council, which was established on September 19, 1996. The Arctic Council is a partnership for sustainable development, addressing environmental, social and economic factors. The Council functions by designating several expert working groups. In February 2003, one of the working groups was assigned the task of developing a strategic plan for the protection of the Arctic marine environment. This plan is to be developed over the next two years, and is led by Iceland and Canada. This same working group contributes to the regional and national implementation of the GPA (*see supra*). The working group does this through further implementation and development of the Arctic Council Regional Programme of Action on the same issues. The Council recognizes that much of the pollution in the Arctic Region is derived from sources outside the region, and thus is working with UNEP for a global approach to the region's problems.

On September 18, 1998, the Arctic Council adopted the Regional Programme of Action for the Protection of the Arctic Marine Environment from Land–Based Activities (RPA). The RPA specifically notes the importance of working with the GPA [art. 1.5]. The RPA adheres to the GPA guidelines in that the severity of land-based activities should be considered in relation to food security public health, coastal and marine resources, ecosystem health, and socio-economic benefits [art. 4.1]. The RPA lays out its priorities for regional action, with POPs and heavy metals of highest concern [Table 2]. It then

sets our specific objectives and strategies for each
source [art. 6], and calls for progress reports to be
submitted to the Arctic Council Ministers [art. 7.2].

In other regions of the world a number of the
UNEP Regional Seas Conventions have spawned
specific Protocols dealing with land-based pollution.
They include the Protocol for the Protection of the
Mediterranean Sea Against Pollution from Land
Based Sources, May 17, 1980 (entered into force
June 17, 1983), (amended in Syracusa, Italy, 6–7
March 1996 as the Protocol for the Protection of the
Mediterranean Sea against Pollution from Land–
Based Sources and Activities), the Protocol for the
Protection of the South–East Pacific Against Pollu-
tion from Land–Based Sources, July 23, 1983 (en-
tered into force Sept. 23, 1986), the Protocol on
Protection of the Black Sea Marine Environment
Against Pollution from Land–Based Sources, 1992
(entered into force 1994), the Kuwait region Proto-
col for the Protection of the Marine Environment
against Pollution from Land–Based Sources, 1990
(entered into force 1993), and the Protocol to The
Convention for the Protection and Development of
the Marine Environment in the Wider Caribbean
Region (WCR), or the "Cartagena Convention," on
the Prevention, Reduction and Control of Land–
Based Sources and Activities Concerning Pollution
from Land-based Sources and Activities to the Convention for the Protection and Development of the
Marine Environment of the Wider Caribbean Region (LBS Protocol), adopted 1999. The LBS Protocol is perhaps the most significant agreement of its

kind with the inclusion of regional effluent limitations for domestic wastewater (sewage) and requiring specific plans to address agricultural non-point sources. Specific schedules for implementation have also been included in the Protocol. In addition, the LBS Protocol sets the stage for the development and adoption of future annexes to address other priority sources and activities of pollution.

The Protocols developed before 1995 typically apply only to the jurisdictional sea area covered by the convention and a land application area measured up to the freshwater limit. However, the more recent Protocols, such as those adopted for the Mediterranean and the Wider Caribbean, take a more comprehensive approach, in that they also apply to the hydrologic basin, and regulate more sources of pollution that affect the marine environment. Additionally, they contain obligations requiring national plans, programs, and specific measures for addressing land-based pollution, as well as other regional or subregional cooperative initiatives.

Thus, we see that the umbrella provisions of UNCLOS are being implemented through a variety of regional treaties. Of these, the OSPAR convention, best addresses the problem of waste and pollution in a comprehensive manner and could prove to be a pilot project for the better control of land-based sources of marine pollution.

CHAPTER ELEVEN

VESSEL–BASED POLLUTION

A. NATURE OF THE PROBLEM

Thousands of miles separate the bulk of the world's oil resources from their markets, and giant oil tankers crisscross the oceans of the world carrying massive quantities of oil to distant destinations. The deliberate release of oil by such tankers in the course of routine shipping operations, oil spills caused by tanker accidents, air emissions from ships, scrapping of ships, and the accidental release of chemical transported by ships can threaten living marine resources and ecosystems [ROBERT CLARK, MARINE POLLUTION 64–72 (5th ed. 2001), hereinafter Clark]. Vessels also pollute the oceans with intentionally discharged garbage, of which plastic debris presents a serious threat to marine life.

The transportation of crude oil or refined products results in the release of approximately 136,000 tonnes of petroleum per year into the oceans of the world. [NATIONAL ACADEMY OF SCIENCE, OIL IN THE SEA 111: INPUTS, FATES, EFFECTS 76 (2002) hereinafter NAS 2002]. The gross volume of oil that is spilled into the sea is declining. In 1971, 6.3 million metric tons of oil were lost to the sea. In 1980, the figure was 3.2 million tons, and in 1989, the figure dropped further to 560,000 million tons. [RONALD MITCHELL, INTENTIONAL OIL POLLUTION AT SEA 70 (1994)]. While the U.S. National Academy of Science puts the current figure at 136,000 tonnes, the International Tanker Owners Pollution Federation (ITOPF) claims that the annual quantity of spilled oil dropped from 435,000 tonnes in 1991 to 8 tonnes in 2001. [*http://www.itopf.com/stats:html*]. If we accept the NAS figures, ships still are responsible only for 11.5% of oil in the oceans.

Nonetheless the visual effect of these accidents is dramatic because of the large volume of oil released in a small area. By way of comparison, land-based sources, including dumping and atmospheric fallout that contribute approximately 40% of all oil pollution (see Chapter Ten), and natural seepages that account for 46% [id.] do not attract attention because they are not visually graphic or arresting. In any event, less than 1/100 of 1 percent of all of the oil that is traded is lost at sea.

In a recent study GESAMP (Group of Experts on the Scientific Aspects of Marine Pollution) which consists of eminent experts jointly sponsored and convened by IMO, FAO, UNESCO–IOC, WMO, WHO, IAEA, and UN/UNEP, undertook an authoritative study of marine pollution. They used the Black Sea, where tanker traffic is heavy, to illustrate the role of vessel pollution and found that the vast bulk of oil entering the Black Sea, is attributable to land-based pollution of which nearly half was conveyed via the Danube River. Even after adding the unquantified inputs through the discharge of oily residues from ships, only 136 tonnes of oil out of a total of 111,000 tonnes in the Black Sea can be attributed to accidental oil spills.

According to GESAMP land-based sources of oil input are likely to remain the most significant polluters even in marine areas with heavy tanker traffic, like the Black Sea. Perhaps more significantly, they opine that vessel pollution may be of negligible importance on oceanic scales. Catastrophic spills such as those from the *Amoco Cadiz, Exxon Valdez* and *Prestige* will cause severe, if transient, problems within regional areas, but they are of limited significance on spatial oceanic, and long-term time scales [GESAMP, PROTECTING THE OCEANS FROM LAND-BASED ACTIVITIES, 23, (2001)].

A few large spills are responsible for a high percentage of oil spilled. Between 1990 and 1999, there were 346 spills over 7 tons, but the ten largest incidents accounted for 75% of the total oil spilled. Figures on a particular year can be distorted by a single large incident. Information on 10,000 incidents show that 85% of spills fall into the smallest category of less than 7 tons. The number of large spills (over 700 tons) is relatively low and decreased significantly during the last 30 years. The average number of spills per year during the 90's was about 1/3 of those during the 70's. Most spills from tankers are small ones that result from routine operations like loading, discharging and bunkering usually in ports or at oil terminals. Larger spills (over 700 tons) are relatively rare and generally result from collisions at sea that have significantly decreased (by about 2/3) during the last 30 years.

While vessel-based pollution may at times create more than a negligible risk, it is not the most dangerous form of marine pollution and does not present as large a risk to human health compared to pollutants released by land-based activities or dumping. It is being treated as a separate subject in this book primarily to reflect the international attention given to it. A number of reasons account for the international response to vessel-based pollution. Oil spills create dramatic and frightening visual effects and lend themselves to graphic photographs and media attention. For example, the oil tanker *Prestige*, which sank 150 miles off the coast of Spain in November 2002 and, resulted in an estimated 1 billion dollar clean up effort, was carrying 70,000 metric tons of oil. This is more than twice the amount of oil spilled by the *Exxon Valdez*, and the resulting spectacle received wide media publicity. Such publicity is heightened by the harm suffered by sea birds and other marine creatures which provokes public indignation and tarnishes the image of the oil industry. Such an impression is worsened by the fact that oil slicks washed ashore effectively prevent the use of beaches and prohibit sea bathing. In response, ship owners, operators of oil tankers and oil companies—who do not cherish their tarnished environmental image—have been willing to take steps to control vessel pollution and to set up their own compensation schemes.

B. ENVIRONMENTAL IMPACTS

1. HARM CAUSED BY THE PHYSICAL PROPERTIES OF OIL

Studies conducted over the last twenty years confirm that the physical properties of oil are harmful to marine life. [NAS 2002 *supra*]. Oil spilled or discharged at sea changes its composition as it spreads over the surface of the water in a thin layer called an *oil slick*. Some components evaporate or dissolve, while others break down and disperse as small droplets. Under some water conditions a thick, sticky mass may form on the surface of the water. The heavy residues of oil from the discharge of oily bilge and ballast water may form tar balls.

Oil that becomes stranded near shore smothers small marine animals and destroys plant life. Heavier oils and mousse-like emulsions clog the bodies of small marine animals, interfering with respiration, feeding and movement. Seabirds, sea otters, and other small marine animals that spend much of their time on the surface of the water, and rely on the insulating properties of feathers or fur to survive, are particularly vulnerable [*see* DWIGHT HOLING, COASTAL ALERT, ECOSYSTEMS, ENERGY, AND OFFSHORE OIL DRILLING 28 (1990)]. Oil destroys the water repellence of a sea bird's plumage, causing it to become waterlogged and drown, or causing it to freeze to death from the loss of thermal insulation. [CLARK, supra at 86–95]. Over 30,000 seabirds died as a result of the 1989 *Exxon Valdez* oil tanker accident in Alaska, but many more seabirds die each year from non-accidental releases of oil in the Northeast Atlantic. Sea otters, which rely on the trapped air in their dense fur for survival in the cold, are likewise vulnerable to floating oil. A sea otter will die of hypothermia if 20–30 percent of its body is covered with oil. The *Exxon Valdez* oil spill caused the deaths of over 1,000 sea otters. Though there is evidence of the deleterious effects of oil pollution on individual organisms and species, there is no reliable evidence of the chronic or acute effects of oil on communities or ecosystems. [NAS supra at 6].

2.   HARM CAUSED BY THE TOXIC PROPERTIES OF OIL

Crude oils as well as refined petroleum products contain toxic substances detrimental to the health of sea birds, plankton, and fish [CLARK, supra at 86–95]. Depending on the toxicity of the oil even small quantities swallowed by birds can prove deadly.

Oils that are dissolved or dispersed in the water can easily penetrate the delicate skin of fish gills, while its aromatic components can irritate and clog the respiratory systems of fish. Adult fish may be able to avoid areas of floating oil, but fish eggs and immature fish that inhabit surface waters cannot do so, and absorb hydrocarbons that cause reduced hatching and early death. Oil that reaches the sediments on the bottom of the ocean impacts the very base of the marine food chain by reducing the production of aerobic bacteria, on which the benthic (bottom-dwelling) organisms depend for their diet.

C. CAUSES OF VESSEL–BASED OIL POLLUTION

Vessel based pollution has declined impressively over the past two to three decades and continues to do so. As we shall see, these dramatic decreases in oil discharges have largely been the result of regulations under the International Convention for the Prevention of Pollution from Ships, Nov. 2, 1973, [12 I.L.M. 1319] as amended, (hereinafter MARPOL 73/78). Two authoritative reports of the U.S. National Academy of Sciences, the first issued in 1985 and the second in 2002, flag these dramatic changes. Accidental spills were estimated at 400,000 tonnes per year according to the 1985 report, and fell to 100,000 tonnes per year according to the 2002 report. Operational discharges, which accounted for 700,000 tonnes in the 1985 report, plummeted to just above 5% of that number: 36,000 tonnes according to the 2002 report. [NAS, 1985, 2002].

It is estimated that intentionally discharged tanker oil accounts for up to one fourth of all ship-generated pollution [NAS, 2002, supra at 76]. Tanker accidents, discharges from non-tankers, and escapes from pipelines and atmospheric depositions account for the rest. Tanker de-ballasting and cleaning used to constitute the major source of oil pollution. When a tanker delivers its cargo, a thin layer of oil remains in the tanks as "clingage." On the return voyage, tankers fill empty cargo tanks with sea water as ballast to stabilize them. They also use sea water in high pressure cleaning procedures to wash down the tanks before receiving a new consignment of oil. Additionally, oil and lubricants from the ship's engines leak into the bilges (bottoms) of tankers and become mixed with sea water. Prior to their arrival at port, captains traditionally discharged the resulting oil/water solutions (or "slops") at sea.

Much of this changed with the regulations made under MARPOL 73/78. Tankers whose deadweight was 20,000 tonnes and over were required to have segregated ballast tanks (SBT), dedicated clean ballast tanks (CBT), or crude oil washing systems (COW). These are tanks completely separated from cargo and fuel oil systems and permanently allocated to the carriage of water ballast. Moreover, pursuant to MARPOL regulations a full two thirds of the tanker fleet now have double hull arrangements. [NAS 2002].

As part of routine operations, ships discharge garbage in addition to oil-contaminated bilge and ballast water. [CLARK supra at 6]. Non-biodegradable plastic debris is an especially serious problem because it may remain in the ocean for 100 years [*see* TONY HARE, POLLUTING THE SEA 14 (1991)]. An estimated 6.5 million tons of plastic per year were discarded by ships in the early 1990's. Seabirds, fish, and mammals die from drowning or injury by getting tangled in plastic packaging, such as six-pack rings and sheeting, or by swallowing plastic objects.

D.   REMEDIAL OBJECTIVES

Remedial objectives for routine operational discharges should include ship design changes, as well as port facilities for receiving "slops" Most tanker accidents occur in high risk areas near shore and close to port entrances where the high volume of shipping traffic multiplies the risk of a collision, and natural hazards such as reefs and rocks increase the risk of ships going aground. Accident prevention should concentrate on construction standards, such as double-hulled oil tankers, and safety standards that ensure seaworthiness and prevent navigational errors that might result in a collision or grounding Ships should be prepared for emergencies and provisions need to be made for intervention in case of an accident. As we shall see, there has been a positive legal response to these issues.

Efforts should also be made to control and contain spilled oil and prevent its reaching land. Floating booms (similar to short curtains) may be used in an attempt to deflect and contain the spilled oil until it can be pumped off the surface, but are most useful in protecting small areas. Devices for mopping up oil slicks, called "slick-lickers," can handle small spills but are not effective on the open sea.

Dispersal techniques need to be improved. All of the components of crude oil are degradable by bacteria but at vastly different rates depending on the state of the oil. The breakdown of oil into droplets that will more easily biodegrade can be accelerated by spraying dispersants on oil slicks. The dispersants are less toxic than in the 1970's, when the surfactants used in the dispersants caused erosion of fish gills and organs. To further accelerate nature's own cleanup mechanism, a new technique, *bioremediation*, stimulates the growth of the naturally occurring oil-eating bacteria.

More progress needs to be made in shore cleaning techniques which have sometimes increased the damage and delayed recovery from oil spills affecting shore lines. [CLARK, supra at 80]. Beach cleaning techniques include high-pressure water, steam, and dispersants. Physical forces, heat, and cleaning-chemical toxicity may kill most naturally occurring organisms on the beach that have not already been killed by the effects of the oil. Physically mopping up the oil on the beach is only partially effective because most of the oil spilled eludes recovery or clean up. Moreover, clean ups are often more apparent than real because the oil is not removed, but drained away or forced to a few inches below the surface. Here, without oxygen to degrade the oil, it may remain for over a year.

"Ex ante" regulations based upon new technology need to be implemented through a liability regime that enables injured parties to seek relief against polluters. As we discuss below, the international response to vessel pollution has been more satisfactory than in many other areas.

E. LEGAL RESPONSE

International law has responded to the two different causes of vessel pollution: (1) the general operation of commercial shipping; and (2) the occasional accident occurring at sea (*see* also Chapter Ten, Land–Based Pollution).

1. OPERATIONAL POLLUTION

As we have noted, most vessel pollution of the marine environment arises from the daily operation of ships, not from the highly publicized, but infrequent, catastrophe. To address this type of pollution, the international community has developed two fundamental and related schemes of governance. The first is (MARPOL 73/78), which set out specific regulations for, among other things, the permissibility of pollution discharge as well as construction requirements for ships. The second important legal regime is the United Nations Convention on the Law of the Sea (UNCLOS), Dec. 10, 1982, [21 I.L.M. 1261] (entered into force Nov. 16, 1994) which potentially alters the jurisdictional structure of MARPOL while generally deferring to its other provisions.

(a) The 1973/1978 International Convention for the Prevention of Pollution From Ships (MARPOL)

The MARPOL Convention is the most important global treaty for the prevention of pollution from the operation of ships; it governs the design and equipment of ships; establishes a system of certificates and inspections; and requires states to provide reception facilities for the disposal of oily waste and chemicals. It covers all the technical aspects of pollution from ships, except the disposal of waste into the sea by dumping, and applies to ships of all types, although it does not apply to pollution arising out of the exploration and exploitation of sea-bed mineral resources.

Regulations covering the various sources of ship-generated pollution are contained in the six Annexes of the London Convention and are updated regularly. Annexes I and II, governing oil and chemicals are compulsory but annexes III, IV, V and VI on packaged materials, sewage, garbage and air pollution are optional. It is a combination of two treaties adopted in 1973 and 1978, respectively, and updated by amendments through the years, and is commonly known as MARPOL 73/78.

The MARPOL treaty and its protocols (most significantly the 1978 Protocol Relating to the International Convention for the Prevention of Pollution from Ships) supply general duties for parties, supplemented by the more detailed Annexes, that are themselves supplemented by Appendices to Annexes. In this way, MARPOL creatively deals with the problem of balancing general duties with specific obligations. The regime also provides a flexible approach to law-making, as various combinations of a two-thirds majority in either the IMO or a convened Conference of the Parties can effectively amend the

Treaty, Protocols, Annexes or Appendices [art. 16(f)(i-v)].

The Convention currently includes regulations aimed at preventing and minimizing pollution from ships—both accidental pollution and that from routine operations—and also includes six technical Annexes: Annex I deals with prevention of pollution by oil, Annex II deals with noxious liquid substances, Annex III with harmful substances in packaged form, Annex IV with sewage, Annex V with garbage and Annex VI with air pollution from ships. Parties to the Convention must accept Annex I and II, but the rest are voluntary. [*Id*].

Annex I, which entered into force in 1983, covers the regulation of oil discharge from ships, mandating both construction requirements and release allowances. The technical requirements of construction and readiness are fairly intricate, and attempt to provide minimum safety standards with respect to tankers. Significantly, 1992 amendments 13[f] and 13[g] call for "double-hulls" on all new oil tankers—a feature long sought by environmentalists to prevent spillage in case of rupture. As for release allowances, Annex I quantitatively limits discharge from all ships, limits the rate at which oil may be discharged to 60 liters per mile traveled, and prohibits discharge in most circumstances within 50 miles of the coastline [Reg. 9]. The Annex also severely limits the release of oil in special environmentally sensitive areas, including the Baltic, Mediterranean, Black and Red Seas, and the Gulfs. [Reg. 10].

Annex II entered into force in 1987 and details the discharge criteria and measures for the control of pollution by noxious liquid substances carried in bulk. There were 250 substances included in the Convention, and the discharge of their residues is allowed only to reception facilities. No discharge of residues containing noxious substances is permitted within 12 miles of the nearest land. Annex III entered into force in 1992 as the first optional annex. It contains general requirements for the issuing of detailed standards on packing, marking, labeling, documentation, stowage, quantity limitations, exceptions and notifications for preventing pollution by harmful substances. As mentioned above, Annex IV contains requirements to control pollution of the sea by sewage and enters into force in September 2003. Annex V entered into force in 1988, deals with different types of garbage, and specifies the distances from land and the manner in which garbage may be disposed of. The most important feature of the Annex is the complete ban imposed on the dumping into the sea of all forms of plastic. Annex VI (the Protocol of 1997 for the Prevention of Air Pollution), has only been adopted as an amendment and has not yet entered into force. The regulations in this annex will set limits on sulphur oxide and nitrogen oxide emissions from ship exhausts and prohibit deliberate emissions of ozone depleting substances. [IMO website: http://www.imo.org].

In allocating responsibility for the monitoring of its regulations, MARPOL creates a role both for the flag state and the port state. To fulfill its obligations, the flag state must certify each ship's compliance with MARPOL's construction and readiness guidelines by issuing an International Oil Pollution Prevention Certificate for each vessel [Reg. 5(2)]. In addition, the flag state must update the certificate, conducting periodic surveys of each ship to ensure continued observance of the regulations [Reg. 4]. The port state, for its part, may inspect any ship within its ports or off-shore terminals in order to verify "that there is on board a valid certificate" [art. 5]. If "clear grounds" exist for believing that the condition of the ship does not correspond to the certificate, the port state may then conduct a full inspection of the vessel [art. 5(2)]. If it finds a violation, the port state must prevent the ship from setting sail until the vessel "can proceed to sea without presenting an unreasonable threat of harm to the marine environment" [art. 5(2)].

Concerning the investigation of discharge violations, the port state has even more latitude than in construction and readiness inspections. In this case, the port state does not need "clear grounds" upon which to proceed with an inspection, but in fact may examine any and all ships within its jurisdiction. When coupled with some reliable evidence, the port state may also investigate any violation alleged by another party to the convention, regardless where the claimed illegal discharge has occurred [art. 6(5)]. If an inspection indicates a violation of MARPOL discharge rules, the port state immediately submits a full report to the flag state [art. 6(4)].

The flag state must then institute appropriate actions against the violating ship, and must notify both the port state and the IMO of the disciplinary steps taken [art. 6]. In applying its own law, the flag state must not allow more lenient treatment of its flag ships, but must impose penalties "adequate in severity to discourage violations" of the MARPOL regime [art. 4(4)].

(b) The United Nations Convention on the Law of the Sea (UNCLOS)

As previously discussed, UNCLOS significantly alters the jurisdictional scheme of the world's oceans. Concluded after MARPOL, UNCLOS makes potentially broad changes in the application of the former, especially in regard to coastal state power under the expanded Exclusive Economic Zone (EEZ). MARPOL does not compel extension of coastal state jurisdiction beyond the territorial sea, but neither does it forbid such an extension. Instead, MARPOL simply gives deference to future application of UNCLOS to its own provisions, stating that "the term 'jurisdiction' ... shall be construed in the light of international law in force at the time of application or interpretation of the present Convention" [MARPOL 9(3); PATRICIA BIRNIE & ALAN BOYLE, INTERNATIONAL LAW AND THE ENVIRONMENT 273 (2002)].

As a jurisdictional matter, the question arises as to when a coastal state may adopt stricter pollution provisions than those provided in MARPOL. Based on traditional notions of sovereignty, UNCLOS codifies a long-held customary rule that a coastal state may adopt more stringent discharge rules in both its internal waters and territorial sea [art. 211(3), 211(4)]. The rigor of these laws, however, must not interfere with a foreign vessel's right of innocent passage [art. 24]. Innocent passage remains a time-honored right, and UNCLOS defines the term as movement which is "not prejudicial to the peace, good order or security of the coastal state" [art. 19(1)]. On the other hand, a coastal state may not adopt stricter construction or readiness requirements for foreign vessels traveling in its internal waters or territorial sea, as clearly this would dramatically hinder the right of innocent passage by limiting access to only certain types of vessels [art. 21(2)].

In the EEZ, in contrast, a coastal state may not adopt more exacting discharge rules than those already in place under MARPOL [art. 211(5)]. In this way, UNCLOS limits the sovereignty of a coastal state within its own jurisdiction. Even for environmentally sensitive areas, a coastal state must first seek approval of the IMO to adopt special pollution discharge rules and, if approved, the adopted rules must follow IMO recommendations [art. 211(6)(a)].

Concerning enforcement of discharge violations, UNCLOS offers several variations from the more limited MARPOL regulations, though nations have yet to put these expanded powers into practice. Under UNCLOS, coastal states have a type of graduated authority in dealing with pollution violations.

For example, if "clear grounds" exist for believing a vessel has committed a state or MARPOL violation in the territorial sea, then the coastal state may undertake physical inspection of the ship, detain the vessel, and institute proceedings against it [art. 220(2)]. For minor violations in the EEZ, a coastal state may only require the ship to provide information concerning its identity as well as its last and next ports of call [art. 220(3)]. However, when "clear grounds" exist for believing a ship has committed "a substantial discharge causing or threatening significant pollution of the marine environment" in the EEZ, then the coastal state may commence an inspection if the vessel fails to provide satisfactory information about the incident [art. 220(5)]. Finally, in the most egregious circumstances, if "clear objective evidence" exists that a vessel has committed a violation causing "major damage or threat of major damage to the coastline," the coastal state may then undertake a broader physical inspection of the ship, detain the vessel, and institute proceedings against it [art. 220(6)].

UNCLOS also gives expanded enforcement jurisdiction to the port state, but again in practice states have yet to employ these powers. Understandably, a port state may institute proceedings against any vessel voluntarily in port that has committed a violation within that state's territorial sea or EEZ [art. 220(1)]. Additionally, however, UNCLOS conveys a qualified universal jurisdiction on the port state, which may institute proceedings against any ship that has committed a MARPOL discharge violation on the high seas or within the jurisdiction of another state, if the latter so requests [art. 218]. The result is an expanded role for the port state, much beyond that bestowed by MARPOL. The universal jurisdiction remains limited only by that of the flag state, which always retains a right of preemption under Article 228, except in cases of "major damage" to coastal states. Whether the international community actually adopts the expanded jurisdictional powers of the port and coastal states remains to be seen, though states now possess the legal wherewithal to do so under UNCLOS. In the meantime, the legal regimes of MARPOL and UNCLOS must take significant credit for the fact that routine shipping operations, once responsible for releasing an estimated 3–6 million metric tons of crude oil each year in the 1970's, declined in the early 90's to only 10 to 20 percent of that level [RONALD MITCHELL, INTENTIONAL OIL POLLUTION AT SEA 70 (1994)].

2. ACCIDENTAL POLLUTION

Over the years, accidental pollution of the marine environment—especially in the form of oil spills—has given rise to an extensive system of international agreements for the prevention and containment of such disasters. At the most general level, UNCLOS provides a requirement that states notify other affected states in the case of imminent danger or damage to the marine environment [art. 198], as well as mandating that states cooperate in the development of contingency plans to respond to these emergencies [art. 199]. To this end, states have added a number of safety protocols to the UNEP Regional Seas Conventions—providing a framework for collaboration and the creation of specific response plans. In addition to these protocols, the International Convention on Oil Pollution Preparedness, Response and Co-operation (OPRC), established a broader role for the IMO in coordinating action among parties [Nov. 30, 1990, 30 I.L.M. 773 (entered into force May 13, 1995)].

(a) International Convention on Oil Pollution Preparedness, Response and Co-operation (OPRC)

Parties to the OPRC convention are required to establish measures for dealing with pollution incidents, either nationally or in co-operation with other countries. Under the treaty each party must require its flag ships to carry on board "an oil pollution emergency plan" that adheres to the criteria put forth in MARPOL Annex I, Regulation 26 [*see* art. 3(1)(a)]. These ships then remain subject to inspection by the port state in accordance with MARPOL art. 5 & 6 [*see* art. 3(1)(b)]. Moreover, operators of offshore units—such as drilling rigs—must now have oil pollution emergency plans [art. 3(2)]. At the state level, each party must develop a "national contingency plan for preparedness and response" as part of a national and regional system designed to deal with major oil spills [art. 6]. Parties also have quite specific procedures for reporting oil pollution incidents [art. 4] and for acting on such reports [art. 5]. Buttressing each of these obligations, the OPRC provides a strong oversight role for the IMO—a function designed to foster efficient use of the organization's expertise, and to effect fairness and universal compliance with its provisions.

(b) International Convention Relating To Intervention on the High Seas In Cases of Oil Pollution Casualties (1969 Intervention Convention and 1973 Protocol)

To clarify extra-jurisdictional powers of states, the international community created one of the earliest environmental pollution treaties with the 1969 Intervention Convention, Nov. 29, 1969, 26 U.S.T. 765 (in force May 6, 1975). Developed in response to another major oil spill, the *Torrey Canyon* disaster, in which a tanker mishap caused massive damage to the coastlines of Britain and France, the 1969 Intervention Convention lays down the requirements for a coastal state's intervention during a high seas accident. Under the treaty parties may take measures on the high seas as necessary "to prevent, mitigate, or eliminate grave and imminent danger to their coastline" [art. I(1)]. The treaty also provides mandatory notification and consultation procedures, except in cases of extreme urgency, with regard to flag states and other interested parties [art. III]. All actions taken by an intervening coastal state must be proportionate to the actual or threatened damage, or the

state may be liable to those unreasonably harmed
[art. V, VI].

In the 1973 Protocol Relating to the Intervention
on the High Seas of Pollution by Substances Other
Than Oil (1973 Intervention Protocol), Nov. 2,
1973, 34 U.S.T. 3407 (in force Mar. 30, 1983), the
parties extended the rules of the original convention
to other hazardous substances. The protocol creates
a list of such substances, but also allows action to
control any accident involving "those other substances which are liable to create hazards to human
health, to harm living resources and marine life, to
damage amenities, or to interfere with other legitimate uses of the sea" [art. I(2)]. Concerning the
latter group of unlisted substances, the burden of
proof shifts to the intervening coastal state to prove
a "grave and imminent danger" analogous to that
of a listed substance [art. I(3)]. In 1991 and 1993
the 1973 Protocol was amended so as to include a
revised list of substances.

The 1982 UNCLOS drops the requirement of
"grave and imminent danger" and allows a coastal
state the right to take any measures proportionate
to the actual or threatened damage [art. 221]. Note
that no reference is made here to the coastal state's
EEZ. Therefore, UNCLOS appears to apply the
same standard of proportionality to actions taken in
the EEZ, as to those taken on the high seas under
the 1969 Intervention Convention and 1973 Intervention Protocol. The only significant difference

exists in UNCLOS discarding the "grave and imminent danger" threshold for both the EEZ and high seas.

(c) Protocol on Preparedness, Response and Cooperation for Pollution Incidents by Hazardous and Noxious Substances, 2000 (HNS Protocol)

This agreement follows the principles of the OPRC and was formally adopted by states Party to the OPCR at a Diplomatic Conference held at the IMO headquarters in March 2000. The HNS Protocol, like OPRC, aims to provide a global framework for international cooperation in combating major incidents or threats to marine pollution. Parties to the agreement are required to establish measures for dealing with pollution incidents, and ships are required to carry a shipboard emergency plan to deal with incidents involving hazardous and noxious substances (HNS).

When the HNS Protocol comes into force, it will ensure that ships carrying hazardous and noxious liquid substances are covered, or will be covered, by regimes similar to those already in existence for oil incidents. In 1996, the IMO adopted the International Convention on Liability and Compensation for Damage in Connection with the Carriage of Hazardous or Noxious Substances by sea, providing for a compensation and liability regime for incidents involving these substances.

3. LIABILITY

(a) State Responsibility

The principle of state responsibility for wrongful actions affecting the marine environment remains a well-settled rule of international law. UNCLOS codifies the principle in article 235(1), asserting that "states are responsible for the fulfillment of their international obligations concerning the protection and preservation of the marine environment." Therefore, both flag and coastal states may find themselves liable for actions taken or not taken in accordance with international law. As to the specific liability imposed, most commentators consider the standard one of "due diligence" rather than "strict liability" [BIRNIE & BOYLE, supra]. In fact, although several instances exist in which flag states have paid compensation for oil tanker accidents, injured parties have not targeted states concerning marine pollution. Instead, given the elaborate compensation scheme outlined below, nearly all claimants for oil pollution accidents have looked to private entities to make them whole.

(b) Civil Liability

i. *1969 International Convention on Civil Liability for Oil Pollution Damage (1969 CLC)*

The 1969 CLC, Nov. 29, 1969 973 U.N.T.S. 3 (entered into force June 19, 1975) creates a system for awarding compensation as well as limiting the liability incurred by the owner of a ship involved in an oil pollution accident. The Convention places the liability for such damage on the owner of the ship from which the polluting oil escaped or was discharged. Subject to a number of specific exceptions, this liability is strict. Upon the coming into force of the 1992 Protocol to the 1969 CLC, the treaty will become the 1992 International Convention on Civil Liability for Oil Pollution Damage, 1992 WL 602598, (1992 Liability Convention). Unlike the 1969 CLC, the 1992 Liability Convention clarifies that "pollution damage" includes damage to the marine environment, though "compensation for impairment of the environment other than loss of profit from such impairment shall be limited to costs of reasonable measures of reinstatement actually undertaken or to be undertaken" [art. I(6)(a)]. In other words, claimants will not receive speculative awards for environmental damage, but will only obtain compensation for actual restoration of the marine ecosystem.

According to an allocation procedure based on gross tonnage, the total compensation of a ship owner remains limited for any particular accident. In arriving at the right total some calculation is involved. For example, each "unit of tonnage"— computed in accordance with measurement regulations—corresponds to a certain number of "units of account." Under the 1992 Liability Convention, this translates into three million units of account for the first 5,000 units of tonnage, and 420 units of account for each unit of tonnage thereafter [art. V(1)]. A ceiling of 59.7 million units of account exists for any specific accident. To qualify for the ceiling, the owner must deposit a fund with the appropriate court constituting the total amount of its liability—converting the specified units of account (or "Special Drawing Rights" (SDR) as defined by the International Monetary Fund (IMF)) into national currency according to IMF procedures. Claimants then receive compensation from the fund "in proportion to the amounts of their established claims" [art. V(4)].

Under the 1969 CLC, the owner cannot take advantage of the limit on liability if the owner's "actual fault or privity" caused the accident [art. V(2)]. The 1992 Convention would change this provision, only disallowing the limit on liability when the owner's actions or omissions intentionally or recklessly caused the pollution damage. Under both conventions, the owner of a tanker must hold insurance in the amount of its potential fund contribution, and the ship must carry a certificate attesting to that fact on board at all times [art. VII]. Significantly, during the transitional phase when the 1969 CLC still remains in force, the 1992 Liability Convention would mandate the satisfaction of claims first from the 1969 CLC and then the 1971 Fund Convention (mentioned below) before allowing claims under its own provisions [art. XII *bis*]. From 16 May 1998, Parties to the 1992 Protocol ceased to be Parties to the 1969 CLC due to a mechanism for compulsory denunciation of the "old" regime established in the 1992 Protocol. However, for the time being, the two regimes are co-existing, since there are a number of States which are Party to the 1969

CLC and have not yet ratified the 1992 regime—which is intended to eventually replace the 1969 CLC. The 2000 amendments raised the compensation limits by 50 percent compared to the limits set in the 1992 Protocol.

ii. International Convention on the Establishment of an International Fund for Compensation for Oil Pollution Damage (1971 Fund Convention)

The 1971 Fund Convention, Dec. 18, 1971, 1971 U.N. Jur. Y.B. 103 (entered into force Oct. 16, 1978) creates a burden sharing system in which the owners of oil cargo, such as oil companies, contribute to the overall cost of a tanker accident. In this way ship owners do not shoulder the entire cost of such a catastrophe. The convention adopts most of the definitions of the 1969 CLC, and by protocol in 1992 incorporates the definitions of the 1992 Liability Convention. Upon the entry into force of the 1992 protocol, the convention will be known as the 1992 International Convention on the Establishment of an International Fund for Oil Pollution Damage (the 1992 Fund Convention). To date, under the 1971 Fund Convention much confusion has occurred concerning the application of the term "pollution damage" to environmental harm; however, in adopting the definition of the 1992 Liability Convention as discussed in the preceding section, the 1992 Fund Convention will now allow compensation for "reasonable measures of reinstatement actually undertaken or to be undertaken" [art. I(2)].

As was the case with the 1992 Protocol to the CLC Convention, the main purpose of the Protocol was to modify the entry into force requirements and increase compensation amounts. The scope of coverage was extended in line with the 1992 CLC Protocol. The 1992 Protocol established a separate, 1992 International Oil Pollution Compensation Fund, known as the 1992 Fund, which is managed in London by a Secretariat, as with the 1971 Fund. In practice, the 1971 Fund Convention and its 1992 counterpart exist solely as additional sources of restitution for injured "persons"—whether individuals, corporations or states. To this end, such persons have access to the 1992 Fund Convention only if "unable to obtain full and adequate compensation" under the 1992 Liability Convention for the following reasons: (a) the 1992 Liability Convention is inapplicable; (b) the owner or its insurance company cannot pay; or (c) the damage exceeds that allowed under the 1992 Liability Convention [art. 4(1)]. As in the 1992 Liability Convention, the 1992 Fund Convention itself establishes a limit on the total contribution the Fund might make to a particular accident, in most cases in the amount of 135 million "units of account" (or "SDRs") as converted into national currency by the International Monetary Fund [art. 4]. An insurance mechanism that attempts to spread the cost of a single accident among all oil cargo owners, the Fund obtains its own contributions from these entities through the contracting parties, basing each assessment on the number of tons of oil cargo received during the preceding year.

CHAPTER TWELVE

DUMPING

A. NATURE OF THE PROBLEM

The wastes generated in today's world need to be neutralized or disposed of in a manner that is both effective and efficient. We have noted that optimal waste treatment includes conversion of wastes into a form that will least tax, and better enable the environment to dilute, degrade, assimilate or absorb them. The conversion or treatment of wastes has included the emission of gases and particles into the atmosphere, discharges of sludge and liquid effluent into the aquatic environment, and burial on land (*see* Chapter Nine, Toxic and Hazardous Substances). To this list must now be added the "dumping" of wastes into the sea. Approximately 10 percent of the pollutants and toxic materials that enter the ocean do so in this way [INTERNATIONAL CHAMBER OF SHIPPING, SHIPPING AND THE ENVIRONMENT: A CODE OF PRACTICE (1997)].

"Dumping" is term of art referring to a particular form of marine pollution that is not included in land-based (*see* Chapter Ten), or vessel-based pollution (*see* Chapter Eleven; *see* § D 2, *infra* for a legal definition). Specifically, it has been confined to a form of marine pollution in which wastes, often containing toxic materials, are taken by ship and dumped, or incinerated, in the high seas. "Dumping" has not, therefore, typically referred to land-based pollution through discharges of wastes into the sea, estuaries or rivers from direct outfalls, or vessel-based pollution caused by accidental or deliberate discharges by oil tankers or other ships. However, since what is dumped is generated on land, it is difficult to refute the rationale of the Convention for the Protection of the Marine Environment of the North East Atlantic (OSPAR Convention), Sept. 22, 1992, [32 I.L.M. 1069] (entered into force Mar. 25, 1998), which treats dumping as a species of land-based pollution.

In the past, dumping hazardous waste into the ocean was seen as an acceptable method of disposal because of the relatively low economic costs and the perception that oceans could readily assimilate unlimited quantities of waste. Ocean dumping became less favored as its effects on marine ecology became apparent. Questions have also arisen concerning the reasonableness of allowing industrialized countries to utilize a shared resource (the oceans) without regard to the risks and costs imposed on future generations [PATRICIA BIRNIE & ALAN BOYLE, INTERNATIONAL LAW AND THE ENVIRONMENT 143 (2002)].

B. SOURCES AND ENVIRONMENTAL IMPACTS

Many types of waste that are difficult to dispose of on land have traditionally been dumped directly into oceans and rivers without regulation. This includes many hazardous materials, such as sewage, industrial effluents, sludges, radioactive wastes and polluted dredged spoils. A more detailed review of the characteristics and environmental impacts of these materials is provided in Chapters Nine (Toxic and Hazardous Substances) & Ten (Land–Based Pollution). Bulky, but relatively harmless materials, such as construction waste, wreckage, sand, and excavation debris, have also been subject to widespread dumping. These activities have had significant repercussions in marine food chains and may impact deep-sea biodiversity and ecosystem health.

C.   REMEDIAL OBJECTIVES

As we have noted in Chapter Nine, dumping is a symptom of the malaise of ever-spiraling wastes. Remedial objectives, generally, have largely failed to deal with the root source of toxic wastes, which lies in human demand for products that can only be met by generating such wastes. Moreover, the international environmental community has failed to adopt a truly integrated approach to waste disposal and pollution control.

We shall see that the United Nations Convention on the Law of the Sea (UNCLOS), Dec. 10, 1982, 21 I.L.M. 1261 (entered into force Nov. 16, 1994), and the Convention on the Prevention of Marine Pollution by Dumping of Wastes and Other Matter (1972 London Convention), Dec. 29, 1972, art. 3(1), 1046 U.N.T.S. 120 (entered into force Aug. 30, 1975) did not prohibit all ocean dumping. Instead, they attempted to control it by prohibiting the disposal of particular wastes based on their toxicity, persistence, bioaccumulation, and likelihood of widespread environmental exposure. Today, this regime has been expanded by the entry into force of the 1992 OSPAR Convention, which takes a more comprehensive view of waste management by including land-based and other sources of pollution along with ocean dumping. In addition, the 1996 Protocol to the 1972 London Convention (1996 Protocol), Nov. 8, 1996, 36 I.L.M. 7, incorporates crucial features of the OSPAR Convention and is more fully discussed below.

D. LEGAL RESPONSE

The international attitude toward ocean dumping has moved from an initial stage of acceptance, through strict regulation, to the present general trend prohibiting the dumping of particular kinds of wastes. Especially in recent years, the international community has tightened the rules related to dumping of hazardous substances by, for example, banning all ocean dumping of radioactive wastes. The general legal regime for dumping is defined by UNCLOS, which sets forth a framework of rules for states to follow. The 1972 London Convention, a global treaty, governs more specific actions, and a system of regional agreements facilitates compliance.

1. UNITED NATIONS CONVENTION ON THE LAW OF THE SEA (UNCLOS)

UNCLOS creates a comprehensive jurisdictional framework defining the features and extent of state jurisdiction for the implementation of IMO regulations. UNCLOS mandates that all states adopt measures "to prevent, reduce and control pollution of the marine environment by dumping" [art. 210(1)]. However, in creating such measures, states may not establish standards that are "less effective" than global rules and standards [art. 210(6)]. In this way, UNCLOS establishes a "floor" of minimum protection that all states must follow, and that floor exists as the 1972 London Convention. Yet within its own territorial sea, Exclusive Economic Zone (EEZ, *see* Chapter 13) or continental shelf, a state has the right to institute more stringent requirements than those of the London Convention [art. 210(5)]. Furthermore, in codifying customary international law, UNCLOS provides the coastal state with the right of prior approval to any dumping within its sovereign waters, which of course now includes both the EEZ and the continental shelf [art. 21(1)ff; BIRNIE & BOYLE, supra at 371 (2002)].

2. CONVENTION ON THE PREVENTION OF MARINE POLLUTION BY DUMPING OF WASTES AND OTHER MATTER (1972 LONDON CONVENTION)

The 1972 London Convention exists as the primary vehicle for the international regulation of dumping. As defined by the convention, dumping includes the "disposal of wastes or other matter from vessels, aircraft, [and] platforms" as well as the deliberate sinking of those structures themselves as a method of disposal [art. III(1)]. "Dumping," however, does not include the discharge of oil and other harmful substances in the normal operation of those structures, which in general is covered by the International Convention for the Prevention of Pollution from Ships (1973/1978 MARPOL Convention), Nov. 2, 1973, 12 I.L.M. 1319 (entered into force July 1, 1992). (see Chapter 11)

In regulating the disposal of wastes, the 1972 London Convention employs a listing and permit system that is intended to cover the entire spectrum of dumping at sea. For substances listed in Annex I, or the "black list," dumping is prohibited except in emergency situations [art. IV(1)(a), V(2)]. In addition to dangerous substances such as mercury, cadmium and crude oil, this list includes "netting and ropes" which may "interfere materially with fishing, navigation or other legitimate uses of the sea" [Annex I(4)]. In contrast, the convention allows the dumping of substances on Annex II, or the "grey list," but requires a prior "special permit" to do so. Materials on this list include trace amounts of the toxic substances listed in Annex I, as well as less hazardous wastes such as chromium and nickel [art. IV(1)(b)]. The convention allows the dumping of all other wastes at sea, requiring only that the vessel obtain a "general permit" [art. IV(1)(c)]. The responsibility for issuing these permits, and thereafter reporting the information to the IMO, falls upon the appropriate authorities of a party for all wastes loaded in its territory [art. VI(2)]. On the other hand, when a flag ship loads wastes in the territory of a state not party to the convention, the responsibility for permitting and reporting remains with the flag state [art. VI(2)]. In considering whether to grant either type of permit, the designated authorities must look to the broad dictates of Annex III, which mandates that they take into account both the characteristics of the material dumped and the dump site.

Especially for an older treaty, the 1972 London Convention creates an innovative and flexible rule-making system. Consultative Meetings of the Parties may adopt an amendment to the treaty by a two-thirds majority of those present, but such a change only comes into force for those parties who accept it [art. XV(1)(a)]. For an amendment to any Annex—which must be based on scientific or technical considerations—again a two-thirds majority at the Consultative Meeting passes the change, but the burden shifts as only parties who denounce the amendment within a certain time frame remain unbound [art. XV(2)]. Finally, a Consultative Party may adopt non-binding resolutions as it sees fit [*see* art. XIV(b)-(f)].

In considering the special example of radioactive waste dumping, we can see the flexibility of the above system at work. For instance, the convention originally placed high-level radioactive wastes on Annex I, and low-level radioactive wastes on Annex

II. In 1983, however, and then again in 1985, the Consultative Meeting passed a non-binding resolution that installed a moratorium on the dumping of all radioactive wastes, including low-level wastes. From this point on the political and scientific debate intensified concerning the potential harm of radioactive dumping, culminating with the Russian admission that the former Soviet Union had repeatedly dumped both high-and low-level wastes for decades. As a final measure, in 1993 the Consultative Committee amended Annex I to include all "radioactive wastes or other radioactive matter" [Annex I(6)]. In response only Russia officially filed a declaration of non-acceptance with the IMO, in effect allowing it legally to continue the disposal of low-level radioactive wastes at sea. For all other parties, the dumping of radioactive material of any type remains illegal.

The case of radioactive dumping, therefore, while reflecting the flexibility of the 1972 London Convention system, also reveals its limitations in controlling all dumping of an environmentally damaging nature. Furthermore, though in theory the permit and reporting system covers the entire spectrum of dumping at sea, nations have had a difficult time in controlling illegal dumping by their own nationals [PHILIPPE SANDS, PRINCIPLES OF INTERNATIONAL ENVIRONMENTAL LAW 310 (1995)]. Nonetheless, as a general rule commentators point to the convention as one of the most successful environmental treaties to date for its significant role in the quantitative worldwide reduction of the disposal of wastes at sea [BIRNIE & BOYLE, supra at 427].

The 1996 Protocol is intended to replace the 1972 London Convention, as is dealt with more fully in Section 3. As of May 31, 2002, sixteen of the necessary 26 parties had ratified the Protocol, and another nine had signed with their ratification pending.

3.   1996 PROTOCOL TO THE CONVENTION ON THE PREVENTION OF MARINE POLLUTION BY DUMPING OF WASTES AND OTHER MATTER, 1972

The 1996 Protocol, which has not yet come into force, flags a significant change in the approach to waste management. Substantively, it replaces the selective restrictions on dumping imposed by the 1972 Convention, with a total ban on waste incineration, dumping of most materials, and exporting wastes to non-parties for the purposes of dumping or incineration at sea. [Art. 5–6]. Even the limited exceptions to these bans that may be granted in cases of serious, unavoidable threats to human health, safety, or the marine environment when there is no feasible, less-harmful alternative, require substantial international consultation and oversight. [Art. 8]. The Protocol joins a number of other international instruments such as the Stockholm Convention on Persistent Organic Pollutants, May 22, 2001, 40 I.L.M. 532 (see Chapter Nine), the Cartagena Protocol on Biosafety to the Convention on Biological Diversity, Jan. 29, 2000, 38 I.L.M.

1027 (see Chapter 5), and the United Nations Framework Convention on Climate Change, May 9, 1992, 31 I.L.M. 849 (see Chapter 6) in incorporating its own version of the elusive and ill defined precautionary principle [Christopher D. Stone, *Is There a Precautionary Principle? 31 Envtl. L. Rep. 10790, 10799 (2001)*] (see Chapter Eighteen for fuller discussion of the precautionary principle). It also embodies the "polluter pays" principle, and moves toward a more comprehensive strategy of waste reduction and prevention.

Unlike the 1972 Convention, which prohibits the dumping of specific listed materials, the 1996 Protocol bans dumping of any material that is *not* listed in Annex 1. [Art. 4, 1.1]. Materials currently listed are dredged materials, sewage sludge, industrial fish processing waste, vessels and offshore platforms, inert, inorganic geological material, organic material of natural origin, and bulky but unharmful materials like iron, steel, and concrete for which no waste disposal on land is possible. [Annex 1, 1]. Dumping of radioactive materials, or of matter that could seriously impede fishing or navigation, is prohibited. [Annex 1, 2].

While the 1972 London Convention permits the dumping of unlisted wastes, the 1996 Protocol allows dumping permits to be issued only for listed substances. To list a new substance, the would-be polluter must conduct a scientific risk assessment of its probable impact on human health and the environment, [Annex 2, 7], including complete information about the product's origins; physical, chemical, biochemical and biological properties; toxicity; persistence; and tendency to accumulate or biotransform in organisms or sediments. [Annex 2, 8.1–8.5]. If this information is incomplete, the waste cannot be listed. [Annex 2, 7].

The Protocol adopts a proactive approach to the generation of wastes. Applicants for dumping permits are required to undertake an exhaustive self-evaluation of waste reduction and disposal strategies, with a view toward avoiding dumping altogether by finding "environmentally preferable alternatives." [Art. 4, 1.2].

To apply for a permit, a polluter must first conduct a "Waste Prevention Audit" to identify sources of the waste and find ways to reduce it at the source. [Annex 2, 2.1]. This entails a complete evaluation of polluters' production systems, and a full assay of the feasibility of waste reduction via product reformulation, clean production technologies, process modification, input substitution, and recycling. [Annex 2, 2.3.1–2.3.5]. If the audit reveals that one or more of these methods could feasibly reduce the amount of waste produced by the permit applicant, the applicant must formulate a general waste reduction strategy incorporating those methods, setting specific target reductions and providing for future audits to ensure compliance.

Once the dumping permit applicant has conducted waste prevention analysis and implementation, the 1996 Protocol also requires it to submit a comparative risk assessment to demonstrate that it is unable to dispose of the waste in less environmentally harmful ways. In order of preference, disposal should be sought via reuse, recycling, destruction of hazardous materials, treatment to reduce or remove hazardous components, and disposal of the waste on land, into air, or in water. [Annex 2, 5]. If the permitting authority finds that the permit applicant could utilize one of these less harmful alternatives without disproportionate cost, it may deny the permit. Similarly, the permit applicant must demonstrate that the specific dump site will be the best feasible choice, taking into account factors like biological sensitivity of the area and the location of other possible uses of the sea. [Annex 2, 11].

Finally, the Protocol requires the permitting authority to conduct an assessment of the potential effects each disposal option could have on human health, its environmental costs, hazards, economics, and exclude the possibility of future uses of the waste, and issue or deny a permit based on that assessment. [Annex 2, 12–13]. Extensive monitoring provisions are also incorporated to ensure compliance with the authority's guidelines and to verify that the environmental and health costs projected in the assessment were correct. [Annex 2, 16]

For settlement of disputes, the 1996 Protocol sets forth a detailed arbitration procedure, paid for by the parties to the dispute [Annex 3]. This is a compulsory system of arbitration that significantly buttresses the role of arbitration, as distinct from judicial settlement, as a form of legal enforcement. (See Chapter Three).

4. REGIONAL TREATIES

A number of regional treaties have dealt with the question of dumping, and in some cases these agreements have led to a tightening of standards beyond those of the 1972 London Convention. These regional treaties include the Convention on the Protection of the Marine Environment of the Baltic Sea Area, Apr. 9, 1992, 1992 WL 675165 (entered into force Jan. 17, 2000); the Convention on the Protection of the Black Sea Against Pollution, Apr. 21, 1992, 32 I.L.M. 1101 (entered into force Jan. 15, 1994), and accompanying Protocol on the Protection of the Black Sea Marine Environment Against Pollution by Dumping, Apr. 21, 1992, 1992 WL 602572 (entered into force Jan. 15, 1994); and the Convention for the Protection of the Natural Resources and Environment of the South Pacific Region, Nov. 24, 1986, 26 I.L.M. 38 (entered into force Aug. 22, 1990), and the accompanying Protocol for the Prevention of Pollution of the South Pacific by Dumping, Nov. 24, 1986, 26 I.L.M. 38 (entered into force Aug. 22, 1990).

By far the most encouraging of the regional conventions is the 1992 OSPAR Convention, which takes an integrated approach and deals with land-based pollution and dumping in one treaty. Like the 1996 Protocol, this demonstrates a more comprehensive ecosystem approach to protection, and more clearly defines the strong presumption against dumping by disallowing the practice entirely—*except* for a small number of listed substances [OS-

PAR Annex II, Art. III]. Along with the Protocol, this treaty points the way to the future and could serve as a pilot project for more ambitious undertakings.

CHAPTER THIRTEEN

CONSERVATION OF MARINE LIVING RESOURCES

A. NATURE OF THE PROBLEM

Ninety percent of marine life exists within ecosystems located in shallow waters above the continental shelves. While the oceans cover 70 percent of the earth's surface, the continental shelves are submerged extensions of the coastline at the edge of the continents, forming only a small fragment of the oceans. The proximity of these shallow waters to land exposes marine resources and ecosystems to increasing environmental impacts from human activities (*see* Chapter Four, Population Growth; and Chapter Ten, Land Based Pollution). Burgeoning population and economic growth gives rise to oceanic over-exploitation, pollution, and habitat destruction that threatens the health and bounty of the environment. Protecting marine living resources and ecosystems from these forces is important not only for maintaining the world's ecological balance, but also for meeting the food needs of an increasing world population [TONY HARE, POLLUTING THE SEA 5 (1991); D. Alastair Bigham, *Pollution from Land Based Sources*, in THE IMPACT OF MARINE POLLUTION 203 (Douglas Cusine & John Grant eds., 1980)].

382

B. SOURCES AND IMPACTS

In this section, we introduce and briefly canvass a few of the major human activities that adversely impact marine ecologies. The following topics will be the focus of our discussion throughout this section: (1) biodiversity decline caused by over-exploitation of fish stocks; (2) ecological damage resulting from human pollutants; and (3) the effect of development and soil erosion on estuarine and coastal habitats.

First, over-exploitation has caused a serious decline in biodiversity in the world's fishing regions. Unsustainable takings have depleted edible fish stocks, while changing the balance of the predator-prey relationship within marine ecosystems. Modern fishing technologies that yield a harvest rate exceeding the reproductive rate of fish have resulted in the depletion or full exploitation of almost every commercial species of fish. Some industrial techniques can be especially harmful. In driftnet fishing, for example, the nylon mesh nets extend for miles and indiscriminately catch all creatures too large to pass through them. The result includes the illegal catch of undersized, pre-reproductive fish of the target species, and non-target species that are then thrown back into the ocean to die. Such illegal and unwanted fish, called "by-catch," may amount to as much as 30 percent of the legal catch. Thousands of marine mammals, seabirds and sea turtles are also killed by drowning or injury in fishing nets each year. Dolphins are frequent victims because commercially valuable tuna swim beneath them, and the dolphins become entangled in the nets intended to catch the tuna. In addition to these problems, the deliberate catching of species in violation of international laws also impacts biodiversity within the world's major fishing areas. For example, the total reported legal catch of the Patagonian toothfish in the Antarctic for the year 2000 was 10,245 metric tones; however, estimates indicate that during this same period the illegal catch of this fish was more than 100,000 metric tones within the Indian Ocean sector of the Southern Ocean alone [*see* UNEP, GLOBAL ENVIRONMENTAL OUTLOOK 2000].

Long before driftnets became a threat, whales and seals were commercially hunted to the verge of extinction, exploited for their meat, fur, oil, and ivory [SIMON LYSTER, INTERNATIONAL WILDLIFE LAW 39 (1985)]. Perhaps two million whales were killed between 1920 and 1980, when at last serious international efforts to protect whales began [J. J. MCCOY, THE PLIGHT OF THE WHALES 11 (1989)]. The killing of perhaps three or four million seals during the 19th century resulted in the serious depletion of seal populations, and led to international efforts to protect seals in the early 1900's. Today, despite international efforts, whales and thousands of seals (including baby harp seals) are still killed illegally or under the guise of legal taking for "scientific purposes." [*see* Chapter Eight, Antarctica, § F(6)(b)].

Furthermore, human demand for fish competes with the demand on those resources by other fish, seabirds, and marine mammals. Natural fishery environments are highly diverse, and fishing one or two commercial species causes imbalances in the many ecosystems in these environs. For example, commercial over-fishing of cod and haddock at New England's Georges Bank depleted a prime feeding area for whales. Similarly, the Antarctic marine food chain has been disrupted by fishing for krill—shrimp-like crustaceans that are an important food source for whales, seals, penguins, and seabirds [STEPHEN SAVAGE, ENDANGERED SPECIES, DOLPHINS AND WHALES 106 (1990); *see also* Chapter Eight, Antarctica § D].

Second, pollution threatens marine living resources by destroying marine habitat and adversely affecting the health effects of species that live there. Some land-based discharges are directly toxic to marine life. The effects of these toxins are worsened by their concentration in the surface layer of the sea containing the marine phytoplankton on which the marine food chain depends. The toxic pollution of marine life has resulted in thinner eggshells of seabirds (decreasing their survival rate), impaired reproduction in some marine mammals, and physical deformities. Other pollutants, though not toxic, contribute to rampant algae growth which kills fish by clogging their gills and depleting the water of oxygen (*see* Chapter Nine, Toxic and Hazardous Substances; and Chapter Ten, Land Based Pollution).

Pollutants are deposited in the oceans by many mechanisms including atmospheric deposition, ocean dumping and oil contamination from commercial activities. Atmospheric deposition is responsible for over 30 percent of marine pollution. Chlorinated hydrocarbons (including pesticides, such as DDT, and PCBs) are released into the atmosphere by evaporation from the earth's surface and during crop spraying. They also are carried on wind-borne dust. These pollutants then precipitate into the marine environment as rain or fallout.

Ocean dumping constitutes ten percent of marine pollution see (Chapter Twelve). The most significant ocean dumping involves dredged spoils, or sediments removed from shipping channels. Because shipping areas are often industrialized, dredged spoils can contain significant amounts of heavy metals, petroleum hydrocarbons, and chlorinated hydrocarbons. Other wastes dumped at sea include sewage sludges, garbage and radioactive wastes. Overall, ocean dumping adversely affects marine habitat in two ways: the solid material settles to the bottom smothering bottom-dwelling marine life, and habitat and the toxic pollutants in the dredged spoils or wastes are released into the water (*see* Chapter Twelve). Oil pollution from tanker operations and accidents, coastal refineries, and offshore oil production also accounts for about ten percent of all marine pollution. For a complete discussion of these activities, *see* Chapters Twelve, Dumping, Eleven, Vessel Based Pollution, and Ten, Land-Based Pollution.

Third, estuarine and coastal habitats, such as coral reefs, mangrove forests, and coastal wetlands, are damaged not only by chemical pollution, but also by development and accompanying soil erosion. Soil sediments clog and destroy estuarine and coastal habitats. Coral reefs, central to some of the most productive and diverse ecosystems, are especially susceptible to sedimentation damage. Mangrove forests along the reef shores that provide essential feeding and breeding habitat for young fish also remain vulnerable to the deleterious impacts of sedimentation and erosion. Additionally, human activities and subsidence destroy coastal wetlands. For example, coastal development in the Mississippi Delta—predicted to continue into the next century—devastates wetlands that act as habitat of much marine biological diversity, including the feeding and breeding ground for many species of fish [WALTER REID & MARK TREXLER, DROWNING THE NATIONAL HERITAGE: CLIMATE CHANGE AND U.S. COASTAL BIODIVERSITY 8 (1991); *see also* UNEP, GLOBAL ENVIRONMENTAL OUTLOOK–3 180 (2002) (hereinafter GEO–3)].

In the discussion above we identified a few of the major ecological impacts effected by human activities on the marine environment. However, to understand the problems presented by these impacts, we must not only investigate the human activities that precipitated them, we must also investigate the pressures behind these human activities. Population growth, urbanization, industrialization, and tourism in coastal areas are just a few of the many topical faces that such an investigation might reveal [*see* GEO–3, at 180]. As a more specific example of this point, consider that in 1997 an estimated 50 percent of the global population lived in coastal areas; and that by 2025, this percentage is expected to increase to 75 percent. The activities of this population profoundly impact the marine environment (and beyond), which in turn markedly affects that population (and beyond). When we see that 37 percent of the population in 1997 is far larger than the total number of people living on the planet in 1950, the phenomenon of population growth becomes apparent as an important factor in developing solutions to the problems created by human-induced damage to the marine environment [*see generally* Chapter 4, Population Growth].

In December of 2002, the U.N. General Assembly adopted a resolution to establish a U.N. process for the global reporting and assessment of the state of the marine environment by 2004. This process is intended to include both the socio-economic aspects of the relevant issues in both their current and foreseeable identities [*see* G.A. Res. 57/141, 57th Sess., Agenda Item 25(a), A/RES/57/141 at 45 (2002)].

C.   REMEDIAL OBJECTIVES

Marine living resources are an integral part of the biodiversity of the world, and the protection of marine biodiversity has to be approached in tandem with the preservation of terrestrial biodiversity under the Convention on Biological Diversity, June 5, 1992, [31 I.L.M. 818] (entered into force Dec. 29, 1993) (*hereinafter CBD see* Chapter Five, Biodiversity). Responding to this reality, the Parties to the Convention on Biological Diversity agreed on a program of action for implementing the Convention. The program called "Jakarta Mandate on Marine and Coastal Biological Diversity" was adopted in 1995. Through its program of work, the Convention focuses on integrated marine and coastal area management, the sustainable use of living resources, protected areas, mariculture and alien species. In this endeavor, the CBD has many partners, including international organizations and initiatives regional organizations such as the Regional Seas Conventions and Action Plans, [see Chapter Ten, Land–Based Pollution], local governments, research facilities and non-governmental organizations.

A twin challenge faces the protection of both marine and terrestrial living resources and ecologies: human population growth and economic development. IEL, on the whole, has attempted to deal with over-exploitation, pollution, and habitat destruction, rather than directly address the more intransigent issues of population growth and economic development that fall within the matrix of sustainable development. This pragmatic attempt to address the more immediate issues can be seen as a necessary first step toward a more complete solution because the international community may not be willing to go further at this stage. It is important, however, that any serious attempt to address marine over-exploitation should at least open the door to a more explicit and concrete recognition of the demands of sustainable development.

The first steps toward a more integrated approach to managing natural resources within the framework of sustainable development have been taken at programmatic as well as treaty levels. In addition to the Jakarta Mandate under the CBD referred to above, Chapter 17 of Agenda 21 (see Chapter Two) titled "Protection of the Oceans, All Kinds of Seas, Including Enclosed and Semi–Enclosed Seas, and Coastal Areas and the Protection, Rational Use and Development of Their Living Resources" provides prescriptions for ocean and coastal management. In Par. 17.5, coastal nations commit themselves to "integrated management and sustainable development of coastal areas and the marine environment under their jurisdiction." The text stresses the need to reach integration (e.g., identify existing and projected uses and their interactions and promote compatibility and balance of uses); the application of preventive and precautionary approaches (including prior assessment and impact studies); and full public participation .

In addition, under art. 4 of the Framework Convention on Climate Change parties commit themselves, inter alia, "to develop integrated plans for coastal zone management." Thus, the Framework Convention on Climate Change reinforces the more general prescriptions concerning integration contained in Chapter 17 of Agenda 21. Furthermore, under the Global Programme of Action on Protection of the Marine Environment from Land–Based

Activities, [see Chapter Ten, Land–Based Pollution]
States agree to ... focus on sustainable, pragmatic
and integrated environmental management approaches and processes such as integrated coastal
area management, harmonized, as appropriate, with
river basin management and land use plans

For both ecological and political reasons it is
important that the conservation of marine resources be located within an integrated legal design
for the oceans. The United Nations Convention on
the Law of the Sea (UNCLOS), Dec. 10, 1982, 21
I.L.M. 1261 (entered into force Nov. 16, 1994) has
responded to this challenge by initiating the development of such a comprehensive regime. UNCLOS
focuses on the protection of marine living resources
as an intrinsic component of the oceanic environment, and contains a number of necessary, general
obligations dealing with the protection of different
marine resources. The comprehensive approach of
UNCLOS to the oceans, which deals *inter alia* with
land-based pollution, sets the stage for further coordination between UNCLOS and the Biodiversity
Convention—as well as international legal regimes
whose topical focus and substantive commitments
are not that of environmental protection.

D. LEGAL RESPONSE

1.   UNITED NATIONS CONVENTION ON THE LAW OF THE SEA (UNCLOS)

(a) Overview

Developed over a period of 30 years, including fifteen years of active negotiation, UNCLOS provides an example of the comprehensive rather than the framework approach to treaty-making. The Convention combines a broad codification of international law and other substantive rules into one authoritative source and addresses a remarkably broad range of issues: e.g., navigational rights, territorial sea limits, economic jurisdictions, passage of ships through narrow straits, conservation, management and protection of the marine environment, a marine research regime and, rather uniquely, a binding procedure for the settlement of disputes between States. It could be described as a "constitution" for the oceans—a convention that incorporates other international rules, regulations, and implementing bodies, and which aspires to be the authoritative voice (with some specified exceptions) on matters pertaining to these things (*see also* Chapter Two, The Historical Continuum, § B).

i.   *Dispute Settlement under UNCLOS—The Bluefin Tuna Case*

The scope and authority of the dispute settlement machinery established by UNCLOS was canvassed in the Southern Blue Fin Tuna Case [*see* Southern Bluefin Tuna Case (N.Z. v. Japan; Austl. v. Japan),

1999 ITLOS Nos. 3 & 4 (Provisional Measures Order of Aug. 27)]. Australia, New Zealand and Japan had signed a trilateral regional fisheries agreement known as the Convention for the Convention for the Conservation of Southern Bluefin Tuna, May 10, 1993, 1819 U.N.T.S. 360 (entered into force May 10, 1994) (hereinafter Bluefin Convention). The Bluefin Convention allocated to each party a quota of allowable catches. Australia and New Zealand alleged that Japan had exceeded its quota by employing "research fishing." When the three countries failed to resolve the issue under the Bluefin Convention, Australia and New Zealand initiated an action before the International Tribunal on the Law of the Sea (ITLOS) charging Japan with violations of UNCLOS. In a decision announced August 27, 1999, ITLOS required Japan to provisionally cease its experimental fishing program until an UNCLOS arbitration panel had the opportunity to decide the issue of whether Japan's actions violated UNCLOS on the merits [*id.*]

However, in August of 2000, a five-member international arbitral tribunal held that it lacked jurisdiction to decide the issue on the merits [Australia and New Zealand v. Japan, Award on Jurisdiction and Admissibility, 39 I.L.M. 1359 (2000) (hereinafter Bluefin Case)]. Accordingly, the tribunal revoked the provisional measures issued by ITLOS which had enjoined Japan's Bluefin experimental fishing program.

The core of Japan's argument before the arbitral tribunal was that (1) the dispute arose solely under the 1993 Convention, (2) a provision of the Bluefin

Convention excluded compulsory settlement procedures without the agreement of all the parties, and (3) thus it could not *ipso facto* be compelled to arbitrate the merits of the dispute. In the alternative, Japan argued (4) that if the tribunal were hold the dispute arose under both conventions, a provision of UNCLOS which entitles parties to avoid compulsory dispute settlement where another treaty to which they are parties excludes such a settlement procedure governed this case and militated in favor of a decision by the tribunal against recognizing its jurisdictional authority.

The arbitral tribunal characterized Japan's argument that the dispute only concerned the Bluefin Convention as relying on an "artificial" distinction and held that the dispute arose under both conventions. However, by a vote of 4 to 1, the Tribunal sustained Japan's contention that a provision of the Bluefin Convention excluded compulsory jurisdiction over disputes arising both under it and the Law of the Sea Convention. According to the arbitral tribunal, the Bluefin Convention had rejected compulsory jurisdiction because article 16(3) allows only for consensual and not compulsory arbitration. Consequently, compulsory adjudication under UNCLOS was unavailable to the parties [Bluefin Case, at ¶ 57]. Curiously, while explaining that the terms of article 16(2) of the Bluefin Convention were determinative of the jurisdictional issue, the arbitral tribunal also stated that the provisions of article 16 "do not expressly and in so many words exclude the applicability of any procedure, including the compulsory procedures of UNCLOS" [id. at ¶ 56].

As regarding the binding nature of UNCLOS, however, the arbitral tribunal was of the view that "UNCLOS falls significantly short of establishing a truly comprehensive regime of compulsory jurisdiction entailing binding decisions." This view is highly contentious and is based on dubious reasoning.

(b) Jurisdiction Zones

UNCLOS resolves a centuries-long debate concerning the jurisdictional boundaries of the world's oceans. In fact its jurisdictional pronouncements have evolved from case law, particularly the ICJ's jurisdictional guidelines as set forth in the *Icelandic Fisheries Cases* (1974) [Fisheries Jurisdiction (Federal Republic of Germany v. Iceland), 1974 I.C.J. 3; Fisheries Jurisdiction (United Kingdom of Great Britain and Northern Ireland v. Ice.), 1973 I.C.J. 302]. For the purposes of marine living resources, UNCLOS delineates four major areas: the *territorial sea*, the *exclusive economic zone*, the *continental shelf* and the *high seas*.

i. *Territorial Sea*

In clear language UNCLOS extends the sovereignty of a coastal state to 12 nautical miles, known as the territorial sea [arts. 2 & 3]. This means that specific utilization of the area remains subject to the laws and regulations of the coastal state. The coastal state can, for example, prohibit all fishing in its territorial sea unless otherwise provided by agreement. In effect UNCLOS only grants other states the right of innocent passage, which the coastal state may strictly control through the adoption of laws and regulations with respect to "the conservation of the living resources of the sea" [art. 21(1)(d)].

ii. Exclusive Economic Zone (EEZ)

Potentially a major breakthrough for the preservation of marine living resources, the EEZ comprises a 200 nautical mile breadth as measured from the same baselines used to measure the territorial sea [art. 57]. UNCLOS bestows sovereignty and jurisdiction over this area to the coastal state [art. 56(1)(a)], in return for which the coastal state must perform a number of obligations, including the conservation and management of living resources in the zone [art. 61(2)]. In this way UNCLOS supersedes the former doctrine of "freedom of fishing," which now applies only in limited fashion on the high seas, and which has long contributed to over-exploitation of resources.

As part of its conservation and management duties, the coastal state must determine the "allowable catch of the living resources in its exclusive economic zone" [art. 61(1)] and must take measures to ensure "that the maintenance of the living resources in the exclusive economic zone is not endangered by over-exploitation" [art. 61(2)]. In doing so, the coastal state must consider the effects of exploitation on species related to the harvested species, which includes other species caught incidentally while trying to catch commercial species [art. 61(4)]. Further, the coastal state must "promote the objective of optimum utilization of living resources" [art. 62(1)], and strive "to maintain or restore populations of harvested species at levels which can produce the maximum sustainable yield" [art. 61(3)].

After setting an appropriate "allowable catch" for a commercial species, the coastal state may then take the entire catch if it desires. If, however, the coastal state cannot harvest the full allowable catch, then the coastal state may grant access to other states in order to harvest the surplus [art. 62(2)]. Contrary to the former freedom of fishing doctrine, other states may therefore only take certain designated species in the EEZ, and then only by permission of the coastal state. In considering which states to give permission to, a coastal state must first look to the needs of developing countries and landlocked states [arts. 62(2) & (3); 69 & 70].

By extending conservation and management duties to the 200 mile limit of the EEZ, UNCLOS provides a potentially effective mechanism to prevent over-exploitation of marine living resources; according to recent figures, over 90 percent of the world's fisheries resources lie within national EEZs. Nonetheless, in practice developing countries have had technical difficulty in determining the allowable catch for all commercial species in their respective EEZs, and in enforcing both their conservation laws and their exclusive rights to development. Organizations such as FAO and UNEP have endeavored to assist developing countries in these efforts, but funds remain scarce. Much work still exists to fulfill this promising aspect of UNCLOS.

iii. Continental Shelf

The coastal state will in all cases have sovereignty over the natural resources of its continental shelf [art. 77(1)]. This means that the coastal state has exclusive rights to the "sedentary species" of the seabed—those "organisms which, at the harvestable stage, either are immobile on or under the seabed or are unable to move except in constant physical contact with the seabed or the subsoil" [art. 77(4)]. In most cases the continental shelf will exist within the EEZ, and so the rules pertaining to the waters above the shelf will be those of the EEZ. In the unusual case of a continental shelf extending beyond the 200–mile limit, however, a special situation arises. The waters above the seabed will remain subject to the rules of the high seas, while the natural resources of the seabed will still fall within the sovereignty of the coastal state [art. 77(1)]. Interestingly, UNCLOS includes no explicit duty to conserve the resources of the continental shelf, but most commentators agree that a duty is implied given the strong emphasis on conservation throughout the convention.

iv. High Seas

In the area beyond the EEZ the former doctrine of freedom of fishing still obtains, though it now exists in qualified fashion. States do have the right for their nationals to engage in fishing on the high seas [art. 116], but certain duties of conservation and management also apply. For example, as necessary states must adopt measures for their respective nationals regarding the conservation of living resources on the high seas [art. 117]. In addition, states have a duty to cooperate with each other concerning the conservation and management of these resources; as appropriate this may include the creation of regional fisheries [art. 118]. Furthermore, through such cooperative arrangements states must endeavor to set "allowable catche[s]," again designed to maintain or restore harvested species at levels of maximum sustainable yield, and take any other conservation measures regarding harvested species [art. 119(1)(a)]. In doing so states must also protect incidentally captured species from becoming "seriously threatened" [art. 119(1)(b)].

The above general obligations have recently been further defined by the 1995 Agreement for the Implementation of the Provisions of UNCLOS Relating to the Conservation and Management of Straddling Fish Stocks and Highly Migratory Fish Stocks (Straddling and Highly Migratory Fish Stocks Agreement or SFSA), Dec. 4, 1995 [34 I.L.M. 1542]. States whose vessels work the high seas must now follow the regulations of SFSA, outlined below, concerning these designated categories of fish stocks.

(c) The Species Approach

In combination with the general obligations laid down for different jurisdictional zones, UNCLOS adopts special rules for several groups of species. This approach acknowledges the wide variety of marine living resources, as well as the commensurate difficulties in dealing with such variability. Unless otherwise noted in the treaty, the general obligations regarding the EEZ and the high seas still remain—such as setting allowable catches and adopting proper conservation and management measures. However, regarding "straddling stocks" and "highly migratory fish stocks," the recent SFSA provides more extensive protections.

i. Straddling Stocks

"Straddling stocks" are fish stocks located both in a coastal state's EEZ and an adjacent area of the high seas. In general UNCLOS article 63(2) mandates that the coastal state and the other states fishing the stocks on the high seas enter into agreed measures "necessary for the conservation of these stocks." In practice, however, the regional fisheries have not successfully addressed this problem, and in particular they have had no power to control the consumption of non-member distant water flagships. In the Northwest Atlantic, for example, when the member states of the Northwest Atlantic Fishing Organization (NAFO) actually reduced their total allowable catch on the high seas (excluding squid) by 8.7 percent from 1986–1992, non-member states over the same period increased their own take by 27.7 percent.

In addressing such difficulties, the 1995 SFSA compels greater cooperation between coastal states and distant-water flag states. Coastal States and States fishing on the high seas must "adopt measures to ensure the long-term sustainability of straddling fish stocks and highly migratory fish stocks and promote the objective of their optimum utilization" [SFSA art. 5(a)]. In short, this means that both coastal states and flags states must cooperate to adopt compatible "conservation and management measures" such as catch limits for certain species [SFSA art. 7]. In most instances this negotiation will take place through the appropriate regional or sub-regional fishery, and all flag states fishing on the high seas must either join the relevant fishery or at least agree to abide by the measures established by that organization [SFSA art. 8].

The new SFSA also provides for enforcement mechanisms on the high seas. This is a major step with regard to the management of high seas fishing. In effect, a member of a subregional or regional fishery organization may board and inspect a flag state ship on the high seas "for the purpose of ensuring compliance with conservation and management measures ... established by that organization ..." [SFSA art. 21(1)]. The inspecting state must notify the flag state of any alleged violation [SFSA art. 21(2)], such as failing to maintain accurate catch data or fishing for a prohibited stock, and the flag state must then respond within three working days [SFSA art. 21(6)]. In the meantime, inspectors may remain on board, and the flag state must choose either to inspect the matter itself or authorize the inspection by the inspecting state [SFSA art. 21(6)]. The result is a new approach to policing the high seas—one that requires all states to follow the rules adopted by regional and sub-regional fisheries organizations as these organizations attempt to protect straddling stocks and highly migratory fish stocks. For a recent, and potentially conflicting, perspective, see the Bluefin Case, [*supra* § D(1)(a)(i)].

ii.   *Highly Migratory Species (HMS)*

UNCLOS creates a special category for highly migratory species listed in Annex I of the treaty. This annex includes some mammals, but the primary focus is on non-mammals such as marlin, swordfish and tuna. Coastal and other fishing states must "co-operate" either directly or through organizations "with a view to ensuring conservation and promoting the objective of optimum utilization of such species throughout the region, both within and beyond the exclusive economic zone" [art. 64(1)]. In addition, states must work to establish appropriate cooperative organizations where none exist [art. 64(1)]. As made clear by article 65, the treaty excludes marine mammals from the article 64(1) requirement of promoting "optimum utilization" of such species if states, collectively or individually, opt for more stringent protection. Again, for non-mammals the 1995 SFSA creates further duties of cooperation between distant-water flag states and coastal states, with the focus of such cooperation taking place through relevant regional and sub-regional fisheries organizations.

iii. *Marine Mammals*

In singling out marine mammals, UNCLOS recognizes their especially fragile circumstances. Through loss of habitat, over-exploitation and incidental taking, the mammals of the oceans have proved particularly vulnerable, and as a rule their populations do not recover as quickly as fish. UNCLOS article 65 allows coastal states or any appropriate international organization "to prohibit, limit or regulate the exploitation of marine mammals more strictly than provided for" in the general articles dealing with the EEZ. UNCLOS article 120 broadens the protections offered by article 65 to include the high seas. Furthermore, states must "co-operate with a view to the conservation of marine mammals," and in the case of cetaceans (whales and porpoises) must "work through the appropriate international organizations for their conservation, management and study" [art. 65]. This latter provision has led to some confusion, both as to the identity of the "appropriate international organizations" and as to the breadth of the phrase "work through." Canada, for example, has taken the stand that it should manage the small cetaceans found in its own EEZ, and that NAFO should play a limited consultative role. Others have argued that the IWC exists as the proper institution for all cetaceans, and that its role should be determinative rather than consultative. As it turns out, a number of countries have instituted outright bans on the taking of many marine mammals, but small cetaceans especially remain at risk of continued depletion without a coherent framework of protection. (For more on the role of IWC, *see* § 3 below).

iv. The Special Case of Seals

The extension of national jurisdiction under UNCLOS has largely supplanted international efforts to protect seals, as nearly all seals live within the 200–mile limit of the EEZ. Formerly, however, the conservation of seals for later exploitation purposes very much occupied the minds of fur industry nations. As early as 1911, Japan, the United States, Russia and Canada signed a treaty to share in the taking of certain Pacific Ocean species [Convention between the United States of America, the United Kingdom of Great Britain and Northern Ireland and Russia, for the Preservation and Protection of Fur Seals]. July 7, 1911, VIII I.E.P. 3682:29 (entered into force Dec. 15, 1911). With the expiration of this convention in 1941, the same parties (Russia replaced by the Soviet Union) concluded the Interim Convention on Conservation of North Pacific Fur Seals, Feb. 9, 1957, 314 U.N.T.S. 105 (entered into force Oct. 14, 1957). The parties amended and renewed this convention a number of times, though the last agreement of 1984 has now expired. In the Atlantic, two different instruments protect seals in the northeast and northwest Atlantic, respectively, though again their importance as conservation instruments has waned. More recently, the treaty for the Conservation of Seals in the Wadden Sea entered into force in 1991 between the Netherlands, Denmark and Germany—a treaty which takes an ecosystem approach to habitat protection and pollution control, while also prohibiting the taking of seals within the region.

Therefore, though bilateral and small multilateral agreements may help in the coordination of regional protection of seals, the more wide-ranging and inclusive treaties of the past no longer possess their former appeal. In the future, more effective protection may be afforded by the listing procedures of both CITES and the Bonn Convention. Finally, for the protection of seals living outside of national jurisdiction in the Antarctic, please see the Chapter Eight, Antarctica.

v. *Anadromous Species*

Anadromous species are those species, such as salmon, which spawn in freshwater rivers, migrate to the high seas, and finally return to the same freshwater rivers to reproduce. UNCLOS allocates a dual role for the state of origin, which has both a "primary interest in and [a] responsibility for such stocks" [art. 66(1)]. This means that the state of origin, after negotiations with other interested states, may set a total allowable catch for such species [art. 66(2)]. The state of origin therefore obtains the first right to exploit these species, and all taking should occur landward of the outer limits of its EEZ. However, other states that might experience economic dislocation without harvesting the species may by agreement receive special allowance to participate in the taking—either in the EEZ or on the high seas [art. 66(3)(a)]. In return for the right to utilize the species, the state of origin has the obligation to "ensure their conservation" by proper regulatory measures [art. 66(2)]. This includes the creation of conservation regulations for all takings landward of its EEZ, and the good faith attempt to establish conservatory agreements for all takings beyond that limit.

vi. Catadromous Species

These are species spawned on the high seas, such as eels, which then migrate to freshwater rivers and lakes. For these species the UNCLOS gives the coastal state—"in whose waters catadromous species spend the greater part of their life cycle"—the responsibility for "management" [art. 67(1)]. Harvesting by any party is prohibited on the high seas [art. 67(2)]. In waters landward of the outer limits of the EEZ, the coastal state assumes the rights and obligations generally allocated for other types of fishing in its EEZ. This means that the coastal state sets an allowable catch and other states may only participate in the harvest by agreement [art. 67(2)].

2. UNEP REGIONAL SEAS PROGRAMME

An umbrella program of UNCLOS, the regional seas programme of the United Nations Environment Programme (UNEP) has evolved into an extremely broad system of marine protection. Covering a number of seas or coastal regions—a majority involving developing countries—the Regional Seas Programme often functions as the primary means for coordinating environmental action within the geographic area. These treaties are more fully discussed in Chapter Ten: Land–Based Pollution section 3 Regional Treaties.

In implementing the programme, UNEP had made use of the convention-protocol approach to international law making. First, UNEP develops an Action Plan for the region, which the potential parties then use to create a framework treaty. Subsequently, the parties negotiate protocols to the treaty dealing with specific areas of concern.

With regard to species conservation, though all the treaties contain general obligations to protect the marine environment, a handful have also generated protocols mandating the establishment of marine or coastal protected areas. For example, the Nairobi Protocol for the Eastern African Regional Sea Convention requires parties to cooperate in the creation of a network of protected areas with the aim of preserving both flora and fauna.

The UNEP Regional Seas Programme has proven successful in providing flexible mechanisms for the coordination of regional responses to marine problems. However, nearly all the conventions remain underfunded and the protocols continue to be unratified and/or poorly implemented. Improvement in these areas will undoubtedly lead to better protection of marine species.

Chapter Ten: Land Based Pollution at section 3 (Regional Treaties) also discusses a cluster of regional treaties that could help the protection of living marine resources

3. INTERNATIONAL CONVENTION FOR THE REGULATION OF WHALING (ICRW)

Signed in 1946, the ICRW still exists as the controlling document for the regulation of whaling throughout the world [Dec. 2, 1946, 161 U.N.T.S. 72 (entered into force Nov. 10, 1948)]. Created more as an exploitation rather than conservation treaty, the ICRW has since evolved into an ideologically strict and somewhat controversial preservation regime. This shift in attitude reflects the current anti-whaling make-up of the International Whaling Commission (IWC)—the supervising body of the convention.

The ICRW creates a relatively simple institutional system. Under the treaty the IWC maintains a Schedule, which fixes "with respect to the conservation and utilization of whale resources" the following regulations [art. V(1)]:

(a) protected and unprotected species;

(b) open and closed seasons;

(c) open and closed waters, including the designation of sanctuary areas;

(d) size limits for each species;

(e) time, methods and intensity of whaling (including the maximum catch of whales to be taken in any one season);

(f) types and specifications of gear and apparatus and appliances which may be used;

(g) methods of measurement; and

(h) catch returns and statistical and biological records

The IWC may amend the Schedule at any time, but any amendments must be "necessary to carry out the objectives and purposes" of the convention [art. V(2)(a)], and must be "based on scientific findings" [art. V(2)(b)]. In addition, each party to the treaty has one vote on the IWC, and each amendment to the Schedule must carry a three-fourths majority for approval.

Originally comprised of predominantly pro-whaling states, the IWC consistently set catch limits too high, resulting in the continued depletion of commercial whale species throughout the 1970s. By 1982, however, as public outrage over whaling reached dramatic proportions, membership in the IWC came to include a majority of non-whaling states, and the commission passed a moratorium on all commercial whaling beginning three years later in 1985.

The moratorium in fact contains a double loophole. First, parties can simply object to the moratorium (or any other amendment) within a timely fashion and the moratorium will not bind them [art.

V(3)]. Norway, for example, immediately did object to the 1982 action. Second, article VIII(1) of the ICRW allows continued whaling "for the purposes of scientific research"—with power to grant permits for such "scientific" action at the discretion of the flag-state. Over the years, Iceland, Japan and Norway have taken hundreds of whales under this guise, all in an attempt to keep their respective whaling industries in business pending the possible lifting of the moratorium.

Nonetheless, the moratorium has proven such a success that the IWC's own Scientific Committee recommended a partial lifting of the moratorium in 1991. The Scientific Committee proposed that up to 2,000 minke whales could be taken each year without damage to the overall viability of the species. The IWC, however, has consistently declined to heed the advice of its Scientific Committee and has refused to relax the ban. If it is assumed the Scientific Committee is correct, the IWC's insistence on maintaining the ban in its current state can be seen as contradicting article V(2)(b), which maintains that amendments of the Schedule "shall be based on scientific findings."

In 1996 the IWC again refused to lift the moratorium on commercial whaling. Iceland has dropped out of the IWC, and Japan continues to conduct its own "scientific" whaling. Japan, in fact, has taken hundreds of minke whales in the Southern Ocean Whale Sanctuary—a sanctuary specifically created in 1994 to protect whales from exploitation in Antarctica. The IWC has loudly requested that Japan stop this action.

The present impasse openly reflects the political vulnerability of some international environmental institutions. Norway, under the leadership of Prime Minister Gro Harlem Bruntland, has continued to promote high environmental standards both at home and abroad. In fact, the Bruntland report offered the original blueprint for sustainable development for the World Commission on Environment and Development in 1986. Anti-whaling states, however, who so importantly voted the moratorium into place in 1982, now find it politically impossible to reverse their position—even when confronted with strong scientific evidence. Of course these states may simply want to ban whaling altogether for a variety of valuable reasons, including moral and aesthetic ones. Nevertheless, the IWC remains committed to conservation *and utilization*, and the international community remains committed to sustainable development under Agenda 21. In this case we find a high profile example of the potential conflict between preservation on the one hand, and sustainable use on the other.

4.   DRIFTNET FISHING

Driftnet fishing is a particularly devastating method of catching (or taking) fish in which a single boat, or several boats working together, suspend a series of nets up to 40 miles wide and 48 feet deep, catching everything—including dolphins—in their

wake [*see* LAKSHMAN D. GURUSWAMY, ET AL., INTERNA-
TIONAL ENVIRONMENTAL LAW AND WORLD ORDER 747 2d
ed., (1999)]. This form of commercial net fishing
often leads to a catch rate that exceeds the breeding
capability of many species that are caught and
killed by it. In the ten years in which they were
used prior to the moratorium, driftnets were responsible for the near collapse of the Albacore Tuna
fishery in the South Pacific, and contributed to the
serious decline of the North American Salmon fishery. On the basis of these and similar findings, the
General Assembly of the United Nations recommended a moratorium on the use of large-scale
pelagic driftnets in high seas fishing. [*see Resolution
on Large–Scale Pelagic Driftnet Fishing and its
Impact on Living Marine Resources of the World's
Oceans and Seas*, U.N. Doc. A/RES/44/225 (1989),
29 I.L.M. 1555, at 4(b)]. It should not go without
note, however, that this view of the causal relation
has long been challenged as ignoring the scientific
evidence [*see e.g.*, William T. Burke, et al., *United
Nations Resolutions on Driftnet Fishing: An Unsustainable Precedent for high Seas and Coastal Fisheries Management*, 25 OCEAN DEV. & INT'L L. 127, 128
(1994)].

The Convention for the Prohibition of Fishing
with Long Driftnets in the South Pacific Nov. 23,
1989, 29 I.L.M. 1454, entered into force on May 17,
1991, entirely prohibits the fishing practice within a
party's EEZ [art. 3]. In the same year, the United
Nations passed a resolution calling for a moratorium on driftnet fishing on the high seas by Decem-

ber 31, 1992 [*UNGA Resolution on Large Scale Pelagic Driftnet Fishing and its Impact on the Marine Living Resources of the World's Oceans and Seas*, Res.46/215, reprinted in 31 I.L.M. 241 (Dec 20, 1991)]. In keeping with the norm, no enforcement measure exists with the resolution, but the progressive development of soft law on the subject makes driftnet fishing on the high seas a politically unacceptable endeavor. Due to this legal pressure Japan and Taiwan, two of the major driftnet fishing nations, have ceased the practice altogether. For a more recent—though mainly hortative—development in the area of driftnet fishing, see G.A. Res. 57/142, 57th Sess., Agenda Item 25(b), A/RES/ 57/142 (2002).

CHAPTER FOURTEEN

TRANSBOUNDARY AIR POLLUTION

A. NATURE OF THE PROBLEM

Human demands lead to a number of physical processes and activities that convert raw materials, energy, and labor into desired finished products. Diverse pollutants are introduced into the environment during various stages of these production and consumption cycles. We have noted in Chapter Nine, Toxic and Hazardous Substances, that the environment is indivisible, interconnected and interdependent, and that contaminants can move within or beyond the original medium (air, water or land) into which they are introduced.

The migration of air pollutants has created major global problems such as climate change, ozone depletion, and nuclear fallout (Chapters Six, Seven, and Seventeen). Pollutants transported through the air also cause problems, and in Chapter Nine, Toxic and Hazardous Substances, we have discussed how pollutants cause human health and environmental problems. This chapter will focus on the residual transboundary problems caused by air pollutants not covered by regimes described elsewhere in this book. We briefly discuss problems caused by ubiquitous pollutants such as sulphur dioxide and nitrous oxides—including acid rain—and how and why they have given rise to customary and treaty regimes.

B. CAUSES AND SOURCES

Pollutants emitted into the atmosphere from industrial and commercial sources and automobile exhausts can form gases—suspensions of small liquid or solid particles—or become dissolved in cloud vapor or raindrops. Depending upon the condition of the atmosphere, these pollutants may become trapped in the air at low levels and high concentrations. Some of them react chemically to produce new or more toxic chemicals that can be transported many hundreds of miles by winds, deposited on soil or in the water (dry deposition) or returned to the earth by rainfall (wet deposition).

Once a contaminant is deposited on the soil, organisms or other chemicals present in the ground may transform it into a more toxic chemical. Whether or not this occurs, the contaminant will eventually be either absorbed by edible plants and possibly consumed by humans or other animals, carried by rainwater into a body of water, returned to the atmosphere through evaporation, or remain in the soil indefinitely.

C. ENVIRONMENTAL IMPACTS

Acid deposition, or acid rain, is a classic example of the global transportation of pollutants. In the

United States, coal and oil-fired electric plants in the midwest release gases which contain sulphur oxide dust. The dust is transported to the eastern states and Canada, where it precipitates [*See* Jurgan Schmandt, et al., *Acid Rain is Different, in* ACID RAIN AND FRIENDLY NEIGHBORS: THE POLICY DISPUTE BETWEEN CANADA AND THE UNITED STATES 31 (Jurgan Schmandt, et al. eds. 1988)]. In Europe, English and French industries were a major source of sulphur, and the Scandinavian countries often received the acid deposition [A.G. Clarke, *The Air, in* UNDERSTANDING OUR ENVIRONMENT 106 (R.E. Hester, ed. 1986)].

Acid rain is often created by the following process. Industrial plants, generally having tall stacks, distribute waste gases into the atmosphere. The gases and dusts are hot when released, so they tend to rise. Once in the atmosphere, the dusts can react with cloud water to form acids, the worst being sulphuric acid, H_2SO_4. Even without encountering atmospheric water, the sulphur eventually falls to earth where it can react to form acids with any terrestrial water. This is called dry deposition. While the sulphur dust is high in the atmosphere the potential remains great for the acid to travel great distances and across national boundaries [*id.*].

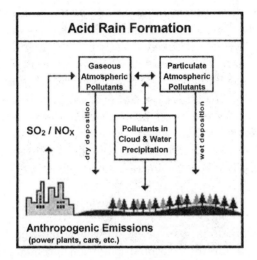

It is important to note, however, that some acid in rain occurs naturally as part of the carbon cycle. Carbon dioxide, for example, results from respiration, fires or volcanoes. These emissions naturally react with rain water forming carbonates, making a mildly acidic solution that actually "buffers" the rain. That is, it forms a solution with the water that can absorb new sources of acidity or basicity before the pH changes. The atmospheric transport of carbon also functions as an important part of the carbon cycle, placing carbon in locations—such as rocky or nutrient poor habitats—where it might not otherwise be available [*id.* at 77].

There are scientific uncertainties associated with a discussion of acid precipitation, and recent United States government studies remain inconclusive about the seriousness of its effects [*See* Marylynn

Placet, *Emissions Involved in Acidic Deposition Processes, in* ACIDIC DEPOSITION: STATE OF SCIENCE AND TECHN.; SUMMARY REPORT OF THE U.S NAT'L ACID PRECIPITATION ASSESSMENT PROGRAM (NAPAP) 25 (1991); H. Simon et al., *Addressing Uncertainty in Envtl Modelling: A Case Study of Integrated Assessment of Strategies to Combat Long–Range Transboundary Air Pollution*, 36 ATMOSPHERIC ENV'T, 5417 (2002)]. The phenomena is difficult to investigate because it traverses entire countries and even seas.

D. REMEDIAL OBJECTIVES

Transboundary air pollution was recognized quite early as an international pollution problem. For example, the facts of the well known *Trail Smelter Arbitration* (United States v. Canada) 3 R.I.A.A. 1938 (Mar. 11, 1941) transpired in the 1920's and 1930's. The principles derived from that case have become the bedrock of customary IEL dealing with transboundary pollution, although the arbitration itself, and the applicable law, were governed by an international agreement between Canada and the United States.

The *Trail Smelter Arbitration* pointed the way to *ex ante* regulatory measures that prevent pollution, establish compliance procedures and enforcement mechanisms, as well as *ex post* grievance-remedial methods such as arbitral and judicial proceedings that are able to assign responsibility and liability for wrongful actions. As we shall see, however, IEL dealing with transboundary pollution is an incomplete patchwork of customary law interwoven with regional agreements of limited jurisdiction.

E. LEGAL RESPONSE

1. CUSTOM

No discussion of transboundary air pollution could begin without mention of the 1941 *Trail Smelter Arbitration* case. As suggested in Chapter One, Sources and Forms of International Law section D, this remains one of the most significant cases in international environmental law, and the only important case dealing with air pollution. The facts actually suggest an unusual transboundary air pollution scenario, without the usual causation problems due to multiple polluters and multiple delivery streams. In this situation a single identifiable polluter—a smelter plant owned by a Canadian corporation and located in Canada—was found by an arbitral tribunal to have caused air pollution damage to a region of the State of Washington. In the next stage of the bifurcated proceedings the tribunal held Canada itself responsible for the pollution damage, providing injunctive relief and a monetary award. In dealing with the doctrine of state responsibility, the tribunal made the following summation:

> The Tribunal, therefore, finds that the above [U.S. domestic] decisions, taken as a whole, constitute an adequate basis for its conclusions, namely, that, under the principles of international law, as well as of the law of the United States,

no state has the right to use or permit the use of its territory in such a manner as to cause injury by fumes in or to the territory of another or the properties or persons therein, when the case is of serious consequence and the injury is established by clear and convincing evidence.

United States v. Canada (Trail Smelter Arbitration), 3 R.I.A.A. 1938 (1941).

This ruling has since become the basis for the general prohibition against transboundary environmental harm that was definitively restated in the 1992 Rio Declaration:

States have, in accordance with the Charter of the United Nations and the principles of international law, the sovereign right to exploit their own resources pursuant to their own environmental and developmental policies, and the responsibility to ensure that activities within their jurisdiction or control do not cause damage to the environment of other States or of areas beyond the limits of national jurisdiction [Principle 2].

Rio Declaration on Environment and Development, Adopted by the U.N. Conference on Environment and Development, Principle 2, U.N.Doc. A/CONF. 151/26, *reprinted in* 31 I.L.M. 874 (June 13, 1992).

In this latter formulation, the parties to the Rio Declaration have discarded both the *Trail Smelter* threshold of harm ("serious consequence") and the standard of causation ("clear and convincing evidence"). The term "damage" in Principle 2, however, does suggest an actionable level of harm, and most commentators have interpreted this to mean "significant harm." As for causation much criticism has been leveled at the high degree of certainty required by *Trail Smelter*, because the "clear and convincing evidence" standard presents a potentially insurmountable obstacle for most environmental cases. Regardless, the basic premise of *Trail Smelter* has evolved into a well-accepted rule of customary international law—restated in a myriad of international, regional and bilateral agreements. Taking into account the sovereign right to development, one country may not cause significant transboundary environmental harm to another [*See* Thomas W. Merril, *Golden Rules for Transboundary Pollution*, 46 DUKE L.J. 931, 951, n. 106–07 (1997)].

2. CONVENTION ON LONG–RANGE TRANSBOUNDARY AIR POLLUTION (LRTAP)

(a) Overview

In the absence of a global international treaty, the Convention on Long-Range Transboundary Air Pollution (LRTAP)—a regional treaty—emerges as the most significant legal regime in the field [Nov. 13, 1979, [18 I.L.M. 1442] (entered into force Mar. 16, 1983)]. Created under the auspices of the UN Economic Commission for Europe (ECE) in 1979, the convention counts most countries in the Northern Hemisphere as parties, including the United States, Canada and Russia. It also represents an early form of the framework convention, though its institutions lack the degree of flexibility and power inherent in more recent framework treaties. Still, LRTAP has evolved to meet the needs of its parties, adding eight protocols that require specific emission limitations for sulphur dioxide (1985, 1994), nitrogen oxides (1988), volatile organic compounds (1991), heavy metals (1998), persistent organic pollutants (1998), and and a protocol which sets 2010 emission ceilings for four pollutants: sulphur, NOx, VOCs and ammonia (1999).

	LRTAP Protocols	Status*	In Force
84	Long-term Financing of the Cooperative Programme for Monitoring and Eval. of the Long-range Transmission of Air Pollutants in Europe (EMEP)	39P	1/28/88
85	Reduction of Sulphur Emissions or their Transboundary Fluxes by at least 30%	22P	9/2/ 87
88	Control of Nitrogen Oxides or their Transboundary Fluxes	28P	2/14/91
91	Control of Emissions of Volatile Organic Compounds or their Transboundary Fluxes	21P	9/29/97
94	Further Reduction of Sulphur Emissions	25P	8/5/98
98	Heavy Metals	36S / 14R	—
98	Persistent Organic Pollutants (POPs)	36S / 14R	—
99	Abate Acidification, Eutrophication and Ground-level Ozone	31S / 4R	—
* P = Parties; S = Signatories; R = Ratifications Current as of Feb. 2003 / Source: UNECE			

The convention, with its strong focus on combating acid rain, embraces the duty to not cause transboundary harm [LRTAP pmbl., para. 5] and mandates that the parties endeavor to limit, reduce and prevent air pollution including long-range transboundary air pollution [art. 2]. The latter phenomenon is defined as air pollution from one state "which has adverse effects in the area under the jurisdiction of another state at such a distance that it is not generally possible to distinguish the contribution of individual emission sources or groups of sources" [art. 1(b)]. As such, the Convention attempts to deal with pollution problems beyond the scope of the original *Trail Smelter* fact pattern, which identified a nearby Canadian polluter as the sole perpetrator of cross-border harm in the United States.

In addition to promoting general calls for consultations, exchange of information, and research and development on the issue, the convention endorses the existing " 'Cooperative programme for the monitoring and evaluation of the long-range transmission of air pollutants in Europe,' " known as EMEP [art. 9]. Each party is asked to join in this program of scientific monitoring and evaluation, which is overseen by a Steering Committee. The convention also establishes a Secretariat, as well as an Executive Body which resembles the Conference of the Parties of more recent framework treaties. However, unlike the newer versions of the framework approach, the Executive Body's powers remain general and unenumerated, and the convention fails to create a formal dispute resolution procedure [*See* art. 13]. Still, as outlined below, the treaty has given birth to a number of substantive protocols.

(b) Sulphur Emissions

Responding to increased anxiety over the threat of acid rain, the parties have made two efforts at controlling sulphur dioxide. The Protocol to the 1979 Convention on Long–Range Transboundary Air Pollution on the Reduction of Sulphur Emissions or Their Transboundary Fluxes by at Least 30 Percent (1985 Sulphur Protocol), July 8, 1985, [27 I.L.M. 707] (entered into force Sept. 2, 1987) required parties to reduce their national annual sulphur emissions by at least 30 percent of their 1980 levels, by the year 1993. This first protocol, which entered into force on January 28, 1988, also mandated that each party develop a national program to this end, and report its national annual sulphur emissions to the Executive Body [art. 4]. It should be noted that the parties as a group succeeded in achieving the goals of the 1985 protocol, in aggregate surpassing the 30 percent reduction called for by 1993.

The Protocol to the 1979 Convention on Long–Range Transboundary Air Pollution on Further Reduction of Sulphur Emissions and Decisions on the Structure and Function of the Implementing Committee, as well as Procedures for Review of its Compliance: United Nations; 1994 (1994 Sulphur Protocol), June 14, 1994, [33 I.L.M. 1540], as its name implies, goes beyond the measures of the 1985 protocol. To begin, parties must not exceed annual sulphur ceilings as set forth in Annex II of the protocol [art. 2(2)]. This annex also creates percentage emissions reductions, again with a base year of 1980, which each party must meet for the years 2000, 2005 and 2010. Unlike the 1985 Sulphur Protocol, however, the percentage of required reduction varies with each party—thus taking into account the different situations of individual countries. The 1994 Protocol also obligates parties to ensure, as far as possible and without excessive costs, that sulphur depositions do not exceed "critical loads"—defined as a level of "exposure to one or more pollutants below which significant harmful effects" do not occur to the environment [art. 1(8)]. In addition, the protocol sets mandatory emission limit values for new stationary combustion sources which existing sources must also strive to meet by 2004 [art. 2(5)]. Specifically, the protocol exempts Canada and the United States from the emission limit values for stationary sources, giving way to the 1991 United States—Canada Air Quality Agreement, Mar. 13, 1991, 30 I.L.M. 676 (1991) [art. 2(5)]. In any event, as of this writing the United States has yet to become a party to the protocol, remaining the only significant economic power outside of LRTAPs requirements.

(c) Nitrogen Oxides

In contrast to the relatively successful endeavor to reduce sulphur emissions, the attempt to control nitrogen oxides (NOx) has proved more difficult.

The UN Protocol to the 1979 Convention on Long–Range Transboundary Air Pollution Concerning the Control of Emissions of Nitrogen Oxides or Their Transboundary Fluxes (1988 Nitrogen Oxides Protocol), Oct. 31, 1988, 28 I.L.M. 212 (entered into force Feb. 1, 1991) has only slightly reduced overall emissions, with some major industrial countries predicting emission increases up to the year 2010 (including the U.K., United States and Canada) [*Negotiation on Pops Treaty Under Way in Geneva, to Continue in Canberra in March*, (Feb 21, 1996) 19 INT'L ENV'T REP. (BNA) 177].

The present protocol requires all parties to control and/or reduce, using 1987 as the general baseline, their national annual emissions of NO_x by the year 1994 [art. 2(1)]. As noted above this stabilization has not occurred across the board. The protocol also mandates that the parties apply national emission standards to major new stationary sources, based on "best available technologies which are economically feasible" (BATEF)[art. 2(2)(a, b & c)]. The parties must likewise apply national emission standards to mobile sources, using the same BATEF approach [art. 2(b)]. As a guideline, the parties are encouraged to look at the Technical Annex for purposes of implementation, though the annex remains strictly recommendatory in nature [art. 10]. Perhaps most important, the protocol places a premium on research and monitoring, while also requiring strenuous reporting and review procedures—all of which may lead to a more effective protocol in the near future.

(d) Volatile Organic Compounds

An as yet unevaluated effort under the umbrella of LRTAP involves the attempt to regulate volatile organic compounds (VOXs), now embodied in the United Nations ECE Protocol to the 1979 Convention on Long Range Transboundary Air Pollution Concerning the Control of Emissions of Volatile Organic Compounds or Their Transboundary Fluxes (the 1991 VOC Protocol), Nov. 18, 1991, 31 I.L.M. 568. This protocol provides parties with three different ways to meet the basic requirement of controlling and reducing VOX emissions, as mandated by article 2(1). First, a party may choose to reduce its national annual emissions "by at least 30 percent by the year 1999, using 1988 levels as the basis or any other annual level during the period 1984–1990" [art. 2(a)]. Second, if its damaging transboundary emissions only originate from a specified area (known as a tropospheric ozone management area or TOMA, and listed in Annex I), then it need only stabilize its total annual emissions while reducing those particularly harmful emissions using the above 30 percent formula [art. 2(b)]. Third, a small polluter may simply choose to stabilize its national annual emissions by 1999, again using 1988 as the baseline [art. 2(c)].

Concerning specific types of sources, the parties must within two years upon entry into force apply national or international standards to new stationary and mobile sources, using BATEF and taking into consideration the respective technical annexes [art. 3(a)(i) & (iii)]. Within five years of entry into force, the parties must apply BATEF to existing stationary sources located in sensitive areas [art. 3(b)(i)]. Again however, the effectiveness of these and other measures remains an open question, as the protocol has only recently arrived on the international scene.

3. UNITED STATES—CANADA

On March 13, 1991, these two countries signed the Agreement on Air Quality, Mar. 31, 1991, 31 I.L.M. 676. The end result of more than a decade of negotiations regarding transboundary air pollution, the agreement primarily attempts to engage the problem of acid rain. The treaty provides that "the parties shall establish specific objectives for emissions limitations or reductions of air pollutants and adopt the necessary programs and other measures to implement such specific objectives" [art. 3(2)(a)]. As a framework agreement, the breadth of the accord allows the United States and Canada to confront both current problems and those which may arise in the future.

Annex I established emissions limitations for sulphur dioxide and nitrogen oxides. As agreed, the United States committed to reducing its annual SO_2 emissions attributable to power plants by 10 million tons relative to 1980 levels by the year 2000—in accordance with Title IV of the 1990 Clean Air Act Amendments (CAAA) [Annex I, art. 1(A)(1)]. The United States further commited to cap such emissions at 8.9 million tons per year by the year 2010

[Annex I, art. 1(A)(2)]. Similarly, Canada committed reducing its annual SO_2 emissions to 3.2 million metric tons annually by the year 2000 [Annex I, art. 1(B)(1)].

As for nitrogen oxides emissions, by 2000 the United States was required to reduce its total annual emissions by approximately 2 million tons—again using 1980 as the baseline [Annex I, art. 2(A)]. For its part, by 2000 Canada pledged to reduce its annual national emissions of nitrogen oxides from stationary sources by 100,000 tons below the forecast level of 970,000 tons [Annex I, art. 2(B)(1)]. Additionally, Canada was required to impose mobile source emissions limitations similar to those found in the CAAA [Annex I, 2(B)(2)].

Concerning institutional arrangements, the agreement establishes an Air Quality Committee to review progress in implementation [art. VIII]. The Committee compiles reports on such matters and presents these to the parties as well as the International Joint Commission (IJC)[art. IX], a body constituted under the Treaty Between Canada and the United States of America Relating to Boundary Waters and Questions Arising Along the Boundary Between the United States and Canada, Jan. 11, 1909, 36 Stat. 2496 (entered into force May 5, 1910), and intended to investigate and make recommendations regarding transboundary air pollution matters generally. The IJC invites public comment on these progress reports, and then submits a synthesis of its findings back to the parties. In this way the Agreement on Air Quality makes use of one of the oldest institutions in international law, the IJC, in an attempt to control a continuing transboundary air pollution problem.

Tropospheric ozone and its precursors (NOx and VOC) are transported across international boundaries, and this phenomena was considered by the Air Quality Committee. Recognizing this fact, Canada and the United States entered into a Protocol in 2000 amending the 1991 agreement on air quality to reduce the transboundary flow of tropospheric ozone and precursor emissions (NOx and VOC), thereby helping both countries attain their respective air quality goals. [http://www.epa.gov/airmarkets/usca/].

As reported by the ICJ in 2002, the total Canadian SO_2 emissions in 2000 were 2.5 million tonnes, or about 20 percent below the national cap of 3.2 million tonnes and a 45 percent reduction from 1980 emission levels [*see* INTERNATIONAL JOINT COMMISSION, AIR QUALITY AGREEMENT: 2002 PROGRESS REPORT 2 (2002)]. The report also indicates the United States achieved a total reduction in SO_2 emissions of about 32 percent when compared to 1990 levels and over 35 percent from 1980 levels. In 2000, U.S. sources emitted approximately 10.6 million tons, some 1.08 million tons more than the allowances granted for the year—reflecting the use of banked allowances. Full implementation in 2010 is expected to result in a 10–million-ton reduction of SO_2 emissions by the U.S. sources—approximately 40 percent below 1980 levels.

4.   UNITED STATES—MEXICO

In 1983, the United States and Mexico signed the Agreement to Cooperate in the Solution of Environmental Problems in the Border Area (La Paz Agreement), Aug. 14, 1983, 22 I.L.M. 1025. The parties agree to take measures, "to the fullest practical extent," to prevent, reduce and eliminate border pollution [art. II], and to coordinate their efforts to address the problems of air, land and water pollution in the area [art. V]. The agreement defines the border area as the region "situated 100 kilometers on either side of the inland and maritime boundaries between the Parties" [art. IV]. In effect, the La Paz Agreement functions as a framework for further action, providing for the creation of annexes to deal with specific problems.

Addressing transboundary air pollution, the La Paz Agreement now contains two separate annexes. The first, Annex IV, entered into force in 1987 and deals with air pollution from all new copper smelters located in the border region. For both parties, sulphur dioxide emissions from all new copper smelters in the area must not exceed .065 percent by volume during any six-hour period [Annex IV, art. I(1) & (3)]. To monitor compliance, smelter owners and operators must track emissions and report any violations exceeding maximum levels, while every six months an "air pollution working group" assesses the progress made in abating smelter pollution. Based on this assessment, the working group then makes specific recommendations to national coordinators in both the United States and Mexico.

Annex V to the La Paz Agreement—intended to reduce pollution caused by urban development—provides for the determination of causes of air pollution in certain United States and Mexican border cities denominated "study areas." The annex requires the United States EPA and Mexico's Social Development Secretariat (SEDESOL) to catalogue emissions from major stationary, mobile, and area sources. The two agencies must then ascertain measures necessary to bring identified pollutants within acceptable control levels (a task facilitated by ambient air quality monitoring and air modeling analysis). Such measures may include, but are not limited to, requiring a given polluter to implement pollution control technology or alter management practice in an effort to bring the polluter into compliance with emissions standards. As an ultimate goal, the parties shall "jointly explore" the harmonization of their air pollution control standards and ambient air quality standards—a process which NAFTA and its progeny may help to spur in the future [Annex V, art. V].

In September 2002, the U.S. and Mexico unveiled an agreement: "Border 2112." U.S. EPA, Border 2012: U.S.–Mexico Environmental Program, EPA–160–3–02–001 (2002). One of the goals of the agreement, vague though it be, is to reduce air pollution. The final objective of the agreement is to reduce air emissions, as much as possible, toward attainment of national ambient air quality standards, and reduce exposure in the border areas by 2012. This is to be done through a phased process in which baselines and alternative scenarios for emissions reduction along the border area, and their impacts on air quality and human exposure are defined. Following upon this, specific emission reductions strategies and air quality and exposure goals are to be drawn up with a view to achieving the final objective by 2012.

CHAPTER FIFTEEN

TRANSBOUNDARY WATER POLLUTION

A. NATURE OF THE PROBLEM

Waters cover the face of the earth, and the oceans occupy seventy percent of the planet's surface. In earlier chapters dealing with Toxic and Hazardous Substances (Chapter Nine), Land–Based Pollution (Chapter Ten), Vessel Pollution (Chapter Eleven), and Dumping (Chapter Twelve), we noted how wastes and pollutants created by our affluent life style are emitted into the air, discharged or dumped into rivers, streams, and the sea, or disposed of on land. While direct discharges into the aquatic environment are obvious sources of pollution, we have seen how indirect sources, such as the atmosphere, can significantly contribute to the problem. Furthermore, all the water on the earth (the hydrosphere) is continually recycled between the oceans, lakes, streams, and groundwater. This recycling process results in the movement of toxic chemicals from one water source to another [DADE MOELLER, ENVIRONMENTAL HEALTH 55 (1992)].

Pollutants can be changed for better or worse within the aquatic environment. Water is a solvent with the ability to dissolve or dilute chemicals and make them harmless to human health or ecosystems. The effectiveness of the diluting process will depend on hydrologic conditions such as the type and location of a water body, the nature of the pollution load, and the concentration and characteristics of the contaminants [ENCYCLOPEDIA OF THE ENVIRONMENT 557 (Ruth Eblen & William Eblen eds., 1994); C.N. Hewitt & R.M. Harrison, *Monitoring, in* UNDERSTANDING OUR ENVIRONMENT 56 (R.E. Hester ed. 1986)]. On the other hand, water can also react with contaminants to form more hazardous or more synergistic reactions, depending on the temperature, acidity, and oxygen level of the water [H. Fish, *Water, in* UNDERSTANDING OUR ENVIRONMENT 136–7 (R.E. Hester ed. 1986)].

As we have seen, the environmental health of the oceans is critical to humanity. Rivers and streams, though they constitute less than one-half percent of the water in the hydrosphere, are essential to the proper maintenance of the global environment and human habitation [*id.* at 119]. The pollution of common pool resources such as the high seas (to which all nations have open access) can create global problems, while the use or abuse of transnational or international rivers and groundwater can cause harm to states sharing these resources. Since all the oceans and over 200 large river basins are shared by two or more countries, competition over the quality and quantity of shared waters can become very intense. In this chapter we concentrate on problems that arise when rivers, lakes, estuaries, coastlines, and groundwater are used in a manner that causes harm to other states.

B. SOURCES OF ENVIRONMENTAL HARM

Pollution introduced into rivers, watercourses, and coastal waters of one state can affect another through transport, diffusion or dispersion. As we have seen in our discussion of Hazardous and Toxic Substances (Chapter Nine), chemicals are usually discharged into waters as part of a waste stream from industrial sources such as pulp and paper mills, iron and steelworks, petroleum refineries, petrochemical industries, fertilizer factories, and other chemistry-based production installations including pharmaceutical plants [*id.*]. Modern agriculture relies heavily on chemical pesticides and insecticides so that significant quantities of these substances enter the aquatic environment as agricultural run-off, and irrigation wastewater. Sediment, too, is swept into the aquatic environment through erosion, agricultural run-off, and irrigation overflows. [PHILLIP FRADKIN, A RIVER NO MORE: THE COLORADO RIVER AND THE WEST 64 (1984)]. In the case of transnational rivers such pollutants are carried downstream into other states or into shared coastal waters or estuaries. Apart from chemicals, organic matter such as untreated or partially treated sewage is discharged into rivers, estuaries and coastal waters [D. Alistair Bigham, *Pollution from Land–Based Sources, in* THE IMPACT OF MARINE POLLUTION

203 (Douglas Cuisine & John Grant eds. 1980), R.B. CLARK, MARINE POLLUTION, 5th ed. (2001)].

Indirect pollution, another major source of fresh water contamination, arises for example from the improper storage of hazardous waste resulting in the leaching of hazardous substances into underground aquifers that lie beneath common borders. Such contamination may affect an entire country's source of drinking water. Additionally, emissions of toxic metals and gases from an industrial park can be transported thousands of miles by the wind and deposited directly on a water body, or on the soil where they can then leach into the groundwater [JOHN HARTE, ET AL., TOXICS A TO Z 77 (1991)].

Both the quality and quantity of water can cause transboundary damage. Water can be extracted in such quantities as to affect its ability to sustain marine life or their supporting ecosystems. The damage caused by the reduction of water volume is not restricted to the ecological health of a river or stream. The overuse of water by an upper riparian state may deprive a lower state of essential water and lead to increased soil salinity, and may even create deserts. Extracting, impounding or diverting water into dams and reservoirs could certainly affect downstream settlements because these flow-regulating projects may restrict sources of potable or agricultural water and may affect human health [FRADKIN, *supra*, at 64]. In the water-deprived areas of the world such as the Middle East, water conflicts may potentially bring nations to the brink of war.

C. ENVIRONMENTAL IMPACTS

The deleterious effects of water pollution vary significantly and range from chemical and biological damage, to physical damage to riverbeds and harbors, to pure economic loss. The chemical and biological effects of chemicals are more fully discussed under the topic of Toxic and Hazardous Substances (Chapter Nine). We take note here of the specific attributes displayed by some of these pollutants in water. For example, organo-chlorines like DDT, dieldrin, aldrin, heptachlor, and mirex are chemicals used as pesticides and insecticides that display three remarkable characteristics. First, they are toxic or poisonous in small doses; at critical concentrations they can affect the marine life in a body of water and humans who drink or are exposed to such water. Second, they are *persistent* or stable. This means that they are not readily broken down by microorganisms, enzymes, heat or ultra-violet light, and have stable and long lives in aquatic environments. Third, they *bioaccumulate*. This means that they are water insoluble, and not readily metabolized though soluble in fatty tissue, and accumulate in the fatty tissue of fish and animals upon ingestion. They then move up the food chain by aggregating in the body fat of predator fish and animals. DDT has been found, for example, to affect condors, osprey, falcons, golden eagles, sea gulls, pelicans and even humans who have eaten such contaminated fish or mammals. A similar profile could be drawn of the impacts of industrial chemicals discharged into the aquatic environment [HARTE, *supra*, at 86–90].

Water polluted by sewage has substantial biological effects, including impacts on human health. Microbial agents can affect people on contact by causing skin infections and respiratory illness, while the ingestion of water or seafood contaminated by pathogens from sewage can cause severe gastrointestinal and respiratory problems. In ordinary circumstances, the microbial activity in water breaks down normal organic wastes by decomposition—a process which takes up oxygen. Large volumes of organic wastes, like sewage, introduce many nutrients to a body of water. The nutrients can spur microbial growth, resulting in an increased demand for dissolved oxygen, thus creating a Biological Oxygen Demand (BOD) that can alter the biological diversity of the body of water. This process is often called "cultural eutrophication" [CHARLES GOLDMAN & ALEXANDER HORNE, LIMNOLOGY 354 (1983)].

Rivers not only carry chemical and biological substances downstream, they also bring sediment caused by erosion, deforestation, agricultural runoff, and irrigation. Such sediment can clog up harbors and cause problems in shipping lanes. Moreover, the inflow of pollutants with attendant human health and environmental problems can adversely affect tourism, an industry upon which many developing countries are heavily dependent [Bigham, *supra*, at 203].

D. REMEDIAL MEASURES

We have observed in our discussion of Toxic and Hazardous Substances (Chapter Nine), and Land–Based Pollution (Chapter Ten) that remedial measures should endeavor to reduce waste generation by addressing consumption demands. In order to achieve such a goal, the control of water pollution should become part of a more comprehensive attempt to integrate pollution control of atmospheric, terrestrial, and aquatic pollution. Without losing sight of this more comprehensive goal, remedial measures need also to address the more immediate problems posed by transboundary river pollution. These problems, which as we shall see have been considered by the International Law Commission (ILC), arise from the disputed rights and duties pertaining to the quality and quantity of water claimed by upper and lower riparian owners of international rivers. Furthermore, water pollution, not unlike other areas of IEL, primarily requires an *ex ante* approach supplemented by *ex post* grievance remedial mechanisms. As discussed below, various regional conventions have attempted to address this challenge.

E. LEGAL RESPONSE

1. CONVENTION ON THE LAW OF THE NON–NAVIGATIONAL USES OF INTERNATIONAL WATERCOURSES

Cooperation concerning the use of transboundary watercourses is well established. As a number of rivers and lakes demarcate international boundaries, nations have found it beneficial to arrive at cooperative relationships regarding utilization of these shared resources. As such, we can now confidently cite several broad-based rules of customary law with regard to the use of international watercourses.

In 1991 the International Law Commission (ILC) expounded and elaborated on these rules in the Draft Articles on the Law of the Non-navigational Uses of International Watercourses (ILC Draft Articles), U.N. GOAR, 46th Sess., Supp. No. 10 at 161, U.N. Doc. A/46/10 (1991). Empowered by the Charter of the United Nations, June 26, 1945, 1 U.N.T.S. xvi (entered into force Oct. 24, 1945), to "initiate studies and make recommendations for the purpose of encouraging the progressive development of international law and its codification," the ILC in its Draft Articles provided a roadmap both to extant law and the law as it "might be." This completed effort at codification and development was the first regarding watercourses since the Helsinki Rules on the Uses of the Waters of International Rivers (1966 Helsinki Rules), Aug. 20, 1966, 52 I.L.A. 484 (1967).

In 1994 the U.N. General Assembly called for an international framework convention to be negotiated based on the Draft Articles. Pursuant to this directive, on May 21, 1997, the General Assembly adopted the Convention on the Law of Non-navigational Uses of International Watercourses [Convention on the Law of the Non-navigational Uses of International Watercourses, G.A. Res. 51/229, U.N. GAOR, 51st Sess., U.N. Doc. A/RES/51/229 (1997), *reprinted in* 36 I.L.M. 700 (1997) (hereinafter Convention)]. The ILC and the Convention share the objective of encouraging the progressive development of international law and its codification regarding the non-navigational uses of international watercourses. These uses encompass the use of watercourses for purposes other than navigation, as well as their protection, preservation and management. [art. 1].

In light of its purposes, and symbiotic relationship to customary law, we have chosen the Convention as our own roadmap in traversing the customary law on the subject. Yet, in approaching the Convention one should keep in mind that it does not distinguish between extant and progressive development of the law, leaving room for debate on the specifics of the present state of affairs. In this section therefore, while entering into the more controversial aspects of the Convention, we have also attempted to separate the general customary law from its progressive development. We shall also take note of the pronouncements the ICJ in the important case between Hungary and Slovakia regarding the Gabcikovo–Nagymaros Project. [Case Concerning the Gabcikovo–Nagymaros Project (Republic of Hungary v. Slovak Federal Republic), [1997 I.C.J. 4] (hereinafter Hungary v. Slovakia).

(a) Communication: Notification, Consultation and Negotiation

Art. 8 of the Convention reinforces the need for communication by institutionalizing a general obligation to cooperate. In discussing the kind of cooperation arising from the obligation to cooperate it would be helpful to clarify some of the relevant terms. Perhaps the best approach is to consider notification, consultation and negotiation on a continuum of governmental interaction. Notification is referred to in arts. 12, 13, 15 16 & 18. While notification *per se* simply requires the providing of information without a mutual exchange, some types of notification under the convention, such as those referred to under art. 17, are tied to a further requirement of consultation and negotiation. Consultations are referred to in arts. 4, 6, 7, 17, 18, 19, 24, 26 & 30, and require a dialogue among participants without an obligation of reasonable compromise, or therefore of result. Art. 17 refers to a special situation where a notification relates to possible infractions of the principle of equitable distribution or the duty not to cause transboundary damage. Art. 17(2) then draws a distinction between consultation and negotiation by noting that the notifying state ". . . shall enter into consultations and if necessary, negotiations with a view to arriving at an equitable resolution of the situation." Negotiation, referred to in arts. 4, 17, 18, 19, 30 & 33, requires a dialogue with an obligation to compromise—if in good faith a reasonable actor would so compromise—but not necessarily an obligation of result. Of course all three terms function within a political context in which the pressures to agree (or disagree) would both inform the terms and promote an outcome.

As an overriding objective, the Convention mandates communication and thus cooperation between watercourse states, requiring that they "shall, at the request of any of them, enter into consultations concerning the management of an international watercourse" [art. 24(1); *see also* arts. 4(2), 5(2), 6(2), 8 & 11]. The Convention thus requires the adoption of "watercourse agreements" among watercourse states and further stipulates that "[e]very watercourse State is entitled to participate in the negotiation of and to become a party to any watercourse agreement that applies to the entire international watercourse, as well as to participate in any relevant consultations" [art. 4(1)].

Concerning the future use of a watercourse, the Convention contains a high degree of specificity regarding states' obligations to communicate. The details—such as time frames to respond—are pragmatic embellishments, but the basic obligations correspond to customary law. For example, before a watercourse state implements "planned measures" having a possibly significant adverse effect, it must provide a potentially harmed state with timely notification [art. 12]. The notifying state must allow the potentially harmed state six months in which to respond [art. 13(a)–(b)], and may not implement the planned measures without consent during this period [art. 14(b)]. If the notified state believes the planned measures to be unacceptable—that is inconsistent with either the rules of equitable utilization or the duty not to cause harm (discussed below)—then the parties must "enter into consultations and, if necessary, negotiations with a view to arriving at an equitable resolution of the situation" [art. 17(1)]. Should the consultations and negotiations fail the Convention offers dispute settlement provisions for impartial fact-finding (if requested by one party), and mediation or conciliation (if agreed to by both parties) [art. 33(3)–(4)].

Given the extensive degree of cooperation found today concerning planned uses of international watercourses, the above requirements of notification, consultation and negotiation appear to follow state practice. In the Lac Lanoux Arbitration (Spain v. France), 12 R.I.A.A. 281 (Nov. 16, 1957), for instance, an arbitral tribunal stated that France could not ignore Spanish interests regarding a planned hydraulic construction project on the Carol River. The tribunal, however, did not go as far as the Convention, explaining that "if, in the course of discussions, the downstream State submits schemes to it, the upstream State must examine them, but it has the right to give preference to the solution contained in its own scheme provided that it takes into consideration in a reasonable manner the interests of the downstream State." The tribunal also disavowed as a rule of law that only a prior agreement between riparian states would allow one state to utilize the hydraulic power of a watercourse.

Nonetheless, the Conventions' mandate of consultations and negotiations (leading finally to impartial fact-finding and possibly mediation/conciliation) reflects contemporary practice in that states nearly always settle these disputes among themselves. In this regard one need only look at the proliferation of regional and bilateral watercourse agreements discussed below to appreciate how the degree of communication—and the perception of that communication as a legal requirement—has significantly increased since the 1957 Lac Lanoux Arbitration Case.

The development of the law since Lac Lanoux is confirmed by the case of Hungary v. Slovakia, where after protracted litigation both parties were ordered by the ICJ to undertake good faith negotiations consistent with both international environmental norms such as sustainable development, and the law of international water courses, to come up with a new management scheme in the context of the already constructed projects in Slovakia.

(b) Equitable Utilization

The status of the doctrine of equitable utilization as the *grund* norm (fundamental law) of international water law has been confirmed by the ICJ in the case of Hungary v. Slovakia. The doctrine enjoys a long lineage. *In re* the Territorial Jurisdiction of the International Commission of the River Oder, 1929 P.C.I.J. (Ser. A) No. 23, at 5, the Permanent Court of International Justice (PCIJ), dealing with a navigable river, declared that each riparian's "community of interest ... becomes the basis of a common legal right, the essential features of which are the perfect equality of all riparian States in the use of the whole course of the river and the exclusion of any preferential privilege of any one riparian State in relation to the others." In reference to non-navigational uses, the Convention requires that "[w]atercourse States shall ... utilize an international watercourse in an equitable and reasonable manner" [art. 5(1)]. The Convention further require the resource be used "with a view to attaining optimal and sustainable utilization thereof and benefits therefrom, taking into account the interests of the watercourse States concerned [and] consistent with adequate protection of the watercourse" [art. 5(1)]. In Hungary v. Slovakia, even though the case did not directly apportion the Danube's flow, the IJC's opinion firmly establishes that international rivers are shared resources and all riparian states have equal rights to enjoy both the commodity and noncommodity ecological benefits of the river, hydrologically connected groundwater, and the riparian corridors.

On its face, this universally accepted rule seems incontrovertible. Who would disagree with a requirement that one state only use a shared river or lake in an equitable and reasonable manner? Problems of interpretation arise, however—as elsewhere in the law regarding standards of reasonableness—because of different operative contexts. Obviously, the very nature of a dispute means that one state does *not* consider another state's use "equitable" or "reasonable." In an effort to overcome this difficulty, the Convention defines the "[u]tilization of an international watercourse in an equitable and reasonable manner" as "taking into account of all relevant factors and circumstances, including:"

(a) Geographic, hydrographic, hydrological, climatic, ecological, and other actors of a natural character;

(b) The social and economic needs of the watercourse States concerned;

(c) The population dependent on the watercourse in each watercourse State;

(d) The effects of the use or uses of the watercourse in one watercourse State on other watercourse States;

(e) Existing and potential uses of the watercourse;

(f) Conservation, protection, development and economy of use of the water resources of the watercourse and the costs of measures taken to that effect;

(g) The availability of alternatives, of comparable value, to a particular planned or existing use. [art. 6(1)].

These clearly remain helpful factors in backing up one's own position (country X's "social and economic needs"), but it is difficult to see how these do not equally aid an adversary's contrary position (country Y's social and economic needs). In other words the list simply offers a language in which to continue the consultations and negotiations mentioned above; it does, however, offer little in the way of proposing solutions. The real benefit is that it may keep the conversation ongoing so that a mutually advantageous political settlement will arise over time. Additionally, should an outside arbiter be brought into the picture, that arbiter may use the listed factors to validate its own interpretation of "reasonableness."

One might also notice the dearth of environmental factors in the list of those factors relevant to equitable and reasonable utilization. This lack is presumably balanced by the duty not to cause transboundary harm [art. 7(1)] and the provisions against ecosystem destruction [art. 20] and pollution [art. 21(2)]. The limited voice given to environmental factors in ascertaining equitable utilization, however, does show the continuing tension between development and environmental protection—a tension the Convention can only attempt to broker and not to resolve.

In the case of Hungary v. Slovakia, The ICJ confirmed inter alia, (a) that multipurpose river basin development treaties may establish a continuing (and environmentally sensitive) management regime that cannot be unilaterally abrogated, (b) recognized that sustainable development and ecological risk assessment are customary rules of international environmental and water law, and (c) held that these customary rules can apply to treaties negotiated prior to the recognition of these emerging norms.

In that case Hungary justified its 1989 suspension of a 1977 river basin treaty involving the construction of a series of locks and dams, as an "ecological state of necessity." To justify termination, Hungary invoked a number of familiar contract defenses, impossibility and changed circumstances, and asserted that the emerging precautionary principle imposed "an *erga omnes* obligation of prevention of damage...." and thus precluded her continued performance of the treaty. To defend its suspension, she invoked Article 33 of the International Law Commission Draft Articles on the International Responsibility of States which allows a state to avoid an international obligation when so doing is the only means to "safeguard an essential interest of the State against a grave and imminent peril."

In a significant expansion of the concept of state necessity, the ICJ agreed that the environmental risks related to an essential state interest. It interpreted Article 33 to require "that a real 'grave' and 'imminent' 'peril' existed in 1989 and that the state's response was 'the only possible response.'" While article 33 embodies a limited precautionary principle, a state invoking it must demonstrate by credible scientific evidence that a real risk will materialize in the near future and is thus more than a possibility. The Court found that Hungary's evidence of risk and the possible range of alternatives did not meet these standards.

In a separate opinion Judge Weeramantry adopted the interrelated principles of environmentally sustainable development and cautionary environmental assessment and management as *erga omnes* customary rules,. In his view they command the same general applicability as the laws of human rights.

(c) Obligation Not to Cause Transboundary Harm

Like the rule of equitable utilization, the rule against causing transboundary harm has long been established for international watercourses. As early as 1937, in the case of the Diversion of Water from the River Meuse (Netherlands v. Belgium), 1937 P.C.I.J. (Ser. A/B) No. 70, at 4, the PCIJ formulated the general rule that "each of the two states is at liberty, in its own territory, to modify them [canals], to enlarge them, to transform them, to fill them in and even to increase the volume of water in them from new sources," provided that the discharge of water outside their respective territories remained at a normal level. This, of course, is an early formulation of Principle 2 of the 1992 Rio Declaration, and art. 21 of the Stockholm Declaration, which assert that "States have ... the sovereign right to exploit their own resources ... and the responsibility to ensure that activities within their jurisdiction or control do not cause damage to the environment of other States."

The Convention makes clear that the harm must be "significant harm," and places a duty of due diligence upon watercourse states not to cause such harm. [art. 7(1)]. The difficulty is determining the proper relationship between "equitable and reasonable utilization" [art. 5] and the no-significant-harm rule [art. 7]. What happens if the two rules are perceived as being in conflict? Suppose, for example, a perceived equitable utilization in State A—such as a municipal power plant—causes significant harm to the watercourse in State B, despite State A's diligent efforts to prevent that harm? The Convention offers this solution:

1. Watercourse States shall, in utilizing an international watercourse in their territories, take all appropriate measures to prevent the causing of significant harm to other watercourse States.

2. Where significant harm nevertheless is caused to another watercourse State, the States whose use causes such harm shall, in the absence of agreement to such use, take all appropriate measures ... in consultation with the affected State, to eliminate or mitigate such harm and, where appropriate, to discuss the question of compensation.

art. 7(1)–(2).

And the Convention backs this up with a further condition: "In the event of a conflict between uses of an international watercourse, it shall be resolved with reference to the principles and factors set out in articles 5 to 7, with special regard being given to the requirements of vital human needs" [art. 10(2)].

Obviously, the Convention does not convey an unequivocal priority of either rule but does soften the absolute prohibition against the causing of transboundary harm. In fact, the Convention stresses an ad hoc consultative resolution of such conflicts, which follows the trend in state practice toward negotiated settlement of such disputes. Taking the Conventions' articles together, we might suggest a new formulation of the customary rule: a use is not *per se* violative of international law if it causes significant transboundary harm, as long as the use is equitable and reasonable, and the parties involved have conducted informed consultations on the matter.

Skeptics, of course, might maintain that the Convention simply offers another level of "reasonable" action in article 7—in effect a tautology which attempts to balance reasonable harm against reasonable use, all in the name of reasonableness. But to be fair the Convention has committed itself to promoting dialogue when conflicts do arise among watercourse states. It has not attempted to lay down the law rigidly with regard to specific and highly contextual problems, but instead has opted for an ongoing conversation among disputants. As long as the conversation is maintained, the chance for a political solution to a problem remains.

(d) Further Protections

The Convention provides a number of additional obligations for watercourse states which, unlike the basic rules regarding communication, equitable utilization and the duty not to cause transboundary harm, do not so clearly follow state practice. As such, these may be seen as part of the "progressive development of the law," or at least as obligations less universally recognized as examples of customary international law. These include: (1) the duty to protect and preserve ecosystems of international watercourses [art. 20]; (2) the duty to harmonize pollution prevention policies [art. 21(2)]; and (3) the duty to take all appropriate measures to prevent or mitigate conditions that may be harmful to other watercourse states, such as flood or ice conditions, water-borne diseases, siltation, erosion, salt-water intrusion, drought or desertification [art. 27]. The last duty (3), though moderated by the qualifier "where appropriate," especially expands the traditional no-significant-harm rule by holding states responsible for both "natural causes or human conduct" of potential harm [art. 27].

(e) The Question of Groundwater

The ILC debated whether to include all types of transboundary groundwaters within the scope of the Draft Articles, the precursor to the Convention. As the Convention now stands, "[w]atercourse means a system of surface waters and groundwaters constituting by virtue of their physical relationship a unitary whole and normally flowing into a common terminus" [art. 2(a)]. The Convention thus excludes so-called "unrelated confined groundwaters" which by definition do not flow into a common terminus.

Though in 1994 the Special Rapporteur strongly recommended the deletion of the phrase "flowing into a common terminus" to the Draft Articles, and therefore the inclusion of confined transboundary groundwaters, the Commission as a whole rejected the proposal. For his part the Special Rapporteur maintained that the ILC should include these transboundary waters to "encourage their management in a rational manner and prevent their depletion and pollution." The Commission, on the other hand, remained reluctant to extend the scope of its work because the Draft Articles had not been formulated with confined aquifers in mind. Instead, as a compromise the ILC adopted a resolution stating its "view that the principles contained in its draft articles ... may be applied to transboundary confined groundwater." In 1986 the ILA reached a similar but more sweeping conclusion, allowing confined groundwaters within the definition of an "international drainage basin" and thus within the regulations of the 1966 Helsinki Rules. Given these two pronouncements, one might plausibly extrapolate the rules regarding international watercourses to the special situation of confined transboundary groundwaters.

2.   REGIONAL AND BILATERAL AGREEMENTS

Over the years a number of regional and bilateral arrangements have provided an extensive body of state practice We have tried to highlight those most important to our prospective readers, but one should be aware that a long list of such agreements now exists. Among the agreements negotiated but not covered here include those for Lake Constance, the River Danube, the River Elbe, the Niger Basin and the Zambezi River System.

(a) 1992 ECE Convention on the Protection and Use of Transboundary Watercourses and Lakes (ECE Treaty)

In 1992, the United Nations Economic Commission for Europe (ECE) codified basic regional rules for the protection and use of transboundary watercourses. The ECE Treaty, March 17, 1992, 31 I.L.M. 1312 (entered into force on October 6, 1996) incorporates much of the customary law discussed above, while further developing the law by affirming the precautionary principle, the polluter pays principle and environmental impact assessments.

The treaty defines "transboundary waters" to mean "any surface waters or ground waters which mark, cross or are located on boundaries between two or more States" [art. 1(1)]. As such, the treaty provides broader coverage than the Convention, which does not officially include isolated or "unrelated" groundwaters (see above). The treaty also contains a broad definition of "transboundary impact" as meaning "any significant adverse effect on the environment" including "effects on human health and safety, flora, fauna, soil, air, water, climate, landscape and historical monuments . . .

[and] effects on the cultural heritage or socio-economic conditions" [art. 1(2)].

Part I of the treaty describes the provision relating to all parties, not just riparian parties, and creates the affirmative duty to take all appropriate measures to "prevent, control and reduce any transboundary impact" [art. 2(1)]. Clearly, this would preclude an upstream state from reducing the water supply to a downstream state if such a reduction would cause significant harm. More specifically, the parties must prevent, control and reduce pollution, and ensure not only the conservation of water resources but also the conservation and restoration of ecosystems [art. 2(2)]. In guiding the obligations of the parties, the treaty also strongly affirms the concept of sustainable development.

Following customary law, the treaty also imposes a duty of equitable and reasonable utilization for international watercourses. As discussed above, this principle is firmly ensconced in international law. The ECE treaty, however—as in the Convention— loosens the absolute prohibition against the causing of transboundary impact—in effect appearing to allow some transboundary harm perpetrated by an equitable use.

The Parties shall, in particular, take all appropriate measures:

To ensure that transboundary waters are used in a reasonable and equitable way, taking into particular account their transboundary character, in the case of activities which cause or are likely to cause transboundary impact.

ECE Treaty art. 2(2)(c).

As the ECE Treaty and the Convention remain the most important pronouncements on the issue, we repeat again our understanding of the customary rule: a use is not *per se* violative of international law if it causes significant transboundary harm, as long as the use is equitable and reasonable, and the parties involved have conducted informed consultations on the matter.

Balanced against the heightened profile of equitable utilization is a detailed enumeration of obligations to prevent, control and reduce transboundary impact. Among these is the requirement that each party set emission limits for discharges from point sources based on "best available technology" (BAT), and that the parties specifically tailor these limits to individual industrial sectors [art. 3(2)]. For diffuse sources, particularly from agriculture, the parties must develop and implement "best environmental practices" (BEP) to reduce the inputs of nutrients and hazardous substances [art. 3(1)(g)]. To aid in the formulation of both types of controls, the treaty defines BAT in Annex I and provides guidelines of developing BEP in Annex II. The treaty further requires parties to define water quality objectives and to adopt water-quality criteria [art. 3(3)], supplying guidelines for these actions in Annex III. As an additional general duty, parties must undertake environmental impact assessments to gauge any future level of harm [art. 3(1)(h)].

In Part II, the ECE Treaty more specifically focuses on the duties of riparian parties, especially emphasizing the need for cooperation. Riparian parties, if they have not already done so, are required to enter into bilateral or multilateral agreements in order to prevent, control and reduce transboundary impact [art. 9(1)]. These agreements must provide for the establishment of "joint bodies" to administer the agreement [art. 9(2)]. A joint body thus acts as the mechanism through which the parties can discharge numerous duties, including joint monitoring and assessment, exchange of information, and the establishment of warning and alarm procedures [art. 9(2)].

Regarding the standard customary obligations of notification and consultation, the treaty mandates that consultations be held in good faith at the request of any riparian party [art. 10], and that each country give prompt notification concerning "any critical situation that may have transboundary impact" [art. 14]. Going beyond custom, the treaty also requires that riparian parties provide mutual assistance upon request should a critical situation arise [art. 15].

At a joint special session held in 2001, the Parties to the ECE Treaty and the Convention on the Transboundary Effects of Industrial Accidents, 31 I.L.M. 1333 (1992), decided that an intergovernmental negotiation process—within the scope of both conventions—should be entered into with the aim of adopting a legally binding instrument on civil liability for transboundary damage caused by hazardous activities. In furtherance of this decision, an open-ended intergovernmental Working Group was established with a mandate to draft a legally binding instrument. As of this writing, that document remains a work in progress [*See Report of the Joint Special Session, U.N. Economic and Social Council*, ECE/MP.WAT/7, ECE/CP.TEIA/5 (Oct. 11, 2001)].

(b) The Rhine

The Rhine River regime offers an example of long-term regional cooperation with regard to an international watercourse. As early as 1950, the riparian European nations of the Rhine created an international commission to oversee the waterway, and in 1963 reformed that institution in the Agreement Concerning the International Commission for the Protection of the Rhine Against Pollution, (1963 Berne Convention), Apr. 23, 1963, 994 U.N.T.S. 3, (entered into force May 1, 1965). Under this agreement the primary function of the International Commission was to research the river's pollution problems and offer guidelines for improvement. Only in 1976, however, did the riparian parties more effectively attempt to arrive at solutions.

In that year the parties amended the 1963 agreement and created two more treaties—the Convention for the Protection of the Rhine against Chemical Pollution (Rhine Chemicals Convention) 1124

U.N.T.S. 375 (entered into force Feb. 1, 1979) and the Convention for the Protection of the Rhine against Pollution by Chlorides (Rhine Chlorides Convention), Dec. 3, 1976, 16 I.L.M. 265 (entered into force July 5, 1985). The Rhine Chemicals Convention is more general and mixes international and national controls.

The Rhine Chemicals Convention, for example, mandates that the parties gradually eliminate the discharge of dangerous substances listed in Annex I, and reduce the discharge of less dangerous substances listed in Annex II [art. 1]. The parties must also draw up a national list of all Annex I substances discharged into the river [art. 2], and must grant prior national approval for any such discharge [art. 3]. In granting approval the national authority must specify emission standards that do not exceed the limits proposed by the International Commission [art. 3(2)]. Any discharge of Annex II substances must also receive prior authorization, but the emission standards are to be established by the national authorities and not the International Commission [art. 6]. Finally, as is widely noted, though the convention contains a provision requiring immediate notification of the commission and affected parties in case of an accident [art. 11], the Swiss government failed to provide timely notice to either following a devastating fire at its Sandoz facility in 1986. The toxic effluent from this accident caused widespread damage to the entire ecosystem of the Rhine and led to the creation of the Rhine Action Programme in 1987 (discussed below).

The Rhine Chlorides Convention more specifically attempts to control pollution of the river by chloride ions. This convention has been supplemented by a 1991 protocol, which further strengthens the obligations of the parties. As it stands, each party is allocated certain discharge limits as set out in Annex IV under the protocol. The strongest measures apply to France, which must reduce its discharges where these exceed 200 milligrams per litre at the Netherlands–Germany border. The excess is to be stored on land and later discharged into the Rhine, pending favorable environmental conditions. The Rhine Chlorides Convention and protocol also provide for cost-sharing with regard to the major obligations of the parties, with percentage shares give to France, Germany, the Netherlands and the Swiss Confederation. Driving the measures of the new protocol is the 1987 Rhine Action Programme, which was adopted in the aftermath of the Sandoz incident. Though not a treaty, the Action Programme establishes as objectives: (1) the restoration of the ecosystem so as to accommodate the return of higher species; (2) the maintenance of the river as a source of drinking water supplies; and (3) the further reduction of pollution by harmful substances. The 1987 Rhine Action Programme hopes to achieve these objectives by the turn of the century.

The "Rhine" Action Program since its inception in 1987 has taken significant steps to achieve these objectives. In particular, the water quality has improved. A sharp reduction of the emissions of communities and industries has been realized. This is

the result of the joint efforts of the International
Commission for the Protection of the Rhine and the
implementation of measures by the contracting Parties. As some hundreds of salmons have ascended
the Rhine, the first ecological success is evident. A
promising start has also been made in the direction
of the other objectives. [www.iksr.org/pdf/Jacobo-
vits].

(c) United States—Canada

A very early example of cooperation by nations
with regard to shared water resources is provided
by the United States and Canada. The 1909 Treaty
Between the United States and Great Britain Relating to Boundary Waters, and Questions Arising
between the United States and Canada (1909
Boundary Waters Treaty), Jan. 11, 1909, X I.P.E.
5158 (entered into force May 5, 1910) deals primarily with issues of navigation, the construction of
dams and other diversion projects. Importantly,
however, this 1909 treaty also states that the "waters flowing across the boundary shall not be polluted on either side to the injury of health or property
of the other" [art. IV]. As such, the document
provides one of the earliest treaty commitments to
control environmental pollution in international
law.

The 1909 Boundary Waters Treaty also establishes the International Joint Commission (IJC)
which is composed of six commissioners—three each
from the United States and Canada [art. VII]. The
IJC must approve any uses, obstructions or diver-

sions that change the level or flow of the boundary waters [art. III]. The IJC additionally acts as both an informal and formal arbiter of disputes, with the power to administer oaths and subpoena witnesses [arts. IX–XIII].

The Agreement Between the United States and Canada on the Water Quality of the Great Lakes (1978 Great Lakes Water Quality Agreement), Nov. 22, 1978, 30 U.S.T. 1383 as amended by protocol in 1987, further expands both the duties of the parties and those of the IJC. Its primary objective is the restoration and maintenance of the chemical, physical, and biological integrity of the waters of the Great Lakes basin ecosystem. The agreement is quite detailed, with numerous annexes and appendices, and creates "General" as well as "Specific Objectives." As "General Objectives," the parties agree that the Great Lakes System should be free from substances or materials that interfere with beneficial uses and/or cause harm to human, animal or aquatic life [art. III]. So as to meet these goals, the treaty provides for "Specific Objectives" which "represent the minimum levels of water quality" for the Great Lakes System [art. IV]. These are set out in Annex 1 and mandate numerical concentration values for Persistent Toxic Substances, such as pesticides and metals, defined as any substance which has a half-life in water of greater that 8 weeks.

Augmenting the General and Specific Objectives, the 1978 Great Lakes Water Quality Agreement requires both parties to develop and implement programs and measures covering a range of problems. The requirements of these provisions are then further detailed in accompanying annexes. As such, the parties must develop programs and measures to combat pollution from municipal sources, industrial sources, non-point sources, shipping activities, dredging activities, off-shore facilities, contaminated sediments and contaminated groundwater and subsurface waters [art. VI]. In addition, the parties must reduce and control inputs of phosphorous and other nutrients which cause eutrophication, as well as other hazardous polluting substances [art. VI]. Emphasizing the ecosystem approach to coordinated action, the treaty further requires the parties to develop and implement both Remedial Action Plans and Lakewide Management Plans [art. VI].

To administer and oversee these obligations, the 1978 Great Lakes Water Quality Agreement places more responsibilities on the IJC. Now backed up by a Water Quality Board and a Science Advisory Board, the IJC must analyze and distribute information relating to both water quality in the Great Lakes System and to pollution entering the system from outside waters [art. VII]. The IJC must also collect and analyze information concerning the General and Specific Objectives and the efficacy of adopted programs [art. VII]. To this end, the IJC is asked to provide biennial reports detailing its assessments, advice and recommendations [art. VII]. The treaty also provides the IJC with the authority to verify independently the data and other information submitted by the parties [art. VII].

In its Eleventh Biennial Report on Great Lakes Water Quality, issued in 2002, the International Joint Commission (IJC) found slow progress in its attempts to restore and maintain the chemical and biological integrity of the waters of the Great Lakes basin ecosystem. Cleaning up contaminated sediments and stopping the invasion of alien species are two top priorities for restoring the chemical and biological integrity of this vast and vital ecosystem. IJC, Eleventh Biennial Report: Great Lakes Water Quality (2002). This means that the parties remain far removed from achieving the ultimate goals of their General Objectives. However, the treaty regime does create sophisticated machinery with which to engage the difficult environmental problems of this heavily industrialized region.

(d) United States—Mexico

Another longstanding relationship of cooperation regarding transboundary waters exists between the United States and Mexico. Treaties drawn in the 1880s deal with navigation, and in this century the two countries signed the 1944 Treaty between the United States and Mexico Relative to the Utilization of Waters of Colorado and Tijuana Rivers and of the Rio Grande from Fort Quitman to the Gulf of Mexico (1944 Colorado River Treaty), Feb. 3, 1944, 3 U.N.T.S. 314. This treaty considers utilization issues such as apportionment, dam construction and flood control. The treaty also establishes the International Boundary and Water Commission (IBWC) (formerly known as the International Boundary

Commission by 1889 treaty), and endows this body with additional powers and duties. These include investigating and developing plans for construction works, overseeing the respective obligations of apportionment, and resolving any disputes between the parties [art. 24]. In addition, in making specific suggestions regarding improvements to the waterways, the Commission proposes official instruments known as "Minutes" that the parties adopt through diplomatic process. In formalizing a Minute, the IBWC publicly announces a written recommendation and the governments then bind themselves to that recommendation through an exchange of diplomatic Notes. An important example of these is Minute No. 242 (1973) which establishes specific responsibilities for both parties regarding the salinity of the Colorado River.

Though the 1944 Colorado River Treaty does require the IBWC "to give preferential attention to the solution of all border sanitation problems" in providing for joint use of the international waters [art. 3], this mandate by itself proved insufficient in protecting the common environment. To address this need more adequately, the parties adopted the 1983 Mexico—United States Agreement to Co-operate in the Solution of Environmental Problems in the Border Area (1983 La Paz Agreement), Aug. 14, 1983, 22 I.L.M. 1025. This agreement commits the two parties to cooperation in the field of environmental protection and conservation in the border area, obligating that they "undertake, to the fullest extent practical, to adopt the appropriate measures to prevent, reduce and eliminate sources of pollution" [art. 1]. To this end the parties conclude annexes that specify more detailed obligations, such as Annex I concerning the San Diego—Tijuana water sanitation problem. Annex I, the only addendum dealing exclusively with water pollution, requires that the parties continue appropriate consultations with regard to the construction, operation and maintenance of disposal and treatment facilities.

The North American Free Trade Agreement (NAFTA) and its progeny, the North American Agreement on Environmental Cooperation between the United States, Canada and Mexico (1993 Environmental Side Agreement), Sept. 14, 1993, 32 I.L.M. 1480, have prompted more extensive cooperation regarding transboundary water resources. The latter document—in addition to restating general objectives of environmental protection—establishes a Commission for Environmental Cooperation (CEC) that oversees the environmental status of the three North American countries. The Council of the CEC considers and develops recommendations concerning pollution prevention techniques, conservation and other transboundary environmental issues [art. 10]. Building on the goals and objectives of the Environmental Side Agreement, Mexico and the United States also created the Border Environment Cooperation Commission (BECC) in 1993 [see Agreement Concerning the Establishment of a Border Environment Cooperation Commission and a North American Development Bank, Nov. 16, 1993, 32 I.L.M. 1545]. The BEEC works closely with the

North American Development Bank and the IBWC with regard to environmental infrastructure projects, facilitating the construction and improvement of border sanitation facilities.

We have noted in Chapter Fourteen that in 1983, the United States and Mexico signed the Agreement to Cooperate in the Solution of Environmental Problems in the Border Area (La Paz Agreement), Aug. 14, 1983, 22 I.L.M. 1025. The parties agree to take measures, "to the fullest practical extent," to prevent, reduce and eliminate border pollution [art. II], and to coordinate their efforts to address the problems of air, land and water pollution in the area [art. V]. The agreement defines the border area as the region "situated 100 kilometers on either side of the inland and maritime boundaries between the Parties" [art. IV]. In effect, the La Paz Agreement functions as a framework for further action, providing for the creation of annexes to deal with specific problems. We also noted that pursuant to the La Paz Agreement the U.S. and Mexico unveiled an agreement: "Border 2112" in September 2002.

One of the major objectives of this agreement relates to water quality. By 2005, it seeks (a) to increase by 1.5 million the number of people connected to potable water and wastewater collection and treatment systems, (b) reduce by 10% the number of days per year of public health advisories in coastal border waters, and (c) assess the water system conditions in 10% of the existing water systems in the border cities to identify opportunities for improvement in overall water system efficiencies, its final objective is to assess significant shared and transboundary surface waters and achieve a majority of water quality standards currently being exceeded in those waters by 2112.

In conclusion, it is evident that the problems of transbondary water pollution form part of the larger picture of land-based pollution, toxics, and biodiversity. Our focus on transboundary river pollution has been based on political and legal developments, and should not obscure the importance of seeing this as one component of a more comprehensive challenge.

CHAPTER SIXTEEN

DESERTIFICATION

A. NATURE OF THE PROBLEM

Desertification refers to the process of climate change and human impacts that create desert environments in "drylands"—the arid, semi-arid, or dry sub-humid regions of the world [*see* U.N. Convention to Combat Desertification in Those Countries Experiencing Serious Drought and/or Desertification, Particularly in Africa, June 17, 1994, art. I (a) [hereinafter Desertification Convention]; Agenda 21, Ch. 12, U.N. Doc. A/CONF. 151/26 (1992)]. Drylands receive less water than forest regions but more than deserts, and are also called "plains" or "grasslands." Climate change may be caused by severe short-term droughts as well as long periods without rainfall. Human impacts arise from the removal of natural vegetation from bio-regions, excessive cultivation, the exhaustion of surface water, and the mining of groundwater [NEW ENCYCLOPEDIA BRITANNICA 2003 (http://search.eb.com)]. Climate change and human impacts destroy the life-supporting quality of drylands and cause erosion, loss of soil fertility, the ability to hold water, salinization of the soil and water, exhaustion of groundwater, and diminution of surface water [Agenda 21 chs.

12.2 & 12.18]. The resulting phenomenon called "desertification" is an advanced stage of land degradation in which the biological potential of the land is destroyed.

Seventy percent of the world's drylands (equal to 3,600 million hectares or 25 percent of the total land area of the world) have been affected by desertification. In Africa, Asia, and South America, 70 percent of the agricultural drylands have experienced degradation, and the remaining drylands are threatened. In Kenya, 85 percent of the total landmass exists in degraded condition, with the figure at 40 percent in India and 20 percent in China, respectively. Desertification has also affected 74 percent of North American agricultural drylands and 65 percent in Europe. The impacts are worse in developing nations that have scant resources for rehabilitating degraded land [see generally William C. Burns, *The International Convention to Combat Desertification: Drawing a Line in the Sand?*, 16 MICH. J. INT'L L. 831, 845–48 (1995)].

The problem of desertification received substantial attention at the World Summit on Sustainable Development (WSSD) both in the Declaration (particularly paragraph 13) and the Plan of Implementation (particularly paragraph 41). [Report of the World Summit on Sustainable Development, A/CONF.199/20, 2002]

B. IMPACTS OF DESERTIFICATION

Agriculture on drylands provides more than 20 percent of the world's food supply. The desertification of agricultural drylands reduces soil fertility and lessens crop yields. In Africa, agricultural production has fallen by 25–50 percent, and worldwide the financial cost of lost agricultural production is approximately $43 billion each year. When degraded, land can no longer sustain plant or animal life, and people who depend on the land are forced to migrate to urban areas or to other land. As more marginally productive land is cultivated or used for grazing, soil degradation advances and once again people must abandon the land. The added stress on urban resources has the potential to create social unrest. In addition to the agricultural, economic, and social impacts, desertification threatens the biodiversity of ecosystems by destroying plants and critical habitat for animals [*see generally*, WORLD RESOURCES INSTITUTE, WORLD RESOURCES 1994–95, A GUIDE TO THE GLOBAL ENVIRONMENT 109–146 (1994) [hereinafter WRI 1995]; *see* Chapter Five, Biodiversity]. The United Nations Environment Programme (UNEP) estimates the global costs of desertification at approximately $42 billion a year [*Agriculture, Land and Desertification: Report of the U.N. Secretary–General*, U.N. Economic and Social Council, E/CN.17/2001/PC/13 ¶ 4 (2001); *see also* INT'L FUND FOR AGRICULTURAL DEVELOPMENT, DRYLANDS: A CALL TO ACTION (1998); UNEP, GLOBAL ENVIRONMENTAL OUTLOOK 2000 (1999)].

C. CAUSES OF DESERTIFICATION

Human activities, driven by population growth, energy needs, and the lack of land have led to over-cultivation—the farming of land beyond its sustainable fertility. Population growth has demanded increased food production and encouraged the farming of marginally productive lands, and the shortening of fallow periods. Over cultivation also arises from economic pressures for revenue-generating cash crops that can be exported. These crops are usually land-intensive, nutrient-depleting and reduce the land area available for food crops. The result of over-cultivation is that drylands, naturally poor in nutrients and organic content, become more susceptible to erosion. Their topsoil is blown or washed away, exposing subsoil that is often infertile and less able to absorb water, thus leading to desertification.

One-half of the world's cattle graze in drylands [WRI 1995, at 296–7]. In developing countries, cattle are raised as a source of food for domestic consumption as well as for export. Overgrazing occurs when land shortages lead to the unsustainable pasturing of livestock. This leads to the loss of vegetation and the replacement of desirable plants such as grasses (which help hold the soil) with shrubs. At the same time, the pulverizing and compacting of soil by cattle hooves leads to soil erosion.

Deforestation exists as another cause of desertification. Forests are cleared in order to provide firewood—an important source of fuel in many developing countries—as well as for crop cultivation and livestock grazing. In developing countries, 90 percent of the population relies exclusively on wood for cooking and heating. The phenomenon of deforestation is most severe in Asia, the Middle East, and Africa, with 90 percent of the forests cleared in Ethiopia and Sudan alone. Often, deforestation acts as a starting point for desertification because destroyed tree and plant roots no longer hold the soil together or provide organic material that fertilizes soil, thereby increasing its water absorbent qualities.

In addition to over-cultivation, irrigation practices that do not properly drain the soil cause the accumulation of salts (salinization) that reduce soil fertility and stunt plant growth. Salinization of irrigated crop land is a serious problem not only in Asia and the Middle East, but also in North America. Salinity of the Colorado River from irrigation practices in the western United States has caused serious land degradation in California and Mexico [*see generally* NEW COURSES FOR THE COLORADO RIVER (Gary D. Weatherford & F. Lee Brown eds., 1986)]. The United States—in order to fulfill its international obligations to Mexico—has built a $260 million desalinization plant, and improved its irrigation practices by lining water canals to reduce salt accumulation (*see* Chapter Twelve, Transboundary Water Pollution).

Some social policies are more responsible for desertification than others. For example, many nations with severe desertification problems have land ownership and tenure systems that do not provide security of tenure for the farmers and ranchers who work the land. Consequently, these groups find no incentives to conserve land or water. Furthermore, some developing nations have encouraged farmers to clear and settle in forests as a means of asserting national sovereignty over native tribes and as a means of appeasing demands for land ownership reform.

D. REMEDIAL OBJECTIVES

Desertification raises questions common to other international environmental problems, and must be addressed within the conceptual framework of sustainable development. In 1992, the United Nations Conference on Environment and Development ("Earth Summit" or UNCED) adopted Agenda 21, a program for sustainable development, which recommended preventive measures for threatened or slightly degraded drylands and rehabilitative measures for moderately or severely degraded drylands. Recommended activities included improved land- and water-use policies, improved agricultural and ranching technologies, soil and water conservation to restore and sustain productivity, reforestation, protection of special ecological areas, and development of alternative energy sources [Agenda 21 ch. 12]. The Desertification Convention entered into force on December 26, 1996. As of January 2002, 178 countries and the European Union have ratified or acceded to the Convention.

E. LEGAL RESPONSE

The Desertification Convention adopts an innovative "bottom-up" approach to an increasingly destructive environmental problem. The convention defines desertification as "[l]and degradation in arid, semi-arid and dry sub-humid areas, resulting from various factors, including climatic variations and human activities" [art. 1(a)]. In other words, desertification is not—as is often misunderstood—the expansion of existing deserts. The convention places significant emphasis on the human role in creating desertification, identifying causation as a "complex interaction among physical, biological, political, social, cultural and economic factors" [pmbl.]. Drought, on the other hand, means the naturally occurring phenomenon brought about by below normal precipitation [art. 1(c)].

The convention seeks to combat desertification and to mitigate the effects of drought, with the goal of promoting sustainable development in affected areas [art. 2(1)]. The emphasis remains on Africa where the problem is seen as most acute, but the Convention contains four Regional Implementation Annexes (RIAs) that also spell out specific provisions for the Northern Mediterranean region, Latin American—the Caribbean, and Asia. Nonetheless, while requiring cooperation and coordination at the sub-regional, regional and international levels, the convention also establishes a strong mandate to involve local communities both in the decision-making and implementation processes. This dedication to a "bottom-up" approach reflects a growing consensus that only a decentralized strategy will work to control environmental degradation, a strategy that includes and rewards local people.

1. COMMITMENTS

(a) Developing Countries

For their part, affected developing country parties must prepare and implement National Action Programmes (NAPs) that seek to meet the objectives of the convention. The purpose of each NAP is to identify the factors causing desertification, as well as practical measures that might ameliorate both desertification and drought [art. 10(1)]. In creating a long-term plan, each developing country must specify the roles of government, local communities and landowners, while also allowing for changing circumstances at the local level [art. 10(2)]. Furthermore, each NAP must provide for participation by Non–Governmental Organizations (NGOs) and "[l]ocal populations, both women and men, particularly resource users, including farmers and pastoralists" at all levels of the decision-making and implementation processes [art. 10(2)(f)]. In the African RIA, the convention notes the necessity of adopting an approach which takes into account the particular conditions of that region, including severe land degradation and poor socio-economic circumstances [art. 3]. In fact, echoing the convention itself at article 4(2)(c), that annex requires African country parties, in accordance with their respective abilities, to "adopt the combating of desertification and/or the mitigation of the effects of drought as a central strategy in their efforts to eradicate poverty" [art. 4(1)(a)]. As of March 2002, 57 NAPs had been prepared and adopted.

In addition to the creation of individual NAPs, the convention requires affected country parties to consult and cooperate, as appropriate, in the development of sub-regional and regional action programmes [art. 11]. The African RIA elaborates on these obligations, requiring, among other things, that affected parties establish sub-regional mechanisms both to manage shared natural resources and to deal with transboundary environmental problems [African RIA art. 11]. At the regional level, the African RIA requires a further action programme that promotes regional cooperation through regular consultations, focusing particularly on capacity-building and the development and exchange of scientific and technological information [art. 13].

At every level, the convention sees the creation of partnership agreements as a means of elaborating and implementing the required action programs [arts. 9(3) & 14]. At the earliest juncture, developing countries should therefore seek the cooperation and involvement of developed countries, intergovernmental organizations and NGOs. In the African RIA these partnership agreements should include both financial and technical assistance, whether attached to national, sub-regional or regional action programmes [art. 18]. In this way the Desertification Convention—again in a "bottom-up" approach that begins at the field level—attempts to create a decentralized system of cooperation and commitment, involving a wide range of prospective donors at the first stages of design.

(b) Developed Countries

The primary obligations of developed country parties remain the transfer of financial resources and technical assistance to developing countries [art. 6]. This means early involvement in partnership agreements, with a focus on addressing the physical, biological *and socio-economic* aspects of the problem [art. 4]. As stated above, fulfillment of these obligations includes strategies for the eradication of poverty in the affected countries [art. 4(2)(c)]. The African RIA further elaborates on these general requirements, while also promoting institutional capacity-building in the areas of administration, science and technology [art. 5].

(c) Implementation

The convention created a number of institutional bodies that will help to implement it. The first is the COP which was established by the Convention as the supreme decision-making body; it comprises ratifying governments and regional economic integration organizations, such as the European Union. One of the main functions of the COP is to review reports submitted by the Parties detailing how they are carrying out their commitments; the COP makes recommendations on the basis of these reports. It also has the power to make amendments to the Convention or to adopt new annexes, such as additional regional implementation annexes. In this way, the COP can guide the Convention as global circumstances and national needs change. To assist the COP, the Convention provides for subsidiary bodies and allows the COP to establish additional ones if necessary. The implementation of the convention was significantly advance when the conference of the parties (COP) decided to set up a permanent secretariat in Bonn, Germany.

The second is the Committee on Science and Technology (CST). The CST is a subsidiary body of the COP; it provides the COP with information and advice on scientific and technological matters relating to combating desertification and mitigating the effects of drought using the most up-to-date scientific knowledge. It is multi-disciplinary, open to the participation of the Parties and composed of government representatives with relevant expertise. It reports regularly to the COP on its work, including at each of the sessions of the COP. The bureau of the CST is responsible for follow-up of the work of the Convention between COP sessions. A revised procedure for the reporting and review process of the implementation of the Convention was established at COP 5. A subsidiary body was established to consider reports from country Parties and observers, as well as information and advice from the CST and the Global Mechanism, and to report to the COP.

Third, A Global Mechanism (GM) helps the COP to promote funding for Convention-related activities and programmes. This mechanism was not conceived to raise or administer funds. Instead, the GM encourages and assists donors, recipients, development banks, NGOs, and others to mobilize funds and to channel them to where they are most needed. It seeks to promote greater coordination among existing sources of funding, and greater efficiency and effectiveness in the use of funds. The GM is under the authority of the COP, which periodically reviews its policies, operational modalities and activities. The GM is hosted by the International Fund for Agricultural Development (IFAD).

Finally, the convention has given NGO's a special place. In recognizes that one of the many strengths of the non-governmental community is that they are the voice and interface of grass roots communities. To the extent that this convention aims to improve the livelihoods of marginalized populations, particularly those communities most threatened by drought and desertification the COP has sought the assistance of the non-governmental community as part of the official programme of work of the Conference of Parties.

To date, over 650 non-governmental organisations have been accredited with observer status to the Conference of the Parties. The participation of these non-governmental organizations in the implementation of the Convention and their contribution to the various meetings is a necessary component of the successful implementation of the Convention.

As with all international environmental regimes, the success of the Desertification Convention rides on tangible contributions from the wealthier parties. In a recent review it was found that the degree of progress made differs from country to country. However, already 27 affected countries in Africa have finalized their National Action Programmes to combat desertification and are starting to implement them. However, the lack of adequate and predictable funding is regarded by all as an obstacle to implementation.

CHAPTER SEVENTEEN

NUCLEAR DAMAGE

A. NATURE OF THE PROBLEM

The military use of nuclear bombs can lead to unparalleled suffering. Civilian deployment of nuclear energy endeavors to turn swords into ploughshares, but has raised concerns about risks associated with exposure to radiation. Consequently, this chapter deals with military weapons production, use, and testing, as well as civilian nuclear energy applications such as power generation, medical uses, and nuclear waste disposal.

Radiation is a form of energy consisting of atomic particles and electromagnetic rays that are emitted from radioactive elements, such as uranium and plutonium. Radiation can cause destructive chemical changes, and when harmful radiation strikes human tissue, it strips (ionizes) electrons or neutrons of the molecules and atoms and thereby kills or damages human cells. The nature of the harm depends on the type and intensity of the radiation and the part of the body that is exposed. High-level (high intensity) radiation kills cells, and can cause excruciating radiation sickness and death within days or weeks. In contrast, low-level radiation only damages cells, allowing them to multiply, but the damaged cells may produce mutations that could lead to cancers and genetic defects years later. While radiation can be harmful, life evolved in the presence of natural ionizing radiation called background radiation, and over time radiation has proven beneficial by facilitating adaptation and change in organisms and species [MARTIN S. SILBERBERG, CHEMISTRY: THE MOLECULAR NATURE OF MATTER AND CHANGE, 1060–1062 (2000)] (herinafter SILBERBERG).

The risk of exposure to radiation arises both from military and civilian uses of nuclear power. While the estimated figures on radiation attributable to nuclear weapons testing and power generation conceal wide variations, it is estimated that 78% of worldwide human exposure to radiation arises from natural causes, 14% from medical treatment and X-rays, and less than 1% from fallout, discharges and occupational exposure resulting from nuclear weapons testing and power generation [R.B.CLARK, MARINE POLLUTION, 5th ed. 167–168 (2001)] (hereinafter CLARK). Nonetheless, there is a strong public perception that radiation caused by nuclear power generation is dangerous. The threat of mass destruction posed by the military use of a nuclear bomb is clearly etched in the public psyche. Such fear is reinforced by the reality of less catastrophic but nonetheless devastating accidents in nuclear power plants, such as the 1986 Chernobyl accident, which is estimated to have caused thousands of cancer deaths [Silberberg, *supra*, at 1060]. Moreover, it is a fact, as distinct from public sentiment or irrational fear, that some high-level nuclear wastes remain radioactive for hundreds of years, and continue to present a yet unsolved problem of waste disposal.

1.   USE AND TESTING OF NUCLEAR WEAPONS

The detonation of a single nuclear bomb or "warhead" would cause a local disaster on a scale that few people in the world have seen and survived. However, it should not be confused with the effects of a nuclear war, in which many nuclear bombs would be exploded. A conflict of that magnitude would likely cause the end of civilization in the countries concerned, and perhaps over the whole world, as well as radioactive contamination of entire continents, and terrible damage to the environment and ecology.

The effect of a single bomb would depend on its power, where it exploded (high in the air or at ground level) and whether it is dropped in a densely populated and built-up area like a city or in open country like an attack on a missile silo. The nuclear bombs available to the great military powers of the world (China, France, Israel, Russia, United Kingdom, United States) range in power from several megatons down to a few kilotons, and some even smaller. A "megaton" is the explosive power of one million tons of TNT (1). A "kiloton" is the power of one thousand tons of TNT.

Bombs likely to be available to terrorist organizations or governments other than the great military powers would be in the 10–to 100–kiloton range.

Bombs made by amateurs might not explode with the full power they were designed for. The two bombs that have been exploded over cities, Hiroshima and Nagasaki in Japan in August 1945, were in the ten-to twenty-kiloton range [Alan F. Phillips, The Effects of a Nuclear Bomb Explosion on the Inhabitants of a City, *at* http://www.pgs.ca /pgs.php/Abolition/8/ (*accessed on* Feb. 21, 2003)].

A 1 megaton hydrogen bomb, hypothetically detonated on the earth's surface, has about 80 times the blast power of the 1945 Hiroshima explosion. The devastation caused by such a nuclear bomb begins at the core with an intensive thermal wave causing pressure damage that creates a crater 200 feet deep and 1000 feet in diameter filled with highly radioactive soil and debris. Casualties from this initial impact decrease with distance from the core: within 1.7 miles of the core, 98% of the people are killed and only a few of the strongest buildings remain standing, while seven miles from the core, only 5% of people are killed instantly, while 45% are injured.

The initial blast and its shock waves are followed by equally deadly radiation. Immediately after the detonation, a great deal of earth and debris, made radioactive by the blast, is carried high into the atmosphere, forming a mushroom cloud. The material drifts downwind and gradually falls back to earth, contaminating thousands of square miles.

The extent to which radiation affects humans is usually measured in Rems which is an abbreviation for "roentgen equivalent man." This is a measurement that seeks to quantify the amount of radiation that will produce certain biological effects. Because uncertainty continues to surround the extent and nature of such biological effects, this discussion, while taking account of Rems, will express effects in qualitative terms.

At a distance of 30 miles from the core, humans will be exposed a greater-than-lethal dose of radiation. Death can occur within hours of exposure, and about it will take about ten years for levels of radioactivity to drop to safe levels. At a distance of 90 miles, radiation exposure will cause death from within two to fourteen days. 160 miles from the core, humans will suffer extensive internal damage, including harm to nerve cells and the cells that line the digestive tract, a loss of white blood cells, and temporary hair loss. 250 miles from the core, humans will suffer a temporary decrease in white blood cells and an uncertain increase in the risk of cancer and genetic diseases. Two to three years will need to pass before radioactivity levels in this area drop low enough to be considered safe, by U.S. peacetime standards. [Office of Technology Assessment, THE EFFECTS OF NUCLEAR WAR (1979)].

The explosion of numerous nuclear weapons of this magnitude could produce global environmental problems and climatic changes. Edible plants, livestock, and marine food sources could be destroyed or become contaminated, resulting in severe food shortages. Water could be contaminated by radioactivity and by pathogenic bacteria and viruses if sewage treatment and waste disposal facilities are destroyed by the initial explosions. Crop failures may also result from "nuclear winters" caused by the accumulation of soot in the atmosphere from explosion-induced fires. Finally, the ozone layer may be damaged by nitrogen oxides released by fires caused by the bomb [John Harte et al., TOXICS A TO Z 153 (1991)]. As we have seen, any damage to the ozone layer will expose the earth to harmful ultraviolet radiation (*see* Chapter Seven, Ozone Depletion).

Since 1945, there have been more than 2,000 nuclear test explosions, primarily underground but also in the atmosphere and underwater. Both the United States and the Soviets conducted nuclear weapons tests in sparsely populated areas within their own borders, as well as without [Stewart L. Udall, *Radiation Nightmare of '50s Guinea Pigs, in* THE ARIZONA REPUBLIC, May 22, 1994, at C1]. However, radioactive fallout from above-ground explosions cannot be contained within borders, but maybe carried hundreds of miles downwind. For example, fallout from aboveground testing in northwest Russia during the cold war was transported into air, land, and water throughout the Arctic [*Environment and Health of Arctic Peoples*, 2 L'AURAVETL'AN INFORMATION BULLETIN (Mar. 13, 1997)].

Underground testing also has potentially harmful effects on health and the environment. For example, at the Nevada Test Site, underground nuclear tests have caused serious radioactive contamination of the groundwater and soil [Danette L. Bloomer,

Comment, *Beyond Our Own Backyard: Considering the Legal Implications and Environmental Risks of Importing Spent Nuclear Fuel,* 10 J. ENVTL. L. & LITIG. 157, 184 (1995)]. The explosion of the first nuclear weapons at the end of the Second World War began the process of radioactive pollution of the sea, which was accelerated by the conducting of nuclear weapons testing until the signing of the Treaty Banning Nuclear Weapon Tests in the Atmosphere, in Outer Space and Underwater, Aug. 5, 1963, 2 ILM 883 (entered into force Oct. 10, 1963), which prohibited all nuclear tests except for those carried out underground. Since then France and China conducted atmospheric testing until 1974 which made a relatively minor contribution to marine radioactive pollution. [Clark, *supra,* at 155]. However, French underground nuclear testing on atolls in the South Pacific has produced fissures in the basalt bases, subsidence, and submarine slides. These side effects have given rise to fears of a massive release of radioactive debris from further testing, and concern about long-term containment of radioactive materials underground [*French Nuclear Testing and the South Pacific Nuclear Free Zone: Testimony on Nuclear Issues in the South Before the Subcomm. on Asia and the Pacific of the House Comm. on Intl Relations,* 104th Cong. (1995) (testimony by Joshua Handler & Thomas W. Clements, Greenpeace), *available at Westlaw,* 1995 WL 12715828]. Some argue that water and plankton samples taken downstream from the atolls may indicate that radiation is already leaking [*id.*].

Nuclear weapons detonated underwater also produced radioactive isotopes that were carried as fine dust into the atmosphere and circled the globe many times before settling back to the earth as fallout. The most important of these isotopes are strontium 90 and caesium 137, which have a half-life of 30 years, and plutonium–239, which has a half-life of 24–400 years. Fallout from nuclear testing peaked in the 1960s, but has fallen significantly with the gradual cessation of weapons testing. [Clark, *supra*, at 156–57].

2. CIVILIAN NUCLEAR ENERGY

The generation of power from nuclear energy amounts to 17% of the electric power generated in the world. In a nuclear power reactor, the chain reaction is controlled to prevent an explosion, using the controlled released of heat to generate power. The risks created by civilian nuclear power generation arise: a) during the operation of power plants; b) by accidents; and c) from waste disposal.

The routine operation of nuclear power plants generates radioactive materials in the form of stack gases, as well as radioactive liquid effluent. The International Atomic Energy Agency (IAEA) has issued standards, regulations, codes of practice, guides and other related instruments dealing with operational safety. Unfortunately, these are voluntary, not obligatory, standards. The continuing absence of universal standards of safety in the operation of nuclear power plants accentuates the dangers of accidents.

Unintentional releases of nuclear radiation, such as occurred at Three Mile Island and Chernobyl [*see generally* Shepard Buchanan, et al., ENVIRONMENTAL COSTS OF ELECTRICITY (1991)], illustrate the perils of civilian nuclear use. The Chernobyl accident in the former Soviet Union, in which a meltdown caused an explosion and massive release of radiation, was the most serious nuclear power reactor accident ever to occur. Within two months of the accident, 31 people had died from severe radiation burns. More importantly, the United States Department of Energy estimates that the long-term health effects of the Chernobyl accident in the northern hemisphere will include an additional 28,000 cancer deaths, 700 additional children born with severe mental retardation in the next generation, and 1,900 additional children born with genetic disorders.

The meltdown during the Three Mile Island accident in the United States did not result in an explosion, and the amount of radiation released was far less than at Chernobyl. Still, abnormal radiation was detected 250 miles from the power plant and in Wales, England.

Because reactor design and operation vary with time and among countries, estimates of the probability of a serious accident that would release a significant amount of radiation are disputed. However, the Nuclear Regulatory Commission has estimated that the probability of a severe accident at a United States reactor is 1 in 3,333 each year.

3. NUCLEAR WASTE

Nuclear wastes are the by-products of nuclear weapons production, nuclear power generation, medical and dental uses, research, and other processes using radioactive elements. By volume, 99% of nuclear waste emits a low level of radiation. Low-level radioactive waste by definition is solid, and has usually been disposed of by packaging in leak-resistant containers and burying in shallow trenches. This creates the potential for environmental problems if radioactive contamination leaks from the waste repository. Disposal sites may have hydrological problems—such as erosion, accumulation of water in the trenches, and groundwater movement—that would allow the radiation to contaminate ground and water, and thereby enter food chains. Contaminated groundwater is the most common pathway for human exposure to radiation from nuclear waste. In addition to waste in repositories, some low-level waste was dumped at sea by both the United States and the Soviets [Jeffrey L. Canfield, *Soviet and Russian Nuclear Waste Dumping in the Arctic Marine Environment: Legal, Historical, and Political Implications*, 7 GEO. INT'L ENVTL. L. REV. 353 (1994)].

High-level wastes are defined as those that are sufficiently radioactive to generate heat, and are composed of spent nuclear fuel. Nuclear weapons production requires plutonium, which is extracted from the fuel of military production reactors, leaving large quantities of highly radioactive liquid waste and fuel rods. Nuclear power plant fuel is replaced about once a year, and the spent fuel rods are temporarily stored at the power plants to cool down in large ponds of water [see Harte, supra, at 162–3]. The water thereby becomes radioactive. The spent fuel itself will remain radioactive for thousands of years. Long-term storage of such high-level waste has been achieved either by placing the waste in repositories in deep geologic formations or by ocean dumping [see RONNIE D. LIPSCHUTZ, RADIOACTIVE WASTE: POLITICS, TECHNOLOGY, AND RISK (1980); Chapter Nine, Toxic and Hazardous Substances]. With both methods, the concern is the possible effect of radioactive waste leaks and the effects of decay heat on the surrounding environment. As we have seen (Chapter Twelve), the London Dumping Convention banned the dumping of high level waste in 1972 and all radioactive waste in 1994. Permanent, land-based nuclear storage sites will not be ready in the United States or Russia until after the year 2010. While spent fuel can be recycled, most countries (including the U.S.) are not currently recycling due to the process' cost and inefficiency. [Nuclear Energy Institute, *High-Level "Nuclear Waste" is really Used Nuclear Fuel*, 2003 (*available at* http://www.nei.org)].

B. REMEDIAL OBJECTIVES

In the Advisory Opinion of the ICJ on the Legality of the Threat or Use of Nuclear Weapons, 1996 I.C.J. No. 95 (July 8) (Legality of Nuclear Weapons case), the court stated: "Nuclear weapons which cannot be contained in either space or time have the potential to destroy all civilization and the entire ecosystem of the planet." Fear of such destruction has led the international community to seek ways of containing and eliminating the nuclear threat from both military and civilian sources. The most obvious and most difficult way to eliminate a nuclear threat is to remove the source: in the military case, this means banning nuclear weapons all together. In the Legality of Nuclear Weapons case, the ICJ appeared to endorse such a method by holding that nations of the world are under a legal obligation to pursue and conclude negotiations with a view to achieving nuclear disarmament. However, the political problems confronting such a course are formidable.

One such obstacle is that the most powerful nations in the world are those in possession of nuclear weapons, and they may be loath to relinquish them. A second, but related roadblock to disarmament is the fact that nuclear weapons maintained the peace for over 50 years during the Cold War and its recent aftermath. Nuclear deterrence and the balance of terror have been the linchpins of Western defense policy. This "balance of terror" based upon nuclear deterrence protected the military use of nuclear weapons, and the environmental devastation they cause, from serious legal scrutiny for over half a century.

However, the end of the cold war has accelerated a sequence of unfolding conventional (treaty) and judicial developments of great importance. These continuing changes, in the view of many commentators, have transformed the mirage of a nuclear weapons-free world into a foreseeable objective. Alternatives to total nuclear disarmament include the non-proliferation of nuclear weapons and the banning of any further nuclear tests. Of course, even if total nuclear disarmament were achieved, it would still leave us with the problem of what to do with the huge quantities of existing nuclear wastes.

In the realm of civilian nuclear energy, an important question is the extent to which preventative and remedial legal responses have been successful. A preventative regime seeks to regulate the construction and operation of nuclear plants in a way that prevents pollution and accidents. It also provides for a system of warning and assistance if accidents do occur. At present the IAEA is not empowered to impose obligatory international safety standards for reactor construction or operations: instead, a remedial regime facilitates the granting of compensation when damages have been caused. The details of how the international community has responded legally call for fuller discussions.

C. LEGAL RESPONSE

As the dangers of nuclear pollution have gradually become more apparent over the years, the international community has struggled to develop rules governing both the civilian and military uses of nuclear energy. In this section, we first outline how the international community has addressed the intractable challenge of nuclear weapons, despite formidable political difficulties. We next outline the response of IEL to the dangers of civilian nuclear power generation. Finally, we discuss the regime governing accidents at nuclear installations and the question of liability.

1. USE AND TESTING OF NUCLEAR WEAPONS

(a) Treaty Overlay

The first steps toward nuclear disarmament were taken by the arms control treaties. The United Soviet Socialist Republics—United States: Treaty on the Elimination of Their Intermediate–Range and Shorter–Range Missiles, Dec. 8, 1987, 27 I.L.M. 84 dealt with the reduction of nuclear missiles, while the Strategic Arms Reduction Talks (START) led to the Treaty on the Reduction and Elimination of Strategic Offensive Arms, Nov. 25, 1991, 32 I.L.M. 246, which reduced the awesome nuclear arsenals of the USA and Russia. Second, a cluster of treaties addressed the testing, deployment, possession and use of nuclear weapons in a variety of locales and conditions. The most important of the treaties restricting nuclear testing are the Treaty Banning Nuclear Weapons Tests in the Atmosphere, in Outer Space and Under Water, and the Treaty on Principles Governing the Activities of States in the Exploration and Use of Outer Space, Including the Moon and other Celestial Bodies, Jan.

27, 1967, 6 I.L.M. 386 (entered into force Oct. 10, 1967). Four significant regional treaties confine the deployment of nuclear weapons in Latin America, the South Pacific, South–East Asia and Africa. The Treaty of Tlatelolco for the Prohibition of Nuclear Weapons in Latin America, Feb. 14, 1967, 6 I.L.M. 52 (entered into force Apr. 22, 1968), prohibits the use of nuclear weapons by the contracting parties; while the parties to the South Pacific Nuclear Free Zone Treaty, Aug. 6, 1985, 24 I.L.M. 1442 (entered into force Dec. 11, 1986), the Organization of African Unity: African Nuclear–Weapon–Free Zone Treaty, June 21–23, 1995, 35 I.L.M. 698, and the South–East Asia Nuclear Free Zone Treaty, Dec. 15, 1995, 35 I.L.M. 635 undertake not to manufacture, acquire or possess any nuclear weapons. These treaties must be read in the context of the Treaty on the Final Settlement with Respect to Germany, Sept. 12, 1990, 29 I.L.M. 1186, and the Treaty on the Non-proliferation of Nuclear Weapons (NPT), July 1, 1968, 7 I.L.M. 809 (entered into force Mar. 5, 1970).

The contours of a general prohibition on nuclear weapons began to take definite shape with the NPT of 1968. This treaty sought to control nuclear damage by prohibiting "horizontal" proliferation (the spread of nuclear weapons to non-nuclear states in a world of five declared nuclear states) and "vertical" proliferation (the further amassing and development of nuclear weapons by nuclear states). The nuclear states were obligated under article VI "to pursue negotiations in good faith on effective measures relating to cessation of the nuclear arms race at an early date and to nuclear disarmament, and on a treaty on general and complete disarmament under strict and effective international control."

In 1995, the NPT was indefinitely extended by the NPT Review and Extension Conference, which endorsed an earlier Security Council resolution [Resolution 988 (1995) of Apr. 11, 1995] that reiterated and re-affirmed the need for "general and complete disarmament" called for by article VI. The Conference did so with a "politically binding" Final Document on Extension of the Treaty on the Non-proliferation of Nuclear Weapons, May 11, 1995, 34 I.L.M. 959 that re-asserted the importance of fulfilling the legal obligation expressed in article VI.

(b) Nuclear Testing

Even at the height of the cold war, the nuclear powers recognized the environmental threat posed by nuclear explosions, and so negotiated the Treaty Banning Nuclear Weapons Tests in the Atmosphere, in Outer Space and Under Water, which, not surprisingly, forbids all nuclear weapons tests in the atmosphere, outer space and under water [art. I(1)(a)]. The agreement also prohibits any other nuclear explosion, such as an underground explosion, that causes a transboundary exchange of radioactive debris [art. I(1)(b)]. The treaty seeks to end the "contamination of man's environment by radioactive substances," and calls upon the parties to continue negotiations toward the banning of all nuclear testing, including underground explosions

[Pmbl.]. Originally, the treaty was signed by all the nuclear powers except France and China.

Since that date there has been considerable pressure to take the final step toward cessation of all nuclear testing. Of their own accord, the U.S. and the former Soviet Union forged two treaties controlling underground explosions in the 1970s—the Treaty Between the Soviet Union and the United States on the Limitation of Underground Nuclear Weapons Tests, July 3, 1974, 13 I.L.M. 906 and the Treaty on Underground Nuclear Explosions for Peaceful Purposes, May 28, 1976, 15 I.L.M. 891.

More recently, efforts to halt nuclear testing took a dramatic step forward when the General Assembly of the United Nations responded to increased concern on the part of non-nuclear nations by calling for the development of a comprehensive ban on all nuclear testing. After many years of arduous negotiation, the Comprehensive Nuclear Test Ban Treaty (CTBT) was opened for signature in late 1996 [35 I.L.M. 1439]. By prohibiting all nuclear testing, the CTBT effectively prevents the development of new nuclear weapons. It was immediately signed by the five major nuclear states: the United States, Russia, China, France and the United Kingdom, and nearly one hundred other nations. The Preparatory Commission for the CTBT began work almost immediately on establishing the International Monitoring System and the International Data Centre, and developing of operational manuals for on-site inspection, all of which will be implemented as soon as the treaty goes into effect.

However, the treaty must be ratified by the 44 presumptive nuclear powers before it comes into force, and this has presented substantial difficulties. The United States, alone among its NATO partners, has thus far declined to ratify the CNTBT. According to its critics this places the U.S. in an ambiguous position vis-a-vis disarmament. In light of the fact that the U.S. has maintained a moratorium on testing for years and has promised to maintain that status at the present time, its abstention from the CNTBT seems to serve no useful function.

Senate opponents of the CTBT have offered four reasons as to why it should not be ratified. First, opponents argue that the CTBT would stop neither proliferation nor testing by current nuclear states. The fact is that states may develop nuclear weapons without testing. North Korea is a case in point. Paul Kerr, *N. Korea's Uranium Program Moving Ahead* ..., 33 ARMS CONTROL TODAY No. 3 (2003). Iran may be close behind. The opponents reject the claim that following the U.S. example of ratifying the CTBT, other countries would stop testing as well. They noted that although the US has observed a unilateral moratorium on nuclear testing since 1992, China, India, and Pakistan subsequently tested nuclear weapons. Second, opponents of the treaty cite the need to keep the U.S.'s options open and note that the CTBT could limit future U.S. flexibility in the event that changed circumstances require new technologies or weapons to deal with unforeseen threats. For example, in light of the threat of terrorism, the U.S. may need to develop and test new nuclear weapons that can destroy underground compounds. Such weapons would likely require testing before deployment. Of course, this presumes that the U.S. would resort to nuclear weapons, rather than traditional missiles or explosives. Third, treaty opponents claimed that the CTBT would have an adverse effect on the safety, reliability, and effectiveness of the U.S. nuclear deterrent. They raise concerns that the current stewardship program for the U.S. nuclear stockpile is inadequate to ensure the safety, security, and reliability of the weapons. In a related vein, they also hold that ongoing tests are necessary to warn off potential attackers, and that without further testing, confidence in the nuclear arsenal's deterrent capacity will be damaged.

Finally, opponents remain concerned about the effectiveness of the CTBT's verification system. Small, low-yield nuclear tests could be used by advanced nuclear states to develop new weapons as well as verify old ones, and such tests may escape detection by the CTBT's monitoring system. Opponents of the treaty argue that there is no way to reliably differentiate between low-yield nuclear explosions and earthquakes, conventional explosions, or other "seismic events."

Proponents of the treaty note, however, that since the U.S. also conducts its own highly sensitive monitoring procedures, the risk of small tests escaping notice would be greatly reduced or eliminated by the two systems acting in concert. Proponents of the treaty further point out that without ratifying the CTBT, the US cannot receive the treaty's benefits, such as monitoring and on-site inspections, and its moral authority to press other nations to disarm is substantially weakened.

In 1998, the prospects of the CTBT were further set back by news of nuclear weapons tests in India and Pakistan. Both nations had been considered presumptive nuclear powers whose ratification was required for the CTBT to enter into force, but neither had signed or ratified prior to their testing. The United Nations Security Council swiftly passed a resolution condemning the tests, urging the cessation of testing in South Asia and the ratification of the CTBT, and calling upon other nations to affirm their commitments to non-proliferation and disarmament [Resolution 1172, June 6, 1998, 37 I.L.M. 1243].

India and Pakistan both refuse to ratify the CTBT, citing three major objections. First, India in particular is wary of agreeing to disarm when the other nuclear states—including the U.S.—have thus far failed to agree to a schedule or time table for total disarmament. A second but related objection is that the CTBT's moratorium on nuclear tests would freeze international nuclear capabilities at their present levels, so that countries like the U.S. and Russia would have sophisticated technology and expansive arsenals that newer nuclear weapons programs would never be able to obtain. Finally, India cites the China–Pakistan alliance, which enabled the rapid development of Pakistani nuclear technology and the buildup of a substantial Pakistani arsenal, as a tangible nuclear threat on its borders justifying its own nuclear weapons program. Pakistan, of course, cites India's own armament as a similar threat. Relations between the two nations are strained at the best of times, and an agreement on this issue does not appear to be forthcoming. Given this impasse, neither country is likely to sign or ratify the CTBT in the near future.

(c) Disarmed Nuclear Materials

In recent years, the United States and Russia have sought to reduce the numbers of nuclear weapons through the Strategic Arms Reduction Talks leading to the START Treaties. [Treaty between the U.S. and the USSR on the Reduction and Limitation of Strategic Offensive Arms, July 31, 1991, entered into force 1994, U.S.–U.S.S.R., S. Treaty Doc. No. 102–20/23 (1991) (START 1); Treaty between the U.S. and the USSR on the Reduction and Limitation of Strategic Offensive Arms, May 23, 1992, entered into force April 14, 2000, U.S.–Russ. S. Treaty Doc. No. 103–1 (1993) (START II); Treaty between the U.S. and the Russian Federation on Strategic Offensive Reductions, May 24, 2002, 4 ILM 799].

Unfortunately, however, we are witnessing the unfolding of unforeseen, albeit serious, consequences arising from this wholly laudatory endeavor. Unlike previous international agreements, such as (the Strategic Arms Limitations Treaties (SALT)) which largely placed caps on arms increases arising from the escalating arms race during the

Cold War, the START Treaties actually *reduce* the number of nuclear weapons and warheads, including submarine launched ballistic missiles. Under START I, signed in 1991, the United States and the former Soviet Union agreed to limit their nuclear weaponry to 1,600 strategic nuclear delivery vehicles and 6,000 warheads. By the end of the implementing period under START II, deployed strategic warheads are reduced to 3000–3500. START III, which has not yet been ratified, will bring this figure down to 2000–2500 warheads.

Under START I, for example, this meant that the two superpowers were obligated to reduce their arsenals by thirty to forty percent. While the launchers were to be destroyed, the warheads themselves had to be removed from their operational delivery vehicles and then stockpiled or destroyed. The destruction of the launchers, a number of which were located on submarines, meant that many submarines were prematurely retired from the submarine fleets of both countries.

Some of the problems confronting the United States and Russia as a result of this decommissioning involved the safe offloading of spent nuclear fuel and fuel assemblies from the decommissioned submarines, the safe transport of nuclear warheads to reprocessing facilities where the nuclear materials could be reprocessed to non-weapons-grade materials, the safe transport of nuclear reactor cores for similar reprocessing, and the interim and final storage of many metric tons of liquid and solid nuclear wastes created by the decommissioning of nuclear submarines and other ships.

The costs of the environmental management of the problems created by START I were estimated in the United States to be about $5–6 billion a year, and the total expenditure for this program was estimated in 1996 to be about $227 billion. Reeling from a failing economy, Russia weakened its already modest environmental programs and is now responsible for massive pollution in the Arctic Ocean. Confronted by this new face of the nuclear challenge created not by arms escalation, but by arms reductions, Russia simply remains unable to meet the significant additional costs to address environmental cleanup.

Soviet nuclear pollution of the Arctic is well documented. The pollution has been caused by numerous factors including accidents on land that released radioactive material into the Arctic environment, land-based discharge of radioactive pollutants into rivers that later migrated into the neighboring Arctic seas, and Soviet Navy activities. The Yablokov Report documents the frightening extent to which these various kinds of dumping took place between 1958 and 1992 [Yablokov et al., FACTS AND PROBLEMS RELATED TO THE DUMPING OF RADIOACTIVE WASTE IN THE SEAS SURROUNDING THE TERRITORY OF THE RUSSIAN FEDERATION; MATERIALS FROM A GOVERNMENT REPORT ON THE DUMPING OF RADIOACTIVE WASTE, COMMISSIONED BY THE PRESIDENT OF THE RUSSIAN FEDERATION (1993)]. It recounts how the huge Russian nuclear fleet, the largest in the world, used the shallow Barents and

Kara Seas of the Arctic Ocean to dispose of the waste that had been generated, and even to dispose of unsafe nuclear reactors.

Russian submarines remain a significant source of pollution. The fleet of over 140 retired nuclear submarines, moored in the Russian naval graveyard ports of Murmansk in the Barents Sea of the Arctic Ocean and Vladivostok in the Sea of Japan in the Pacific Ocean, are of particular concern. These shipyards do not have safe or adequate facilities for storing the spent nuclear waste generated by the nuclear submarines. While military secrecy surrounds their operations, informed observers conclude that they are not managed according to recognized international standards. The dangerous waste generated by the reactors in Murmansk is stored or disposed of in unsafe conditions, in a manner that presents danger to human health and to the natural environment both on land and at sea. The problems of disposing of Russian nuclear wastes are formidable.

Science and Technology (S & T) agreements have led to the greater involvement of more technical agencies and private company experts, and has also led to a greater depth and complexity of cooperation among the states involved. These S & T cooperative exchanges override ideological or national aims, and reduce future conflicts. For example, when nuclear weapons are disarmed, plutonium sequestered in weapons systems need to be safely managed. One way of doing so is to stabilize and transform them into fuel for nuclear power reactors. In 1998, the

United States and the Russian Federation formed a joint steering committee on plutonium management, intended to research and review scientific efforts to improve plutonium conversion capabilities. [U.S–Russian Federation: Agreement on Scientific and Technical Cooperation in the Management of Plutonium that has been Withdrawn from Nuclear Military Programs, July 24, 1998, 37 I.L.M. 1296 (1998)].

Cooperative exchanges of this kind are currently also being facilitated by the Cooperative Threat Reduction Program (CTR) of the U.S. The CTR is the program that the U.S. Congress created to help Russia carry out their obligations under the START agreements. One aspect of this program is addressed to Chain of Custody activities. These Chain of Custody activities enhance security, safety, and control of nuclear weapons and fissile material in Russia by assisting in centralizing fissile material in a limited number of storage areas and strengthening safety, security, and control during movement and interim storage. Projects provide assistance to enhance effective controls over nuclear weapons and the fissile materials removed from them throughout the drawdown and dismantling of these weapons. This includes providing safe and secure transportation of nuclear weapons from operational sites and storage areas to dismantlement facilities; improved security and accountability for weapons in transit; safer and more secure storage and transport of fissile material removed from nuclear weapons by providing storage containers; and designing, equipping, and assisting in construction of centralized fissile material storage facilities [See generally, Cooperative Threat Reduction Annual Report for FY 2002 GAO–03–341 (2002).

However, so far Congress has only funded CTR plans to decommission submarines if they pose a strategic threat to the United States. Congress has hitherto not considered the environmental threat alone significant enough to fund the dismantling of 120 or so multi-purpose submarines (SSNs). But Russia maintains that the SSNs are the more immediate threat, given the poor technical conditions and the fact that on some of these boats the nuclear fuel has been on board for 30 years [T. Jandl "Proliferaton Ahead of Remediation". THE NUCLEAR CHRONICLE FROM RUSSIA (2000)] An EIA is not required for CTR plans because the program only concerns itself with military rather than environmental threats.

One possible solution to this problem is for the U.S. Congress to expand the scope of the CTR and deal with all aspects of Arctic nuclear pollution, including the decommissioning of SSNs. Congress could also include additional funding to be used in conducting an environmental analysis of each future proposal for a CTR project. In this way a single agency would share the twin objectives of arms control and environmental protection [*see generally* ARMS CONTROL AND THE ENVIRONMENT (Lakshman D. Guruswamy & Suzette R. Grillot eds., 2001)].

(d) Customary Law

i. Nuclear Testing

Until the total phase-out of nuclear testing occurs, the customary international law status of such explosions remains in doubt. Given the general international support for the CTBT, coupled with state practice in this area, one can make a strong claim that customary international law forbids the atmospheric, outer space, or under water testing of nuclear weapons. This would appear to be the rule even in the absence of transboundary environmental harm. On the other hand, the status of underground testing remains problematic. Should the testing cause significant environmental damage or a threat of such damage to another state, the well-settled general prohibition against such damage would control. Without transboundary environmental harm, however, and until the CTBT comes into its own, it seems doubtful that underground testing *per se* would violate customary international law.

Though the Nuclear Tests Cases did not resolve the issues surrounding underground nuclear testing, they remain some of the most important cases in international environmental law for their discussion of important issues. And, as they dealt first with the issue of atmospheric testing, and only more recently considered underground testing, they track the evolution in thinking concerning nuclear weapons testing. More generally, the cases also provide a glimpse into the evolution of international environmental law over a twenty year period. The cases also highlight the severe limitations of the World Court—both real and self-inflicted—that continue to hamper the development of international environmental law. For all of these reasons, and to provide a window into the actual functioning of the World Court, we offer an extended analysis of these decisions.

The Nuclear Tests Cases (Round One)

In 1973 both Australia and New Zealand brought separate, but similar, actions against France in the World Court, complaining of France's imminent atmospheric tests on the Mururoa Atoll in the South Pacific [*see* Nuclear Tests (Australia v. France), 1973 I.C.J. 99 (June 22); 1973 I.C.J. 320 (July 12); 1974 I.C.J. 253 (Dec. 20); 1973 I.C.J. 338 (Aug. 28); 1974 I.C.J. 530 (Dec. 20); Nuclear Tests (New Zealand v. France), 1973 I.C.J. 135 (June 22); 1973 I.C.J. 341 (Sept. 6); 1973 I.C.J. 324 (July 12) 1974 I.C.J. 457 (Dec. 20); 1974 I.C.J. 535 (Dec. 20)]. From 1967 to 1972 France had conducted atmospheric tests within its own territory there, and appeared about to begin another series of tests in 1973. In its application to the court Australia claimed:

(i) The right of Australia and its people, in common with other States and their peoples, to be free from atmospheric tests by any country is and will be violated;

(ii) The deposit of radio-active fall-out on the territory of Australia and its dispersion in Australia's airspace without Australia's consent:

(a) violates Australia's sovereignty over its territory;

(b) impairs Australia's independent right to determine what acts shall take place within its territory and in particular whether Australia and its people shall be exposed to radiation from artificial sources;

(iii) the interference with ships and aircraft on the high seas and in the super-adjacent airspace, and the pollution of the high seas by radio-active fall-out, constitute infringements of the freedom of the high seas.

[Nuclear Tests (Australia v. France), 1973 I.C.J. 99, 103 (June 22)].

New Zealand's claim was somewhat different, presenting a *jus cogens* argument and also referring to nuclear testing in general, not just atmospheric nuclear testing. According to New Zealand's application,

(a) [France's action] violates the rights of all members of the international community including New Zealand, that no nuclear tests that give rise to radio-active fall-out be conducted;

(b) it violates the rights of all members of the international community, including New Zealand, to the preservation from unjustified artificial radio-active contamination of the terrestrial, maritime and aerial environment and, in particular, of the environment of the region in which the tests are conducted....

(c) it violates the right of New Zealand that no radio-active material enter [its] territory...., including [its] air space and territorial waters, as a result of nuclear testing;

(d) it violates the right of New Zealand that no radio-active material, having entered [its] territory..., including [its] air space and territorial waters, as a result of nuclear testing, cause harm, including apprehension, anxiety and concern to the people and government of New Zealand...;

(e) it violates the right of New Zealand to freedom of the high seas, including freedom of navigation and overflight and the freedom to explore and exploit the resources of the sea and the seabed, without interference or detriment resulting from nuclear testing.

[Nuclear Tests (New Zealand v. France), 1974 I.C.J. 457, 512 (Dec. 20)].

Though it had previously accepted the compulsory jurisdiction of the ICJ under article 36 of the Statute of the International Court of Justice, France disavowed the court's competence to hear the cases, denied jurisdiction and declined to appear. In spite of France's rejection, the case remained on the court's official list or docket.

Interim Measures

The two petitioners also asked for interim measures, and the court supported these requests in 1973, stating that "no action of any kind [should be] taken which might aggravate or extend the dispute ... in particular, the French Government should avoid nuclear tests causing the deposit of radio-active fall-out" on the respective territories of Australia and New Zealand [Nuclear Tests (Australia v. France), 1973 I.C.J. 99, 106 (June 22); Nuclear Tests (New Zealand v. France), 1973 I.C.J. 135, 142 (June 22)]. France, in turn, ignored the decision and actually conducted two nuclear tests.

Jurisdiction

In 1974 the court then had to decide the question of jurisdiction. As this phase of the World Court proceedings approached, however, the French government suddenly shifted direction—making a number of public declarations to the effect that it would discontinue its atmospheric nuclear tests and would move on to underground tests. Neither Australia nor New Zealand was reassured by these unilateral statements, and both continued to press their respective claims.

In the decision on its competence to hear the cases, the court first had to deal with France's request that the court remove the two cases from its list, based on the fact that France now did not accept the court's jurisdiction. Without elaboration, the court simply stated in both instances that "the present case was not one in which the procedure of summary removal from the list would be appropriate" [Nuclear Tests (Australia v. France), 1974 I.C.J. 253 (Dec. 20); Nuclear Tests (New Zealand v. France), 1974 I.C.J. 457, 460 (Dec. 20)].

In the next step, the court focused on whether a present dispute still existed between France on the one hand, and Australia and New Zealand on the other. On this matter—though France's unilateral promise to stop atmospheric testing was not embraced as sufficient by either applicant—the court decided that France had made a binding commitment. Therefore, with the objective of both applicants presumably met and the "dispute having disappeared," the court dismissed both cases without reaching the merits [Nuclear Tests (Australia v. France), 1974 I.C.J. 253, 271 (Dec. 20); Nuclear Tests (New Zealand v. France), 1974 I.C.J. 457, 475 (Dec. 20)].

The environmental significance of the first round of the Nuclear Tests Cases primarily lies with the granting of interim measures. Though the court did not base its decision on the merits of the Applicants' cases, it did admit that both had established *prima facie* cases of possible harm and that the rights of all parties needed to be preserved for later adjudication. The granting of interim measures thus lends support to the general rule that one country may not inflict transboundary environmental harm on another. On the other hand, the decision on jurisdiction shows how ready the court is to dispose of cases on procedural grounds when faced with controversial substantive issues. Here the court creatively and very narrowly dispensed with a case—following an out-dated formalism—in which it might have made important pronouncements of law.

To its credit, however, the court did provide an opportunity to reopen the cases, stating that "if the basis of this Judgment were to be affected, the Applicant could request an examination of the situation in accordance with the provisions of the statute" [Nuclear Tests (Australia v. France), 1974 I.C.J. 253, 271 ¶ 60 (Dec. 20); Nuclear Tests (New Zealand v. France), 1974 I.C.J. 457, 477 ¶ 63 (Dec. 20)]. It is this opening which lead to round two of the dispute.

The Nuclear Tests Case(s) (Round Two)

With a newly elected, conservative administration firmly in control, France declared its intention to conduct another series of underground tests in the South Pacific beginning in 1995. Outraged by what they perceived as the continued arrogance of France and the renewed threat of environmental harm, the South Pacific countries loudly denounced the action. New Zealand swiftly moved to reopen its 1974 case against France, claiming that "the basis of the Judgment had been affected" by the new underground tests proposed by France [Request for an Examination of the Situation in Accordance with Paragraph 63 of the Court's Judgment of 20 December 1974 in the Nuclear Tests (New Zealand v. France) Case, 1995 I.C.J. 288, 298 ¶ 33 (Sept. 22)]. As France no longer accepted the compulsory jurisdiction of the court under article 36 of the ICJ Statute, New Zealand could not institute new proceedings but could only hope to gain access through the older case. Australia, as you will remember, had based its original complaint more narrowly on atmospheric testing, and apparently for this reason did not try to reopen its own case. Instead, it later attempted to intervene in New Zealand's proceedings.

In its Application to the court, New Zealand stated:

(i) that the conduct of the proposed nuclear tests will constitute a violation of the rights under international law of New Zealand, as well as of other States; further or in the alternative;

(ii) that is unlawful for France to conduct such nuclear tests before it has undertaken an Environmental Impact Assessment according to accepted international standards. Unless such an assessment establishes that the tests will not give rise, directly or indirectly, to radioactive contamination of the marine environment the rights under international law of New Zealand, as well as the rights of other States, will be violated.

[*Id.* at 290 ¶ 6].

New Zealand asked that the court make a broad interpretation of the words "the basis of the Judgment"—that the phrase should not be restricted to France's atmospheric testing only, but that it referred more generally to the cessation of environmental contamination by nuclear testing [Id. at 293 ¶ 18]. According to New Zealand, as current scientific evidence now showed that the environmental risks of underground nuclear testing were greater than had been thought in 1974, the resumption of such tests would alter the underlying protection afforded by the judgment. Indeed, New Zealand's original Application in 1973 did not even mention atmospheric tests, but instead focused on the right to be free from nuclear damage.

In addition, through its application and oral argument, New Zealand now backed up its complaint with specific advances in international environmental law. first, it maintained that the duty not to cause transboundary harm—in an early stage of crystallization in 1974—was now a well-settled principle of customary international law. Second, it noted that the principle of inter-generational equity was at stake, that the 20,000 year by-product of nuclear testing invoked a consideration of the rapidly developing principle of inter-generational rights. Third, it claimed that the precautionary principle mandated a shift of the burden of proof to France, and that France should have to conduct an Environmental Impact Assessment before proceeding with its tests. Fourth, it stated that a number of treaties disallowed the introduction of radioactive wastes into the marine environment, and that France's action violated the high standard afforded that medium [*id.*].

Once again, however, the court adopted an extremely narrow interpretation of the law. By a vote of twelve to three, the court refused to reopen the case, agreeing with France's argument that the "basis of the Judgment" in the 1974 adjudication had only to do with "atmospheric" testing. As New Zealand knew that France would begin conducting underground tests in 1974, it could not now complain of those tests but only the threatened commencement of atmospheric tests. France, of course, was not proposing atmospheric tests, and New Zealand had no legitimate fears that pertained to the earlier case.

The significance of this second round of the Nuclear Test Cases, however, resides in the opinions of the dissenting judges. In dissent Judge Weermantry, supported by Judge ad hoc Palmer, devastatingly criticised the unnecessary formalism of the decision, pointing out the dangers of strict construction. Judge Weermantry explained:

> If X should complain to the village elder that Y is threatening him with a sword in a manner causing reasonable apprehension of an intention to cause grievous harm, and the village elder orders Y to drop his sword, is that order to be construed as an order to refrain from causing bodily harm, whatever the weapon used? If Y thereafter proceeds to harm X with a club, Y would surely not be able to contend that the order issued on him related to the use of a sword and that he did not violate it in any way by using a club. Clearly, a larger reason lies behind the order than the mere prohibition against inflicting harm with a sword. The unexpressed rationale lying behind the order, namely, the desire to protect X from bodily harm, lies at the very heart of the order, if it is to be construed in the light of common sense. [*Id*. at 334]

Clearly, according to Weermantry, the original decision back in 1974 had attempted to protect New

Zealand from harm caused by nuclear weapons testing, not just the fall-out from atmospheric tests. If at this juncture progress in scientific knowledge reveals underground testing as causing greater harm than thought in 1974, then a *prima facie* case has been established. The case should then proceed to the merits and the court should engage, rather than by-pass, the very important legal issues at hand.

Judge Weermantry argued against the narrow formalism of the majority, and showed a willingness to discuss all the important issues brought forward—including transboundary environmental harm, inter-generational equity, the precautionary principle and environmental impact assessment, and protection of the marine environment. Unfortunately, due to the reticence of the present court, a majority decision on these issues of general customary international law must wait until another day. And regarding the specific status of underground nuclear testing, in the near future it is unlikely that the court will obtain jurisdiction over a seminal case. More probably, a ratified Comprehensive Test Ban Treaty will provide primary guidance in this area.

ii. Use of Nuclear Weapons

The Advisory Opinion of the ICJ in the Legality of the Threat of the Use of Nuclear Weapons, 35 I.L.M. 809 (July 8, 1996) forms an important part of the emerging customary law on nuclear weapons. The General Assembly of the United Nations requested the World Court for an Advisory Opinion on the question: Is the threat or use of nuclear weapons in any circumstances permitted under international law? The Court was urged by the United States and other nuclear powers to decline the question. Instead it held, by a wafer-thin majority secured by the double vote of the president, that the threat or use of nuclear weapons would generally be contrary to the rules of international law applicable in armed conflict and in particular the principles and rules of humanitarian law. The Court refrained from ruling unequivocally that the threat or use of nuclear weapons would be illegal under any circumstances. According to the majority, the inadequacy of facts at its disposal precluded the Court from concluding definitively that the threat or use of nuclear weapons would be lawful or unlawful in extreme cases of self defense where the very survival of the state would be at stake.

However, in light of the horrendous threats posed by nuclear weapons, and the growing consensus among the community of nations as evidenced in the treaties referred to above, the Court was of the unanimous opinion that these treaties foreshadowed "a future general prohibition of the use of such weapons" although not presently constituting a prohibition on the use or possession of nuclear weapons [*Id.* at 825 ¶ 62]. Addressing article VI of the NPT, it concluded that: "The legal import of that obligation goes beyond that of a mere obligation of conduct; the obligation involved here is an obligation to achieve a precise result—nuclear disarmament in all its aspects—by adopting a particular course of conduct, namely, the pursuit of negotiations on the matter in good faith" [*Id.* at 830]. This means that nuclear states are under a legal obligation—an "obligation of result"—to bring to a conclusion negotiations leading to nuclear disarmament in all its aspects under strict and effective international control.

Even though the Court did not declare every threat or use of nuclear weapons illegal, it carved out a rule of illegality and confined its exception to cases of extreme self defense where the survival of the state is at stake. Judge Schwebel, the American judge, dissented, arguing that neither law, state practice nor comity supported the conclusion that the use or threat of use of nuclear weapons are generally illegal. On the other hand, Judge Weermantry reasoned that the decision did not go far enough. He asserted that use or threat of use of nuclear weapons is illegal in any circumstances, and that self defense did not constitute an exception. The implications of this decision are noteworthy. First, it may assail and dismantle the legal foundations of nuclear defense policies premised on first use of nuclear weapons. Second, it confronts the permanent members of the Security Council (United States, England, Russia, France and China, all of which are nuclear powers) with the illegality of the threat or use of their nuclear weapons except in self defense when their very existence is at stake. Third, it directs all nuclear powers that they must enter into good faith negotiations to achieve total nuclear disarmament. While it is true that the last finding is not as imperative as it may seem because good faith negotiations could go on indefinitely, it appears that the nuclear powers have not taken such a cynical view of their obligations.

2. CIVILIAN NUCLEAR ENERGY

(a) Nuclear Safety

IAEA Standards

Concerning the uses of nuclear energy, three international organizations have primary responsibility. The Nuclear Energy Agency (NEA), created by the OECD, has played a limited role in promoting common safety standards through national legislation in its member countries, but its fundamental function remains that of disseminating information. EURATOM, an EU entity, has developed mostly health-related safety directives that member countries must implement and enforce, but the organization has yet to expand into the area of siting, design and operation. Thus the most significant is the IAEA, created by statute under the auspices of the United Nations in 1956 and supported by nearly all the nations of the world as parties. According to its statute, the IAEA's principal objective is "to accelerate and enlarge the contribution of atomic energy"—though as a secondary function it is required to establish "standards of safety for protection of health and minimization of danger to life and property" [Statute of the International Atomic Energy Agency (IAEA Statute), Art. III (A)(6), Oct. 26,

1956, art. II, 276 U.N. T.S. 3 (entered into force July 29, 1957)]. Thus the IAEA operates with the twin purposes of fostering the development of nuclear power and controlling its dangers.

Though undertaking the function belatedly, and to its critics at cross-purposes with its development function, the IAEA has gradually assumed the leadership role in health and safety standards. Over the years the agency has generated a broad set of nonbinding rules covering virtually every area of nuclear safety, including the siting, design and operation of nuclear installations. Though in practice many countries rely on these in setting national requirements, and the IAEA itself remains bound by its own provisions, the standards legally exist as technical guidelines. Only if by agreement the IAEA helps establish a particular facility—through the providing of IAEA materials and expertise—do the standards as well as follow-up inspections become binding on that facility. As detailed below, the recent adoption of the 1994 Convention on Nuclear Safety has raised the profile of the IAEA standards, but these still remain guidelines rather than obligatory measures.

(b) 1994 Convention on Nuclear Safety

Following the Chernobyl accident in 1986, the international community—led by the Group of Seven (G–7) economic powers—worked toward the adoption of a treaty on nuclear safety. As the preamble states, the Convention on Nuclear Safety, [Sept. 20, 1994, 33 I.L.M. 1514] functions as an "incentive convention," mandating the creation of appropriate national standards for civil nuclear installations but not requiring the use of IAEA provisions. To that end, the convention "entails a commitment to the application of fundamental safety principles for nuclear installations rather than of detailed safety standards," [pmbl. (viii)] and ensures that "there are internationally formulated safety guidelines which ... provide guidance on contemporary means of achieving a high level of safety" [*Id.*]. Though many non-nuclear states desired more stringent and specific standards, the requirements of the convention remain largely hortatory, with the parties simply charged with taking "appropriate steps" at the national level. The hope is that "appropriate" national standards will follow IAEA or other international standards, fostering an improved level of nuclear safety throughout the world.

Under the convention, each party must install "a legislative and regulatory framework to govern the safety of nuclear installations" [art. 7]. The convention actually only covers power plants, and does not deal with nuclear fast breeder reactors or any aspect of the nuclear fuel cycle, most notably radioactive waste. In addition to the establishment of national safety standards, each party must develop a competent regulatory authority which, unlike the IAEA itself, does not engage in the promotion of nuclear energy [art. 8]. As to general areas of action, each nation must take "appropriate steps" to ensure emergency preparedness [art. 16], assessment and verification of safety [art. 14], quality assurance [art. 13] and radiation protection [art. 15]. More specifically, concerning the safety of installations, each party must develop "appropriate" standards and procedures regarding siting [art. 17], design and construction [art. 18], and operation [art. 19].

The convention is stricter regarding existing nuclear plants. Each party must make "all reasonably practicable improvements" of existing nuclear installations and, if upgrading cannot be undertaken, should close the nuclear installation "as soon as practically possible" [art. 6]. In considering the timing of any necessary shut-down, the party may weigh "the whole energy context and possible alternatives as well as the social, environmental and economic impact" [art. 6].

The IAEA acts as the secretariat of the convention, though as such it has little independent power. Instead, the convention again relies on national implementation and oversight, requiring parties to submit compliance reports to the contracting parties at review meetings [arts. 5 & 20]. At these meetings each party may discuss and seek clarification of another party's report, but no official dispute resolution machinery exists by which to challenge that report's content [art. 29]. Following the same logic, neither the IAEA nor any other institution created by the convention possesses formal enforcement powers [art. 20].

(c) The 1986 IAEA Convention on Early Notification of a Nuclear Accident (Notification Convention)

Another treaty prompted by the Chernobyl accident, the Notification Convention, Sept. 26, 1986, 25 I.L.M. 1369 (entered into force Oct. 27, 1986) attempts to prevent delay by parties in reporting accidents to its neighbors. Presently in force and signed by nearly all the nuclear capable nations, the Notification Convention covers any civilian accident in which the "release of radioactive material occurs or is likely to occur and which has resulted or may result in an international transboundary release that could be of radiological safety significance for another State" [art. 1]. In short the treaty encompasses present as well as probable nuclear accidents, if these cause significant or potentially significant transboundary harm. Unfortunately, a major shortcoming of the convention exists in the broad discretion given to parties in interpreting the word "significance." In another important limitation, the treaty does not mandate notification regarding accidents at military facilities. This problem has since been ameliorated by the declaration of the five nuclear states that they will extend the convention's provisions to these incidents.

Faced with such a nuclear accident, a party must "forthwith notify" either the IAEA or the potentially "physically" affected states as to the nature, time and location of the accident [art. 2(a)]. Furthermore, the party must promptly provide any information that might minimize the radiological effects of the accident, such as the possible cause, general release characteristics and any results of environmental monitoring [arts. 2(1) & 5]. A party also must "promptly" respond to any request for consultations by an affected state, when such consultations would seek to minimize the radiological consequences inside the latter's territory [art. 6].

(d) The 1986 IAEA Convention on Assistance in the Case of a Nuclear Accident or Radiological Emergency (Assistance Convention)

Complementing the Notification Convention, the Assistance Convention, Sept. 26, 1986, 25 I.L.M. 1377 (entered into force Sept. 26, 1987) creates a framework of cooperation that strives to facilitate aid among countries in the event of a nuclear accident. The treaty situates the IAEA as the conduit of such assistance, but also encourages other bilateral or multilateral arrangements [Art. 1]. Though nothing in the convention forces a party to request assistance, upon doing so it must "specify the scope and type of assistance required and, where practicable, provide the assisting party with such information as may be necessary for that party to determine the extent to which it is able to meet the request" [Art. 2(2)]. In turn, the providing party must promptly respond concerning the availability, scope and terms of any assistance [Art. 2(3)]. For its part, the IAEA proactively collects and distributes information as to each party's available experts, equipment and material in the event of a nuclear accident and, if requested, assists parties in the preparation of emergency plans and the development of personnel training and radiation monitoring programs [Art. 5(1)]. The convention also provides for immunity from legal proceedings for the assisting party and its agents, though any party may at the time of accepting the convention declare itself not bound by these specific provisions [*see* Arts. (8, 10)]. In short, the convention seeks to expedite voluntary assistance by other nations, removing administrative and legal roadblocks.

(e) Liability

i. State Responsibility

The legal fallout from Chernobyl has arguably undermined the strength of the customary law rule prohibiting states from causing transboundary environmental harm. In the specific area of liability for nuclear accidents, the necessary doctrinal component of state practice appears lacking as no aggrieved state brought a formal claim against the former Soviet Union (though several reserved the right to do so). The result obviously questions whether states are legally responsible for this type of nuclear harm under customary international law. Simply put, if, in the face of widespread damage, no claims were filed and no compensation volunteered or awarded, then how can liability for nuclear accidents exist under international law?

The fact that states declined to press claims does not necessarily mean that they believed the claims legally unwarranted. It is perfectly feasible that states declined to prefer claims for fear of establishing precedents that could be used against them. The states harmed by Chernobyl fallout were themselves nuclear states and may have decided it was in their self interest not to create a legal weapon that might be used against them. Moreover, in the particular case of Chernobyl the harmed states may only have decided that the costs of pursuing compensation outweighed the benefits—especially given the inability to pay on the part of the former Soviet Union.

In fact, evidence of a liability regime applicable to radioactive contamination is supplied by another case. In 1979 Canada pressed a claim against the USSR for damages caused by a nuclear-powered satellite that broke up over its territory. Canada made its claims both under general principles of international law and the 1972 Convention on International Liability for Damage Caused by Space Objects (1972 Space Objects Convention), Mar. 29, 1972, 961 U.N.T.S. 187 (entered into force Sept.1, 1972). This time the USSR agreed to pay Canada US $3 million as compensation. As the legal basis for liability remained unnamed in the concluding document, the result permits an argument in favor of applying both custom and the 1972 Space Objects Convention. More recently, by resolution on Dec.14, 1992 the U.N. General Assembly adopted Principles Relevant to the Use of Nuclear Power Sources in Outer Space, which again provides for state responsibility for damage caused by outer space operations utilizing nuclear power [Principle 8].

Furthermore, the general rule against transboundary environmental harm—first provided in the Trail Smelter Arbitration case, (United States v. Canada), 3 R.I.A.A. 1938 (1949)—continues to find universal support in international environmental treaties and declarations. Therefore, to carve out an exception to the rule for nuclear accidents seems premature, as nations have consistently embraced the rule in such important documents as the Rio Declaration on Environment and Development, and in major international treaties such as the Biological Diversity Convention and Climate Change Convention.

As for the standard of liability, this question also obviously remains unresolved. Some scholars argue for strict or absolute liability because nuclear energy is an ultra-hazardous activity. The 1972 Space Objects Convention, for example, makes the launching state "absolutely liable to pay compensation for damage caused by its space object on the surface of the earth or to aircraft in flight" [art. II]. Similarly, in the civil liability conventions described below, the standard is one of strict liability.

Others have argued for a due diligence standard regarding nuclear accidents, in which liability would arise for a state in whose territory an accident occurred only if the state acted negligently in the development, application and monitoring of appropriate safety standards. Adherents of this view look to Chernobyl as an incident *not* causing a breach of due diligence, pointing out that the plant in question was built according to national standards set by the Soviet Union. Though these standards may not rise to the level of the plants built in the West, the argument goes, this does not necessarily mean that the Soviet Union acted negligently.

Striving for coherence in the aftermath of Chernobyl, the IAEA created a Standing Committee on Nuclear Liability, which in attempting to revise the Vienna Convention on Civil Liability for Nuclear Damage (1963 Vienna Convention), May 21, 1963, 7 I.L.M. 727 (entered into force Nov. 12, 1977) continues to discuss the issue of state responsibility. However, with a number of nuclear powers rejecting the notion, it now appears unlikely that any form of state responsibility for nuclear accidents will make its way into that treaty. On the other hand, the 1994 Convention on Nuclear Safety asserts in the preamble that responsibility for nuclear safety rests with the state having jurisdiction over a particular nuclear installation. This is to be contrasted with Article 9 of the same convention, which holds that prime responsibility lies with the operator of an installation. The result is a double-tiered program of responsibility under this treaty, with the state's duty one of regulation and monitoring, and the operator's one of stringent compliance.

ii. Civil Liability

With no global regime in place for state responsibility, the international community relied largely on civil liability to assign responsibility for nuclear damage. Prior to 1997, civil liability for nuclear damage was defined by two separate conventions, the 1963 IAEA Vienna Convention on Civil Liability for Nuclear Damage, May 21, 1963, 1063 U.N.T.S. 265 (Vienna Convention), and the 1960 OECD Paris Convention on Third Party Liability in the Field of Nuclear Energy July 29, 1960, 956 U.N.T.S. 264 (1960 Paris Convention). The two conventions share a number of characteristics, including strict liability for the operator, compulsory insurance and a monetary limit on compensation for damage. In considering these one should keep in mind that the former U.S.S.R. was not a party to either convention, and so neither could be invoked in the case of Chernobyl. One should also be aware of the existence of another treaty—the Convention on the Liability of Operators of Nuclear Ships, May 25, 1962, 57 A.J.I.L. 268 (entered into force July 15, 1975)—which creates similar obligations but, because it has limited acceptance and scope, is not discussed further.

Because the Paris Convention and Vienna Convention were signed by different parties and at times expressed contradictory mandates, it was necessary to agree upon which treaty should apply in any given case of nuclear damage. This issue was addressed in the 1988 Joint Protocol Relating to the Application of the Vienna Convention and the Paris Convention, Sept. 21, 1988, 42 Nuclear Law Bulletin 56 (entered into force Apr. 27, 1992). Under the protocol, which is now in force, the convention ratified by the installation state governs liability for damage incurred by a state-party to the other convention [Arts. II & IV]. In addition, each convention applies to each incident to the exclusion of the other [Art. III]. Though offering a more unified approach, the protocol only points out the necessity of completing negotiations for a global convention that would uniformly deal with civil liability for nuclear damage.

The 1960 Paris Convention on Third Party Liability in the Field of Nuclear Energy (1960 Paris Convention)

Created under the auspices of the OECD, the 1960 Paris Convention, July 29, 1960, 956 U.N.T.S. 264 strove to unify civil liability rules for nuclear damage in Western Europe. Nearly all western nuclear nations in the region are parties, including France, Germany and the United Kingdom. The convention channels all liability to the operator of the nuclear installation for "damage to or loss of life of any person" and "damage to or loss of any property" [Art. 2]. Whether this includes environmental damage remains unclear. The treaty does cover transport of nuclear substances, for which the operator in charge remains liable and not the carrier [Art. 4]. If an incident occurs, the operator's liability is strict rather than absolute, though the convention actually only exempts responsibility in the few cases of armed conflict, hostilities, civil war, insurrection or grave natural disasters of an exceptional character [Art. 9].

To pay for any liability, each operator must carry insurance in the amount specified under the convention [Art. 10]. The liability remains limited—an important feature of this convention—to 15 million Special Drawing Rights (SDR) as defined by the International Monetary Fund [Art. 7]. (At 2002 values, one unit of SDR approximately equals one and one-third U.S. dollars ($1.33)). In fact, under the 1960 convention a party may even set the liability limit as low as 5 million units of account. As the parties quickly perceived, however, a maximum of 15 million SDR would not cover an accident of any magnitude, and so they adopted the 1963 Brussels Convention Supplementary to the 1960 Convention on Third Party Liability in the Field of Nuclear Energy (Brussels Convention), Jan. 31, 1963, 2 I.L.M. 685.

This convention, which has been updated by later protocol, leaves the operator's liability at the same level and establishes a supplementary system of public funding [Art. 3]. Thus, in the event of an accident in its territory, a state party must provide up to an additional 170 million SDR to compensate worthy claimants. Furthermore, should the damage exceed that amount, the other parties to the convention would provide up to 125 million SDR according to a formula based on thermal power and GNP [Art. 12]. This party-state contribution limit was further defined in the Convention on Supplementary Compensation for Nuclear Damage, Sept. 12, 1997, 36 I.L.M. 1473, which is open to all nations regardless of their party status in the Paris Convention. In total, accident liability under the amended Paris Convention was limited to 300 million SDRs. On the other hand, if the damage results from fault by the operator, the party in whose territory the installation exists may pass legislation allowing both itself and other contracting parties recourse against that operator [Art. 5(b)].

In 2001, parties to the amended Paris Convention agreed to a new protocol, again revising liability limits upwards to accommodate the high costs of nuclear damage. Under that protocol, which is expected to be ratified as soon as the parties have enacted complementary domestic legislation, liability will be limited to 700 million Euros for operators, 500 million Euros for public funds from the installation state, and a collective party-state contribution of 300 million Euros. Consequently, the new total liability for nuclear accidents will be 1.5 billion Euros.

In general, jurisdiction over nuclear incidents lies with the courts of the party in whose territory the nuclear incident occurred [Art. 13(a)], and final judgments must be honored and enforced by all the contracting parties [Art. 13(d)]. Moreover, though a state may actually be the installation operator in many cases, no party may invoke jurisdictional immunities to avoid actions [Art. 13(e)].

The 1983 IAEA Vienna Convention on Civil Liability for Nuclear Damage (1963 Vienna Convention)

The 1963 Vienna Convention, May 21, 1963, 1063 U.N.T.S. 265 closely resembles the 1960 Paris Convention, and was amended in 1997 to modernize its provisions. As the most comprehensive and up-to-date instrument currently dealing with civil liability for nuclear damage, it has the potential to emerge as a unified global convention on the issue. At the moment, however, only 32 nations (none of which possess significant nuclear industries) are parties to the Convention, and only four have also ratified the Protocol. The Protocol contains inter alia a better definition of nuclear damage (now also addressing the concept of environmental damage and preventive measures), extends the geographical scope of the Vienna Convention, and extends the period during which claims may be brought for loss of life and personal injury. It also provides for jurisdiction of coastal states over actions incurring nuclear damage during transport. Taken together, the two instruments should substantially enhance the global framework for compensation well beyond that foreseen by existing Conventions.

Prior to the 1997 amendments, the Vienna Convention—like the Paris Convention covered damage to persons and property but made no mention of environmental damage—though the Paris Convention did allow national courts expansive interpretive power in providing for "nuclear damage" [Art. I(k)(ii); PHILLIPE SANDS, PRINCIPLES OF INTERNATIONAL ENVIRONMENTAL LAW: FRAMEWORKS, STANDARDS AND IMPLEMENTATION, 655 (1994)]. Under the new Protocol to Amend the Vienna Convention, Sept. 12, 1996, 36 ILM 1462, the definition of "nuclear damage" is expanded to encompass "the costs of measures of reinstatement of impaired environment," "loss of income derived from an economic interest in any use or enjoyment of the environment, incurred as a result of significant impairment of that environment," and "the costs of preventive measures" [Art. 2, 2(k)iv-vi]. Liability for such damage extends to radiation emitted by any nuclear installation, including from waste produced by those installations.

The Vienna Convention's standards for operator liability, award limits, and jurisdiction generally mirror those of the Paris Convention. Unlike the OECD regime, however, the Vienna Convention contains no provision for supplemental funding by the parties themselves. Instead, the convention sets the floor for operator liability at $5 million US dollars (value in gold on April 29, 1963). An upper ceiling is not fixed for operator liability, leaving open the possibility of massive awards directly from the operator. This is in conflict with the Paris Convention's formula of operator, state, and contracting party contributions. For the treaty to become the global instrument on civil liability that the IAEA envisions, the future parties must resolve this inconsistency. Given the recent attention that has been paid to the precise amounts allowable under the Paris Convention's formula, it is likely that compensation amounts on a global treaty will follow that scheme instead of the Vienna Convention's.

CHAPTER EIGHTEEN

THE FUTURE OF IEL

We have seen how an expanding IEL patrols an increasingly interconnected and interdependent world. It is a world in which practitioners and judges, at many levels of international and national law, are coming alive to the impact and import of IEL. Not surprisingly, IEL is now an established subject, firmly ensconced in the law school curriculum with a burgeoning scholarly literature.

What of the future? Understanding the present must pave the way for even the most faltering prognostication, and we begin by taking a synoptic view of the present status of IEL. In so doing this chapter does not venture to re-conceptualize the subject in conformity with the author's own ideas of success or failure. Rather, the chapter looks objectively and realistically at what is. It begins by examining the foundational and systemic norms of IEL: sustainable development (SD), and the common law of humankind. It then reviews other primary rules and principles.

Primary rules and principles are those obligations found either in treaty or customary law. The examination of the primary rules is followed by a quick survey of the secondary rules of state responsibility, and the legal phenomena created by a developing international civil society. We have resisted the urge to offer utopian blue prints for future action, but have settled instead for some modest, pragmatic and incremental suggestions for future developments. Overall, we paint a mottled yet generally optimistic picture of IEL.

A. FOUNDATIONAL & SYSTEMIC NORMS

1. SUSTAINABLE DEVELOPMENT

As noted in Chapter Two IEL is part of a historical continuum and we use the Johannesburg Declaration on Sustainable Development, Sept. 4, 2002 [41 I.L.M. 1480] (hereinafter Johannesburg Declaration), and the Rio Declaration on Environment and Development, June 13, 1992, 31 I.L.M. 874 (hereinafter Rio Declaration) as our baseline to focus on SD.

SD—the syncopated foundational concept of IEL—continues to soften its environmentalism, and place even greater emphasis on development. In Chapter Two, we noted how the Rio Declaration retreated from the high watermark of environmental protection embodied in the Stockholm Declaration. The Johannesburg Declaration also continues to drift away from demanding environmentalism.

What is most striking about the re-articulation of SD at Johannesburg is that it introduces a third element of social development into the definition of

SD. Hitherto unseen, social development has now been unveiled as a full grown concept. This change is significant because SD only consisted of two components (economic development and environmental protection) but has now been invested with a third (social development). Viewed differently, the two stick package of SD has now become a three stick bundle.

The emphasis on economic development and the eradication of poverty may effectively have diminished the importance demanding environmentalism, and this development can be disquieting to some environmentalists. In fact it has been argued by some commentators that the Rio Declaration institutionalized a preeminent right to economic development that enfeebled and attenuated the imperative of sustainable development. [Marc Pallemaerts, *International Environmental law in the Age of Sustainable Development: A Critical Assessment of the UNCED Process*, 15 J. L. & COM. 623, 630–635 (1996)].

Nonetheless, it is important to appreciate that the present tension between the concerns and needs of the poor developing world and the crusading environmental agenda sometimes espoused by the developed world, may well be a passing phase. One explanation for the behavior of the developing countries may be found in the Kuznet curve model of environmental protection. The Kuznet curve is an economic model that explains how rising incomes will result in decreases in pollution, and posits that international environmental regulation only becomes a reality to governments once the basic needs of their people are met. If that be correct then developing countries which achieve economic growth may well reinstate a more demanding environmental agenda.

Regardless of the theoretical explanations for their position, the Johannesburg Declaration and the Plan of Implementation emphasizes the undeniable extent to which the eradication of poverty, clean water, sanitation, energy, health care and food security, as distinct from certain kinds of environmental protection, have become the central concern of the developing world. As against this, we need also to take account of the paradoxical extent to which environmental protection has become a part of the common law of humankind.

2. THE COMMON LAW OF HUMANKIND

National environmental laws govern environmental problems within nation states. A review of the environmental laws of various nations that make up the international community reveals the extent to which environmental problems—whether arising from air and water pollution, land use or exploitation—are omnipresent. Uniformities of biophysical reactions are part of nature's writ that runs ubiquitously and universally, and the laws of nature can give rise to identical biophysical reactions. If, for example, the receiving medium is the same, discharges of wastes or residuals, whether in Los Angeles, Liverpool, Dusseldorf or Auckland lead to pollution. Common biophysical reactions take place regardless of where in the world the environment is abused. If the necessary conditions exist, sulphur dioxide and nitrogen oxide will react and result in acidic deposition in the Ruhr, Northern England, or in the Raquette, New York. Polychlorinated biphenyls (PCBs) act to cause cancers in West Virginia in the same way as they do in Newcastle upon Tyne, UK, or Colombo, Sri Lanka.

In responding to these common problems, nation states have often arrived at common regulatory patterns of control. Time does not permit any systematic exploration of the compass of comparative environmental law, but we know from the examples of acid rain and PCBs that, when faced with this common problem, nation states hardly ever deny their deleterious effects or decide to ignore them. The actions nations take, of course, are dependent upon their state of economic development and national priorities. While recognizing the evil of pollution, nations may be economically unable to take action to remedy these evils whether in the form of technological, emission, or ambient standards placed on industry or with other restrictions placed on the consumers or society at large. This denotes that there is a near universal recognition of the damage caused by pollution and a resolve to address this problem. Such action may, therefore, be postponed while states remain cognizant of what is required, and may even solicit international assistance to do so.

National boundaries do not, however, constitute biophysical or chemical boundaries, and pollution sometimes migrates from one state to another causing transboundary legal problems that fall within the province of international, not national law. The customary IEL principle prohibiting a state from using its property so as to injure that of another responds to this phenomena, reflects the climate of world opinion, and symbolizes the confluence of national and international law. It is restated in numerous declarations and treaties founded upon a universal appreciation of the need to control damage caused by pollution. These articulations recognize a principle, rooted as much in national law as in international comity, that has become part of the common law of humankind.

Hersch Lauterpacht authenticated the extent to which international law is molded by domestic sources, analogies, and experience [See HERSCH LAUTERPACHT, PRIVATE LAW SOURCES AND ANALOGIES OF INTERNATIONAL LAW (1970)]. He also demonstrated how article 38 of the Statute of the International Court of Justice directs the ICJ to apply the "general principles of law recognized by civilized nations" [Id. at 69]. By "general principles" he referred to principles of law expressing rules "of uniform application in all or in the main systems of private jurisprudence" [Id]. While Lauterpacht applied his reasoning to private law analogies, the principle underlying his thesis, on a parity of reasoning, is equally applicable to domestic public and regulatory law analogies. The general principles of environmental law universally recognized by States enables us clearly to see that the formidable body of IEL dealing both with global and non-global problems is itself part of the greater universal rubric of the common law of humankind—a system of law that the international community and judicial tribunals are obliged to recognize and embrace.

In this context, a fecund recommendation of Agenda 21 is worthy of exploration. It urges that NGOs be given the opportunity of vindicating treaty rights in national forums [¶ ¶ 27.10 & 27.13]. In addition, principle 13 of the Rio Declaration provides that "[s]tates shall develop national law regarding liability and compensation for the victims of pollution and other environmental damage...." These expressions of international consensus underscore the importance of giving: 1) national courts jurisdiction; and 2) individual plaintiffs access and standing in national courts to pursue environmental rights and duties created by treaty. We have seen that such remedies are unusual and effectively remain confined to the subjects of nuclear and oil pollution.

Some commentators view the Rio Declaration's emphasis on adjudication by national courts, based on civil liability as distinct from international state liability, as illustrative of "inertia" that has deflected the development of the latter (PHILIPPE SANDS, PRINCIPALS OF INTERNATIONAL ENVIRONMENTAL LAW 630 1995). While we have noted the lack of progress at Rio, it seems that on this occasion national liability may be a functional and practical way to develop the concept of liability for environmental harm. We have already reviewed the shortcomings of international judicial remedies, and are confronted with having to deal with the stubborn political fact that in the absence of strained political relationships, states do not generally take each other to court. Whether based on self-interest arising from the mutual vulnerability of a state to actions by others, or a desire not to offend friendly states, the crop of cases has been meager.

On the other hand, environmental litigation in national courts is proliferating and it makes sense to use national courts to advance international remedies. The Convention *on the Law of the Non-navigational Uses of International Watercourses, May 21 1997 [36 I.L.M.700]* recognizes the importance of national remedies in a curiously named article on "Non-discrimination" [art. 32]. Article 32 prohibits states from discriminating on the basis of nationality or residence in granting judicial remedies to any natural or juridical person who has suffered appreciable harm. Although this principle has not been accepted by states either by enacting national legislation *en mass,* or agreeing to an international treaty, the fact that it has received some acceptance in the Rio Declaration and Agenda 21 is evidence of an evolving "soft" law. As we have seen, the Nordic Convention establishes this principle and it is to be hoped that it could be built upon through implementing mechanisms of other treaties.

B. PRIMARY RULES AND PRINCIPLES

1. PRINCIPLES

It is necessary at this point to underline two trends that countervail developments, referred to in Section A above, that restrict or restrain environmental protection. We have already seen that environmental skepticism has not stood in the way of a rising environmental common law of humankind. We should also note that international law has not gone to the extreme of equating SD with economic development alone. Environmental protection continues to play an important role and serve the mutual interests of all parties. The prevention of transboundary harm, and conservation are two such areas. The resilience and dynamism of the principles applicable to these areas helps to confirm that there environmental protections still remains an important component of SD.

The prohibition on transboundary pollution, which we have referred to above, was codified by Principle 21 of Stockholm, is now entrenched in numerous provisions of pre-Rio treaties and declarations, and has received such strong support through the practice and *opinio juris* of states that it has become a principle of customary international law [*see* Chapter One, Sources of IEL]. The attempt in the Rio Declaration to undermine the illegality of transboundary pollution by emphasizing the suzerainty of developmental policies, fails to overcome the overwhelming body of law that mirrors Principle 21 of Stockholm, and defines it as an environmental wrong.

Furthermore, principle 21 of Stockholm, and not principle 2 of Rio, is reaffirmed in article 3 of the Biodiversity Convention—a post Rio treaty. The significance of this fact is that an instrument of hard law (the Biodiversity Convention) is normatively superior to the non-legal Rio Declaration. The Biodiversity Convention's prohibition on transboundary pollution makes no exceptions for transboundary pollution arising from developmental policies.

The principle of conservation asserts the equality of environmental protection, not its subordination to development, within the dynamic of sustainable development. We have seen how the Biodiversity Convention has sought to strike this balance (*see* Chapter Five, Biodiversity). Moreover, post Rio developments such as the 1995 Agreement for the Implementation of the Provisions of UNCLOS of 10 Dec. 1982, relating to the Conservation and Management of Straddling Fish Stocks and Highly Migratory Fish Stocks (Straddling and Highly Migratory Fish Stocks Agreement or SHMFSA), and other instruments discussed in Chapter Thirteen have reiterated the importance of conservation.

However, it is necessary to reinforce the importance of conservation by moving toward a World Forestry Convention—something that was repudiated at Rio. Such a Forestry Convention should protect old forests, particularly tropical forests, that are home to up to 50% of the plant and insect biological diversity of the world. It is necessary that the world be presented with a plan to save its tropical forests, and conserve the gene banks of the planet.

Given the foundational character of SD it may well be that the principle of common but differentiated responsibility (CBDR) found in Principle 7 of Rio, and article 4 of the Climate Change Convention has now become part of customary law. It is difficult to accept the equitable and distributional thrust of SD without the need for common but differentiated responsibility. Such a conclusion is reinforced by the fact that numerous treaties institutionalize CBDR and establish financial mechanisms for doing so, while institutions such as the Global Environmental Facility (GEF)(see Appendix) were re-invented to better act as a mechanism for implementing CBDR.

2. RULES

While we have covered a host of treaties and conventions, there is little doubt that global warming dominates the attention given to IEL. Consequently we will focus on the primary obligations governing global warming and observe how they have been implemented. The Kyoto Protocol which binds developing (Annex A) countries to reduce their emissions of carbon dioxide from 5%–7% below their 1990 levels between 2008–2012 [art. 3] has been the subject of interminable discussion and debate. These duties constitute primary rules of obligation. We have noted in Chapter Six that the U.S. has refused to ratify Kyoto, and that most countries who have ratified the Protocol will not be able to meet their obligations.

In this context, the position of the developing countries at the 8th Conference of the Parties under UNFCC held in New Delhi in November 2002 (discussed in Chapter Six) throws light on their mindset. The developing countries, to the consternation of some environmentalists, prevailed on the conference to move from mitigation (direct reductions of carbon dioxide emissions) to adaptation (taking defensive action to adapt to any adverse changes). They wanted help from the developed countries to adapt to the possible effects of increased global warming. Their actions cannot be seen as encouraging developed countries to spend huge sums of money on meeting the Kyoto regulations which, as we have seen in Chapter Two, will resulted only in minimal gains.

The common sense and logic of what happened at New Delhi is difficult to refute. Lomborg, in an editorial to the New York Times [August 26, 2002] asserts that the money expended by the United States alone in meeting the Kyoto Protocol in a year could provide every person in the world with access to basic health, education, family planning and water and sanitation services. He inquires: "Isn't this a better way of serving the world?" Lomborg's figures have not been refuted [http://courses. dce.harvard.edu/ ?envre115/sept19/LomborgOpEd.doc] and there seems little doubt as to how the developing world would answer that question.

Moreover, we have pointed out in Chapter Six that a major initiative on alternative fuels is a prerequisite for implementing Kyoto. There are compelling reasons a to why this should be undertaken and the next UN summit should focus on alternative sources of energy. New sources of energy are desperately needed in the developing world and such an effort will form an integral and essential component of SD.

3. EMBRYONIC RULES AND PRINCIPLES

There are a number of embryonic primary principles of soft law that could develop either into widely accepted legislative treaties, or into customary IEL. This would transform them from being aspirational and hortatory norms into legal obligations. Candidate principles begin with the precautionary principle, (PP) which according to some is already a principle of customary international law.

Such a conclusion is difficult to justify for a number of reasons. First, the Dispute Settlement Body of WTO after examining the evidence expressed doubt as to whether the precautionary principle was in fact a principle of customary international law or a general principle of law under article 38(c) of the Statute of the International Court of Justice. [WTO Appellate Body Report on EC Measures Concerning Meat and Meat Products (Hormones), Jan. 16, 1998, WT/DS48/AB/R, ¶ 123, at http:// *www.wto.org/english/docs_e/docs_e.htm*.]

Second, the precautionary principle does not admit to any workable definition. While there is no authoritative legal definition of the "Precautionary Principle," the concept of precaution, as distinct from a legal norm or term of art, is recognized in a small number of broadly adopted international, and a larger number of more restricted regional legal instruments. The broadly adopted international instruments include the following provisions: Principle 15 of Rio ("precautionary approach"); Chapter 17.22 in Report of the United Nations Conference on the Environment and Development, U.N. Doc.A/CONF.151/26 (1992) ("preventive, precautionary and anticipatory approaches"); the preamble in Cartagena Protocol on Biosafety to the Convention on Biodiversity, [Jan. 29, 2000, *39 I.L.M. 1027, (2000)*] ("precautionary approach"); the preamble and articles 1, 8, and 9 in Stockholm Convention on Implementing International Action on Certain Organic Pollutants, May 22, 2001, pmbl, arts. 1, 8, 9, http://www.chem.unep.ch/sc/documents/convtext/convtext_en.pdf ("precaution," "precautionary manner"); and article 3 in United Nations Framework Convention on Climate Change, May 9, 1992, art 3(3), [*31 I.L.M. 849, 854 (1992)*] ("precautionary measures").

The indeterminacy of the PP makes it an inappropriate and ineffective regulatory decision-making tool. The PP provides no guidance on any of the fundamental questions that are faced in making any risk decision. The PP is ambiguous as to what level of risk is acceptable, what role costs should play in risk decisions, what quantum of scientific evidence is sufficient for making decisions, and how potential risk-risk tradeoffs should be addressed. Proponents of the PP disagree not only on these important questions, but also on whether the PP should apply in the risk assessment process, the risk management process, in both risk assessment and risk management processes, or as a substitute for the current risk assessment/risk management paradigm.

Third, the PP, at least as defended by some of its strongest proponents, would appear to be directed at hazard, as opposed to risk, by calling for precautionary measures once some indicia of hazard exist. Yet every substance or product has the intrinsic potential for some hazard, which may or may not translate into real-world risks of concern. Because hazard potential is ubiquitous, basing regulatory decisions on hazard alone creates the potential for arbitrary, unfair, and inefficient regulations.

Finally, there is a paucity of practice and *opinion juris* supporting PP, and it does not therefore rise to the level of customary law. This does not preclude the evolution of a more refined and restricted version of PP which could emerge as principle of customary international law.

The polluter pays principle (PPP) is articulated for example in Principle 16 of Rio The Johannesburg Plan of Implementation encourages countries to "... Continue to promote the internalization of environmental costs and these of economic instruments, taking into account the approach that the polluter should, in principle, bear the costs of pollution." [19(b)] However, the objections based on indeterminacy and lack of *opinion juris* directed at PP apply equally to PPP.

4.   CLASH OF PRIMARY OBLIGATIONS

While trade as an instrument of economic growth is another component of sustainable development, the clash of environmental and trade norms has assumed an importance that warrants separate treatment. The reliance on free trade to achieve economic growth—a foundational premise of post-World War II international development strategies—appears to have been strongly endorsed in the Rio Declaration. Articles 4, 11 and 12 lean toward interpreting sustainable development as economic development. Principle 12, for example, is strongly supportive of "an open international economic system that would lend itself to economic growth and sustainable development...." It goes on to state that "unilateral actions to deal with environmental challenges outside the jurisdiction of the importing country should be avoided...." The Plan of Implementation of the Johannesburg World Summit on Sustainable Development devotes all of Section V to "sustainable development in a Globalizing World" and emphasizes the importance of free trade.

The General Agreement on Tariffs and Trade, [Oct. 30, 1947, 61 Stat. A–3, 55 U.N.T.S. 187] [hereinafter GATT 1947], institutionalized the universality of free trade, while the World Trade Organization (WTO) establishes an international organization to implement it [General Agreement on Tariffs and Trade, Final Act Embodying the Results of the Uruguay Round of Multinational Trade Negotiations, Apr. 15, 1994, LEGAL INSTRUMENTS— RESULTS OF THE URUGUAY ROUND vol. 1, 33 I.L.M. 1125] [hereinafter WTO]. Together, GATT and WTO (GATT/WTO) are perceived by its advocates as semi-constitutional treaties aimed at eliminating interference and intrusion in international trade.

The tension between free trade and environmental protection is an important aspect of this dispute between economic growth and environmental protection, and requires resolution within the conceptual framework of sustainable development. The future of IEL will be critically affected by how this conflict is settled. A potential clash may well hinge on the extent to which the restrictions on trade in GMOs, or living modified organisms (LMOs) as they are called in the Cartagena Protocol on Biosafety to the Convention on Biodiversity, Jan. 29, 2000, [39 I.L.M. 1027, (2000)] are consistent with SD are consistent with the GASTT regime.

The World Trade Organization (WTO) and the Agreement on Sanitary and Phytosanitary Measures (SPS Agreement) [Agreement on the Application of Sanitary and Phytosanitary Measures, Apr. 15, 1994, Marrakesh Agreement Establishing the World Trade Organization [hereinafter WTO Agreement], Annex 1A, 69 (1994) (hereinafter SPS

Agreement), available at *http://www.wto.org/english/docs_e/legal_e/15-sps.pdf*] are part of the GATT. To the extent that a decision to ban GMOs obstructs free trade, the SPS Agreement requires that such decisions be justified on principles of scientific risk assessment. The Cartagena Protocol on the other hand, focuses on environmental protection, not free trade. The Biosafety Protocol allows nations pursuing biosafety to ban GMOs by using the precautionary principle, even where strict scientific proof may be lacking.

Any judicial dispute over this issue will fall within the jurisdiction of the Dispute Settlement bodies of the WTO, because neither the Convention on Biological Diversity (CBD) nor the Cartagena Protocol creates binding dispute settlement procedures. Environmentalists, including this author, have justifiably been suspicious about the judicial machinery of the WTO. To assuage such fears, it is necessary that any decisions taken by the judicial bodies of the WTO be based on the international customary law principles of fairness and reasonableness. (see Lakshman D. Guruswamy, *Sustainable Agriculture: Do GMO's Imperil Biosafety?* 9 IND. J OF GLOBAL LEGAL STUDIES 461 (2002)).

C. SECONDARY RULES AND STATE RESPONSIBILITY

Chapter Three deals somewhat extensively with the ILC codification of the Law of State Responsibility. The jural status of this codification could rest:

(a) on customary law, (b) a treaty or on (c) both. It remains to be seen as to what extent this codification is treated as an expression of existing customary law, and/or the extent to which it generates or leads to the growth of customary law. If institutionalized in a treaty it is binding on the parties as a treaty. It becomes equally binding if it is considered a re-statement of existing customary law. In any event the fact of an authoritative codification will serve as a reference point for any elucidation of state responsibility and this is a major step forward for IEL.

What the ILC draft articles has done is to fill a big hiatus in international treaty law. Many treaties embodying primary obligations do not provide for the consequences of the breach of these obligations. Where there is a breach the absence of particularized relief or remedies often has parties groping for ways of implementing the convention. The draft articles fills this gap by stipulating the responsibility of the parties, and the nature of the remedies. Admittedly, it does not create a new system of compulsory dispute resolution, but given the undeveloped stage of the international legal system, rules of state responsibility signal a significant advance.

D. THE ACTORS IN IEL

World actors are changing from state actors to others, such as NGOs, businesses, and other nongovernmental entities. While the 1648 Treaty of

Westphalia ushered in the nation-state, which then became the sole subject of international law and policy, we are now perceiving a return to a pre-Westphalian world centered around civil society. The concept of civil society has a long political genealogy. It originated in the works of Thomas Paine and George Hegel in the late eighteenth century. After lying dormant for almost 200 years, the Marxist theorist Antonio Gramsci resuscitated the concept in the post World War II era. [Thomas Carothers, *Civil Society*, FOREIGN POL'Y, 18, 18–19, (Winter 1999–2000)]

In essence, civil society is a domain parallel to, but separate from, the state in which citizen actors associate and coalesce according to their own interests and needs. It encompasses political parties and interest groups that include both for-profit as well as not-for-profit groups. Civil society thus encompasses labor unions, professional associations, chambers of commerce, ethical and religious groups, and environmental NGOs.

Domestically and internationally, NGOs work at gaining considerable expertise on a topic, then urge governments and businesses to act on the basis of their findings and conclusions. Their efforts sometimes result in "soft law" as opposed to treaties and agreements. Environmental NGOs aggressively try to keep governments accountable through protest and debate.

It is almost obvious that IEL needs to develop innovative means of overcoming the deficiencies of a sovereignty-based system of international governance. Global environmental problems have to be solved within a consensual legal system of sovereign states who alone are empowered to make legal and political decisions about them. Legal or economic theories support the plain fact that nation states act in their own best interests and not that of the global community. While they might act to save the global commons where their own self-interest is affected, their actions are premised on individual, not community needs. Not surprisingly, there are many situations in which the cries for legal measures to arrest or avert environmental perils are left unanswered.

Despite attempts to re-conceptualize international legal society along different lines, there is little evidence to support a fundamental change in the present sovereignty-based legal system. The suggestions for reform we propose accept that sovereignty will remain the basis of decision-making, and are of an incremental and functional nature premised on what appears possible. Even so, it is perfectly feasible for the present sovereignty based system to give better status and delegate more functions to NGOs.

As we have seen, NGOs are a fact of international life and they have long played an active role in IEL [see Appendix]. As such, it does not take a big leap to institutionalize them as actors entitled to contribute in the law-making and implementing processes. This has already been done by the International Labor Organization (ILO) [see Appendix] and it is achievable for the various international organizations to take measures to accord NGOs a similar status in their deliberations. We have also taken note in Chapter Two of the key role played by NGO's at the Johannesburg WSSD and in Chapter Sixteen of their important positions in the Desertification convention. There will, of course, be some problems concerning selection and accountability, but these are not insurmountable obstacles, and could be resolved along the same lines as the ILO. We have also already seen how that the Commission on Sustainable Development (CSD) entertains reports from NGOs. Since such a move was based on consensus, it is well within reach to hope that other organizations created by treaty will do likewise. In addition, Agenda 21 envisions a greater role for NGOs and calls on the UN system to give them increased administrative and financial support. [¶ 27.12] It further calls on the UN system to enhance the contribution of NGOs to decision-making, implementation and evaluation of its projects. [¶ 27.9 (a)]. The infusion of people power into the law-making and implementing process will help to reduce the "democratic deficit" in international law-making and implementation.

APPENDIX

A. COMMISSION ON SUSTAINABLE DEVELOPMENT

The Commission on Sustainable Development (CSD) is a functional commission of the UN Economic and Social Council (ECOSOC). It was established in 1992 by the ECOSOC at the request of the UN General Assembly. The CSD facilitates and reviews the progress of commitments made under the final documents of the Earth Summit. To serve this purpose, the CSD promotes a dialogue between governments and seeks to build partnerships and facilitate projects that further sustainable development. Many important conferences and meetings are held each month in New York City which seek to bring governmental officials together to work towards implementing protection for biological diversity, reducing global warming and managing and conserving the world's forests. The CSD also provides written policy guidance on implementing the Earth Summit's principle documents. Five years after the Earth Summit, the Special Session of the General Assembly adopted a document entitled Programme for the Further Implementation of Agenda 21, which was prepared by the CSD.

The CSD has 53 members who are elected for three year terms of office by the ECOSOC from UN member countries. States that are not represented, UN organizations, accredited inter-governmental and non-governmental organizations can observe CSD sessions when they meet each year for two to three weeks. To learn more about the CSD, see http://www.un.org/esa/sustdev/.

B. EARTH COUNCIL

The Earth Council is a non-governmental organization (NGO) that was formed as a direct result of the "Earth Summit" or the "United Nations Conference on Environment and Development" (UNCED) held in Rio de Janeiro, Brazil in 1992. The Earth Council provides advice on environmentally sound, conservation-oriented approaches to sustainable development, and promotes public awareness of environmental and conservation issues. Membership includes interested scientists, non-governmental organizations, and individuals. The organization has completed an Earth Charter that has established principles for a sustainable way of life. The general principles include respecting and caring for the community of life [Chapter I], ecological integrity [II], social and economic justice [III], and democracy, nonviolence, and peace [IV]. The Earth Council's headquarters are in San Jose, Costa Rica. For more information visit http://www.ecouncil.ac.cr/.

C. THE EUROPEAN UNION

The European Union (EU), presently consisting of 15 European member states, was first conceived as the European Coal and Steel Community by the Treaty of Paris in 1951, and became the European Economic Community (EEC) pursuant to the Treaty of Rome of 1957. In 1986, the Single European Act (SEA) changed the EEC into the European Community (EC), and its present incarnation, the European Union (EU), is the result of the Maastricht Treaty of European Union of 1993. The Treaty of Rome did not confer express or explicit power to make environmental laws upon the EC. Despite this fact, commencing in 1973 the EEC made environmental laws dealing with a variety of problems traversing air, aquatic, and terrestrial pollution, in addition to the protection of natural resources. It did so primarily on the legal basis—subsequently approved by the European Court of Justice—that such environmental laws removed non-trade barriers and harmonized trading conditions. The EC was given express power to legislate on environmental matters by the SEA, and this was reinforced by the Maastricht Treaty.

The law-making, enforcing, and judging powers of the EU are without parallel in other international organizations. The Commission and Council, with the advice of the Parliament, are empowered to make environmental laws (Regulations and Directives) within all areas of the EU's activities. To date, there are Directives and Regulations on a whole range of environmental issues, including air and water pollution issues, waste disposal and management, nuclear waste, and the protection of biodiversity. The Commission supervises the enforcement of these laws, and can bring a defaulting Member State before the compulsory jurisdiction of the European Court of Justice. In 1990, the EU established a European Environmental Agency that provides scientific and technical support to the EU and its Member States.

The EU is a unique international polity with an ambiguous legal character. It possesses a constitutional structure that approximates more closely to a non-unitary confederation than to an international organization. To the extent that it is created by treaty and derives its legal status under international law, it can be treated—at least functionally—as a new legal order or organization within international law. To learn more about the European Union, visit *http://europa.eu.int/*.

D. FOOD AND AGRICULTURE ORGANIZATION OF THE UNITED NATIONS

The Food and Agriculture Organization of the United Nations (FAO) is an intergovernmental organization working to alleviate hunger and poverty through agricultural development, improved nutrition and the pursuit of food security. Since FAO was founded in 1945, food production has increased dramatically, and has kept up with the growing population of the world. The FAO seeks to meet the needs of both present and future generations by developing long-term strategies for sustainable agriculture and rural development. To reach this aim, the FAO provides practical assistance to developing countries, advises governments, provides a neutral forum for conflicts between countries, and serves as the collector and disseminator of information about nutrition, food, agriculture, forestry and fisheries. The FAO hosted the World Food Summit in both 1996 and 2002, where hundreds of countries gathered to pledge alliance to end hunger. There are 183 member countries plus one member organization, the European Community, in FAO. For more information, visit http://www.fao.org/.

E. GLOBAL ENVIRONMENTAL FACILITY

The Global Environmental Facility (GEF) is a funding institution jointly created by the World Bank, the United Nations Environment Program (UNEP) and the United Nations Development Program (UNDP). It was formed in 1990, initially with $1.2 billion to be used to fund environmental protection efforts. The GEF is designed to aid developing countries with six primary environmental issues: 1) climate change, 2) stratospheric ozone depletion, 3) loss of biological diversity, 4) pollution of international waters, 5) land degradation, and 6) persistent organic pollutants (POPs).

The Biodiversity and Climate Change Conventions designate the GEF as their financial mechanism. Pursuant to the restructuring agreed to in Agenda 21, the GEF was partially reinvented in order to enhance the methods of governance and guarantee a more balanced and equitable division of resources between the interests of developing and donor (developed) countries. To summarize the restructured GEF, the entity now has both a Council and an independent Secretariat. The Council employs a voting method known as "the double-weighted majority," in which affirmative decisions require a 60 percent majority of the total number of participants as well as a 60 percent majority of the total contributions. UNEP monitors GEF projects to ensure they have been brought into conformity with other international environmental agreements and projects, while the UNDP provides the GEF with expertise on institution building and personnel training. Because of the GEF's broad and important environmental goals, and the careful attention given to it by the Earth Summit and other environmental organizations, the GEF has been reshaped to play an important role in future efforts to protect the environment.

Administratively, the GEF Secretariat is located in the World Bank which also oversees the disbursement of GEF funds. The GEF maintains a WWW site at: http://www.gefweb.org/.

F. GREENPEACE

In 1971, Greenpeace developed out of a Canadian citizens committee that was named "Don't Make a Wave." The organization was renamed and redirected with the purpose of "creating a green and peaceful world." Greenpeace, by its own definition, is only concerned with protecting the environment. It seeks to influence the use of the seas by "bearing witness" and by drawing attention to what it perceives to be abuses of the environment.

Greenpeace exploits, and the boats that carried Greenpeace members have become legend. The first Greenpeace action was undertaken by 12 crew members who sailed a small boat into a United States atomic test site off the Alaskan coast. In the 1970s Greenpeace's first ship, the Rainbow Warrior carried out actions in the South Pacific that helped to focus world-wide attention on atmospheric bomb testing. In the 1990s the ship the Mv Greenpeace protested the use of the Antarctic as a testing ground for Trident missiles. It was rammed and nearly sunk by the United States Navy. In the 1990s the Mv Greenpeace monitored environmental damage in the Arabian Gulf during the Gulf War, and lead a campaign to designate a whaling sanctuary in the Southern Atlantic.

Today, Greenpeace maintains a network of 43 offices in 40 countries; it is headquartered in Amsterdam. It is privately funded, with 5 million contributors in 130 countries. Its staff exceeds 1300 persons, and it speaks for 2.8 million supporters worldwide. To learn more about Greenpeace, "surf" over to http://www.greenpeace.org/homepage/.

G. INTERNATIONAL ATOMIC ENERGY AGENCY

The International Atomic Energy Agency (IAEA) was established by the Statute of the International Atomic Energy Agency Oct. 26, 1956, 276 U.N.T.S. 3 (entered into force July 29, 1957). It is the product of a compromise following the failure of a United States proposal for an international body to manage and supervise all civilian nuclear operations. It is an independent intergovernmental organization that has close associations with the UN but has not been given specialized agency status. It is comprised of 113 members states, that meet annually, and a Board of Governors of 35 member states including 10 of those most advanced in atomic energy technology.

According to its Statute, its main purpose is to encourage the research, development and application of atomic energy for peaceful purposes, and to ensure through safeguards that nuclear materials are not used for military purposes [art. III (1) & (5)]. It was also required "where appropriate" to establish health and safety standards [art. III (6)]. The Chernobyl accident transformed this marginal safety mandate into a central mission, though the standards do not have the force of law, and States are not obliged to comply with them.

Despite their non-legal character, IAEA standards, regulations, codes of practice and guides cover all aspects of radiation protection and radioactive waste disposal, and are widely followed. Under the Treaty of the Non Proliferation of Nuclear Weapons, July 1, 1968, 7 I.L.M. 809 (entered into force Mar. 5, 1970) (*see* Chapter Seventeen), which was extended indefinitely in 1995, non-proliferation safeguards are made obligatory through bilateral agreements with the IAEA, and periodic compulsory inspections by the Agency are also mandated. In the result, the IAEA has assumed the role of an important international environmental organization.

Please visit http://www.iaea.org/worldatom/ to learn more.

H.   INTERNATIONAL COURT OF JUSTICE

The International Court of Justice (ICJ) hears disputes between nation-states that have accepted its jurisdiction and provides advisory opinions to international organizations authorized to request them [*see* 48 Y.B.U.N. 1518 (1994)]. The ICJ, located in The Hague, Netherlands, was established by the Charter of the United Nations, June 26, 1945, 1 U.N.T.S. xvi (entered into force Oct. 24, 1945) and the Statute of the International Court of Justice, June 26, 1945, 59 Stat. 1031 (entered into force Oct. 24, 1945).

The ICJ consists of 15 judges who each are appointed for 9 year terms that can be renewed. The Court cannot be composed of more than one judge of any nationality. Sixty states have accepted the compulsory jurisdiction of the ICJ (often with reservations) and 20 international organizations have the authority to request advisory opinions on legal questions that arise in the scope of their activities. However, the UN General Assembly and the Security Council can request an advisory opinion from the ICJ on any legal question. In July 1993, the ICJ established a seven member Chamber for Environmental Matters to aid in the formulation of an international environmental jurisprudence. But the ICJ's impact on international environmental law begins much earlier in cases [*see* Chapter One, Sources], and it continues to play a significant role in the development of IEL. Though reticent at times to flex its power, the ICJ has provided authoritative restatements on many aspects of international law that have an important bearing on environmental matters. To learn more about the ICJ, visit http://www.icj-cij.org/.

I. INTERNATIONAL LABOR ORGANIZATION

The International Labor Organization (ILO), located in Geneva Switzerland, was established in 1919 as an independent international body associated with the League of Nations. Currently, the ILO is a UN intergovernmental organization. The ILO promotes social justice and works to improve labor conditions and living standards. Substantively, the ILO's work has focused on nuclear hazards, carcinogenic substances, construction safety, and occupational health services. In a consortium with the World Health Organization and the United Nations Environment Programme, the ILO established an intergovernmental forum on chemical safety at the 1994 Stockholm International Convention on Chemical Safety. Additionally, the ILO was one of six intergovernmental organizations that finalized and adopted International Basic Safety Standards for Protection Against Ionizing Radiation.

An outstanding feature of the ILO is its tripartite character, consisting of government, employers, and employees. Each member state is represented in the ILO by a delegation made up of two members from government, one from the employers and one from the employees. Delegates vote independently, and a resolution requires a two-thirds majority.

One of the principle achievements of the ILO is its conventions (treaties) dealing with a variety of safeguards, which member states are obliged to implement. The ILO requires such compliance with a unique supervisory system, annual reports, and a complaint system granting any member the right to complain about non-observance of any ILO convention. More information on the ILO can be found at *http://www.ilo.org/*.

J. INTERNATIONAL LAW COMMISSION

The International Law Commission (ILC), comprised of eminent jurists from various countries, was created by the UN General Assembly in 1947 to help the progressive development and codification of international law. It currently has thirty-four members, each representing a different country. "Progressive development" is defined as "the preparation of draft conventions on subjects which have not yet been regulated by international law or ... not yet been sufficiently developed in the practice of states" (art. 15). The ILC's first priority is acting upon requests by the General Assembly for legal work. In reality, this rarely takes place. The ILC customarily initiates draft articles which are sent to Member States, who are then requested to make comments. This preparatory work meets the definition of "progressive development," and is intended to lead to codification and the eventual formation of customary international law. The ILC is involved in various projects traversing IEL. These projects include the Convention on the Law of the Non–Navigational Uses of International Watercourses, the Draft Articles on Responsibility of States for internationally wrongful acts, the Draft Articles on International Liability, Draft Articles on Prevention of Transboundary Harm from Hazardous Activities, and its current project on International Liability for Injurious Consequences Arising out of Acts Not Prohibited by International Law. See http://www.un.org/law/ilc/ for information.

K. INTERNATIONAL MARITIME ORGANIZATION

The International Maritime Organization (IMO) was established by the United Nations Maritime Conference in March, 1948. In May, 1982, the IMO adopted its current name. The IMO fosters international cooperation and exchange of information on technical matters among member states affecting international merchant shipping, encourages the general adoption of maritime safety standards, and works to prevent and control maritime pollution. The IMO makes recommendations upon issues presented to it by member states and convenes international conferences on other matters within its competence.

The IMO worked towards the prohibition on the dumping of low level radioactive substances at sea, which was adopted by amendment to the 1972 London Dumping Convention that also bans the dumping or incineration of industrial wastes at sea. The IMO has also been involved in strengthening the requirements of the International Convention for the Prevention of Pollution from Ships, 1973/1978 (MARPOL). In 1994, the IMO (with $5.5 Million from the Global Environment Facility and the World Bank) began the Wider Caribbean Initiative for Ship–Generated Waste in an effort to reduce vessel pollution in the Caribbean.

The IMO has aided in the establishment of major IEL conventions designed to protect the environment, including the Convention on Safety of Life at Sea 1974; the International Regulations for Preventing Collisions at Sea 1972; Standards of Training, Certification, and Watchkeeping 1978; Prevention of Pollution from Ships 1973–1978; the Establishment of an International Fund for Compensation for Oil Pollution Damage 1969; and, the International Convention on Oil Pollution Preparedness, Response, and Cooperation 1990.

The IMO consists of an Assembly, a Council, a Maritime Safety Committee, a Secretariat, and small subsidiary bodies, created to address specific issues, such as the Legal Committee or the Facilitation Committee. Currently, the organization has 162 members, 300 staff members, and its headquarters are in Geneva, Switzerland. For more information regarding the IMO please see: *http://www.navcen.usca.mil/marcomms/imo/* or http://www.imo.org/index.htm.

L. ORGANIZATION OF AMERICAN STATES

The Organization of American States (OAS) is an intergovernmental organization whose origin dates back to 1890, beginning with a series of conferences called the International Union of American Republics, a conference that met for commercial purposes. The OAS charter was signed in Bogota in 1948 and entered into force in 1951. The charter has since been amended many times, most recently in 1996.

The OAS has a history of promoting environmental awareness, dating back to 1938 with the Convention on Nature Protection and Wildlife Preservation in the Western Hemisphere, and most recently in the creation of an Inter–American System of Nature Conservation.

The OAS strengthens the peace and security of the Western Hemisphere and OAS member states, seeks the solution of political, juridical and economical issues, and promotes economic, social and cultural development.

The OAS meets annually and has 35 member states. Cuba's present government has been excluded from participation since 1962, but remains a member as a national entity. For more information on the OAS, see http://www.oas.org/.

M. ORGANISATION FOR ECONOMIC CO–OPERATION AND DEVELOPMENT

The Organisation for Economic Co-operation and Development (OECD) was established as the Organisation for European Economic Co-operation (OEEC) on April 16, 1948 to administer United

States aid granted under the Marshall Plan and the Economic Co-operation Administration. In 1960— after Europe had attained economic recovery—the OPEC was transformed into the OECD. Attempts to strengthen the organizational structure of OECD to create a stronger institution have not been successful; it lacks supra-national legal powers which results in Members acting merely on a voluntary basis.

Article 2 of the OECD constitution requires it "to promote the efficient use of the [member] resources." Under this mandate, the OECD fosters sustainable economic growth and economic development, contributes to sound economic expansion and the expansion of world trade on a multilateral, non-discriminatory basis. The OECD began addressing environmental concerns in 1970 with the creation of the Environment Committee which is affiliated with the OECD's Executive Committee. The Committee evaluates the impact of international exchanges on the environment. The OECD was the first organization to legally define pollution. And in 1972, OECD was among the first to develop the influential "polluter-pays principle."

The OECD's Headquarters are in Paris. It is comprised of 30 Members including the European states, Canada, the United States and Japan. The administration of the OECD includes of a Council, an Executive Committee, a secretariat and various committees. Membership in the OECD is open to any government. For further information on the OECD see http://www.oecd.org/.

N. SOUTH PACIFIC REGIONAL ENVIRONMENT PROGRAMME

The South Pacific Regional Environment Programme (SPREP) was founded jointly by UNEP and the South Pacific Commission in 1982. Originally under the auspices of the Regional Seas Programme, it is now an autonomous organization promoting the environmental protection of the region. It helps countries form environmental policies, educates the general population about environmental issues and conducts tests and experiments on pollution, as well as protected area management. It consists of 26 members, most of which are Pacific island countries but also including Australia, France, New Zealand, and the United States. One of SPREP's current projects is the South Pacific Biodiversity Conservation Programme, which is working on a regional strategy for international waters. The South Pacific Regional Environment Program maintains a website at *http://www.sprep.org.ws/*.

O. UNITED NATIONS

The United Nations (UN) has a membership of 191 States. Article 7 of the UN Charter creates seven "principal organs": 1) the General Assembly; 2) the Security Council; 3) the Economic Council; 4) the Social Council; 5) the Trusteeship Council; 6) the International Court of Justice; and 7) the Secretariat. It also maintains fourteen specialized agencies: the International Labour Organization

(ILO), the Food and Agriculture Organization of the UN (FAO), the UN Educational, Scientific and Cultural Organization (UNESCO), the World Health Organization (WHO); the World Bank, the International Monetary Fund (IMF), the International Civil Aviation Organization (ICAO), the Universal Postal Union (UPU), the International Meteorological Organization (WMO), the International Maritime Organization (IMO), the World Intellectual Property Organization (WIPO), the International Fund for Agricultural Development (IFAD), and the UN Industrial Development Organization (UNIDO). Two other important agencies are affiliated with the United Nations that cooperate with it and its various organs, but are structured as independent organizations—the International Atomic Energy Agency (IAEA) and the World Trade Organization (WTO). The UN has no specialized agency committed to the protection of the international environment, although many specialized agencies carry out functions that impact upon the environment adversely as well as beneficially. The United Nations Environment Program, though not a specialized agency, has played a vital role. The UN has also supported major environmental conferences including Stockholm in 1972, and Rio in 1992. The UN maintains an extensive WWW site at: http://www.un.org/.

P.   UNITED NATIONS CONFERENCE ON TRADE AND DEVELOPMENT

The United Nations Conference on Trade and Development (UNCTAD) was created by the UN

General Assembly as a one-time conference, but was later established as a permanent organ. The UNCTAD encourages international trade to stimulate economic growth and development. It also formulates procedures and policies on international trade, and makes proposals to place those procedures and policies into effect. In 1992 UNCTAD adopted "A New Partnership for Development," a program that seeks to foster economic development and environmental protection through "proper management of natural resources with a view to achieving sustainable development."

The UNCTAD has 192 member countries, drawn from the United Nations or its specialized agencies, and the International Atomic Energy Agency. To learn more about the UNCTAD take your computer for a visit to http://www.unctad.org.

Q. UNITED NATIONS DEVELOPMENT PROGRAM

The United Nations Development Program (UNDP) was formed by the UN General Assembly in 1965 from the UN Expanded Program of Technical Assistance and the UN Special Fund. UNDP's environmental efforts have primarily filled the role of strengthening existing programs and institutions. For example, UNDP played a major role in the development of the GEF. As its listed goals, UNDP works to advance human development and to serve as a consultative resource in efforts to eliminate poverty, regenerate the environment, create jobs, and advance the role of women. UNDP also helps developing countries increase the efficient use of human and natural resources. Towards its goal of ensuring environmental sustainability, UNDP hopes, by the year 2015, to cut the number of people without access to safe drinking water by half. It could emerge as an important agency for advancing sustainable development in the future. The UNDP maintains a WWW site at http://www.undp.org/.

R. UNITED NATIONS EDUCATIONAL, SCIENTIFIC, AND CULTURAL ORGANIZATION

Founded in 1946, the United Nations Educational, Scientific, and Cultural Organization (UNESCO)—a subsidiary organization of the UN—advances peace through the promotion of education, science, and culture. UNESCO has played an important role in IEL in that it has attempted to influence public opinion in environmental matters. For example, UNESCO initiated the Man and Biosphere Program in 1970 and the Intergovernmental Oceanographic Commission in 1960. It also aided in the formulation of and acts as a secretariat for the Ramsar Convention 1971 and the World Heritage Convention 1972. In addition, UNESCO works to eliminate illiteracy through worldwide elementary education programs. It also safeguards world culture, books, and art, encouraging member countries to cooperate and provide access to their intellectual and cultural enterprises.

UNESCO maintains a General Conference, an Executive Board and a Secretariat. It has 188 members, and its main office is located in Paris, France. To learn more about UNESCO, see its web site at http://www.unesco.org/.

S.   UNITED NATIONS ENVIRONMENT PROGRAM

The United Nations Environment Program (UNEP) was founded in 1972 as a result of recommendations made at the Stockholm Conference on the Human Environment. It may be seen as the "environmental conscience" of the UN. UNEP coordinates solutions of different countries and agencies to environmental problems, addressing on a global scale such issues as ecology, sustainable development, methods of connecting development with environmental problems, and environmental management. UNEP seeks partnerships with other UN agencies, private businesses, non-governmental organizations, scientists, and all others who might have something to contribute to environmental solutions. One of UNEP's major functions is the maintenance of information systems. The Global Environmental Monitoring System (GEMS) is a worldwide effort to keep track of changes in the terrestrial ecosystem. The Global Resource Information Database (GRID) is a global network that maintains information referenced by the Global Environmental Outlook (GEO), which has produced the State of the Environment Report since 1994. Environment and Natural Resource Information

Networking (ENRIN) coordinates local institutions, creating regional and national state-of-the-environment reports which keep those regions updated on important environmental changes.

UNEP has helped to formulate programs and treaties. For instance, UNEP was involved in the Regional Seas Programme, encompassing more than thirty environmental agreements, the Zambezi Agreement and Action Plan, the Vienna Convention on Ozone, Montreal Protocol, the Basel Convention, the Stockholm Convention on POPs, the Rotterdam Convention, and the Biodiversity Convention. The World Summit on Sustainable Development was a milestone for UNEP. Moreover, the UNEP provides supportive functions as well as Secretariat functions in many of these treaties.

UNEP's Headquarters are maintained in Nairobi, Kenya. Policies are directed by its Governing Council, whose 58 members are elected to four year terms by the UN General Assembly. UNEP highlights its current activities at http://www.unep.no/.

T.   UNITED NATIONS INSTITUTE FOR TRAINING AND RESEARCH

The United Nations Institute For Training And Research (UNITAR) was established in 1965 as an independent organization maintained within the UN. Primarily, it trains UN officials, diplomats, officials of developing countries and staff of the specialized agencies within the UN. UNITAR publishes papers on such international topics as multilateral cooperation in regional development, women's roles in decision making, disaster preparedness and the elimination of racism. UNITAR plays a vital role in the formulation of IEL in that it adopts training programs and initiates research programs that foster environmental issues. The UNITAR maintains a WWW site at http://www.unitar.org/.

U. WORLD BANK

The World Bank began with the formation of the International Bank for Reconstruction and Development (IBRD) at the United Nations Monetary and Financial Conference held at Bretton Woods in 1944. The Bank's original purpose was the rebuilding of post-WWII Europe. Today, the Bank provides funds and expertise for the improvement of developing nations. The World Bank is a group composed of five organizations: 1) the International Bank for Reconstruction and Development (IBRD—established in 1944), 2) the International Development Association (IDA—established in 1960), 3) the International Finance Corporation (IFC—established in 1956), 4) the Multilateral Investment Guarantee Agency (MIGA—established in 1988), and 5) the International Centre for Settlement of Investment Disputes (ICSID—established in 1966). In the 1980's, the World Bank responded to environmental concerns by creating an Environment Department and Operational Directives that addressed involuntary resettlement, indigenous people, the involvement of non-governmental organizations, and environmental assessments. Moreover, it operates the Tropical Forest Action Plan with the World Resources Institute, and the Global Environmental Facility (GEF), which assists developing countries in offsetting costs incurred from adopting environmental measures. To learn more about the World Bank, visit http://www.worldbank.org/.

V. WORLD CONSERVATION UNION

The World Conservation Union (IUCN), founded in 1948, is a non-governmental organization whose broad capabilities include the development of conservation strategies. The IUCN seeks "to influence, encourage and assist societies throughout the world to conserve the integrity and diversity of nature and to ensure that any use of natural resources is equitable and ecologically sustainable." The IUCN has 865 members which include both governments and non-governmental organizations. Although it has played an important role in the formulation of IEL jurisprudence, its resolutions are non-binding. It has helped formulate a Convention on Preservation of Biological Diversity, The 1972 World Heritage Convention, the 1973 Convention on Trade in Endangered Species, The 1971 Convention on Wetlands of International Importance, and the 1979 Convention on Conservation of Migratory Species of Wild Animals. The IUCN has established an Environmental Law Program (ELP) which seeks to "lay the strongest possible legal foundation at the international, regional and national levels for environmental conservation in the context of sustainable development." The ELP's activities are administered by the Commission on Environmental Law (comprised of over 800 volunteering environmental law specialists) and the Environmental Law Centre (comprised of 15 highly skilled legal and information specialists). To learn more about the IUCN, log on to http://www.iucn.org/.

W. WORLD HEALTH ORGANIZATION

The World Health Organization (WHO), formed in 1948, is affiliated with the Economic and Social Council of the United Nations. The WHO is a directing and coordinating authority on health issues, establishing international collaboration while assisting governments as they strengthen health services and promote medical research and training. WHO's objective since 1977 has been "health for all by the year 2000."

WHO's environmentally related activities stem from the 1992 Earth Summit's declaration that countries should implement development in a sustainable fashion. It recognizes that a safe environment is a sustainable basis for human health. Since then, the WHO has assisted a number of countries in incorporating health and environmental concerns in their development plans. In 1994 the WHO created "Africa 2000" in an effort to universally provide water and sanitation services on the continent. Together with the UNEP, WHO maintains air quality monitoring devices in more than 60 countries, and the WHO has also contributed to the study of the ozone layer and climate change. In 1993, the WHO requested the ICJ to issue an advisory opinion on the Legality of the Threat or Use of Nuclear Weapons. Currently, the WHO is planning a meeting to address the impact of climate change on human health.

WHO is given authority to promote conventions on the international health issues, often in consort with other organizations. One hundred ninety-two governments are members. Located in Geneva, Switzerland, the WHO has a full-time staff of more than 4,000 people from more than 100 nations, and a billion dollar per year budget. To learn more about the WHO, make a virtual stop at http:// www.who.int/en/.

X. WORLD METEOROLOGICAL ORGANIZATION

The World Meteorological Organization (WMO), which came into existence in 1950, became a specialized member of the UN in the same year. The WMO establishes international networks that work together to monitor the atmosphere and standardize measurements and statistics. The WMO has a number of programs, including the World Climate Programme (WCP). As part of the WCP, the WMO and the United Nations Environment Programme (UNEP) established the Intergovernmental Panel on Climate Change (IPCC) in 1988, which has become the platform for leading authorities on the climate change issue. WMO is developing the World Hydrological Cycle Observation System (WHYCOS) which will work towards the reduction of desertification and tempering the effects of drought.

The WMO has 185 members and is comprised of an Executive Council, a Congress and a Secretariat, employing a full time staff of about 300 people from 50 different countries. To learn more about the WMO, visit http://www.wmo.ch/.

Y. WORLD TRADE ORGANIZATION

The World Trade Organization (WTO) is a permanent institution, established in 1995 as a result of the Uruguay Round trade negotiations and the Marrakesh Declaration. It is a centralized international agency for promoting free trade. The WTO is at once a platform for international trade relations, a provider of framework trade legislation, an overseer of trade policies and a forum for the resolution of trade disputes. In a tentative and hesitant attempt to incorporate an environmental dimension in its policies, a WTO General Council Committee on trade and the environment reported to the WTO ministerial conference at Singapore in December of 1996. While the WTO has no specific agreement dealing with the environment, a number of WTO agreements include provisions dealing with environmental concerns. Indeed, the preamble to the Agreement Establishing the WTO identifies sustainable development and environmental protection as part of its objectives. Potentially, 152 countries could join the WTO, and current membership is at 145. To learn more about the WTO, see http://www.wto.org/.

Z. WORLD WILDLIFE FUND

The World Wildlife Fund (WWF) is a non-governmental, public and charitable organization that was established by a group of scientists and public relations experts, and was closely aligned with the World Conservation Union (IUCN). Originally, the WWF was a fund, established through charitable fund raising, that donated money to conservation efforts throughout the world. Today, WWF is an organization that also works directly with government and business to focus attention on key environmental issues like energy conservation, climate change, habitat destruction, and education. The WWF's mission is "to reverse the destruction of the Earth's natural environment and build a future in which humans can live in harmony with nature." To learn more about the WWF, go to http://www.wwf.org/.

*

Index

References are to Pages

589

WORLD CONSERVATION UNION
See appendix at section V

WORLD COURT
See International Court of Justice (ICJ), appendix at section H

WORLD HEALTH ORGANIZATION
See also, appendix at section W

WORLD METEOROLOGICAL ORGANIZATION
See also, appendix at section X

WORLD PARK
Alternative to Antarctic Treaty, as, 265

WORLD WILDLIFE FUND
See also, appendix at section Z

WRITERS
See Publicists

†